Contents

Acknowledgement		v
Introduction		vii
Studying Evidence		ix
Revision and Examination Technique		xi
Table of Cases		xvii
Table of Statutes		xxvii
1	Introduction to Evidence	1
2	Competence and Compellability	4
3	Corroboration	23
4	Burdens and Standards of Proof	37
5	Hearsay – General Exclusion	55
6	Hearsay – Statutory Admissibility in Civil Cases	75
7	Hearsay – Statutory Admissibility in Criminal Cases	83
8	Character Evidence	103
9	Similar Fact Evidence	127
10	Privilege	148
11	Evidence Illegally or Unfairly Obtained	169
12	Opinion Evidence	188
13	Public Policy	205
14	Proof Without Evidence	220

REVISION WORKBOOK

Evidence

Third Edition

ROSAMUND REAY
LLM, MA, Solicitor,
Senior Lecturer in Law, University of Hertfordshire

OLD BAILEY PRESS

OLD BAILEY PRESS
at Holborn College, Woolwich Road,
Charlton, London, SE7 8LN

First published 1997
Third edition 2002

ISBN 1 85836 463 9

British Library Cataloguing-in-Publication.

A CIP Catalogue record for this book is available from the British Library.

Printed and bound in Great Britain.

Acknowledgement

Some questions used are taken or adapted from past University of London LLB (External) Degree examination papers and our thanks are extended to the University of London for their kind permission to use and publish the questions.

Caveat

The answers given are not approved or sanctioned by the University of London and are entirely our responsibility.

They are not intended as 'Model Answers', but rather as Suggested Solutions.

The answers have two fundamental purposes, namely:

a) to provide a detailed example of a suggested solution to an examination question; and

b) to assist students with their research into the subject and to further their understanding and appreciation of the subject.

Introduction

This Revision WorkBook has been designed specifically for those studying evidence to undergraduate level. Its coverage is not confined to any one syllabus, but embraces all the major evidence topics to be found in university examinations.

Each chapter contains a brief introduction explaining the scope and overall content of the topic covered in that chapter. There follows, in each case, a list of key points which will assist the student in studying and memorising essential material with which the student should be familiar in order to fully understand the topic.

Additionally in each chapter there is a key cases and statutes section which lists the most relevant cases and statutory provisions applicable to the topic in question. These are intended as an aid to revision, providing the student with a concise list of materials from which to begin revision.

Each chapter usually ends with several typical examination questions, together with general comments, skeleton solutions and suggested solutions. Wherever possible, the questions are drawn from the University of London external evidence papers, with recent questions being included where possible. However, it is inevitable that, in compiling a list of questions by topic order rather than chronologically, not only do the same questions crop up over and over again in different guises, but there are gaps where questions have never been set at all.

Undoubtedly, the main feature of this Revision WorkBook is the inclusion of as many past examination questions as possible. While the use of past questions as a revision aid is certainly not new, it is hoped that the combination of actual past questions from the University of London LLB external course and specially written questions, where there are gaps in examination coverage, will be of assistance to students in achieving a thorough and systematic revision of the subject.

Careful use of the Revision WorkBook should enhance the student's understanding of evidence and, hopefully, enable you to deal with as wide a range of subject matter as anyone might find in an evidence examination, while at the same time allowing you to practise examination techniques while working through the book.

Studying Evidence

The study of Evidence, whether as a first degree subject or for Bar examinations, requires an awareness that topics cannot be learned in isolation. Evidence is very closely integrated, in that very few topics can be compartmentalised; in most instances material studied at any one point will impinge upon and relate to materials studied at other points. Whatever the approach taken by lecturers, or authors of textbooks, on Evidence, there will invariably be cross-referencing.

In the early stages the subject will appear disjointed and difficult to rationalise and therefore understand; only towards the end of a course of study of the subject will the pieces of the jigsaw start to interlock. A recommended approach, therefore, is to read, several times, an introductory book on Evidence before beginning study of the subject in depth – thus acquiring a somewhat superficial but usefully coherent and cohesive awareness which will be invaluable when examining specific areas and relating them to others. The same introductory book can also be used to good effect as part of the revision process, to reinforce the 'lateral thinking' needed in Evidence.

Evidence is never taught as a first year undergraduate subject. Whether studying for a law degree or Bar examinations, an Evidence student must have some knowledge of law, especially Criminal Law, and of basic procedure (both criminal and civil) to excel in this adjectival subject. However, in Evidence examinations it is not detailed knowledge of substantive law which is required, but merely a very basic knowledge of substantive law and procedure, and detailed knowledge of the evidentiary issues involved. Evidence 'problem questions' may appear to require the examinees to deal with Criminal, Company, Tort, Contract Law etc, but the examiner is testing knowledge of Evidence – using as a realistic vehicle some criminal or other scenario.

In studying Evidence, therefore, the student must be aware of the integrated nature of the subject, be basically conversant with principles of substantive law; and be wary of concentrating on a few topics – as they might well be covered in only one or two examination questions!

Revision and Examination Technique

Revision Technique

Planning a revision timetable

In planning your revision timetable make sure you do not finish the syllabus too early. You should avoid leaving revision so late that you have to 'cram' – but constant revision of the same topic leads to stagnation.

Plan ahead, however, and try to make your plans increasingly detailed as you approach the examination date.

Allocate enough time for each topic to be studied. But note that it is better to devise a realistic timetable, to which you have a reasonable chance of keeping, rather than a wildly optimistic schedule which you will probably abandon at the first opportunity!

The syllabus and its topics

One of your first tasks when you began your course was to ensure that you thoroughly understood your syllabus. Check now to see if you can write down the topics it comprises from memory. You will see that the chapters of this WorkBook are each devoted to a syllabus topic. This will help you decide which are the key chapters relative to your revision programme, though you should allow some time for glancing through the other chapters.

The topic and its key points

Again working from memory, analyse what you consider to be the key points of any topic that you have selected for particular revision. Seeing what you can recall, unaided, will help you to understand and firmly memorise the concepts involved.

Using the WorkBook

Relevant questions are provided for each topic in this book. Naturally, as typical examples of examination questions, they do not normally relate to one topic only. But the questions in each chapter will relate to the subject matter of the chapter to a degree. You can choose your method of consulting the questions and solutions, but here are some suggestions (strategies 1–3). Each of them pre-supposes that you have read through the author's notes on key points and key cases and statutes, and any other preliminary matter, at the beginning of the chapter. Once again, you now need to practise working from memory, for that is the challenge you are preparing yourself for. As a rule of procedure constantly test yourself once revision starts, both orally and in writing.

Strategy 1

Strategy 1 is planned for the purpose of quick revision. First read your chosen question carefully and then jot down in abbreviated notes what you consider to be the main points at issue. Similarly, note the cases and statutes that occur to you as being relevant for citation purposes. Allow yourself sufficient time to cover what you feel to be relevant. Then study the author's skeleton solution and skim-read the suggested solution to see how they compare with your notes. When comparing consider carefully what the author has included (and concluded) and see whether that agrees with what you have written. Consider the points of variation also. Have you recognised the key issues? How relevant have you been? It is possible, of course, that you have referred to a recent case that is relevant, but which had not been reported when the WorkBook was prepared.

Strategy 2

Strategy 2 requires a nucleus of three hours in which to practise writing a set of examination answers in a limited time-span.

Select a number of questions (as many as are normally set in your subject in the examination you are studying for), each from a different chapter in the WorkBook, without consulting the solutions. Find a place to write where you will not be disturbed and try to arrange not to be interrupted for three hours. Write your solutions in the time allowed, noting any time needed to make up if you are interrupted.

After a rest, compare your answers with the suggested solutions in the WorkBook. There will be considerable variation in style, of course, but the bare facts should not be too dissimilar. Evaluate your answer critically. Be 'searching', but develop a positive approach to deciding how you would tackle each question on another occasion.

Strategy 3

You are unlikely to be able to do more than one three hour examination, but occasionally set yourself a single question. Vary the 'time allowed' by imagining it to be one of the questions that you must answer in three hours and allow yourself a limited preparation and writing time. Try one question that you feel to be difficult and an easier question on another occasion, for example.

Misuse of suggested solutions

Don't try to learn by rote. In particular, don't try to reproduce the suggested solutions by heart. Learn to express the basic concepts in your own words.

Keeping up-to-date

Keep up-to-date. While examiners do not require familiarity with changes in the law during the three months prior to the examination, it obviously creates a good impression if you can show you are acquainted with any recent changes. Make a habit of looking through one of the leading journals – *Modern Law Review*, *Law Quarterly Review* or the *New Law Journal*, for example – and cumulative indices to law reports, such as the *All England Law Reports* or *Weekly Law Reports*, or indeed the daily law reports in *The Times*. The *Law Society's Gazette* and the *Legal Executive Journal* are helpful sources, plus any specialist journal(s) for the subject you are studying.

Examination Skills

Examiners are human too!

The process of answering an examination question involves a communication between you and the person who set it. If you were speaking face to face with the person, you would choose your verbal points and arguments carefully in your reply. When writing, it is all too easy to forget the human being who is awaiting the reply and simply write out what one knows in the area of the subject! Bear in mind it is a person whose question you are responding to, throughout your essay. This will help you to avoid being irrelevant or long-winded.

The essay question

Candidates are sometimes tempted to choose to answer essay questions because they 'seem' easier. But the examiner is looking for thoughtful work and will not give good marks for superficial answers.

The essay-type of question may be either purely factual, in asking you to explain the meaning of a certain doctrine or principle, or it may ask you to discuss a certain proposition, usually derived from a quotation. In either case, the approach to the answer is the same. A clear programme must be devised to give the examiner the meaning or significance of the doctrine, principle or proposition and its origin in common law, equity or statute, and cases which illustrate its application to the branch of law concerned. Essay questions offer a good way to obtain marks if you have thought carefully about a topic, since it is up to you to impose the structure (unlike the problem questions where the problem imposes its own structure). You are then free to speculate and show imagination.

The problem question

The problem-type question requires a different approach. You may well be asked to advise a client or merely discuss the problems raised in the question. In either case, the most important factor is to take great care in reading the question. By its nature, the question will be longer than the essay-type question and you will have a number of facts to digest. Time spent in analysing the question may well save time later, when you are endeavouring to impress on the examiner the considerable extent of your basic legal knowledge. The quantity of knowledge is itself a trap and you must always keep within the boundaries of the question in hand. It is very tempting to show the examiner the extent of your knowledge of your subject, but if this is outside the question, it is time lost and no marks earned. It is inevitable that some areas which you have studied and revised will not be the subject of questions, but under no circumstances attempt to adapt a question to a stronger area of knowledge at the expense of relevance.

When you are satisfied that you have grasped the full significance of the problem-type question, set out the fundamental principles involved.

You will then go on to identify the fundamental problem (or problems) posed by the question. This should be followed by a consideration of the law which is relevant to the problem. The source of the law, together with the cases which will be of assistance in solving the problem, must then be considered in detail.

Very good problem questions are quite likely to have alternative answers, and in advising a party you should be aware that alternative arguments may be available. Each stage of your answer, in this case, will be based on the argument or arguments considered in the previous stage, forming a conditional sequence.

If, however, you only identify one fundamental problem, do not waste time worrying that you cannot think of an alternative – there may very well be only that one answer.

The examiner will then wish to see how you use your legal knowledge to formulate a case and how you apply that formula to the problem which is the subject of the question. It is this positive approach which can make answering a problem question a high mark earner for the student who has fully understood the question and clearly argued their case on the established law.

Examination checklist

a) Read the instructions at the head of the examination carefully. While last-minute changes are unlikely – such as the introduction of a compulsory question or an increase in the number of questions asked – it has been known to happen.

b) Read the questions carefully. Analyse problem questions – work out what the examiner wants.

c) Plan your answer before you start to write.

d) Check that you understand the rubric before you start to write. Do not 'discuss', for example, if you are specifically asked to 'compare and contrast'.

e) Answer the correct number of questions. If you fail to answer one out of four questions set you lose 25 per cent of your marks!

Style and structure

Try to be clear and concise. Fundamentally this amounts to using paragraphs to denote the sections of your essay, and writing simple, straightforward sentences as much as possible. The sentence you have just read has 22 words – when a sentence reaches 50 words it becomes difficult for a reader to follow.

Do not be inhibited by the word 'structure' (traditionally defined as giving an essay a beginning, a middle and an end). A good structure will be the natural consequence of setting out your arguments and the supporting evidence in a logical order. Set the scene briefly in your opening paragraph. Provide a clear conclusion in your final paragraph.

Table of Cases

A T & T Istel v Tully [1992] 3 All ER
523   *149, 166*

Abrath v North Eastern Railway Co (1886) 11
App Cas 247; (1883) 11 QBD 440   *240*

Air Canada v Secretary of State for Trade (No
2) [1983] 2 AC 394; [1983] 1 All ER 910
HL   *205, 210, 212, 215, 216, 218*

Alexander v Rayson [1936] 1 KB 169   *240*

Alfred Crompton Amusement Machines Ltd
v Customs and Excise Commissioners (No
2) [1974] AC 405   *155, 166, 213, 216, 217,
218*

Ashburton (Lord) v Pape [1913] 2 Ch
469   *81, 150, 155, 158, 161, 167*

Associated Provincial Picture Houses Ltd v
Wednesbury Corporation [1948] 1 KB
223   *25*

Attorney-General v Hitchcock (1847) 1 Exch
91   *116*

Attorney-General for Hong Kong v Lee
Kwong-Kut [1993] AC 951   *39*

Attorney-General of Hong Kong v Wong
Muk-Ping [1987] 2 All ER 488   *27, 28, 30*

Attorney-General's Reference (No 3 of 2000):
R v Looseley [2001] 4 All ER 897   *173, 174*

Autospin (Oil Seals) Ltd v Beehive Spinning
(A Firm) (1995) The Times 9 August   *191*

Bairstow v Queen's Moat Houses plc (1997)
The Times 31 January   *79*

Baker v Rabetts (1954) 118 JPN 303   *21*

Balabel v Air India [1988] Ch 317; [1988] 2 All
ER 246   *149*

Balfour v Foreign and Commonwealth Office
[1994] 2 All ER 588   *167*

Banbury Peerage Case, The (1811) 1 Sim & St
153   *227, 241, 244*

Barkway v South Wales Transport Executive
[1949] 1 KB 54   *249*

Berryman v Wise (1791) 4 Term Rep
366   *229*

Bilbie v Lumley (1802) 2 East 469   *235*

Blunt v Park Lane Hotel [1942] 2 KB
253   *157, 166*

Blyth v Blyth [1966] AC 643   *247*

Brandao v Barnett (1846) 12 Cl & Fin
787   *235*

Bratty v Attorney-General for Northern
Ireland [1963] AC 386; [1961] 3 All ER
523   *248*

British Steel Corporation v Granada
Television Ltd [1982] AC 1096; [1980] 3
WLR 774; [1981] 1 All ER 417   *149, 207,
216*

Broome v Broome [1955] P 190   *213*

Brown v Bennett (Witness Summons) (2000)
The Times 2 November   *189*

Brown v Foster (1857) 1 H & N 738   *161*

Brown v Matthews [1990] 2 All ER 155   *207,
213*

Buckinghamshire County Council v Moran
[1989] 3 WLR 152   *152*

Burmah Oil v Bank of England [1980] AC
1090; [1979] 3 WLR 722 HL; [1979] 3 All ER
700   *205, 208, 210, 212, 216, 218*

Burr v Ware RDC [1939] 2 All ER 688   *149*

Butler v Board of Trade [1971] Ch 680   *151,
159, 161*

Buttes Gas and Oil v Hammer (No 3) [1981] 1
QB 223   *206*

Calcraft v Guest [1898] 1 QB 759   *80, 81,
150, 153, 155, 158, 161, 166, 167*

Calderbank v C [1976] Fam 98   *156*

Camelot Group plc v Centaur
Communications Ltd [1999] QB 124
CA   *153*

Castle v Cross [1984] 1 WLR 1372   *64*

Chandrasekera v R [1937] AC 220   *66, 73*

Chard v Chard [1956] P 259   *223, 225, 241,
244*

Chipchase v Chipchase [1939] P 391   *245*

Chocoladefabriken Lindt v The Nestlé Co Ltd
[1978] RPC 287   *159*

Conway v Rimmer [1968] AC 910   *167, 205,
208, 209, 210, 211, 212, 215, 217, 218*

D v NSPCC [1978] AC 171; [1977] 1 All ER
589   *152, 159, 162, 206, 207, 208, 210, 213,
214, 215, 216, 218*

Davey *v* Harrow Corporation [1958] 1 QB 60   *235*

Derby & Co Ltd *v* Weldon (No 8) [1990] 3 All ER 762   *150, 151, 159*

DPP *v* A and BC Chewing Gum [1968] 1 QB 159   *190, 193, 195, 203*

DPP *v* Blake (1989) 89 Cr App R 179   *86*

DPP *v* Boardman [1975] AC 421 HL; [1974] 3 All ER 887   *128, 131, 132, 133, 135, 136, 137, 138, 140, 141, 144, 145, 146, 202, 204*

DPP *v* Hester [1973] AC 296   *27, 28, 30*

DPP *v* Kilbourne [1973] AC 729   *27, 28, 131, 132*

DPP *v* M [1997] 2 All ER 749   *5*

DPP *v* Marshall [1988] 3 All ER 683   *214*

DPP *v* Smith [1961] AC 290   *232*

Duff Development Co *v* Government of Kelantan [1924] AC 797   *234, 236*

Duncan *v* Cammell Laird & Co Ltd [1942] AC 624   *167, 205, 206, 208, 209, 210, 211, 215, 217, 218*

Ellis *v* Home Office [1953] 2 QB 135   *210, 213*

Emmanuel *v* Emmanuel [1946] P 115   *233*

Fay *v* Prentice (1845) 14 LJ CP 298   *234, 236*

Folkes *v* Chadd & Ors (1782) 3 Doug 157   *167, 199*

Francis & Francis *v* Central Criminal Court [1988] 3 All ER 775   *150*

Francisco *v* Diedrick (1998) The Times 3 April *38*

G *v* DPP [1997] 2 All ER 755   *6*

Gatland *v* MPC [1968] 2 QB 279   *53*

Gibson *v* Wales [1983] 1 WLR 393   *221*

Goddard *v* Nationwide Building Society [1986] 3 WLR 734   *81, 159*

Goodwin *v* UK (1996) 22 EHRR 123   *153*

Governor of Brixton Prison, ex parte Osman (1991) 93 Cr App R 202   *207*

Greenhough *v* Gaskell (1833) 1 MY & K 98   *160*

Grobbelaar *v* Sun Newspapers Ltd (1999) The Times 12 August   *170*

Guiness Peat Properties *v* Fitzroy Robinson [1987] 1 WLR 1027; [1987] 2 All ER 716   *81, 150, 164*

H and Others (Minors) (Sexual Abuse: Standard of Proof), Re [1996] AC 563; [1996] 1 All ER 1   *38, 51*

Halford *v* Brookes (1991) The Independent 1 October   *50, 51*

Hall *v* R [1971] 1 WLR 298; [1971] 1 All ER 322   *16, 35, 87, 102*

Hargreave *v* Spink [1892] 1 QB 25   *235*

Harmony Shipping Co *v* Saudi Europe Line [1979] 1 WLR 1380   *155, 189, 204*

Harris *v* DPP [1952] AC 694   *140, 141, 145*

Hehir *v* Commissioner of Police for the Metropolis [1982] 1 WLR 715   *213*

Helliwell *v* Piggott-Sims [1980] FSR 582   *81*

Hill *v* Baxter [1958] 1 QB 277   *224, 225*

Hollington *v* Hewthorn [1943] KB 587   *192*

Hornal *v* Neuberger Products Ltd [1957] 1 QB 247; [1956] 3 All ER 970   *50, 51, 80, 82*

Hoskyn *v* Metropolitan Police Commissioner [1979] AC 474   *13, 18, 19*

Howe *v* Malkin (1878) 40 LT 196   *59*

Hunter *v* Chief Constable of the West Midlands Police [1982] AC 529; [1981] 3 All ER 727   *192*

Huyton-with-Roby UDC *v* Hunter [1955] 1 WLR 603   *233*

Ingram *v* Percival [1969] 1 QB 548   *222, 238*

Inquiry under the Company Securities (Insider Dealing) Act 1985, Re an [1988] 1 All ER 203   *153*

ITC Film Distributors Ltd *v* Video Exchange Ltd [1982] Ch 431   *151, 158–159, 169*

Jeffery *v* Black [1978] QB 490   *179, 183*

John *v* Humphreys [1955] 1 WLR 325; [1955] 1 All ER 793   *45*

Jones *v* DPP [1962] AC 635; [1962] 1 All ER 569   *106, 115, 117*

Jones *v* Godrich (1845) 5 Moo PCC 16   *161*

Jones *v* Metcalfe [1967] 1 WLR 1286   *102*

Joseph Hargreaves Ltd, Re [1900] 1 Ch 347   *213*

Kershaw *v* Whelan [1996] 1 WLR 358   *151*

Kite, The [1933] P 154   *249*

Konigsberg, Re [1989] 3 All ER 289   *150, 155*

Kuruma *v* R [1955] AC 197   *179*

L (A Minor) (Police Investigation: Privilege), Re [1997] AC 16   *151, 153, 162*

La Roche *v* Armstrong [1922] 1 KB 485   *159*

Lam Chi-ming *v* R [1991] 2 WLR 1082; [1991] 3 All ER 173   *182*

Langham *v* Governors of Wellingborough School [1932] LJ KB 513   *249*

Leyland DAF Ltd, Re [1994] 1 BCLC 264   *118*

Lillycrap *v* Nalder & Sons [1993] 1 All ER 724   *161*

Lobban *v* R [1995] 1 WLR 877   *172, 187*

Lowery *v* R [1974] AC 85   *190, 193, 196, 199, 204*

McNally *v* Chief Constable of the Greater Manchester Police (2002) The Times 6 March   *206, 208*

McQuaker *v* Goddard [1940] 1 KB 687   *221*

M'Naghten's Case (1843) 10 Cl & Fin 200   *44, 50, 201, 232, 240*

Machine and General Investment Co Ltd *v* Austin [1935] AC 346   *11*

Makin *v* Attorney-General for New South Wales [1894] AC 57 PC   *127, 131, 132, 135, 137, 145*

Manchester Brewery Co Ltd *v* Coombs (1901) 82 LT 347   *73, 74*

Mancini *v* DPP [1942] AC 1   *248*

Marks *v* Beyfus (1890) 25 QBD 494   *213, 216, 218*

Matto *v* Crown Court at Wolverhampton [1987] RTR 337   *170, 181*

Maxwell *v* DPP [1935] AC 309   *12, 106, 114*

Metropolitan Police Commissioner *v* Hills [1980] AC 26   *118, 119*

Miller *v* Minister of Pensions [1947] 2 All ER 372   *50*

Mohammed (Allie) *v* The State [1999] 2 AC 111   *171, 174*

Mole *v* Mole [1951] P 21   *152*

Monckton *v* Tarr (1930) 23 BWCC 504   *224*

Monroe *v* Twistleton (1802) Peak Add Cas   *7, 21*

Mood Music Publishing Co Ltd *v* De Wolfe Publishing Ltd [1976] 1 Ch 119; [1976] 1 All ER 463   *130, 164–165*

Morris *v* Davies (1837) 5 Cl & Fin 163   *52, 249, 250*

Murdoch *v* Taylor [1965] AC 574; [1965] 1 All ER 406   *107, 108, 114, 116, 117, 118, 119, 121, 204*

Myers *v* DPP [1965] AC 1001   *35, 57, 62, 63, 64, 67, 97, 101*

National Justice Compania Naviera SA *v* Prudential Assurance Co Ltd (Ikarian Reefer) [1995] 1 Lloyd's Rep 455   *191, 193*

Neill *v* North Antrim Magistrates' Court [1992] 1 WLR 1220; [1992] 4 All ER 846   *69*

Neilson *v* Laugharne [1981] 1 QB 736   *155, 164, 213*

Nembhard *v* R [1982] 1 All ER 183   *62*

Ng Chun Pui *v* Lee Chuen Tat (1988) The Times 25 May   *249*

Nimmo *v* Alexander Cowan & Sons Ltd [1968] AC 107   *45, 53*

Noor Mohamed *v* R [1949] AC 182; [1949] 1 All ER 365   *139, 141*

Parkes *v* R [1976] 1 WLR 1251; [1976] 3 All ER 380   *35, 87*

Peach v Commissioner of Police for the Metropolis [1986] QB 1064; [1986] 2 All ER 129   *151, 213*

Peete, Re; Peete *v* Crompton [1952] 2 All ER 599   *223*

Phene's Trusts, Re (1870) 5 Ch App 139   *245*

Piers *v* Piers (1849) 2 HL Cas 331   *223, 225, 244, 250*

Powell *v* Chief Constable of North Wales (2000) The Times 11 February   *207*

Practice Direction [1975] 1 WLR 1065   *124*

Practice Direction (Crown Court: Evidence: Advice to Defendant) [1995] 2 All ER 499   *173*

Preston-Jones *v* Preston-Jones [1951] AC 391   *52*

Prudential Assurance Co *v* Edmonds (1877) 2 AC 487   *249*

R *v* Abadom [1983] 1 WLR 126; [1983] 1 All ER 364 CA   *190, 193, 203*

R *v* Acton Justices, ex parte McMullen (1991) 92 Cr App R 98   *69, 89*

R *v* Agar (1990) 90 Cr App R 318   *206, 213, 216, 218*

R v Ahmed [1993] Crim LR 946   *26*

R v Alath Construction Ltd [1990] 1 WLR 1255   *54*

R v Alladice [1988] Crim LR 608; (1988) 87 Cr App R 380   *85, 90, 91, 170, 175, 176, 179, 214*

R v Ananthanarayanan (1994) 98 Cr App R 1   *143*

R v Anderson [1988] QB 678; [1988] 2 All ER 549   *106, 129, 141*

R v Andrews [1987] AC 281; [1987] 1 All ER 513   *59, 60, 62, 65, 69, 98, 99, 198*

R v Apicella (1985) 82 Cr App R 295; [1986] Crim LR 238 CA   *183*

R v Askew [1981] Crim LR 398   *92*

R v Ataou [1988] QB 798; [1988] 2 All ER 321   *150, 158*

R v Aziz [1995] 3 WLR 53   *105*

R v B (RA) (1997) 2 Cr App R 88   *136*

R v Bailey and Smith [1993] Crim LR 681   *86*

R v Bains [1992] Crim LR 795   *18, 22*

R v Baker (1912) 7 Cr App 252   *122, 123*

R v Baldwin [1986] Crim LR 681   *9, 20*

R v Ball [1983] 1 WLR 801; [1983] 2 All ER 1089   *232*

R v Barrett (1991) 92 Cr App R 61   *84*

R v Barrington [1981] 1 WLR 419   *128, 142*

R v Barton [1973] 1 WLR 115   *150, 158, 161*

R v Baskerville [1916] 2 KB 658   *23, 26, 28*

R v Beales [1991] Crim LR 118   *179*

R v Beck [1982] 1 WLR 461   *25, 26*

R v Bedingfield (1879) 14 Cox CC 341   *59, 62, 65, 99*

R v Beveridge [1987] Crim LR 401   *32*

R v Birtles (1911) 6 Cr App R 177   *223*

R v Bishop [1975] QB 274   *107*

R v Blackburn (1992) The Times 1 December   *94*

R v Blake and Tye (1844) 6 QB 126   *187*

R v Blastland [1986] AC 41; [1985] 2 All ER 1095   *55, 60, 63, 99*

R v Bleakley [1993] Crim LR 203   *25*

R v Boyes (1861) 30 LJQB 301; 1 B & S 311   *157*

R v Boysen [1991] Crim LR 274   *193*

R v Bradford Justices, ex parte Wilkinson [1990] RTR 59   *9, 14*

R v Bradshaw (1986) 82 Cr App R 79   *203*

R v Brasier (1779) 1 Leach CC 199   *31*

R v Britzman; R v Hall [1983] 1 WLR 350; [1983] 1 All ER 369; (1983) 76 Cr App R 134   *108, 113, 117, 122, 125*

R v Brookes (1991) 92 Cr App R 36   *128*

R v Brown (1991) The Times 13 December   *25*

R v Brown and Daley (1988) 87 Cr App R 52   *206*

R v Bruce [1975] 1 WLR 1252   *119*

R v Bryant; R v Oxley [1979] QB 108   *95, 104, 106*

R v Buckley (1873) 13 Cox CC 293   *60, 62*

R v Burke (1985) 82 Cr App R 156   *125–126*

R v Butler (1987) 84 Cr App R 12   *128, 130, 131, 133*

R v Butterwasser [1948] 1 KB 4   *114*

R v C (2002) The Times 21 January   *39, 40*

R v Cain [1994] 2 All ER 398   *105*

R v Callender [1998] Crim LR 337   *59*

R v Carr-Briant [1943] KB 607   *51, 232*

R v Carrington [1990] Crim LR 330   *129*

R v Chalkley and Jeffries [1998] 2 All ER 155   *171, 173, 174, 176*

R v Chance [1988] QB 932; [1988] 3 All ER 225   *23, 35*

R v Chandler [1976] 1 WLR 585; [1976] 3 All ER 105   *16, 87, 102*

R v Chapman [1969] 2 QB 436   *142*

R v Chard (1971) 56 Cr App R 268   *189, 195, 199*

R v Cheema [1993] NLJR 1439; [1994] 1 All ER 639   *30, 180*

R v Christie [1914] AC 545   *31, 33, 35*

R v Christou [1996] 2 All ER 927   *146, 147, 171, 177*

R v Clare; R v Peach (1995) The Times 4 April   *191*

R v Clark [1955] 2 QB 469   *125*

R v Cole [1990] 2 All ER 108   *88*

R v Condron [1997] 1 WLR 827; [1997] 1 Cr App R 185   *17*

R v Cook [1959] 2 QB 340   *12*

R v Cook [1987] 1 All ER 1049   *65*

R v Coulman (1927) 20 Cr App R 106   *123*

R v Cowan [1995] 4 All ER 939   *10, 17, 173*

R v Cox and Railton (1884) 14 QBD 153   *149, 150, 155, 158, 161*

R *v* Cramp (1880) 14 Cox CC 390   *26, 33*

R *v* Crampton [1991] Crim LR 277   *85, 181*

R *v* Crawford [1998] 1 Cr App R 338   *119*

R *v* Cresswell (1876) 1 QBD 446   *229*

R *v* Cross (1990) 91 Cr App R 115   *42*

R *v* Crown Court at Snaresbrook, ex parte DPP [1988] 1 All ER 315   *150, 158*

R *v* Cruttenden [1991] 3 All ER 242   *7*

R *v* Davies [1962] 1 WLR 1111; [1962] 3 All ER 97   *192, 201*

R *v* Davison-Jenkins [1997] Crim LR 816 CA   *107*

R *v* Dowley [1983] Crim LR 168   *26*

R *v* Edwards [1975] QB 27   *38, 40, 43, 45, 47, 48, 50, 51, 54, 232, 240*

R *v* Edwards [1991] NLJ 91   *104*

R *v* Eleftheriou [1993] Crim LR 947   *102*

R *v* Ellis [1910] 2 KB 746   *118, 119*

R *v* Evans [1965] 2 QB 295   *25*

R *v* Ferguson (1909) 2 Cr App R 250   *122, 123*

R *v* Flemming (1987) 86 Cr App R 32   *92*

R *v* Fletcher [1917] 1 Ch 339   *94*

R *v* Foster [1984] 3 WLR 401   *192*

R *v* Freebody (1935) 25 Cr App R 69   *29*

R *v* Fulling [1987] QB 426; [1987] 2 All ER 65   *70, 84, 86, 90, 96, 97, 99*

R *v* Galbraith [1981] 1 WLR 1039; [1981] 2 All ER 1060   *42, 240*

R *v* Garbett (1847) 1 Den CC 236   *157*

R *v* Garrod [1997] Crim LR 445 CA   *105*

R *v* Gibson (1887) 18 QBD 537   *94*

R *v* Gill [1963] 1 WLR 841   *248*

R *v* Gill and Ranuana [1989] Crim LR 358   *170*

R *v* Goldenberg (1989) 88 Cr App R 285   *85, 91*

R *v* Goodway [1993] 4 All ER 894   *92, 114*

R *v* Governor of Pentonville Prison, ex parte Osman [1989] 3 All ER 701   *150*

R *v* Grant [1960] Crim LR 424   *44*

R *v* Groves [1998] Crim LR 200   *131, 133*

R *v* Gurney [1994] Crim LR 116   *129*

R *v* H *See* R *v* Hepburn

R *v* Hagan (1873) 12 Cox CC 357   *94*

R *v* Hampshire [1995] 3 WLR 260   *31*

R *v* Hardy (1794) 24 State Trials 199   *206*

R *v* Harry (1988) 86 Cr App R 105   *56, 64, 66, 71, 72*

R *v* Harvey [1988] Crim LR 241   *85*

R *v* Hatton (1977) 64 Cr App R 88   *118, 120*

R *v* Hayes [1977] 1 WLR 234; [1977] 2 All ER 288   *6, 7, 22*

R *v* Hedges (1909) 3 Cr App R 262   *110*

R *v* Hennessey (1978) 68 Cr App R 419   *211*

R *v* Hepburn [1995] 2 AC 596   *129, 131, 143, 144, 145, 146, 147*

R *v* Hepworth & Fearnley [1955] 2 QB 600   *232*

R *v* Hill (1851) 2 Den 254   *201*

R *v* Hinds; R *v* Butler [1993] Crim LR 111   *109, 111*

R *v* Hoggins [1967] 1 WLR 1233   *120*

R *v* Horn (1912) 7 Cr App R 200   *44*

R *v* Horne [1990] Crim LR 188   *16, 26*

R *v* Hudson [1971] 2 QB 202   *97*

R *v* Hunt [1987] AC 352; [1987] 1 All ER 1   *37, 38, 40, 41, 42, 43, 44, 45, 46, 47, 48, 49, 50, 53, 54*

R *v* Hunt [1992] Crim LR 582   *186*

R *v* Hutchinson (1822) 2 B & C 608n   *198*

R *v* Inch (1990) 91 Cr App R 51   *189*

R *v* Inder (1977) 67 Cr App R 143   *123, 126, 137, 146*

R *v* Islam (1999) 1 Cr App R 22   *109, 110*

R *v* Ismail [1990] Crim LR 109   *84*

R *v* Jackson [1996] 2 Cr App R 420   *190*

R *v* Jelen and Katz (1989) 90 Cr App R 456 CA   *172*

R *v* Jenkins (1945) 31 Cr App R 1   *126*

R *v* Johanssen (1977) 65 Cr App R 101   *128*

R *v* Johnson [1961] 1 WLR 1478   *32, 248*

R *v* Johnson [1989] 1 All ER 121   *206, 218*

R *v* Keane (1994) 99 Cr App R 1   *207*

R *v* Kearley [1992] 2 All ER 345; [1991] Crim LR 282   *56, 57, 60, 66, 67, 70, 71, 72, 74, 91, 93*

R *v* Keeling [1942] 1 All ER 507   *102*

R *v* Keenan [1989] 3 WLR 1193   *70, 171*

R *v* Kelly (1985) The Times 27 July   *10, 14*

R *v* Kempster (1990) 90 Cr App R 14   *193*

R *v* Khan (1981) 73 Cr App R 190   *18, 22*

R *v* Khan (Sultan) [1997] AC 558   *175, 176, 184*

R *v* Kirkpatrick [1998] Crim LR 63   *118, 119, 120*

R *v* L [1999] Crim LR 489   *25*

R *v* Laidman; R *v* Agnew [1992] Crim LR
  428 *146*

R *v* Lake (1977) 64 Cr App R 172 *88*

R *v* Lamb (1980) 71 Cr App R 198 *25*

R *v* Lambert [2001] 3 All ER 577 *38, 39, 40,*
  45, 47, 49

R *v* Lanfear [1968] 2 QB 77 *189*

R *v* Lasseur [1991] Crim LR 53 *107*

R *v* Latif [1996] 1 All ER 353 *172, 173, 183*

R *v* Leatham (1861) 8 Cox CC 498 *169, 175,*
  183

R *v* Lee [1976] 1 WLR 71 *107*

R *v* Levy (1966) 50 Cr App R 238 *122, 125*

R *v* Levy [1987] Crim LR 48 *104*

R *v* Lewes JJ [1973] AC 388 *215, 216*

R *v* Lewis [1989] Crim LR 61 *220*

R *v* Lobell [1957] 1 QB 547 *248*

R *v* Loughran [1999] Crim LR 404 *189*

R *v* Lovell [1990] Crim LR 111 *25*

R *v* Lovett [1973] 1 WLR 241 *120*

R *v* Lucas [1981] QB 720 *26, 63, 92, 113, 114*

R *v* Lumley (1869) LR 1 CCR 196 *230*

R *v* Lunt (1987) 85 Cr App R 241 *128*

R *v* Lydon [1987] Crim LR 407 *64, 198, 199*

R *v* McCarthy [1998] RTR 374 *88*

R *v* McCay [1990] Crim LR 338 *60, 65, 198,*
  199

R *v* McGillvray [1993] Crim LR 530 *63*

R *v* McGovern (1991) 92 Cr App R 228 *85,*
  181

R *v* McGuirk (1963) 48 Cr App R 75 *119*

R *v* McLean (1968) 52 Cr App R 80 *102*

R *v* McLeod [1994] 3 All ER 254 *108, 116,*
  117, 123, 124, 126

R *v* Makanjuola [1995] 3 All ER 730 *25, 26*

R *v* Manji [1990] Crim LR 512 *86*

R *v* Marsh [1994] Crim LR 52 *122, 123*

R *v* Martin [2000] Crim LR 615 *104*

R *v* Martinez-Tobon [1994] 2 All ER 90 *95,*
  179

R *v* Masih [1986] Crim LR 395 *194, 195, 196*

R *v* Mason [1988] 1 WLR 139; [1987] 3 All ER
  481 *86, 170, 175, 176, 177, 179, 181, 214*

R *v* Mathias (1989) 139 NLJ 1417 *7*

R *v* Mattison [1990] Crim LR 117 *193*

R *v* Menga and Marshalleck [1998] Crim LR
  58 *207*

R *v* Miah [1997] Crim LR 351 *105*

R *v* Mitchell (1892) 17 Cox CC 503 *16*

R *v* Mullen [1999] 2 Cr App R 143 *173*

R *v* Myers [1998] AC 124 *84*

R *v* Nathaniel [1995] 2 Cr App R 565 *183*

R *v* Neale (1977) 65 Cr App R 304 *132*

R *v* Nelson (1978) 68 Cr App R 12 *107*

R *v* Newton and Carpenter (1859) 1 F & F
  641 *198*

R *v* Norton [1910] 2 KB 496 *16*

R *v* Novac (1976) 65 Cr App R 107 *128, 146*

R *v* Nye & Loan (1977) 66 Cr App R 252 *65*

R *v* Okafor [1994] 3 All ER 741 *171*

R *v* Okorudu [1982] Crim LR 747 *65*

R *v* Olaleye (1986) 82 Cr App R 337 *27*

R *v* Osborne [1905] 1 KB 551 *31, 33, 34, 109,*
  110

R *v* Osbourne; R *v* Virtue [1973] 1 QB
  678 *33, 35, 65, 181, 198, 199*

R *v* Owen (1986) 83 Cr App R 100 *108*

R *v* P (1991) 93 Cr App R 267 *129, 131, 135,*
  138, 139, 140, 141, 142, 143, 144, 145, 146,
  147, 202

R *v* Parker (1994) 26 HLR 508 (CA) *70*

R *v* Parris (1989) 89 Cr App R 68 *172, 177*

R *v* Patel [1981] 3 All ER 94 *66*

R *v* Peach [1990] 2 All ER 966 *24*

R *v* Perry [1909] 2 KB 697 *99*

R *v* Perry [1984] Crim LR 680 *130*

R *v* Peters (1995) 2 Cr App R 77 *131, 134*

R *v* Pike (1829) 3 C & P 598 *62, 99*

R *v* Podola [1960] 1 QB 325 *44*

R *v* Powell [1986] 1 All ER 193; [1985] 1 WLR
  1364 *116, 122, 123, 126*

R *v* Prater [1960] 2 QB 464 *25, 180*

R *v* Pryce [1991] Crim LR 379 *30*

R *v* Putland [1946] 1 All ER 85 *46*

R *v* Quinn [1990] Crim LR 581 *170, 171, 214*

R *v* R [1994] 4 All ER 260 *155*

R *v* Rankine [1986] QB 861; [1986] 2 All ER
  566 *206, 218*

R *v* Rappolt (1911) 6 Cr App R 156 *125*

R *v* Reading [1966] 1 WLR 836 *142*

R *v* Redd [1923] 1 KB 104 *105*

R *v* Redgrave (1981) 74 Cr App R 10 *204*

R *v* Rice [1963] 1 QB 857 *64, 66, 91, 93, 198,*
  199

R *v* Rimmer & Beech [1983] Crim LR
  250 *190*

R *v* Robertson [1968] 1 WLR 1767   44

R *v* Robertson; R *v* Golder [1987] QB 920;
[1987] 3 All ER 231   *193*

R *v* Rodley [1913] 3 KB 468   *142*

R *v* Rouse [1904] 1 KB 184   *113, 125*

R *v* Rowson [1985] 2 All ER 539   *117*

R *v* Rowton (1865) 34 LJMC 57; Le and Car
520   *95, 204*

R *v* Ryder [1994] 2 All ER 859   *143*

R *v* Samuel (1956) 40 Cr App R 8   *106, 123*

R *v* Samuel [1988] 2 WLR 920; [1988] 2 All ER
135   *86, 90, 170, 172, 175, 177, 186, 214*

R *v* Sanders (1991) 93 Cr App R 245   *203*

R *v* Sang [1980] AC 402   *170, 171, 175, 183,
184*

R *v* Sanghera [2001] Crim LR 480   *171, 174*

R *v* Sat-Bhambra [1988] Crim LR 453   *85*

R *v* Sawoniuk [2000] Crim LR 506   *131, 135*

R *v* Scarrott [1978] QB 1016   *23, 128, 137*

R *v* Scott [1991] Crim LR 56   *179*

R *v* Seaman (1978) 67 Cr App R 234   *128*

R *v* Seigley (1911) 6 Cr App R 106   *114*

R *v* Shannon [2001] 1 WLR 51   *171, 172, 174*

R *v* Sharp [1988] 1 All ER 65   *96, 97*

R *v* Shellaker [1914] 1 KB 464   *114*

R *v* Shepherd [1904] 1 Ch 456   *247*

R *v* Shepherd [1993] 1 All ER 225   *64*

R *v* Shore (1983) 76 Cr App R 72   *66*

R *v* Silcott [1987] Crim LR 765   *88, 187, 195*

R *v* Silcott; R *v* Braithwaite; R *v* Raghip (1991)
The Times 9 December   *178, 181*

R *v* Simbodyal (1991) The Times 10
October   *192*

R *v* Simpson [1983] 1 WLR 1494   *221, 225*

R *v* Simpson (1993) 99 Cr App R 48   *138*

R *v* Smith [1979] 1 WLR 1445   *190, 203*

R *v* Smith (Percy) [1976] Crim LR 511   *65*

R *v* Smith (Robert William) (1985) 81 Cr App
R 286   *26*

R *v* Smurthwaite and Gill (1994) 98 Cr App R
437   *86, 170, 171, 175, 177, 184*

R *v* Sokialiosis [1993] Crim LR 872   *134*

R *v* Spiby (1990) 91 Cr App R 186   *57*

R *v* Spinks [1982] 1 All ER 587   *192*

R *v* Stannard [1965] 2 QB 1   *120*

R *v* Steane [1947] KB 997   *232*

R *v* Stewart [1999] Crim LR 746   *193*

R *v* Stewart; R *v* Schofield [1995] 3 All ER 159
CA   *183*

R *v* Stockwell (1993) 92 Cr App R 260   *195*

R *v* Straffen [1952] 2 QB 911; [1952] 2 All ER
657   *131, 132*

R *v* Summers (1953) 36 Cr App R 14   *50*

R *v* Sutton (1816) 4 M & S 532   *237*

R *v* Swendsen (1702) 14 How St Tr 559   *95*

R *v* Tanner (1977) 66 Cr App R 66   *107, 114*

R *v* Taroy (1794) 24 State Tr 199   *211*

R *v* Taylor (1923) 17 Cr App R 109   *142*

R *v* Thompson (1976) 64 Cr App R 96   *9, 69*

R *v* Thomson [1912] 3 KB 19   *62*

R *v* Tompkins (1977) 67 Cr App R 181   *150,
161*

R *v* Toner (1991) 93 Cr App R 382   *190, 199*

R *v* Treacy [1944] 2 All ER 229   *117*

R *v* Tricoglus (1976) 65 Cr App R 16   *128*

R *v* Turnbull [1977] QB 224; [1976] 3 All ER
549   *25, 30, 32, 33, 34, 35, 91, 92, 102*

R *v* Turnbull (1984) 80 Cr App R 104; [1984]
Crim LR 620   *65, 99*

R *v* Turner [1944] 1 KB 463   *107, 193*

R *v* Turner [1975] QB 834; [1975] 1 All ER
70   *95, 189, 190, 194, 195, 196, 197, 199,
201, 204*

R *v* Tyrer (1990) 90 Cr App R 446   *85*

R *v* Varley (1982) 75 Cr App R 242; [1982] 2
All ER 519 CA   *108, 114, 118, 119, 120*

R *v* Venna [1976] QB 421   *97*

R *v* Vye [1993] Crim LR 604   *95, 105, 108,
117, 135*

R *v* W [1994] 2 All ER 872   *143*

R *v* Wainwright (1875) 13 Cox CC 171   *35,
60, 62*

R *v* Wainwright (1925) 19 Cr App R 52   *32,
92*

R *v* Waite [1892] 2 QB 600   *230*

R *v* Walker [1998] Crim LR 211   *194, 196*

R *v* Wallwork (1958) 42 Cr App R 153   *6, 7,
9, 18, 20, 32*

R *v* Walsh [1989] Crim LR 822   *171*

R *v* Warwickshall (1783) 1 Leach 263   *96,
179, 182*

R *v* Watts [1983] 3 All ER 101   *114, 124*

R *v* Weightman (1991) 92 Cr App R
291   *189, 194, 197, 199, 201, 204*

R *v* Whartin [1998] Crim LR 668   *138*

R *v* Whitaker (1977) 63 Cr App R 193   *180*

R *v* White (1999) 1 Cr App R 153   *109, 110*

R *v* Whitehead [1929] 1 KB 99   *26, 28, 102*

R *v* Wilkinson; R *v* Fraser, Trans Ref: 9700349W2, 9700870W2, 7 August 1997, CA (Criminal Division)   *146*

R *v* Willshire (1881) 6 QBD 366   *224*

R *v* Winfield [1939] 4 All ER 164   *105, 106*

R *v* Wood (1982) 76 Cr App R 23   *64*

R *v* Woodcock (1789) 1 Leach 500   *198*

R *v* Wren [1993] Crim LR 952   *105*

R *v* Wright [1994] Crim LR 55   *179, 183*

R *v* Wright; R *v* Ormerod (1987) 90 Cr App R 91   *20*

R *v* Z [1990] 3 WLR 940   *18, 129, 131*

Ratten *v* R [1972] AC 378   *56, 60, 61, 64, 66, 68, 69, 70–71, 94, 98, 198*

Reynolds *v* Llanelly Associated Tinplate Co [1948] 1 All ER 140   *237*

Rio Tinto Zinc Corporation *v* Westinghouse Electric Corporation [1978] AC 547; [1978] 1 All ER 434   *149, 157, 158*

Rogers *v* Home Secretary [1973] AC 388   *207, 209*

Rush & Tompkins *v* GLC [1988] 3 WLR 939   *159*

Sarah C Getty Trust, Re [1985] 2 All ER 809   *166*

Sastry Velaider Aronegary *v* Sambecutty Vailalie (1881) 6 App Cas 364   *244, 250*

Science Research Council *v* Nassé [1980] AC 1028; [1979] 3 WLR 762   *207, 211, 216*

Secretary of State for Defence *v* Guardian Newspapers [1984] 3 WLR 986; [1984] 3 All ER 601   *153, 167, 219*

Selvey *v* DPP [1970] AC 304; [1968] 2 All ER 497   *12, 107, 108, 109, 112, 113, 114, 122, 125*

Sharples *v* Halford [1992] 3 All ER 624   *207*

Shenton *v* Tyler [1939] Ch 620   *7, 21*

Sodastream *v* Thorn Cascade [1982] RPC 459   *188*

South Shropshire District Council *v* Amos [1987] 1 All ER 340   *152, 159*

Sparks *v* R [1964] AC 964; [1964] 1 All ER 727   *56, 199*

Statue of Liberty, The [1968] 1 WLR 739   *64, 82, 164*

Stirland *v* DPP [1944] AC 315   *106, 108*

Subramaniam *v* Public Prosecutor [1956] 1 WLR 965   *94, 109, 110*

Sussex Peerage Case, The (1844) 11 Cl & Fin 85   *58, 63*

Tate Access Floors Inc *v* Boswell [1990] 3 All ER 303   *167*

Taylor dec'd, Re [1961] 1 WLR 9   *223*

Taylor *v* Chief Constable of Cheshire [1986] 1 WLR 1479; [1987] 1 All ER 225   *57, 64*

Taylor *v* Taylor [1967] P 25; [1965] 2 WLR 779; [1965] 1 All ER 872   *224*

Teixeira de Castro *v* Portugal (1998) 28 EHRR 101   *171*

Teper *v* R [1952] AC 480   *60, 66, 70, 71, 94*

Theodoropoulas *v* Theodoropoulas [1964] P 311   *152*

Thomas *v* Connell (1828) 4 M & W 267   *94–95*

Thompson *v* R [1918] AC 221   *131, 133, 134, 140, 142*

Tomlin *v* Standard Telephone and Cables Ltd [1969] 1 WLR 1378   *156*

Toohey *v* MPC [1965] AC 595   *95, 189, 190*

Tweny *v* Tweny [1946] 1 All ER 564   *250*

V *v* C (2001) The Times 1 November   *149*

Ventouris *v* Mountain, The Italia Express [1991] 3 All ER 472   *81, 149, 164*

W *v* Edgell [1990] 2 WLR 471   *208*

Waugh *v* British Railways Board [1981] 1 QB 736; [1980] AC 521; [1979] 2 All ER 1169   *81, 151, 154, 155, 158, 161, 162, 164, 166*

Waugh *v* R [1950] AC 203   *62*

Webster *v* James Chapman [1989] 3 All ER 939   *150, 151*

Wentworth *v* Lloyd (1864) 10 HL Cas 589   *157*

Westminster City Council *v* Croyalgrange (1986) 83 Cr App R 155   *54*

Wetherall *v* Harrison [1976] QB 773   *238, 239*

Wheeler *v* Le Marchant (1881) 17 Ch D 675   *154*

Williams *v* Home Office [1981] 1 All ER 1151   *216*

Woodhouse *v* Hall [1980] Crim LR 645; (1981)
72 Cr App R 39   *64, 109, 110*
Woolmington *v* DPP [1935] AC 462   *41, 44,*
47, 48, 49, 50, 51, 52, 53, 54, 240, 248, 249, 250
Wright *v* Doe d Tatham (1837) 7 Ad & E
313   *66, 70, 71, 73, 74*

X *v* Y [1988] 2 All ER 648   *153*
X Ltd *v* Morgan Grampian Ltd [1990] 2 WLR
1000   *153, 154*

Ymnos, The [1981] 1 Lloyd's Rep 550
164

Table of Statutes

Administration of Justice Act 1985
  s33   *149*

Children and Young Persons Act 1933
  s38(1)   *24*
  s50   *227*
Children and Young Persons Act 1963
  89
    s16(1)   *227*
    s42   *89*
    s43   *89, 101*
Children Act 1989
  s4   *22*
  s96   *5, 22*
  Part IV   *151, 162*
Children Act 1996   *21*
  s96   *21*
  s96(2)(a)   *22*
  s96(2)(b)   *22*
  s105   *21*
Civil Evidence Act 1965   *21*
  s14   *21*
Civil Evidence Act 1968   *52, 77, 78, 81, 89*
  s2   *235*
  s4   *88, 89, 235*
  s5   *168*
  s6   *89*
  s9   *78*
  s9(1)   *78*
  s9(2)(a)   *78*
  s11   *52, 192*
  s12   *192*
Civil Evidence Act 1972   *79, 80, 190, 191, 193, 195, 203*
  s3   *80, 190, 193, 203*
  s3(2)   *191*
  s3(3)   *190*
Civil Evidence Act 1995   *2, 18, 22, 57, 58, 60, 75, 76, 77, 78, 79, 80, 81, 163, 164, 166, 188*
  s1   *75, 81, 163, 164, 167*
  s1(1)   *75, 76*
  s1(2)(b)   *75*
  s2   *188*
  s2(1)   *76, 77*

Civil Evidence Act 1995 (*contd.*)
  s2(1)(a)   *76, 164*
  s2(1)(b)   *76*
  s2(2)   *76*
  s2(3)   *77*
  s2(4)   *77*
  s2(4)(b)   *77*
  s3   *76, 81*
  s4   *77, 80, 164*
  s4(2)   *77*
  s5   *163*
  s5(1)   *79*
  s6(2)   *163*
  s7   *60, 78, 80, 188*
  s7(1)   *57, 80*
  s7(2)   *58, 78*
  s7(3)   *78*
  s8   *78, 81*
  s8(1)   *82*
  s9   *78, 80, 81*
  s9(5)   *78*
  s11   *75*
  s13   *75, 79, 163, 168*
  s14(1)   *80*
Civil Procedure Rules 1999   *75, 76, 80, 161, 163, 167, 169, 170, 191, 192*
Company Securities (Insider Dealing) Act 1985   *42*
  s1(1)   *42*
  s3   *42*
Contempt of Court Act 1981
  s10   *153, 154, 167, 208, 217, 219*
Criminal Evidence Act 1898   *6, 7, 10, 11, 13, 16, 103, 105, 108, 113, 115, 118, 122, 127, 202, 203, 204*
  s1   *6, 7, 10, 11, 103, 105, 108, 118, 122*
  s1(1)   *11*
  s1(a)   *16*
  s1(b)   *16*
  s1(c)   *11*
  s1(2)   *11, 103, 105, 106, 123*
  s1(3)   *12, 103, 105, 106, 115, 116, 117, 121, 122, 123*
  s1(3)(i)   *11, 12, 106, 116, 123*

Criminal Evidence Act 1898 (*contd.*)
  s1(3)(ii)   *10, 12, 106, 107, 110, 112, 113,*
    114, 116, 117, 118, 120, 122, 123, 124,
    125, 126, 203, 204
  s1(3)(iii)   *12, 107, 108, 113, 114, 115,*
    116, 117, 118, 119, 120, 121, 123, 202,
    204
  s2   *118*
  s3   *118*
Criminal Evidence Act 1979   *118*
Criminal Justice Act 1967
  s8   *232*
  s9   *89, 101*
  s10   *220, 225*
  s10(2)   *220*
  s10(4)   *220*
Criminal Justice Act 1988   *5, 8, 23, 58, 68,*
  69, 70, 88, 89, 93, 193
  s23   *68, 69, 70, 88, 89, 93, 94, 101, 109,*
    110, 200
  s23(1)   *101*
  s23(1)(ii)   *101*
  s23(2)   *200*
  s23(2)(a)   *68, 101*
  s23(3)   *89*
  s23(3)(b)   *69, 101*
  s24   *58, 70, 88, 89, 102*
  s24(1)   *88, 102*
  s24(4)   *88, 102*
  s25   *68, 88, 89, 102, 200*
  s25(2)   *88*
  s26   *69, 88, 89*
  s27   *88*
  s28   *88*
  s30   *191, 193, 201, 203*
  s30(3)   *201, 203*
  s32   *89, 102*
  s32A   *102*
  s33A   *5, 8*
  s33A(1)   *31*
  s33A(2A)   *5, 6, 9, 31*
  s33A(3)   *5*
  s34   *23*
  s34(1)   *24*
  s34(2)   *102*
  Schedule 2   *88, 89*
    para 3   *89*
Criminal Justice Act 1991   *5, 9, 102*

Criminal Justice Act 1991 (*contd.*)
  s52   *5*
  s52(1)   *5*
  s52(2)   *9, 24*
Criminal Justice and Public Order Act 1994
  10, 17, 23, 26, 173, 178, 179
  s31   *107*
  s32   *23, 25, 26, 29, 31, 180*
  s33(1)   *24*
  s34   *17, 102, 173, 179*
  s35   *10, 11, 17, 95, 114, 173, 174, 179*
  s36   *17*
  s37   *17*
  s38   *17*
  s38(3)   *17*
  s39   *17*
  s168   *179*
Criminal Law Act 1967
  s6   *99*
Criminal Law Amendment Act 1867
  s6   *100*
Criminal Procedure Act 1865
  s3   *69*
  s4   *91, 92, 117*
Criminal Procedure (Attendance of
  Witnesses) Act 1965   *9, 14, 19*
Criminal Procedure (Insanity) Act 1964
  s6   *44*
Criminal Procedure (Insanity and Unfitness
  to Plead) Act 1991   *44*
Criminal Procedure and Investigation Act
  1996   *207*

European Communities Act 1972
  s4(2)   *235*
European Convention on Human Rights
  39, 40, 50, 153, 184
  art 6   *39, 40, 49, 171, 184*
  art 6(2)   *39, 49*
  art 8   *40, 171, 184*
Evidence Amendment Act 1853   *18*
  s1   *7, 21*
Evidence Further Amendment Act 1869   *7,*
  18, 21

Factories Act 1961
  s29(1)   *45*
Family Law Reform Act 1969
  s26   *223, 227, 245*

Financial Services Act 1986   *40, 41, 42*
   s27   *40, 41, 42, 43*
   s58   *40, 42*
   s207(3)   *40, 42*

Homicide Act 1957   *38, 48*
   s2(2)   *38, 45, 203*
Human Rights Act 1998   *39, 171*

Insolvency Act 1986   *40*
   s206(1)(a)   *40*
Interception of Communications Act 1985
   176
Interpretation Act 1978
   s3   *235*

Magistrates' Courts Act 1952
   s81   *45*
Magistrates' Courts Act 1980   *40, 49, 100*
   s101   *38, 40, 45, 47, 48, 49, 51, 52, 53,*
     54, 240
   s102   *89*
   s103   *89*
   s105   *89, 101*
Misuse of Drugs Act 1971   *45, 53*
   s5   *46*
   s28   *39*
   s28(2)   *39, 45*
   s28(3)   *39*
Misuse of Drugs Regulations 1973   *46*

Official Secrets Act 1911
   s1(2)   *130*

Perjury Act 1911
   s13   *24, 29*
Police and Criminal Evidence Act 1984   *3,*
   4, 6, 8, 13, 14, 17, 18, 19, 26, 58, 60, 68, 70,
   83, 84, 85, 87, 88, 89, 90, 91, 92, 96, 99, 100,
   131, 169, 174, 175, 176, 177, 178, 180, 182,
   183, 184, 185, 187, 192, 212, 214
   s6   *181*
   s10   *150, 154, 181*
   s10(2)   *150*
   s16   *181*
   s17   *179*
   s17(2)(a)   *179*
   s18   *179*

Police and Criminal Evidence Act 1984
(*contd.*)
   s58   *96, 176, 178, 179, 181, 186*
   s58(8)   *178*
   s62   *183*
   s62(1)(b)   *183*
   s62(10)   *26*
   s63   *183*
   s64(3B)   *183*
   s65   *183*
   s65(3)   *26*
   s66   *86, 96, 170*
   s67   *96*
   s67(11)   *86*
   s68   *89*
   s69   *88, 89, 94*
   s74   *192, 193*
   s74(1)   *193*
   s74(2)   *193*
   s76   *58, 68, 70, 83, 84, 85, 86, 87, 90, 91,*
     92, 99, 100, 116, 117, 169, 174, 178, 179,
     180, 185, 187
   s76(2)   *84, 186*
   s76(2)(a)   *70, 86, 96, 99, 179, 181, 185,*
     186
   s76(2)(b)   *70, 85, 86, 96, 97, 99, 179, 181,*
     185, 196, 197
   s76(3)   *84*
   s76(4)   *96, 182, 185*
   s76(4)(a)   *179, 182, 186*
   s76(5)   *87, 96, 100, 179, 182, 185, 186*
   s76(6)   *87, 100, 182*
   s76(8)   *84, 86, 97, 100*
   s77   *83, 185, 186*
   s78   *3, 58, 67, 68, 70, 83, 84, 86, 87, 90,*
     91, 96, 116, 130, 131, 170, 171, 172, 173,
     174, 175, 176, 177, 178, 179, 180, 181,
     182, 183, 184, 185, 186, 187, 193, 212,
     214
   s78(1)   *86, 170, 174*
   s80   *4, 6, 8, 9, 11, 13, 14, 15, 18, 19, 62*
   s80(1)   *18, 19*
   s80(1)(a)   *8, 99*
   s80(1)(b)   *14*
   s80(2)   *14*
   s80(2A)   *18, 19*
   s80(3A)   *18, 19*
   s80(4A)   *18, 19*

Police and Criminal Evidence Act 1984
  (*contd.*)
    s80(3)   *8, 9, 14, 19*
    s80(3)(a)   *9, 14*
    s80(3)(b)   *14*
    s80(5)   *7, 14*
    s81   *191, 203*
    s82(1)   *16, 83, 87, 91, 97, 116, 181, 182,*
      185
    s82(3)   *83, 86, 87, 91, 96, 175, 181, 182,*
      184
    s116   *178*
Prevention of Corruption Act 1916   *45, 48*
    s2   *45*
Prevention of Crime Act 1953   *45*
    s1(1)   *45*

Rehabilitation of Offenders Act 1974   *122,*
  124, 126
    s4(1)   *124*
    s7(2)(a)   *124*
Road Traffic Regulations Act 1967
    s78A   *231, 233*
Road Traffic Regulations Act 1984   *24*
    s89   *24*
    s89(2)   *29*

Sexual Offences Act 1956   *24, 45, 101*
    s9   *200*
    s32   *45*
Sexual Offences (Amendment) Act 1976   *111*
Summary Jurisdiction Act 1848
    s14   *45*

Theft Act 1968
    s27(3)   *130*
Treason Act 1895   *24*
    s1   *29*

Youth Justice and Criminal Evidence Act
  1999   *4, 10, 14, 18, 19, 21, 89, 109, 118,*
  122
    s41(1)   *107, 111*
    s41(2)   *111*
    s41(2)(b)   *112*
    s41(3)   *112*
    s41(3)(b)   *111*
    s41(3)(c)   *111*
    s41(3)(c)(ii)   *111*
    s41(4)   *111*
    s41(5)   *111*
    s42(1)   *111*
    s53   *4, 18, 20*
    s53(1)   *18, 19, 20*
    s53(2)   *20*
    s53(3)   *20*
    s53(4)   *20*
    s54   *4, 18, 20*
    s54(1)   *18, 19, 20*
    s54(6)   *20*
    s55   *4, 18*
    s55(2)   *20*
    s56   *4, 18*
    s57   *4*
    s60   *89*
    Schedule 7   *103*
      para 4   *103*

Chapter 1

Introduction to Evidence

1.1   **General**

1.2   **Types of evidence**

1.3   **Cogency of evidence**

1.1 General

Rules of evidence are mainly exclusionary, because many of them developed at a time when trial by jury was the rule rather than the exception, and it was thought that jurors would be unduly influenced by knowledge of previous convictions of the accused; by hearsay evidence; by character evidence; by opinion evidence of a non-expert etc. Despite many recent reforms, it is still generally true to state that the courts in England are not apprised of all the facts, not even of all the relevant facts, but only of those facts which the laws of evidence allow – and even some of these facts may be excluded in the discretion of the judge.

To be capable of admissibility, evidence must be legally relevant, ie must have reached a sufficiently high point on the scale of relevance. For example, if D is charged with theft, it is not legally relevant (although it may be logically relevant) that he has several previous convictions for theft. It is legally relevant that he was seen in the store at the time and that he had the goods – alleged by the prosecution to have been stolen by him – in his possession.

However, although his being seen in the store is legally relevant, the fact of his being seen is not necessarily admissible – eg the prosecution may wish to inform the court that a customer, or a store detective, not available to give evidence at the trial, saw D in the store. Such evidence would be hearsay if it is to be related by a person other than said customer or store detective, and may therefore not be admissible. Thus, the hearsay rule may exclude relevant evidence. Further, relevant evidence may be excluded by other exclusionary rules, such as that giving protection against a person's incriminating himself (self-incrimination privilege); evidence may be in a communication between a person and his legal adviser and therefore protected by legal professional privilege; evidence may be excluded as a matter of public policy on the grounds that disclosure would be injurious to state security or some other protected public interest (public interest immunity). Therefore, it is vital that at the outset one realises that in evidence relevance and admissibility are not synonymous. To be admitted in court, evidence must be legally relevant – but legally relevant evidence will not necessarily be admitted in court, because of one or more of the exclusionary rules which comprise most of the law of evidence.

1.2 Types of evidence

Admissible evidence may take one of several forms, as shown below.

Testimony

This is the oral evidence of a witness. It may be evidence of what that witness perceived, ie 'direct testimony', or alternatively it may be what another person perceived and the witness is reporting that to the court as evidence of its truth, ie 'hearsay'. In civil trials hearsay is now admissible, since the passing of the Civil Evidence Act 1995; in criminal trials hearsay is inadmissible unless it falls into one of the recognised categories of admissible hearsay, eg res gestae statements, freely made confessions, or dying declarations.

Documentary evidence

Here, a document is adduced in evidence. For the purposes of evidence, there is no all embracing definition of 'document'. It includes not only a document in writing but also photographs, maps, plans, drawings, blue-prints, cassettes, micro-dots etc. The document may be admitted because its content, or its existence, is relevant. As regards content of a document, the 'best evidence' rule would dictate production of the original, but increasingly the law of evidence provides for the admissibility of copies of documents. The original document is 'primary' evidence, the copy is 'secondary' evidence.

Real evidence

Real evidence comprises objects produced for inspection by the court in order that the court may draw inferences from the condition, existence etc of the object. Real evidence would therefore include a document produced purely as evidence of its condition or existence rather than of its contents. In the case of both documentary and real evidence there must be some testimony as to, for example, the authenticity of the documents, the location where the real evidence was discovered, otherwise the documentary or real evidence will have little if any cogency in itself.

Circumstantial evidence

Circumstantial evidence may be contrasted with 'direct' evidence, in that the latter relates to some fact in issue of which the witness has 'direct' or first-hand knowledge, whereas the former comprises evidence of facts from which an inference may, or may not, be drawn as to the fact in issue. For example, in a murder trial a witness may give testimony which is 'direct' evidence of his seeing the accused stab the victim, or may give circumstantial evidence of the accused's motive, eg that on several occasions he had heard the accused voice his violent disposition toward, hatred of, and/or intention to kill the victim. Circumstantial evidence may be in the form of testimony, documentary or real evidence; examples are evidence of motive, opportunity, identity (eg fingerprints of the accused at scene of crime).

1.3 Cogency of evidence

Evidence may be admissible, but mere admissibility does not further the cause of the party adducing the evidence. What must be assessed, and what will be crucial in deciding the case, is the cogency, ie the probative value, or the weight of the admissible evidence. Cogency is a matter of degree, from technical admissibility with little or no probative value at one end of the spectrum to cogency so strong as to be probative to the extent of being conclusive at the other end.

Admissibility of evidence is a question of law to be determined by the judge, often in a voir dire ('trial within a trial') in the absence of the jury. Cogency of such admissible evidence is a question of fact, to be determined by the jury; for example, in a criminal trial the jury will evaluate the cogency of prosecution and defence evidence which they have been allowed to hear (ie which the judge has ruled admissible) in deciding whether the prosecution has proved the guilt of the accused beyond reasonable doubt.

However, in deciding on the admissibility of an item of evidence, the judge will be influenced by the degree of relevance of that evidence and thus to some extent by its cogency. Also a judge may withdraw an issue from the jury where a party has failed to discharge an evidential burden, eg if the defence in a criminal trial attempts to run a defence of sane automatism in an effort to secure an acquittal, the judge will withdraw that defence from the jury unless the defence adduce sufficient evidence in support of the alleged automatism. So, although the jury, as the tribunal of fact, is not concerned with the admissibility of evidence, the judge, when deciding the legal question of admissibility, cannot divorce this completely from the cogency, or weight, of the evidence under scrutiny.

Finally, to add to the uncertainty in evidence, the judge in a criminal trial has a discretion to exclude admissible evidence where its probative value is outweighed by its prejudicial effect on the defence; here again the judge is concerned with the cogency of evidence. This overriding discretion is, apparently, in addition to the statutory discretion given by s78, Police and Criminal Evidence Act 1984, to exclude 'unfair evidence'.

All these concepts, all these issues, will be examined in depth in the ensuing chapters, and constitute the major part of the law of evidence.

Chapter 2
Competence and Compellability

2.1   **Introduction**

2.2   **Key points**

2.3   **Key cases and statutes**

2.4   **Questions and suggested solutions**

2.1 Introduction

Following the enactment of s80 Police and Criminal Evidence Act (PACE) 1984 the competence and compellability of the spouse of an accused person was simplified and drastically changed.

New rules governing competence and compellability are to be introduced by ss53–57 Youth Justice and Criminal Evidence Act 1999. These new rules have been described as 'much simpler' (*Murphy on Evidence*, 7th edition, Blackstone Press). Section 53 states that all persons are competent to give evidence in criminal proceedings, regardless of their age, provided that they can understand questions put to them as witnesses and give answers which can be understood. A witness who is under the age of 14, or who lacks an appreciation of the solemnity of the occasion and of the particular responsibility to tell the truth involved in taking the oath , must give evidence unsworn. In the case of a witness over the age of 14, there will be a presumption of the necessary appreciation (and so a presumption that such a witness will give sworn evidence). The defendant and his spouse will remain competent, but the rule that the defendant is not compellable is maintained and, in general, a spouse will only be compellable at the instance of the defendant (there are certain exceptions to this rule). Murphy comments that 'this simplification of the law in a field which has no obvious need for complexity had been suggested by many commentators, including previous editions of this work, and is to be welcomed'.

2.2 Key points

Distinguish competence and compellability

Competence

General rule is that all persons are competent as witnesses, ie they may give evidence.

Exceptions to the general rule include children; persons of defective intellect; the accused as a prosecution witness.

Compellability

General rule is that all competent witnesses are compellable, ie they can be compelled (under threat of punishment for contempt of court as a last resort) to give evidence. This does not mean that the witness will always have to answer every question put to him (he may claim that his answer will tend to incriminate him, for example, or the matter may be the subject of legal professional privilege). Exceptions to the general rule of compellability are only two – the accused and his/her spouse.

Children

The law used to be that a child's competence was tested by inquiring into his or her understanding of the oath. According to the result of that test, the child could give sworn or unsworn evidence in criminal proceedings, but could only give sworn evidence in civil proceedings. Now s52 of the Criminal Justice Act 1991 has changed this as far as criminal proceedings are concerned. Now all children's evidence in such proceedings is given unsworn, whether they understand the oath or not – s52(1) inserts this as s33A into the Criminal Justice Act 1988. A 'child' is defined for these purposes as someone under the age of 14: s33A(3). The question of competence is now governed by s33A(2A) which provides that 'a child's evidence shall (ie must) be received unless it appears to the court that the child is incapable of giving intelligible evidence'. For children over 14 the general rule is that the child is competent to give sworn evidence subject only to the inability to understand an oath because of unsoundness of mind.

The court must assess the competence of each child. In *DPP* v *M* [1997] 2 All ER 749 the defence contended that a child of five was incapable of giving intelligible testimony by reason of her age alone. The prosecution submitted that the court should assess whether the child was capable of giving intelligible evidence by watching the video tapes of the child's interviews with the police or otherwise. The court refused to watch the tapes on the basis that by reason of her age, the child was not a witness on whom reliance should be placed. The prosecution appealed and the Court of Appeal held that it was not open to a judge to exclude a child's evidence by reason of age alone, since according to the words of s33A(2A) Criminal Justice Act 1988, a child's evidence should be received unless it appears to the court that the child is incapable of giving intelligible testimony.

As for civil proceedings, s96 Children Act 1989 (which came into force at the end of 1991) allows a child to give unsworn evidence in certain circumstances, for the first time.

Section 96 applies to any civil proceedings, and any child witness (which is defined in the Act as someone under the age of 18). If, in the opinion of the court, the child does not understand the nature of the oath, the child's evidence can be heard by the court if, in its opinion:

a) he understands that it is his duty to speak the truth; and

b) he has sufficient understanding to justify his evidence being heard.

In civil cases there is no fixed age, obviously, at which a child becomes competent to give sworn evidence, though it has been suggested that this will normally be between the ages of eight and ten: *R v Hayes* [1977] 2 All ER 288. It has also been stated that it would be most undesirable to call as a witness to give unsworn evidence in a criminal trial a child aged five: *R v Wallwork* (1958) 42 Cr App R 153. This has clearly been overtaken by s33A(2A) with its mandatory form of wording. In *G v DPP* [1997] 2 All ER 755 it was held that in considering the test as to whether a child is capable of giving intelligible testimony, the court does not require the assistance of any expert such as a child psychologist, since this is a simple test well within the capability of a judge or magistrate.

Persons of defective intellect

If a proposed witness appears to suffer from some impairment of intellect, which could be the result of mental illness or handicap, or drink or drugs, then his competence to give sworn evidence must be tested by the judge; if he does not understand the nature and solemnity of the oath, he is incompetent; if of defective intellect but nevertheless adjudged competent, the jury must decide how much weight, if any, to attach to the evidence of the witness. If the defect appears to be caused by drink or drugs there will be an adjournment before competence is tested.

The accused

The accused is incompetent as a witness for the prosecution. A co-accused is similarly incompetent unless he has already been acquitted or convicted or unless he has otherwise ceased to be a co-accused, eg a successful application for separate trials has been made. Once the co-accused becomes competent for the prosecution he is also compellable.

Section 1 Criminal Evidence Act 1898 (as amended by the Police and Criminal Evidence Act 1984) states: 'Every person charged with an offence shall be a competent witness for the defence at every stage of the proceedings, whether the person is charged solely, or jointly with any other person. Provided as follows: (a) A person so charged shall not be called as a witness in pursuance of this Act except upon his own application ...' Therefore the accused may given evidence for the defence, but is not compellable either as a witness in his own defence or that of a co-accused.

Spouse of the accused

Section 80 Police and Criminal Evidence Act 1984 has drastically changed the competence and compellability of the accused's spouse:

a) spouse is always competent for the prosecution unless husband and wife are jointly charged with an offence, and is always competent for co-accused of other spouse;

b) spouse is compellable as witness for the prosecution or for co-accused of other spouse only if the offence charged involves assault on, or injury or threat of injury to the spouse of the accused or a person under 16, or if the offence charged is a sexual offence in respect of a person under 16;

c) spouse is always competent to give evidence on behalf of the accused (even if both spouses jointly charged) and is always compellable unless both spouses are jointly charged;

d) prosecution cannot comment on failure of spouse to testify, although there is no such prohibition upon the judge.

Ex-spouses

Civil cases

The effect of s1 Evidence Amendment Act 1853 and the Evidence Further Amendment Act 1869 is to make the spouse of a party in a civil trial competent and compellable. The 1853 Act has been construed strictly: *Shenton v Tyler* [1939] Ch 620, and therefore the decision in *Monroe v Twistleton* (1802) Peak Add Cas appears to remain binding, ie that an ex-spouse is incompetent to give evidence about events which occurred during the subsistence of the marriage.

Criminal cases

Section 80(5) Police and Criminal Evidence Act 1984 states:

'In any proceedings a person who has been but is no longer married to the accused shall be competent and compellable to give evidence as if that person and the accused had never been married.'

The wording is unambiguous, and the effect is that an ex-spouse is competent and compellable whether for prosecution or defence, and whether or not the evidence relates to occurrences during the subsistence of the marriage: *R v Mathias* (1989) 139 NLJ 1417. The case of *R v Cruttenden* [1991] 3 All ER 242 made it clear that the divorced spouse is competent and compellable in any proceedings which take place after s80(5) came into effect even if the events about which he or she was to give evidence occurred before it came into effect.

2.3 Key cases and statutes

- *R v Hayes* [1977] 1 WLR 234
- *R v Wallwork* (1958) 42 Cr App R 153
- Criminal Evidence Act 1898, s1

- Criminal Justice Act 1988, s33A
- Police and Criminal Evidence Act 1984, s80

2.4 Questions and suggested solutions

QUESTION ONE

Albert Jones was driving the family car with his wife Bertha in the front passenger seat and their 15-year-old son Charles and seven-year-old daughter Diane in the rear seats. The car was knocked off the road by an oncoming lorry which failed to stop. Charles was killed instantly, and Bertha and Albert both sustained cuts and bruises. Immediately before the incident Diane shrieked: 'Look out, Daddy!'; she was very shocked, but sustained no physical injury.

Albert has been charged with causing death by reckless driving. Bertha made a statement to the police to the effect that Albert was driving far too fast, could not negotiate a bend in the road and thus hit the lorry and was swept off the road; she now does not wish to testify for the prosecution. Diane made a statement: 'Daddy was on the proper side of the road – Mummy's side was near the fence – I shouted very hard when I saw a great big lorry slide across the road towards Daddy's car'.

Discuss the evidentiary problems.

Written by the Author

General Comment

Several issues are raised in this question, and each issue should be addressed as it arises. This method will ensure that nothing is overlooked.

Skeleton Solution

Competence and compellability generally – compellability of spouses: s80 Police and Criminal Evidence Act 1984 and its interpretation – competence of children in criminal trials.

Suggested Solution

The prosecution will have to prove beyond reasonable doubt that Albert was driving the car recklessly; and that reckless driving was a cause of the death of Charles: it is not necessary to prove that it was the only cause, so long as it was a cause of the death.

Bertha, as the spouse of Albert, the accused, is now a competent witness for the prosecution (as she is not charged jointly with them – see Police and Criminal Evidence Act 1984, s80(1)(a)), but whether she is compellable depends on the interpretation of s80(3) Police and Criminal Evidence Act 1984.

Diane, aged seven, being a 'child' for the purposes of s33A Criminal Justice Act 1988 (as amended by the Criminal Justice Act 1991), will have her competence tested in accordance with s33A(2A). She can only give unsworn evidence, and there is therefore now no need to test her understanding of the oath. The case law before the 1991 Act suggested a child of the age of five should not be called to give evidence in a criminal case: *R v Wallwork* (1958) 42 Cr App R 153, but above that age it was more likely that he or she would be called. However, the new test is, arguably, much less stringent and does not impose any particular burden of understanding concepts such as truth or lies.

If Diane gives evidence in Albert's defence her evidence does not need to be corroborated: s52(2) Criminal Justice Act 1991, and the judge is not required to warn the jury of the dangers of convicting without corroborative evidence, but the jury themselves may attach little or no weight to Diane's evidence, dependent on how she gives her evidence and withstands cross-examination by prosecuting counsel.

Section 80 Police and Criminal Evidence Act 1984 makes the spouse of an accused person a competent witness for the prosecution whatever the charge, unless the spouse is a co-accused. However, competence means that the spouse may give evidence if she wishes; Bertha can be compelled to give evidence against Albert only in the limited class of cases stipulated in s80(3), of which the relevant paragraph is s80(3)(a) which makes the spouse of the accused a compellable prosecution witness if:

> '… the offence charged involves an assault on, or injury or a threat of injury to, the wife or husband of the accused or a person who was at the material time under the age of 16.'

Section 80(3)(a) is not very clear, but in the situation in the question the offence charged involves injury to a person under 16, Charles, who was allegedly killed by Albert's reckless driving. If Charles had not died, but had suffered some non-fatal injury, the charge against Albert would have been reckless driving – therefore arguably it would not have been covered by s80(3)(a) as it would not have been in issue that Charles (and Bertha) had been injured, nor that Diane had feared immediate injury to herself. However, since Charles, under 16 years of age, has been fatally injured, and that injury must be part of the prosecution's case against Albert, then Bertha is a compellable witness for the prosecution against her spouse. Her attendance would probably be secured by a witness order or summons (Criminal Procedure (Attendance of Witnesses) Act 1965): if she does not attend when ordered or summoned to do so, a warrant may be issued for her arrest: *R v Bradford Justices, ex parte Wilkinson* [1990] RTR 59; if, having been sworn, she refused to testify, she would be in contempt of court. If she gave evidence, but contradicted her previous statement, and showed enmity to the prosecuting counsel, then with leave of the judge she could be treated as a hostile witness, and her examination by prosecuting counsel would resemble a cross-examination, with questions being put to her on her previous statement as to her husband's driving (see, for example, *R v Baldwin* [1986] Crim LR 681 and *R v Thompson* (1976) 64 Cr App R 96).

Albert cannot be compelled to testify in his own defence; if he does so testify then he can (and probably will) be subjected to rigorous cross-examination. If he elects not to testify, the matter is now governed by s35 Criminal Justice and Public Order Act 1994 which will allow for appropriate comments to be made upon his silence and for proper inferences to be drawn by the court in accordance with the guidelines suggested in *R* v *Cowan* [1995] 4 All ER 939.

Given the unwillingness of Bertha to testify for the prosecution, her evidence if she is compelled is unlikely to carry much weight, therefore it could be that a plea by Albert's counsel of 'no case to answer' would be successful at the conclusion of the prosecution's case, ie the prosecution have not even discharged the evidential burden, therefore there is not even a prima facie case. If such a plea is unsuccessful, or is not made, then Albert would be well advised to testify in his own defence if the only other defence witness is a child of tender years who may be adjudged incompetent as a witness; and if allowed to testify, she is not an independent, disinterested witness. Bertha, once she has been called as a prosecution witness, is not permitted to give evidence for the defence (*R* v *Kelly* (1985) The Times 27 July). Albert's counsel should also bear this in mind when deciding whether or not to call Albert (who must be called, if he is going to testify, before other defence witnesses).

QUESTION TWO

'When Parliament by the Act of 1898 effected a change in the general law and made the prisoner in every case a competent witness, it was in evident difficulty and it pursued the familiar English system of compromise.' (Viscount Sankey)

Discuss.

University of London LLB Examination
(for External Students) Law of Evidence June 1994 Q3

General Comment

This question permits wide discussion of the 1898 Act and its effects, especially with regard to the accused and evidence of his bad character. An understanding of the background to the Act is required, so as to put the quotation into context: the progression from the defendant being incompetent to the position today. Coupled with this, a critical assessment of the Act and its objectives is needed – does the defendant deserve protection and, if so, is it afforded by the Act?

Skeleton Solution

The historical development of the competence of the accused – Criminal Evidence Act 1898 – the balance/compromise of interests especially s1(f)(ii) (as amended to s1(3)(ii) by the Youth Justice and Criminal Evidence Act 1999) – judicial discretion to disallow cross-examination – discussion of the implications of this balance/compromise.

Suggested Solution

In criminal cases prior to the passing of the Criminal Evidence Act 1898, the accused was incompetent at common law. He was thus not permitted to give evidence in his own defence. This was because it was felt first that the defendant's personal interest in the outcome of the proceedings ought to preclude him from giving evidence and second that if competent, it was feared the defendant might be compelled to incriminate himself.

In the years leading up to the Criminal Evidence Act 1898 a number of statutes were passed, rendering the defendant competent in relation to certain offences. This piecemeal approach was clearly unsatisfactory; it was recognised that the defendant should be permitted to give sworn evidence in his own defence in all criminal cases. This was brought into effect by s1 of the Criminal Evidence Act 1898 (hereafter 'the Act').

The Act also changed the position relating to the competence of spouses. Spouses became competent (but not compellable) for the defence, subject to the consent of the defendant (s1(c)). Spouses remained incompetent for the prosecution (although various statutory exceptions were enacted). Since this part of the Act has now been repealed, and the spouse's competence and compellability is now governed by s80 Police and Criminal Evidence Act 1984, it is not proposed to deal with this area of the law in this suggested solution.

Returning to the defendant, s1 of the Act made defendants competent but not compellable in all criminal cases. However, it was recognised that whilst it was just for the defendant to be able to give evidence in his own defence, this also brought about serious potential risks – in particular the fear that he might be torn apart by cross-examination and be forced to incriminate himself. Cross-examination is 'a powerful weapon entrusted to counsel' (per Lord Sankey LC in *Machine and General Investment Co Ltd* v *Austin* [1935] AC 346).

The Act was with drafted with these issues in mind, attempting to strike a balance between these apparently conflicting considerations. How was this balance struck? The defendant was made competent but not compellable, hence he could give evidence in his own defence but only 'upon his own application' (s1(1)). The provisions in the 1898 Act concerning who could comment if the accused chose not to testify were repealed and replaced by s35 Criminal Justice and Public Order Act 1994.

The Act places restrictions on cross-examination of the accused: s1(e) provides that the defendant may be asked any question notwithstanding that it would tend to criminate him as to the offence charged (but not as to any other offences).

As regards other offences (and the defendant's bad character in general) the Act places restrictions on cross-examination. The defendant may be cross-examined as to other offences for the purpose of proving guilt, if the evidence of the other offences is admissible under the similar fact evidence doctrine (s1(f)(i), now s1(3)(i)).

The balance (or compromise) is apparent when one considers cross-examination with regard to offences which are not similar fact offences. The defendant is not fully protected, nor is he fully exposed to cross-examination.

Questions tending to show commission of, or convictions of, other offences (other than similar fact offences) or which show the defendant to be of bad character, are not permitted unless:

a) the defendant's good character is put in issue; or

b) imputations are cast on the prosecution or prosecution witnesses (s1(f)(ii), now s1(3)(ii)); or

c) the defendant gives evidence against a co-accused (s1(f)(iii), now s1(3)(iii)).

Hence, the defendant has the 'shield' of s1(f) (now s1(3)) unless one of the circumstances laid out in s1(f)(i), (ii) or (iii) (now s1(3)(i), (ii) or (iii)) arises, in which case the 'shield' is lost. Questions under s1(3)(ii) and (iii) go to credibility (although arguably questions under s1(3)(ii) indirectly go to guilt) (*Maxwell* v *DPP* [1935] AC 309). It should be added that the judge has a discretion to disallow such cross-examination by the prosecution (*R* v *Cook* [1959] 2 QB 340), but this is purely a discretion, not a general rule to be relied upon by the defence (*Selvey* v *DPP* [1970] AC 304).

How successfully has this balance been struck? The compromise reached in s1(3)(ii) acts as a powerful disincentive to cross-examination of prosecution witnesses by defence counsel. If 'imputations' are cast, then the defendant loses his 'shield'. Whilst prima facie this may seem fair (ie that if a defendant seeks to sully the reputation of prosecution witnesses he should be equally open to such treatment) it is submitted that in reality this is rather unfair – prosecution witnesses are not on trial and are not at risk of conviction and penalty. The defendant is! Surely the defendant's interests are compromised as a result of this apparent balance. It may be said that this is redressed by the judge's discretion to disallow cross-examination but it is submitted that this cannot be used to justify the compromise. As explained above, the House of Lords has said that the judicial discretion is not an absolute rule (*Selvey* v *DPP*).

When one considers the Act in the light of these points it becomes apparent that a compromise has been reached; regrettably, this includes a compromise of the interests of the person most at risk – the defendant.

QUESTION THREE

Bill and Denis are charged with indecent assault on Freda, aged 17, and with raping Gertie, aged 15. Agnes, Bill's wife, made a statement to the police in which she stated that she had witnessed both incidents, but she is now unwilling to give evidence. Bill and Denis assert that they have never touched the girls.

Consider whether Agnes is a competent, or compellable, witness for:

a) the prosecution;

b) Denis;

c) Bill.

Written by the Author

General Comment

This is a straightforward question on competence and compellability. Each part of the question should be considered in turn.

Skeleton Solution

Introduction: spouses as witnesses – whether Agnes competent/compellable for: prosecution; Denis; Bill – brief discussion of problems raised by s80 Police and Criminal Evidence Act 1984.

Suggested Solution

The general rule at common law was that a spouse of an accused person was incompetent as a witness for the prosecution; by virtue of the Criminal Evidence Act 1898 the spouse was competent as a witness for the accused and competent, provided the accused consented, as a witness for a person charged jointly with the accused. The rationale of this general rule was that the law respected the sanctity of marriage and, recognising the unity of husband and wife, considered it undesirable (even abhorrent) that one spouse testify against the other, whether as a witness for the prosecution or as a witness for a person jointly charged with the other spouse as that evidence could be unfavourable to the other spouse's defence.

Even prior to the Police and Criminal Evidence Act 1984 there were numerous statutes which created exceptions to the general rule governing the spouse as a prosecution witness, but in 1979 the House of Lords held that, in all these exceptional situations, the spouse of the accused was competent as a witness for the prosecution, but never compellable (*Hoskyn* v *Metropolitan Police Commissioner* [1979] AC 474). Pre-1984, therefore, the law in this area was very complex; as a prosecution witness the spouse of the accused was generally incompetent, but was competent by virtue of numerous statutory exceptions; as a witness for the accused she was competent but not compellable; as a witness for a person charged jointly with the accused spouse the other spouse was competent with the consent of the accused spouse but not compellable. So, pre-1984 a spouse was either generally incompetent, competent by virtue of statute or competent by virtue of the accused spouse's consent with regard to a co-accused, but never compellable as a witness.

Section 80 Police and Criminal Evidence Act (PACE) 1984 swept aside these, presumably archaic, restrictions on competence and further made the spouse compellable in specified circumstances. The spouse is now competent in every situation, unless charged jointly with the other spouse, and is compellable as a prosecution witness if the offence is a sexual offence against a person under 16, or is an offence involving injury to that spouse or a person under 16.

Applying s80 to the given facts, Agnes is compellable as a prosecution witness to the rape of Gertie, as the offence with which Bill, her spouse, is charged is 'a sexual offence alleged to have been committed in respect of a person who was at the material time under 16' (s80(3)(a) and (b)). Note that parts of s80(3) PACE 1984 will be abolished by the Youth Justice and Criminal Evidence Act 1999, although it appears that the overall effect will not be changed. Whether she is compellable as a prosecution witness to the indecent assault on Freda depends on the age of Freda 'at the the material time', ie if, at the time of the alleged indecent assault Freda was under 16, then Agnes is a compellable prosecution witness; if Freda was 16, then Agnes is merely competent. Despite her reluctance, if Agnes is compellable then her attendance can be secured by a witness order or witness summons (Criminal Procedure (Attendance of Witnesses) Act 1965). If she still refuses to attend a warrant can be issued for her arrest – *R v Bradford Justices, ex parte Wilkinson* [1990] RTR 59. If, having attended, she refuses to testify, she may be punished for contempt of court; if she shows enmity towards the prosecutor in giving her evidence and contradicts her previous statement, then, with leave of the judge, she may be treated as a hostile witness – in which case her examination-in-chief will take the form of a cross-examination, and consequently her evidence will lack the cogency it might otherwise have had. The prosecutor, therefore, may be reluctant to call Agnes if she shows hostility and is adamant that she does not intend to testify against her husband. (Regarding the competence and compellability of Agnes, it is irrelevant that they were not married at the time of the alleged incidents giving rise to the charges – s80 is concerned with the marital status of the accused and the potential witness at the time of the trial. Conversely, if Agnes and Bill had divorced by the time of the trial, then Agnes will be competent and compellable as if she had never been Bill's wife (s80(5)).)

Agnes is now competent as a witness for Denis whether or not Bill consents to her giving evidence for his co-accused at their joint trial (s80(1)(b)). However, her compellability as a witness for Denis is subject to the same restrictions as outlined above regarding her compellability as a prosecution witness. Whether competent or compellable as a witness to testify for Denis, the competence or compellability of Agnes is not subject to the consent of Bill – since s80 became law the wishes of the accused spouse in this context are irrelevant.

Agnes is a compellable witness for Bill, despite her previous apparent willingness to give evidence against him (s80(2)). However, if Agnes is compelled to give prosecution evidence in respect of the rape charge (and, subject to Freda's age at the time of the incident, the indecent assault charge), then she is no longer available as a witness for the defence, whether for her spouse, Bill, or his co-accused, Denis (*R v Kelly* (1985) The Times 27 July).

Several problems are caused by s80, not all of them by some ambiguities in its wording, and not all of them relevant to this problem. Those which are relevant are as follows.

a) If a successful defence application is made for separate trials of Bill and Denis, then Agnes is compellable as a witness for the prosecution, or defence, at Denis's trial, and her marital status is irrelevant.

b) Whether or not Bill and Denis are jointly tried, if the counts of rape and indecent assault are severed, and therefore tried separately, then Agnes may be compellable as a prosecution witness at the trial for rape, but not at the trial for indecent assault, but at both trials she would be compellable as a witness for Bill, but not Denis.

c) If there are separate trials of Bill and Denis, or if they are tried jointly, and Agnes gives prosecution evidence under compulsion, she may have to be treated as a hostile witness, but if the compulsion is permissible only in respect of the alleged rape, not the indecent assault, it may be difficult to the point of impossibility to put her previous statement to her in her examination-in-chief without referring to both alleged incidents as they may be inextricably linked in her statement.

QUESTION FOUR

'It is the principle behind the right to silence, not its practical effect, which makes it necessary to reverse the recent reforms.'

Discuss.

University of London LLB Examination
(for External Students) Law of Evidence June 1997 Q4

General Comment

This question gives a considerable latitude to the candidate in deciding the form and shape of answer, but there is a proposition here that must be supported or rebutted. Any answer that fails to do either is likely to receive low marks. It will be necessary to discuss the scope and rationale for the so-called right of silence as well as the arguments and process that led to the erosion of the rights. The legislative changes and the guidance given by the case law should be looked at if a complete view of the defendant's situation is to be achieved. By way of conclusion, a firm view, supported by reasoning, should be taken of the proposition.

Skeleton Solution

The defendant's right to silence: extent of the right and legal rationale – the evidential effects of silence – the pressure for change and the legislative changes – case law development – conclusion.

Suggested Solution

The so-called 'right to silence' of an accused person consists of various identifiable options open to him, ranging from matters occurring before he is even a suspect right up to the events occurring during his trial. A person may quite properly refuse to answer to police at all stages from initial questioning right through to interviews under detention conditions. He may properly refuse to give evidence or, having been sworn, to answer particular questions and be free from compulsion on the matter. A person had, until relatively recently, the right to fail to give evidence or to answer questions and not have the consequence of permitting prosecution comment or jury inferences drawn which would be adverse to his position. These rights were, until the legislative changes, subject only to minor legislative inroads and they have their origins in the reaction to the legally permissible compulsion of accused persons formerly associated with prerogative powers and institutions, such as the Star Chamber Court. Since the Civil War swept away such compulsion, the common law and statute (s1(a) and (b) Criminal Evidence Act 1898) has largely seen these rights as inviolate both as to freedom from compulsion as well as from adverse effects.

Quite a different matter is the evidential effect of silence and an understanding of this is necessary for a proper perspective on silence. There is ample authority for the proposition that, as between persons who are speaking 'on even terms', a reaction of silence in the face of an accusation which would normally call for some answer is capable of constituting evidence that the accused acknowledged the truth of the accusation: *R v Mitchell* (1892) 17 Cox CC 503; *R v Norton* [1910] 2 KB 496; *R v Chandler* [1976] 3 All ER 105. Such a silence, equating to acceptance, is admissible along with the accusation because the silence equates to a confession by conduct within s82(1) Police and Criminal Evidence Act (PACE) 1984 and to an informal admission at common law. The matter changes rapidly, however, once the accused and accuser cease to be speaking 'on even terms'. According to Lord Diplock in *Hall v R* [1971] 1 All ER 322, silence cannot give rise to an inference of acceptance in the latter situation, usually where the police are questioning a person as a suspect. Nevertheless, there are many cases where *Hall* has been distinguished and an accused taken to have been on even terms with the accuser (usually the victim) despite the presence of the police as in *R v Horne* [1990] Crim LR 188 and also in *Chandler*. The trend has been away from *Hall* in recent years.

Despite the fundamental nature of the rights involved in silence, very great public dissatisfaction arose at the ease with which many defendants appeared able to evade justice by resorting to silence in the knowledge that this could do their case no harm and might well allow their very silence, as a right, to inject reasonable doubt into the trial. There was also great unease at the idea of defendants being permitted to advance defences and matters at trial for the first time, long after any satisfactory investigations into the matter had ceased to be possible. A Royal Commission under Lord Runciman in 1993 recommended that no inferences should be drawn based on silence under police questioning, but the experience of Northern Ireland legislation, based on recommendations of the Criminal Law Revision Committee, showed that there was a supportable case for allowing inferences to be drawn from silence. Parliament took the initiative in ss34–39 Criminal Justice and Public Order Act (CJPOA) 1994. Experience with Northern Ireland legislation had also paved the way for allowing adverse comment by the prosecution and adverse inferences to be drawn from failure to give evidence. The effects of ss34–39 CJPOA 1994 allow for proper inferences and comment upon failure to mention facts when questioned under caution or when charged (s34), upon a defendant of 14 years or older declining to give evidence or, once sworn, refusing to answer a question without good cause (s35), failing to account for marks, substances etc after arrest (s36), and failure to account for his presence at the time and place of arrest (s37).

The massive changes have been developed and complemented by case law development such as the possibility that remaining silent on the advice of a legal advisor will not, of itself, be 'good cause' for the purposes of s34: *R v Condron* [1997] 1 WLR 827. *R v Cowan* [1995] 4 All ER 939 has provided the Court of Appeal guidelines on the drawing of appropriate inferences under s35 and the width of the judicial discretion whether to direct or not against drawing inferences seems very considerable. The judge does not have so much discretion as to the matters that he must direct the jury about but, undoubtly, a much greater responsibility falls upon the judge since these changes.

It would be folly to pretend that the legal right to silence has not been greatly reduced and weakened by the cumulative effect of these changes, but it should be also remembered that the evidential effect of silence has long shown the risks attendant on maintaining silence where some answer might be expected. No compulsion has crept in here at all. There are no echoes of the Court of Star Chamber; all that has happened is the recognition of drawing logical inferences where it is proper to do so and, even then, no conviction can follow on the inferences alone: s38(3) CJPOA 1994. The principle underlying the right to silence never was based as much on a privilege against self-incrimination as on a protection against compulsion of accused persons. This principle is unaffected by the changes and it is submitted that there are no good arguments for reversing the reforms. The notion that there is a right to silence should not, in today's enlightened climate with a comprehensive evidence code under the Police and Criminal Evidence Act 1984, carry with it a certain consequence that remaining silent should have no adverse effect whatever for an accused. This would be totally illogical.

QUESTION FIVE

a) Andrea has been charged with assaulting Brian in an incident at a wedding reception, where both were guests. Andrea in a police interview said that she was acting in self-defence. The prosecution wish to call the following as witnesses. They have both given written statements to the police.

i) Charles, who is Andrea's husband. He stated that Andrea was drunk and had hit Brian without any provocation. Charles has recently told the police that he no longer wishes to give evidence against his wife.

ii) Davina, a girl aged eight, who was present when the assault took place.

Advise the prosecution on the competence and compellability of Charles and Davina.

b) Andrea has now been prosecuted in respect of the alleged assault on Brian and acquitted. Brian wishes to bring civil proceedings against her for assault. He wishes to call Charles and Davina as witnesses. Advise Brian as to their competence and compellability in his proposed civil action.

University of London LLB Examination
(for External Students) Law of Evidence June 2000 Q5

General Comment

Competence in criminal trials is governed by the Youth Justice and Criminal Evidence Act 1999 (ss53–56) and that Act also amends s80 Police and Criminal Evidence Act (PACE) 1984 to some extent. A good understanding of these provisions is required so that relevant information which is not supplied can be identified. The Evidence Amendment Act 1853 makes the spouses of parties to civil actions competent witnesses and competence is governed by the common law. In a question such as this, it is best to consider the position of each potential witness in turn.

Skeleton Solution

Competence and compellability – explanation of terms – Charles: s80(1) PACE 1984 as amended; *Hoskyn* v *Metropolitan Police Commissioner*; s80(2A)–(4A) PACE 1984; witness summons; contempt of court – Davina: s53 Youth Justice and Criminal Evidence Act 1999; *R* v *Wallwork*; *R* v *Z* – the civil proceedings: Charles; Evidence Amendment Act 1853; Evidence Further Amendment Act 1869; Davina; s96 Children Act 1996; *R* v *Khan*; *R* v *Bains*; Civil Evidence Act 1995.

Suggested Solution

This question raises issues concerning the competence and compellability of witnesses in both criminal and civil proceedings. A witness is described as competent to give evidence if he may be called to give evidence and compellable if, being competent, he may be compelled by the court to do so. The general rule is that all persons are competent to give evidence and that competent witnesses may also be compelled to give evidence. This rule applies in both criminal and civil proceedings, but it has been placed on a statutory basis in the former by s53(1) Youth Justice and Criminal Evidence Act 1999 which provides that: 'At every stage in criminal proceedings all persons are (whatever their age) competent to give evidence'. However, there are exceptions to the rule, and it is the nature and extent of two exceptions which are raised in the question.

a) The criminal proceedings

Charles

Before the enactment of the Police and Criminal Evidence Act (PACE) 1984, the spouse of the accused was generally not competent to give evidence for the prosecution. There were several common law and statutory exceptions making the spouse competent in certain situations but generally, even where such an exception applied, the spouse was not compellable for the prosecution. The situation was reviewed by the Criminal Law Revision Committee in its 11th Report. The Committee recommended that the spouse should continue to be competent for the prosecution in all cases. This view was initially reflected in s80(1) PACE 1984. That provision was repealed by the Youth Justice and Criminal Evidence Act 1999 and the spouse of an accused is now competent to give evidence for the prosecution under s53(1) of that Act. Accordingly, Charles is competent to give evidence for the prosecution and if his evidence is in the same terms as his written witness statement, it seems that his testimony will be valuable to the prosecution. However, the prosecution may be placed in some difficulty by the fact that it now appears that Charles is reluctant to give evidence against Andrea. The question that then arises is whether Charles can be compelled to give evidence for the prosecution.

At common law, a spouse is competent for the prosecution but not compellable (*Hoskyn* v *Metropolitan Police Commissioner* [1979] AC 474). The House of Lords in *Hoskyn* was reluctant to compel a wife to give evidence against her husband on a charge of violence, however trivial, and regardless of the consequences for herself, her marriage and her family. Lord Edmund Davies was the only Law Lord to disagree with this view. He took the view that prosecutions based on trivial violence were unlikely to be brought, and said that cases of serious violence by one spouse against the other were too grave to depend on the willingness of one spouse to testify against the other and 'ought not to be regarded as having no importance extending beyond the domestic hearth'. The Criminal Law Revision Committee recommended that a spouse should be compellable only in cases of personal violence by the accused against his or her spouse. These recommendations were not only accepted but were extended by Parliament in s80(2A)–(4A) PACE 1984.

Under s80 PACE 1984 Charles is compellable for the prosecution if the offence with which Andrea is charged is a 'specified offence'. Specified offences are defined in s80(3) to include an assault on a person who was at the material time under the age of 16. Thus the factor which will determine whether Charles may be compelled to give evidence for the prosecution against Andrea will be Brian's age at the time of the alleged assault.

If Charles is compellable, his attendance may be secured by a witness summons or order (Criminal Procedure (Attendance of Witnesses) Act 1965); if he does not attend when ordered or summoned to do so, a warrant may be issued for his arrest. If, having been sworn, he refused to testify, he would be in contempt of court. If

Charles gave evidence, but contradicted his previous statement, and showed enmity to the prosecuting counsel, then with the leave of the trial judge, he could be treated as a hostile witness and his examination by prosecuting counsel would resemble a cross-examination, with questions being put to him on his previous statement concerning the incident (as in, for example *R* v *Baldwin* [1986] Crim LR 681).

The difficulty for the prosecution may be that, if Charles is unwilling to testify against Andrea, his evidence may be of little weight.

Davina

Davina's competence to give evidence is also governed by s53 Youth Justice and Criminal Evidence Act 1999. Section 53(1) applies to make Davina competent (whatever her age) but is qualified by s53(3) which states that a person is not competent to give evidence in criminal proceedings if it appears to the court that he is not a person who is able to understand questions put to him as a witness, and give answers to them which can be understood.

The procedure for determining competence under s53 of the Act is contained in s54. This section provides that competency may be raised either by one of the parties or by the court acting on its own motion (s54(1)). The party seeking to call the witness (in this case the prosecution) bears the burden of proof to satisfy the court on a balance of probabilities that the witness is competent to give evidence (s53(2)). The determination of competency must take place in the absence of the jury (s53(4)). Any questioning of the witness by the court must take place in the presence of the parties (s54(6)).

Since Davina is aged eight, a point may be taken as to her competency. It seems that this issue cannot be determined by reference to her age alone. In *R* v *Wallwork* (1958) 42 Cr App R 153 Lord Goddard CJ disapproved the calling of a child of five to give evidence and this dictum was approved in *R* v *Wright; R* v *Ormerod* (1987) 90 Cr App R 91. However, in *R* v *Z* [1990] 3 WLR 940, Lord Lane CJ expressed the opinion that *Wallwork* had been overtaken by events.

If Davina is competent to give evidence, the next question which will arise concerns whether she should do so as a sworn witness. Section 55(2) of the 1999 Act provides that a witness may not be sworn for the purpose of giving evidence unless he has attained the age of 14 and has a sufficient appreciation of the solemnity of the occasion and of the particular responsibility to tell the truth which is involved in taking an oath. Applying this section, it is apparent that if Davina gives evidence, she will do so unsworn. Since Davina will be unsworn as the result of the application of the statute, the fact that she is unsworn should not itself affect the weight to be attached to her evidence, although her young age may, of course, affect the credibility of her evidence. The Act does not provide for a particular direction to be given where evidence is unsworn.

In principle, as a competent witness, Davina will also be compellable. However, the prevailing view is that it will rarely be appropriate to compel a child to give evidence and the prosecution case is unlikely to be assisted by the production of an obviously unwilling child witness. In such a case, the court will consider exercising its residual discretion as to the conduct of its own proceedings to prevent oppression; there are a number of provisions in the Youth Justice and Criminal Evidence Act 1999, and elsewhere, whose purpose it is to prevent the victimisation of child witnesses.

b) The civil proceedings

Charles

The effect of s1 Evidence Amendment Act 1853 and the Evidence Further Amendment Act 1869 is to make the spouse of a party competent and compellable in civil proceedings. Accordingly, Charles could be compelled to attend court and give evidence for Brian by the issue of a witness summons. Failure to attend court would be a contempt, and could result in arrest. Similarly, if having come to court Charles refused to answer questions, this would again be a contempt which could lead to criminal penalties. The 1853 Act has been construed strictly (*Shenton* v *Tyler* [1939] Ch 620) and therefore the decision in *Monroe* v *Twistleton* (1802) Peak Add Cas appears to remain binding. This result has been described as preposterous and the effect will be that if Charles and Andrea were married at the time of the incident, but divorced by the time of the civil trial, Charles will be incompetent to give evidence about the incident since it occurred during the subsistence of the marriage.

Section 14 Civil Evidence Act 1965 provides that no witness can be required in civil proceedings to answer any question or to produce any document or thing if to do so would expose that person, or that person's spouse, to proceedings for any criminal offence in the UK. This provision is of no assistance to Charles, however, since Andrea has already been acquitted in the criminal proceedings.

Davina

At common law in civil cases, a child who did not understand the nature of the oath was not competent and could not be called as a witness (*Baker* v *Rabetts* (1954) 118 JPN 303). Section 96 of the Children Act 1996 now provides that where, in the opinion of the court, a child called as a witness does not understand the nature of the oath, the child may give evidence unsworn if, in the opinion of the court:

i) he understands that it is his duty to tell the truth; and

ii) he has sufficient understanding to justify the reception of his evidence.

A child for these purposes is a person under the age of 18 (s105). Accordingly, so far as Davina is concerned, there are two questions which the court will have to determine: first, whether Davina is competent to give sworn evidence and, if not, whether she is able to give unsworn evidence.

The issue of competency to take the oath is a matter for the discretion of the court, and the judge will put preliminary questions to Davina in order to enable him to form an opinion. Prior to the introduction of statutory provision in criminal proceedings, the criminal courts would also have occasion to embark on such investigations in appropriate cases and there are a number of decisions in which the court discuss such cases. In *R v Khan* (1981) 73 Cr App R 190 the three members of the Court of Appeal held that much will depend on the type of child before the court, but noted that, in the experience of the three members of the Court, inquiry is generally necessary in the case of a child under the age of 14. This was an observation and not a rule of inflexible application (*R v Bains* [1992] Crim LR 795) but it is probable that there would be such an inquiry into the ability of Davina to take the oath. Questions put to Davina would probably test her appreciation of the solemnity of the occasion and the added responsibility to tell the truth involved in taking the oath, rather than whether she had any understanding of the divine sanction of the oath (*R v Hayes* [1977] 2 All ER 288). The court in *Hayes* appeared to accept the concession made by the defence that the dividing line between children able to take the oath and those not capable of taking the oath probably falls between the ages of eight and ten.

If it appears to the court that Davina is not capable of taking the oath, her evidence may be given unsworn, if in the opinion of the court, the conditions in s96(2)(a) and (b) are satisfied. The general rule concerning compellability would apply to Davina, so that if she is a competent witness she would also be compellable.

In civil proceedings, hearsay evidence may be adduced under the Civil Evidence Act 1995 and this would enable Brain to adduce the evidence of both Charles and Davina without calling either. This provision would not allow Brian to circumvent any difficulty in connection with Davina's competency, since it would have to be shown that she satisfied the test imposed by s96 Children Act 1989. However, such a course of action might prove more attractive than compelling attendance at court, particularly in Davina's case, and in assessing the weight to be attached to the evidence the court would take into account whether it would have been reasonable and practicable for Brian to have produced Charles or Davina as a witness (s4).

Chapter 3
Corroboration

3.1   **Introduction**

3.2   **Key points**

3.3   **Key cases and statute**

3.4   **Questions and suggested solutions**

3.1 Introduction

The requirement for evidence to be corroborated is exceptional in English law, and the exceptional circumstances where the court will concern itself with corroboration have been whittled away by s34 Criminal Justice Act 1988 (and now, significantly, in s32 of the Criminal Justice and Public Order Act (CJPOA) 1994 which finally abolished the mandatory requirements for corroboration) as well as rendered more complex by decisions such as that in *R v Chance* [1988] 3 All ER 225. In law degree and Bar Final examinations it is unusual to be faced with a question dealing solely with corroboration; as happens so often in Evidence papers questions about the area dealt with in this chapter will include a test of the students' knowledge of other, overlapping, areas such as burdens of proof, right of silence etc. Nevertheless, corroboration is an important issue in the law of evidence in criminal trials, although the effect of s32 CJPOA 1994 reduces its importance considerably.

3.2 Key points

The following should be understood by the student who wishes to be conversant with corroboration.

Definition of corroboration

The best definition is a combination of that given in *R v Baskerville* [1916] 2 KB 658 and *R v Scarrott* [1978] QB 1016, ie 'relevant, admissible and credible evidence, originating from a source independent of the witness requiring corroboration, and implicating the accused in a material particular'.

Functions of judge and jury

It is the function of the judge to decide whether evidence (either in itself, or aggregated with other evidence) is capable of amounting to corroboration. If the judge decides this in the affirmative, he must then leave it to the jury to decide whether the evidence is corroborative. If the judge decides this in the negative, he must direct the jury to disregard that evidence because, for example, it is not credible, not independent etc.

Corroboration a pre-requisite to conviction

Three statutes stipulate that an accused person cannot be convicted of the offences stipulated on the evidence of only one witness.

a) The offence of driving a motor vehicle on a road at an excessive speed, contrary to the Road Traffic Regulations Act 1984. Section 89 provides that a driver cannot be convicted of exceeding the speed limit on the uncorroborated opinion evidence of one witness as to the speed of the vehicle. There are two caveats:

   i) the corroboration requirement arises only when the charge is exceeding the speed limit – so if the charge were driving at a speed or in a manner which was reckless, the corroboration requirement would not have to be met;

   ii) corroboration is required of the opinion evidence of one witness, therefore if the evidence is of fact, eg a police officer's reading of a radar speed device, corroboration is not required.

b) The Treason Act 1895 requires the evidence of two or more witnesses for a conviction of high treason.

c) Section 13 Perjury Act 1911 provides that a person cannot be convicted of perjury on the uncorroborated testimony of only one witness as to the falsity of any statement made by the accused which is alleged to be false. Therefore, if the statement was believed to be false, but unbeknown to the maker happened to be true, then there is no corroboration requirement. Where corroboration as to the falsity is required, it does not matter if two witnesses give evidence as to the falsity of the defendant's statement, and each heard him admit its falsity together, on the same occasion: *R v Peach* [1990] 2 All ER 966.

The stipulation that an accused person could not be convicted of offences of procuration – for sexual intercourse or prostitution – of women contrary to the Sexual Offences Act 1956 has now been abrogated by s33(1) CJPOA 1994.

Corroboration warning required as a matter of practice

a) The evidence of children – always now to be given unsworn – does not require corroboration nor a corroboration warning: s52(2) Criminal Justice Act 1991 abolishing s38(1) Children and Young Persons Act 1933, and s34(1) Criminal Justice Act 1988. However, judges may continue as a matter of practice, rather than law, to give a corroboration warning.

b) Accomplices testifying for the defence. An accomplice giving evidence in his own defence obviously has his own axe to grind, and will often give evidence which is unfavourable to his co-accused. Therefore, as a matter of practice, it is desirable that the jury be alerted to the dangers of convicting on that evidence if it is not corroborated. Every case must be treated according to its own particular circumstances, and the omission of a warning will not always lead to a conviction being quashed on appeal: *R v Prater* [1960] 2 QB 464. Where there is no evidence pointing to the involvement of the witness in the crime of which the accused is charged, but nevertheless the witness may have some ulterior motive in testifying for the defence or for the prosecution, then the judge may direct the jury to treat that evidence with some scepticism, but a failure to do so will not necessarily result in the quashing of the conviction of the accused: *R v Beck* [1982] 1 WLR 461; *R v Lovell* [1990] Crim LR 111. The case of *R v Brown* (1991) The Times 13 December in the Court of Appeal, also makes it clear that even if the witness is not an accomplice, but his evidence might be suspect, the judge should not give a corroboration warning, but warn the jury of danger of relying on that evidence.

Similarly, where the spouse of an accomplice gives evidence which is supportive of the accomplice's evidence, the judge may give a warning to the jury to treat the spouse's testimony with caution: *R v Evans* [1965] 2 QB 295.

The requirement to give an accomplice corroboration warning as a matter of practice was abrogated by s32 CJPOA 1994 and the judicial discretion involved is now summarised in *R v Makanjuola* [1995] 3 All ER 730, in which Lord Taylor CJ made it clear that attempts to reimpose the straitjacket of the old corroboration rules were strongly to be depreciated. It seems that where the trial judge bases any warning on that suggested in *Makanjuola* it will be very difficult for an appellant to show that the exercise of the discretion to give the warning was *Wednesbury* (*Associated Provincial Picture Houses Ltd* v *Wednesbury Corporation* [1948] 1 KB 223) unreasonable (*R v L* [1999] Crim LR 489).

Section 32 CJPOA 1994 also ended the requirement, as a matter of practice, to warn about the evidence of sexual offence victims, and *Makanjuola* also applies to these cases.

Identification of accused

Evidence of identification does not need to be corroborated, and a warning against convicting on such uncorroborated evidence is not mandatory. However, because a witness identifying the accused can often be mistaken, albeit genuine, guidelines were laid down by the Court of Appeal (Criminal Division) in *R v Turnbull* [1977] QB 224, and any student of evidence should be conversant with the gist of what the court said, and of subsequent appellate decisions which qualify or amplify the *Turnbull* guidelines. Note further that identification from police photographs ought not to be put in evidence because it infringes similar fact rules: *R v Bleakley* [1993] Crim LR 203 and *R v Lamb* (1980) 71 Cr App R 198.

Corroboration provided by the accused

The accused may provide the necessary, or desirable, corroboration of the evidence of prosecution witnesses in these cases.

a) If the accused tells a material lie (usually by making one statement, then retracting some, or all, of it and making another contradictory statement) then this may amount to corroborative evidence. Whether it will or not was exemplified in *R v Lucas* [1981] QB 720; briefly, to be corroborative the lie must be material, deliberate, and told because of fear of the truth because of a realisation of guilt. So, if the accused can give an explanation of his lies which is consistent with innocence, the lies will not amount to corroboration: *R v Dowley* [1983] Crim LR 168; *R v Ahmed* [1993] Crim LR 946.

    Similarly, lies told by the accused when testifying in his own defence may corroborate other evidence, but do not necessarily, and the same criteria apply as those for lies told pre-court.

b) The silence of the accused in court, ie the fact that he elects not to testify, can never amount to corroboration. But if the accused is accused of an offence by a person on equal terms with him, and he remains silent where it would be reasonable to expect some reply (such as a denial, an indignant retort etc), then his silence is capable of corroborating other evidence of prosecution witnesses: *R v Cramp* (1880) 14 Cox CC 390. Whether or not the defendant and his accuser are on equal terms is a question for the jury: *R v Horne* [1990] Crim LR 188.

    Where the accuser is a person in authority, eg a police officer, then the silence of the accused, as the law stands at present, cannot be corroboration: *R v Whitehead* [1929] 1 KB 99.

c) If the accused refuses, without any reasonable explanation, to provide samples or specimens when he is told the purpose for which they are required, then his refusal is capable of amounting to corroboration: *R v Smith (Robert William)* (1985) 81 Cr App R 286. This decision has been adopted in s62(10) Police and Criminal Evidence Act 1984, in respect of refusal by suspects to give intimate body samples, the phrase used being 'without good cause' rather than 'without reasonable explanation' as in *Smith*. (With regard to non-intimate samples, s65(3) of the 1984 Act provides for these to be taken without consent.)

3.3 Key cases and statute

*   *R v Baskerville* [1916] 2 KB 658

*   *R v Beck* [1982] 1 WLR 461

*   *R v Makanjuola* [1995] 3 All ER 730

*   Criminal Justice and Public Order Act 1994, s32

3.4 Questions and suggested solutions

QUESTION ONE

'The purpose of corroboration is not to give validity or credence to evidence which is deficient or suspect or incredible but only to confirm and support that which as evidence is sufficient and satisfactory and credible ...' (Lord Morris)

Discuss.

University of London LLB Examination
(for External Students) Law of Evidence June 1994 Q4

General Comment

To attempt this question, a knowledge of the context of this quotation is vital since it is a dictum which has been disapproved! The quotation should be put in context and discussed with regard to the decision in *Attorney-General of Hong Kong* v *Wong Muk-Ping* [1987] 2 All ER 488. There is then ample room for discussion of the purpose of corroboration and the various scenarios in which questions of corroboration arise.

Skeleton Solution

Put quotation in context: *DPP* v *Hester* – discuss this dictum as considered in *Wong Muk-Ping* – define corroboration and consider its need and purpose more fully with regard to types of case involving corroboration – corroboration required as matter of law; corroboration warning as matter of law; corroboration warning as matter of practice; identification cases.

Suggested Solution

This dictum is taken from the case of *DPP* v *Hester* [1973] AC 296. Its clear implication is that the purpose of corroboration is to support evidence which is 'sufficient, satisfactory and credible' in its own right (ie when considered without any corroborative evidence). If evidence is not 'sufficient, satisfactory and credible' in its own right, then, Lord Morris suggests, it is not the purpose of corroboration to support it. (Dicta to similar effect can be found in other cases, eg per Watkins LJ in *R* v *Olaleye* (1986) 82 Cr App R 337 and per Lord Hailsham LC in *DPP* v *Kilbourne* [1973] AC 729.)

This proposition came before the Privy Council in the case of *Attorney-General of Hong Kong* v *Wong Muk-Ping* [1987] 2 All ER 488, where it was submitted that where a judge gives a corroboration warning, the jury should be told to consider the credibility of the witness desiring corroboration (the 'suspect witness') in isolation from any other evidence. If they are satisfied as to the credibility of that witness, only then may they go on to consider any corroborative evidence, in order to decide whether or not to accept the evidence of the 'suspect witness'.

This submission was rejected. Lord Bridge said that it is precisely because the evidence of a suspect witness might be unreliable that the corroboration warning is given. Hence, the credibility of a suspect witness is not to be considered in isolation, but in the light of the corroborative evidence, which may assist in establishing its reliability. It should be added that in rare cases, if the suspect witness admits that his evidence-in-chief was false (and the prosecution depends upon it) *then* the judge should direct an acquittal: *Attorney-General of Hong Kong* v *Wong Muk-Ping* [1987] 2 All ER 488.

A more detailed examination of the purpose of corroboration can be undertaken by briefly considering first what corroboration entails, and second, when it arises in the law of evidence.

What is corroboration?

'It is a matter of common sense that the risk of conviction of the innocent is reduced if a conviction is based on the testimony of more than one acceptable witness:' per Lord Morris in *DPP* v *Hester* [1973] AC 296. Such additional evidence is termed 'corroboration'. However, there is no general requirement for corroboration in criminal law. A conviction, generally speaking, may properly and safely be founded on uncorroborated evidence. Therefore, generally, whilst corroboration may assist in proving a case, there is no general requirement for it to exist before a jury may convict.

There are, however, exceptions to this general rule. The reasons underlying these exceptions are simple:

a) the gravity of the allegation; and/or

b) the danger of acting on certain categories of evidence, if uncorroborated.

In order to amount to corroboration, evidence must meet certain requirements:

a) it must be relevant – this is true of all evidence;

b) it must be admissible – that is to say, not excluded by other rules of evidence (again this is true of all evidence);

c) it must be credible – the evidence providing corroboration must be credible. If a witness's testimony falls of its own inanition, the question of the witness being capable of giving corroboration does not arise: per Lord Hailsham in *DPP* v *Kilbourne* [1973] AC 729. It should be noted that this is a quite different scenario from the witness desiring corroboration (the 'suspect witness'), whose evidence does not fall of its own inanition but should be considered in the light of any corroborative evidence, as explained above in *Attorney-General of Hong Kong* v *Wong Muk-Ping*;

d) it must be independent – that is to say, extraneous to the witness who is to be corroborated: *R* v *Whitehead* [1929] 1 KB 99; and

e) it must implicate the accused in a material particular – it must confirm both a material circumstance of the case and the identity of the defendant: *R* v *Baskerville* [1916] 2 KB 658.

When, and why, do questions of corroboration arise? These queries can be answered with reference to four types of case:

a) cases where corroboration itself is required as a matter of law;

b) cases where a corroboration warning must be given as a matter of law;

c) cases in which a corroboration warning is given as a matter of practice;

d) cases involving identification.

Corroboration required as a matter of law

Corroboration itself is required in very few scenarios. However, when required, if there is no evidence capable of amounting to corroboration, the judge will direct an acquittal.

Corroboration is required in the following cases.

a) Speeding – a conviction cannot be based on the opinion evidence of just one witness; corroboration is required (eg another witness's opinion evidence!): s89(2) Road Traffic Regulations Act 1984.

b) Perjury – s13 Perjury Act 1911. The reason underlying this section is unclear, but may be a policy decision – it is felt that if prosecutions for perjury were too easy, witnesses might be discouraged from giving evidence (Criminal Law Revision Committee, 11th Report (Cmnd 4991, paras 178 and 180)).

c) Treason – s1 Treason Act 1895. Technically, treason is punishable by the death penalty, hence corroboration (understandably) is required.

Corroboration warning required as a matter of law

A warning used to be given because of the inherent unreliability of certain types of evidence. The warning was to the effect that it was dangerous to convict on the uncorroborated evidence of a witness, but if satisfied as to the truth of such evidence, the jury could nonetheless do so: *R v Freebody* (1935) 25 Cr App R 69. It should be stressed that corroboration itself was not required – the requirement was that the warning be given.

The warning was given as a matter of law in only two types of case.

a) Accomplices giving evidence for the prosecution – the obvious danger was that the accomplice may minimise his own part, and maximise the roles of others!

b) Sexual offences – allegations are easy to make and difficult to refute. Dangers arise because allegations may be motivated by spite, shame, fantasy and so on (Criminal Law Revision Committee, 11th Report (Cmnd 4991, paras 178 and 180)).

Both of these requirements are now abrogated by s32 CJPOA 1994.

Corroboration warning given as a matter of practice

Two examples will suffice.

a) Accomplices giving evidence on their own behalf – a warning is desirable (but not required) because the witness may seek to minimise his own role, and increase the role of his co-defendants: *R v Cheema* [1994] 1 All ER 639.

b) Children – a warning is desirable because of the risks of childish imagination, suggestibility or poor memory: *R v Pryce* [1991] Crim LR 379.

Identification cases

Such cases carry with them the risk of mistaken identification. Whilst neither corroboration nor a corroboration warning is required, a warning is given to the effect that there is a 'special need for caution' in such cases, and telling the jury to look for 'supporting evidence' (which need not meet the strict requirements of corroboration), although the jury may convict in the absence of such supporting evidence. A detailed examination of this warning as laid down in *R v Turnbull* [1977] QB 224 is beyond the ambit of this question.

In conclusion, the quotation discussed has a flawed foundation. The very purpose of corroboration is to enable the jury to consider the credibility of the 'suspect witness'. The categories of case in which a question of corroboration arises have been discussed, showing that in each category there is potentially unreliable evidence, hence the suspect witness's evidence should be considered in the light of any corroborative evidence so as to enable the jury to accept or reject it. The Privy Council's decision in *Attorney-General of Hong Kong* v *Wong Muk-Ping* [1987] 2 All ER 488 thus firmly rejects Lord Morris' dictum from *DPP v Hester* [1973] AC 296.

QUESTION TWO

A is charged with indecently assaulting B, a six-year-old boy, and C, a ten-year-old girl. Both B and C are pupils at the same school. B's story is that A offered him a lift home in his car while B was walking to the bus stop just after school had finished and the assault took place in the car shortly before A dropped him off just round the corner from where B lived. D, B's mother, noticing a mark on B's leg that evening exclaims, 'Did someone do that to you?' and B describes what happened. He describes A as a short person with a beard, who wore sunglasses and 'had a funny smell'. C's story is that, the day after the assault on B, a man, wearing sunglasses and smelling of garlic, sat on the seat next to her at the bus stop while she was going home from school. He then put his hand on her thigh. She screamed and ran away. E, a passerby, can confirm that he heard C scream but that he only got a glimpse of a short man, who disappeared very quickly.

F, a policeman, sketches a picture in accordance with B's description and B subsequently picks out A in an identification parade. B is overwhelmed by the events of the trial and is unwilling to give evidence. C picks out A from five photographs shown to her from the police records. A claims an alibi for each charge.

Advise the prosecution on any evidential issues that might arise.

University of London LLB Examination
(for External Students) Law of Evidence June 1992 Q6

General Comment

This is a very wide question covering many important evidential issues. You will not be expected to go into each evidential point in great detail; marks will be awarded for recognising the issues.

Skeleton Solution

Children – children's evidence – competence and compellability – corroboration – warnings – previous consistent statement – complaints in cases of sexual nature – identification evidence – alibi.

Suggested Solution

The most important issue here is the competence of a child to give evidence. The general rule in criminal cases is that if a child is competent to give evidence for the prosecution, the child can be compelled to give evidence for the prosecution. B is overwhelmed by the events of a trial and is unwilling to give evidence. The prosecution will be able to compel B to give evidence.

It was established in the case of *R v Brasier* (1779) 1 Leach CC 199 that the competence of a young child to give sworn evidence in criminal proceedings depends upon whether the child understands the nature of the oath but now the matter is determined by s33A(2A) Criminal Justice Act (CJA) 1988 which requires that the child is capable of giving intelligible testimony. The question should be decided in open court but without the jury: *R v Hampshire* [1995] 3 WLR 260. The evidence must be given unsworn: s33A(1).

The former requirements for obligatory corroboration warnings in respect of child witnesses and sexual complainants have now been removed by s32 CJPOA 1994.

The prosecution will wish to adduce evidence of B's complaint to his mother, D. It is well established that in sexual cases the fact that the victim made a voluntary complaint shortly after the alleged offence is admissible to show the victim's consistency. This rule applies even if the complainant is male: *R v Christie* [1914] AC 545.

In the case of *R v Osborne* [1905] 1 KB 551, evidence of a complaint by a victim to his mother was admissible despite the fact that his mother's initial question elicited the complaint. The court held that a question such as 'what is the matter?' does not deprive the complaint of its voluntariness. The prosecution in this case may face difficulties in adducing the evidence of the complaint due to the fact that D's question went beyond the normal inquiry allowed; it could have prompted the complaint. Accordingly, the defence may wish to challenge the evidence in a voir dire.

If B does not give evidence then D will not be allowed to give evidence of the complaint as a witness can only give evidence of a previous complaint if the victim gives evidence: see *R v Wallwork* (1958) 42 Cr App R 153.

E's evidence may be challenged by the defence on the ground that its prejudicial effect outweighs its probative value. In any event, if it is held to be admissible, the judge will give a warning to the jury about the dangers of convicting on identification evidence. The case of *R v Turnbull* [1977] QB 224, set out the guidelines for identification evidence. The judge will give a warning as to the circumstances of the identification. For example, factors such as visibility, light, time of day, length or duration of identification will all be pointed out by the judge.

It is highly unlikely that the court will allow evidence as to the identification of A by C from the police photographs. The general rule is that where a witness identifies the accused from a photograph such an identification is admissible provided that the photograph does not come from the police files. The ratio behind this rule is that the prejudicial effect of such an identification outweighs its probative value (see generally: *R v Wainwright* (1925) 19 Cr App R 52).

The identification of A by B in the identification parade would be admissible provided that the identification parade was carried out in accordance with Code D of the Code of Conduct. Evidence of the identification of A can be given by B or by a police officer who witnessed the identification (see generally: *R v Beveridge* [1987] Crim LR 401).

As to the alibi of A, the general position is that the defendant does not bear the evidential burden of proving his defence of alibi as the burden is on the prosecution to prove the defendant's presence at the scene of the crime. However, in the case of *R v Johnson* [1961] 1 WLR 1478 dicta can be found to the effect that the defendant does bear the evidential burden of proving his alibi. If the jury rejects the defendant's alibi the judge should tell them that the evidence that the defendant has lied about his location does not prove that the identifying witness was correct.

QUESTION THREE

N is charged with the rape of O, aged 16. O says that she was coming home from a disco late at night when N came up behind her and dragged her into some undergrowth where the rape took place, and that N then ran off. P, O's mother, says that when O came home she looked very dishevelled but said nothing until the next morning when, in reply to P's question 'Did something nasty happen last night?', O said 'I was raped'. Later that day, O said that it was someone who was tall, with fair hair and a purple jumper, who raped her. Q, a passer-by at the time of the alleged offence, can confirm that he heard a scream from O and that he got a brief glimpse of a tall person with fair hair who ran away. Two policemen go to N's place that night; when N opens the door, one of them says 'You raped O, didn't you?'. N's response is to go bright red and slam the door in their faces. Later he denies to the police that he has ever met O. O picks N out at an identification parade, but in court, she cannot remember who it was that she selected. A policeman is able to give evidence both of O's selection of N at the parade, and of O's selection from police records of a photograph of N.

Advise the prosecution of any evidential issues that might arise.

University of London LLB Examination
(for External Students) Law of Evidence June 1993 Q8

General Comment

This is a question on disparate items of admissibility; again, none of them is particularly difficult but it requires some skill to pick them all out. Basically they have to do with items arising during the course of evidence. This sort of question requires a good understanding of the rule against narrative and its exceptions and, particularly, its relation to the rule against hearsay. Remember that the rule against narrative is about witness credibility, whereas the rule against hearsay is about the truth of what is said. Credibility is supported by consistency and attacked by inconsistency and truth does not come into it. Many candidates come a cropper because they do not appreciate this distinction.

Divide this question up into a number of smaller questions; this makes it much more manageable. Note how, in all the problem questions answered, the answers go straight into the question; there is no beating around the bush in the form of 'I am asked to advise in the matter of ...' or a boring and silly repetition of the facts given!

It is not difficult. That does not mean that you should answer it in one page; rather, it gives you a chance to show the examiner what you know about the rationale for the rules (in particular, here, the operation and scope of the so–called 'rule against narrative').

Skeleton Solution

The rule against narrative – sexual complaints (*R v Osborne*) and voluntariness – question of corroboration – silence in face of accusation (*R v Christie* and *R v Cramp*) – parties dealing on uneven terms – identification evidence: 'fleeting glimpses' and *R v Turnbull* warning; breach of hearsay rule (*R v Osbourne; R v Virtue*) – use of photograph from police records prejudicial.

Suggested Solution

O has made the serious accusation of rape against N and this amounts to a sexual complaint. Sexual complaints are admissible in evidence in the following way: they are to show that the testimony of the witness in court is consistent; the complainant gives evidence as to the rape in court and her evidence is bolstered by the fact that she complained a very short time after the alleged rape took place. It is not corroborative of that fact, since you cannot corroborate your own testimony, but it is thought to boost credibility (provided certain conditions are met) and, for that reason, sexual complaints are admitted as an exception to the rule against narrative. What is this rule? It prevents witnesses, in general, giving their own later testimony added strength: it prevents them from manufacturing their own evidence. Imagine the defendant who, having murdered his wife, races around saying 'It was an accident; it was an accident' (a fairly common occurrence, sad to relate). However many priests testify to this fact, it should not be seen to bolster his defence of accident in court!

But for sexual complaints to be admissible, two conditions, laid down in *R v Osborne* [1905] 1 KB 551, have to be met; the complaint must be as soon as is reasonably possible after the event and it must be voluntary, in the sense that it should not have been elicited by leading questions (it need not only go to consent, incidentally, and applies to sexual complaints other than rape). What is the position here? O doesn't complain immediately; however, this doesn't seem too important because she may have been so shaken that she needed to get rest immediately, and whether this was so would depend upon what would be reasonable to expect in the circumstances, which would obviously involve reference to O's age. Is the complaint elicited by a leading question? It is not as if O's mother had just asked if anything was the matter; she asks 'Did something nasty happen last night?' and it could be argued that this is a leading question, negativing voluntariness, which suggests the answer 'yes'. But it is not a leading question so far as suggesting rape, or even a sexual offence of a lesser sort. In fact, given that O is dishevelled and P is O's mother, this would be a reasonable sort of question to put. It is fairly clear, therefore, that this sexual complaint would be admissible (not as truth of the facts contained within it) but to support the credibility of O's later testimony in court.

Another exception to the rule against narrative relates to identification evidence; the rationale is that identification being so fraught with inaccuracy, the closer the statement of identification to the time of the actual identification the better. Dock identifications are always frowned upon because of the obvious possibilities of mistake (an assumption that the police have got the right person; embarrassment on the part of the witness that he may have got it all wrong, etc) and so identification evidence in court (given by testimonial description as opposed to pointing to the dock) can be so bolstered. Clearly, O's statement about the assailant being tall, fair and with a purple jumper may be admitted to support her evidence and P will be able to go into the witness box to confirm what O said. Q's evidence is different though, because he only obtained a 'passing glimpse' of whoever might have been the assailant (he only hears a shout). This evidence is possibly admissible but, if so, the judge will have to give what is known as a *R v Turnbull* [1977] QB 224 warning. This case actually gives the power to a judge to withdraw 'fleeting glimpse' type evidence from the jury where the evidence is largely or wholly of the circumstantial identificatory evidence sort. But there is other evidence (eg N's behaviour in the presence of the police) which might suggest otherwise; it would be sensible to consider the items of evidence separately before urging the judge to take this action, however.

A *Turnbull* (*R v Turnbull* [1977] QB 224) warning requires the judge to warn the jury of the dangers of convicting a person on the basis wholly or largely of identification evidence alone; outside the fleeting glimpse type cases the jury may convict but only if the appropriate warning is given. The judge should point out such things as the circumstances obtaining at the time (light, distance, length of time of sighting), the state of mind of the witness (was he familiar with the person identified? Did he have a special reason to notice?), the distinctiveness of the person's appearance (clothing, colour of skin, peculiar features) and so on. Note that it was held in *R v Chance* [1988] QB 932 that where the identity of the alleged rapist is in issue, a *Turnbull* direction will suffice, and no separate corroboration warning as to the sexual nature of the offence is called for. The reason is that no question of the fantasising of the complainant arises. Why? Because the issue of the trial is the identity of the complainant, and not the question whether in fact the complainant has been raped. It would be different, of course, if the defence were that O had consented.

N's response to the policemen's accusation appears damning; but care is needed. In the first place, as has often been pointed out, going bright red, or remaining silent in the face of an accusation, is consistent with many things other than acknowledgement of guilt; one can question the relevance, therefore. On the other hand, the accusation is very direct and clear, specifying O and the circumstances, and an innocent person would, in the normal way, have responded by an angry denial (although sometimes denials, coupled with demeanour, can amount to admissions of guilt: see *R v Christie* [1914] AC 545). However, the real point here is that this evidence is not admissible; a person has a right to remain silent in the face of an accusation (in the sense that this silence will not be used as evidence against him) where the parties are not dealing on even terms (see *Parkes v R* [1976] 3 All ER 380 and *Hall v R* [1971] 1 All ER 322). The police behaved disgracefully here; if they had grounds to suspect that he did this, they should have cautioned him immediately and arrested him; he could then not be questioned unless he was willing and had a solicitor present.

The policeman is allowed to give evidence of O's selection at the identity parade; this is in direct contravention of the hearsay rule because the policeman can only be giving evidence of a statement made by O ('this is the man') made out of court for the purpose of proving the truth of that statement; the policeman's statement cannot be bolstering the credibility of O's testimony in court because O cannot give evidence on this point in court in order for it to be bolstered. Nevertheless, despite *Myers v DPP* [1965] AC 1001, *R v Osbourne; R v Virtue* [1973] 1 QB 678 permits this position in the law. (A lazy counsel and a sleepy judge obviously were in that case – an astute counsel would have insisted that the policeman's hearsay evidence be excluded and would not have been dissuaded by the judge's remark – as occurred in *Osbourne and Virtue* – that 'it was not practical otherwise'.)

The policeman's evidence of a photograph from police records is not allowed as clearly prejudicial because it informs the jury that the defendant has had dealings with the police before: *R v Wainwright* (1875) 13 Cox CC 171.

To conclude, there is little evidence here to maintain a conviction; basically is relies only on a sexual complaint and a 'fleeting glimpse'. If the judge, and he should be urged to do so by the defendant, withdraws the identification evidence of Q from the jury, we only have the sexual complaint and identification by O. The case by the prosecution therefore looks rather weak.

Chapter 4

Burdens and Standards of Proof

4.1   Introduction

4.2   Key points

4.3   Key cases and materials

4.4   Questions and and suggested solutions

4.1 Introduction

The most important distinction is that between the legal burden – the burden of proof – and the evidential burden – the burden of adducing evidence. Only when this distinction is clearly understood can a student do justice to the express and implied exceptions in criminal cases where the legal, as opposed to evidential burden, is on the accused. The House of Lords' decision in *R v Hunt* [1987] AC 352 has made this a popular area for examiners.

4.2 Key points

It is vital that students understand the following concepts and issues.

a) Legal burden is the obligation placed on a party to prove a fact in issue, eg on the prosecution to prove the guilt of the accused and to prove all other issues they raise during the trial.

b) Evidential burden is the obligation placed on a party to adduce enough evidence about an asserted fact for that fact to become a justiciable issue, eg the prosecution must adduce enough evidence of the guilt of the accused for the court to be satisfied that there is a case for the defence to answer.

c) Evidential burden is considered at only two points in a trial:

   i)   at the beginning, to decide which party begins;

   ii) at any time during the trial in deciding whether enough evidence has been adduced in support of an asserted fact for it to become a justiciable issue, ie require the opposing party to adduce evidence in rebuttal.

d) Which party must prove the issue in dispute, and other issues raised during the trial, ie which party must discharge the legal burden, is decided by rules of law, either statute or case law. This aspect may be further complicated by the impact of various types of presumptions, both of law and of fact. These matters are dealt with in detail in Chapter 14 below and a thorough understanding of the incidence of burdens will require an understanding of presumptions, particularly in civil evidence.

e) The rule in civil cases is, generally, that the party who asserts must prove, ie he must discharge the legal burden of proof. For example, in a suit in negligence, the plaintiff (as well as having to discharge the evidential burden) has the legal burden of proving duty, breach and consequential damage. The defendant, if the defence is a simple denial, bears no legal burden, but if some defence is raised which goes beyond that, eg an assertion that the plaintiff was contributorily negligent, then the defendant has the legal burden of proving that assertion. Thus, generally, the party asserting an affirmative bears the legal burden; there are exceptions to this, where a negative assertion is an essential element of a party's case, eg in a suit in malicious prosecution the plaintiff must prove the absence of reasonable cause for the defendant's institution of proceedings.

f) The rule in criminal cases is, generally, that where a burden is borne by the accused it is an evidential burden only. There are three types of defences which, exceptionally, will require the accused to discharge a legal burden of proof if they are to succeed:

i)   insanity and unfitness to plead;

ii) express statutory exceptions – ie where a statute expressly stipulates that the accused must prove an issue (eg a defence of diminished responsibility to a charge of murder, per s2(2) Homicide Act 1957);

iii) implied statutory exceptions – s101 Magistrates' Courts Act 1980 in summary trials and *R v Edwards* [1975] QB 27 in jury trials provide that if the accused relies for his defence on any 'exception, exemption, proviso, excuse or qualification', then he has the legal burden of proving that defence. In this area of the incidence of the legal burden in criminal trials, the House of Lords' decision in *R v Hunt* [1987] AC 352 is important. However, bear in mind *R v Lambert* [2001] 3 All ER 577 (on p39).

g) The standard of proof, which determines how much evidence a party must adduce to discharge a legal burden of proof, varies depending on whether it is a civil or a criminal trial. In civil trials the standard is on balance of probabilities; the more serious the allegation made by a party the more evidence the court will require to be satisfied: *Re H and Others (Minors) (Sexual Abuse: Standard of Proof)* [1996] 1 All ER 1, HL, but even where the allegation by a party is of the commission of a crime by his opponent the standard remains the civil one, ie he must prove that what he alleges is more likely than not the truth. In *Francisco v Diedrick* (1998) The Times 3 April a civil case was brought against an alleged murderer. The court applied *Re H and Others (Minors) (Sexual Abuse: Standard of Proof)* and held that the standard of proof to be applied was the civil standard, ie on the balance of probabilities while bearing in mind that the allegation was of utmost gravity and could only be established by truly cogent evidence. In criminal trials the prosecution must prove the guilt of the accused to the criminal standard, ie beyond reasonable doubt; additionally, whenever the prosecution bears a legal burden of proving any issues during the course of the trial it must prove beyond reasonable doubt. In the exceptional situations where the accused bears a legal, as opposed to merely evidential, burden (see (f)(i), (ii) and (iii) above) the standard of proof is always the civil standard.

h) Article 6 of the European Convention on Human Rights has been incorporated into UK domestic law by the Human Rights Act 1998. Article 6(2) states that 'Everyone charged with a criminal offence shall be presumed innocent until proved guilty according to the law'. This principle may well be offended by the large number of offences which require the defence to prove some or all defences. In *Attorney-General for Hong Kong* v *Lee Kwong-Kut* [1993] AC 951 the Privy Council interpreted the presumption of innocence declared by the Hong Kong Bill of Rights, in identical terms to art 6(2), so as to strike down a reverse onus provision. It remains to be seen fully how the provision in art 6(2) will be interpreted by the courts.

In *R* v *Lambert* [2001] 3 All ER 577 the appellant was convicted of possession of a Class A drug with intent to supply and appealed on the ground that the requirement that he prove his defence on the balance of probabilities was contrary to the presumption of innocence guaranteed by art 6(2) of the European Convention on Human Rights and Fundamental Freedoms, as incorporated by the Human Rights Act 1998. The appeal was from a decision made before 2 October 2000 when the Human Rights Act 1998 came into force. The majority held that as a consequence the appellant was not entitled to rely on Convention rights. Despite this finding, the House went on to give full consideration to the question of whether the imposition of the legal burden of proof in ss28(2) and (3) Misuse of Drugs Act 1971 is compatible with the presumption of innocence contained in art 6(2) of the Convention. This consideration is, however, obiter.

The House of Lords held that a provision which derogates from the presumption of innocence must be objectively justified. The majority went on to hold that it was not justifiable and proportionate to transfer the legal burden of proof to the accused and require him to prove on the balance of probabilities that he did not know that the bag contained a controlled drug. However, their Lordships found that it was possible to read the words of s28 as imposing only an evidential burden rather than a legal burden on the accused, and such a requirement was not in contravention of the Convention.

In *R* v *C* (2002) The Times 21 January the Court of Appeal considered *R* v *Lambert* and held that the proper approach was that a reverse legal burden imposed on an accused had to be justified, and it had to be demonstrated why a legal or persuasive burden (rather than an evidential burden) was necessary. On the facts of the case, the Court held that it was appropriate to read the word 'prove' in s206(1)(a) Insolvency Act 1986 as meaning to 'adduce sufficient evidence so that the burden imposed on the defendant was evidential only'.

4.3 Key cases and materials

* *R* v *C* (2002) The Times 21 January

* *R* v *Edwards* [1975] QB 27

* *R* v *Hunt* [1987] AC 352

* *R* v *Lambert* [2001] 3 All ER 577

* European Convention on Human Rights

  * art 6

  * art 8

* Magistrates Court Act 1980, s101

4.4 Questions and suggested solutions

QUESTION ONE

Section 27 of the Financial Services Act 1986 provides that 'subject to s58 below, no person other than an authorised person shall issue ... an investment advertisement in the United Kingdom, unless its contents have been approved by an authorised person'.

Section 58 provides that 'Section 27 does not apply to ... any advertisement which ... consists of ... any document permitted to be published by listing rules ...' of the International Stock Exchange in London.

Section 207(3) provides that 'for the purposes of this Act an advertisement issued outside the United Kingdom, shall be treated as issued in the United Kingdom if it is directed to persons in the United Kingdom ...'.

Suppose that Makeabuck is charged with contravening s27 in that he had issued such an advertisement in the UK inviting investors to buy shares of Hong Kong companies without obtaining approval of its contents from an authorised person. Suppose that Makeabuck's position is that though some of his advertisements did appear on video screens in the UK, they were issued in Hong Kong and were not directed at persons in the UK; that all documents which were issued in the UK were permitted by the International Stock Exchange's listing rules; and that in any case his advertisements were approved by the Bang-On Bank which was an 'authorised person' under the Act.

Consider the burden and standard of proof in the case under English Law in the context of the following items of evidence:

a) a document produced by a computer containing a register of all persons authorised to carry on investment business in the UK kept under the Financial Services Act, but which does not contain the Bang-On Bank's name;

b) a copy of an authorisation issued to Bang-On Bank under the Act which is in Makeabuck's possession.

Adapted from University of London LLB Examination
(for External Students) Law of Evidence June 1988 Q1

General Comment

No difficulty should be caused by the requirement to state the standard of proof placed on the prosecution and defence in a criminal case. But the placing of the burden is more difficult. There is no authority on the Financial Services Act provisions in question, so general principles must be applied. Necessarily the examiner may disagree with the candidate in his application of the rule in *R v Hunt* [1987] AC 352, but provided the principles are stated clearly full credit will be given.

Skeleton Solution

Elements of the offence: burden and standard in general – burden and standard on each element.

Suggested Solution

In general it is for the prosecution to prove every element of a criminal charge, both actus reus and mens rea, beyond reasonable doubt (*Woolmington v DPP* [1935] AC 462). But this general principle is subject to exceptions and, in particular, to an exception that where statute expressly or by implication places a burden on the defendant then that is where the burden lies (*R v Hunt* [1987] AC 352).

The offence under s27 of the Financial Services Act 1986 has five elements: (a) the publication of an investment advertisement; (b) which is not permitted to be published by listing rules of the International Stock Exchange in London; (c) in the UK; (d) by an unauthorised person; and (e) without the approval of an authorised person.

Whether, as regards any element of the offence, the burden of proof is on the prosecution or defence is a matter of the proper construction of the Act. In *R v Hunt* the House of Lords held that the presumption must be that it is for the prosecution to prove everything which needs to be proved. Where an offence is committed by someone who does an act without first obtaining a licence or some other permission from an official body this presumption will be rebutted provided it is simple for the defendant to prove that he had the necessary permission, but very difficult for the prosecution to prove that he did not. Lord Griffiths recognised in his speech that the vast majority of cases in which a burden is placed on the defendant will be cases where he is accused of doing something without the necessary permission. But he also recognised that a careful definition must be made of the act which is prohibited so that it is known whether the defendant really is asserting a defence. For example, in *R v Hunt* [1987] AC 352 the offence charged was the possession of a certain type of morphine. The Court of Appeal held that once it was established that the defendant had possession of morphine it was for him to prove that it was not of the type alleged, but the House of Lords disagreed. In other words the defendant was not putting forward the defence that the substance was not as alleged, rather it was a necessary ingredient of the prosecution case for the prosecution to prove that it was of the alleged type.

The prosecution will have to call its evidence first and if at the close of its case it has failed to call evidence which could amount to proof beyond reasonable doubt on those issues on which it bears a legal burden, the judge will have no option but to accede to a submission from Makeabuck that there is no case to answer (*R v Galbraith* [1981] 2 All ER 1060).

In Makeabuck's case the five elements of the offence must be considered separately because the burden may not be on the same party on each. Undoubtedly it will be for the prosecution to prove that the advertisements about which complaint is made are investment advertisements. This is a matter on which the prosecution is certainly as competent as the defence to call evidence. Makeabuck does not raise as his defence that the advertisements were not investment advertisements, but that does not preclude the prosecution from having to prove that they were.

Section 58 of the 1986 Act provides that s27 does not apply to any document permitted to be published by listing rules of the International Stock Exchange in London. The effect of this section depends upon whether it means: (a) it is an offence to publish an investment advertisement unless it is permitted by the rules; or (b) only those advertisements which are not permitted by the rules should not be published. The difference between these meanings is one of substance and not just emphasis, in that the first construction means that Makeabuck is putting forward a defence when he says the advertisements are permitted by the rules, whereas the second makes it a necessary part of the prosecution case that the advertisements are not permitted. The case of *R v Cross* (1990) 91 Cr App R 115 involved similar wording to the present statute. It concerned s1 of the Company Securities (Insider Dealing) Act 1985, s1(1) of which creates the offence and is said to be subject to s3, which allows the dealing where it is not done by the individual for profit, or avoidance of loss. The Court of Appeal held that the burden to prove the applicability of s3 lay with the defendant. However, the Court seemed to place emphasis on the fact that the matters in s3 were peculiarly within the defendant's own knowledge. Here, we are concerned with a document permitted to be published by listing rules, and the absence of permission in the rules is something which can be proved just as simply by the prosecution as by the defence. In effect this element of the offence is in the same position as the requirement in *R v Hunt* [1987] AC 352 that the morphine was of the prohibited type. Naturally Makeabuck should call what evidence he has if he wishes to allege that the advertisements were authorised by the listings rules, but there would not formally be a burden on him to do so.

The need for the advertisement to be issued in the UK raises a different point. Section 207(3) extends the definition of issuing in the UK from its obvious starting point of advertisements which are issued in the UK for use in the UK to cover also advertisements issued outside the UK but directed to persons in the UK. In the same way the prosecution would have to prove that any advertisement was an investment advertisement, so it would be necessary for it to call evidence of the origin of the advertisement. There is no reason in principle why the prosecution should not have to prove that the advertisement was of the prohibited type. It is submitted that the origin of the advertisement is just as much a vital element of the prosecution case as is whether or not it is an investment advertisement. It may be that all the prosecution has to do is prove that the advertisement was received in the UK, and then it will be for the defence to bring forward evidence that it was issued outside the UK. But the burden on the defence may be no more than an evidential burden so that it would then be for the prosecution to prove that although it was issued outside the UK, it was directed to persons in the UK.

Whether or not Makeabuck is an authorised person is a matter on which he is likely to bear a legal burden, that is a burden to prove authorisation on a balance of probabilities. The position is effectively the same as where someone charged with selling alcohol without a licence claims that he has a licence, in which case the burden is on the defence to establish that a licence has been granted (*R v Edwards* [1975] QB 27). It appears, in any event, that Makeabuck does not claim that he is authorised. It if is correct that the burden is on the defence, the prosecution will not have to call evidence with a view to establishing that Makeabuck is not authorised because it will be presumed that he is not unless he raises the issue.

Makeabuck does argue that the Bang-On Bank is authorised and that he issued the advertisements with its approval. It would, it is submitted, be unreasonable to expect the defence to have access to information from which it could prove whether someone who approved an advertisement was authorised to do so. We are told that Makeabuck may be in a position to do so in this case, but where the burden lies under s27 must be the same in every case and not all defendants can expect to be in Makeabuck's position. The prosecution may not know that Makeabuck is going to raise the defence that his advertisement was approved by the Bang-On Bank. Therefore it will be for Makeabuck to raise the issue. He will bear an evidential burden; in other words he must raise some credible evidence that the Bang-On Bank gave approval. But it will then be for the prosecution to prove beyond reasonable doubt that the Bang-On Bank is not authorised.

QUESTION TWO

The decision in *R v Hunt* [1987] AC 352 'fashions some workable guidelines out of unpromising material and encourages courts to seek out and apply the intentions of Parliament in a consistent way'.

Discuss.

University of London LLB Examination
(for External Students) Law of Evidence June 1989 Q5

General Comment

A mere narrative on the express and implied reversal of the burden of proof in some criminal statutes leading to the decision in *R* v *Hunt* [1987] AC 352 would not be sufficient to achieve high marks. A critical analysis of the law pre-*Hunt* and discussion of the guidelines in that case is imperative for a comprehensive answer.

Skeleton Solution

Incidence of the legal burden of proof generally in criminal cases: *Woolmington* v *DPP* – exceptions, where defence bears the burden: at common law; express statutory exceptions; implied statutory exceptions – discussion, and criticism, of *R* v *Hunt*.

Suggested Solution

The general rule in criminal cases is that the prosecution bears the legal burden of proving every element of its case; whether the prosecution assertions be positive or negative is immaterial, thus once the defence discharges the evidential burden in respect of any defence, that defence, even if affirmative in its nature, must be disproved beyond reasonable doubt by the prosecution if the accused is to be convicted. Thus, for example, the prosecution has the burden of proving absence of consent if that is raised as a defence to a charge of rape (*R* v *Horn* (1912) 7 Cr App R 200).

This general rule was enunciated by Lord Sankey LC in the celebrated case of *Woolmington* v *DPP* [1935] AC 462. From his now famous speech, the following passage is notorious:

'Throughout the web of the English criminal law one golden thread is always to be seen, that it is the duty of the prosecution to prove the prisoner's guilt subject to what I have already said as to the defence of insanity and subject also to any statutory exception. No matter what the charge … the principle that the prosecution must prove the guilt of the prisoner is part of the common law of England and no attempt to whittle it down can be entertained.'

Implicit in Lord Sankey's classic statement are exceptions to the 'golden thread', ie, where the defence of insanity is raised, and where the legal burden is placed by statute on the defence.

In the case of insanity the legal burden is affected by the presumption of sanity – therefore the accused pleading insanity (*M'Naghten's Case* (1843) 10 Cl & Fin 200) or unfitness to plead because of defective intellect (*R* v *Podola* [1960] 1 QB 325) bears the burden of proving that assertion; the standard of proof in such cases is merely the civil standard of balance of probabilities (*R* v *Podola*). (Where the prosecution raises the issue of unfitness to plead, or alleges insanity or diminished responsibility under the provisions of s6 Criminal Procedure (Insanity) Act 1964 (which is not changed by the provisions of the Criminal Procedure (Insanity and Unfitness to Plead) Act 1991), then the prosecution bears the burden of proof but to the criminal standard of beyond reasonable doubt: *R* v *Grant* [1960] Crim LR 424; *R* v *Robertson* [1968] 1 WLR 1767.)

Evidentially, insanity causes few problems, and was recognised as a loose strand of the 'golden thread', as were statutory exceptions. Again, in the case of express statutory provisions, Parliament has in those situations decreed that on some issue the defence shall exceptionally bear a burden of proof, although obviously the prosecution still bears the legal burden of proof to the criminal standard on all other issues. For example, s32 Sexual Offences Act 1956 provides that regarding the offence of knowingly living on the earnings of prostitution, a man who lives with a prostitute 'shall be presumed to be knowingly living on the earnings of prostitution, unless he proves the contrary'. Another example is provided by s1(1) Prevention of Crime Act 1953, whereby it is an offence for a person to have an offensive weapon in a public place 'without lawful authority or reasonable excuse, the proof whereof shall lie on him'. (There are other express provisions in s2 Prevention of Corruption Act 1916; s2(2) Homicide Act 1957; s28(2) Misuse of Drugs Act 1971, but this last provision must now be interpreted in the light of *R* v *Lambert* [2001] 3 All ER 577.) The reasons for the reversal of the burden of proof on these specific issues are mainly of public policy, and although purists disagree with these exceptions there is no scope for inconsistency in the courts' applying Parliament's intentions.

The 'unpromising material' where inconsistency abounded was in the area of implied, as opposed to express, statutory provisions. Section 101 Magistrates' Courts Act 1980 (formerly s81 Magistrates' Courts Act 1952 which revised s14 Summary Jurisdiction Act 1848) provides in essence that where a defendant in a summary trial relies for his defence on 'any exception, exemption, proviso, excuse or qualification', the burden of proof shall be on the defence, 'notwithstanding that the information or complaint contains an allegation negativing the exception, exemption, proviso, excuse or qualification'. This provision applies to summary trials, but in 1975 it was held that similar principles applied to trials on indictment (*R* v *Edwards* [1975] QB 27); this was confirmed by the House of Lords in *R* v *Hunt* [1987] AC 352.

A clear-cut example of a provision to which s101 applies is the offence of driving a motor vehicle on a road without being the holder of a current driving licence. Once the prosecution prove that the defendant was driving a motor vehicle on a road, the defendant will be convicted of the offence unless he proves the qualification on which he must rely for his defence, ie proves that at the relevant time he held a current driving licence for that class of motor vehicle (*John* v *Humphreys* [1955] 1 All ER 793). Although whether a driver is qualified or not is easily checked by the prosecution, s101 has been held to apply to this and other 'licence' cases; the reason for the application of s101 is not that the court is dealing with facts peculiarly within the knowledge of the defendant (and thus easier for him to prove the affirmative than the prosecution prove the negative) but that s101 is undoubtedly applicable so the burden of proving the qualification is on the defendant.

A case giving rise to some difficulty was that of *Nimmo* v *Alexander Cowan & Sons Ltd* [1968] AC 107. Under s29(1) Factories Act 1961: 'every place at which any person has at any time to work ... shall, so far as is reasonably practicable, be made and kept safe for any person working therein'. An employee alleged that his place of work had not been made and kept safe, and although the case was a civil one, it has substantial relevance in the present context. In the House of Lords it was made clear that where the burden of proof lay would be the same whether the proceedings were criminal or civil. The House of Lords, on their interpretation of the statute, decided that the employee did not have to show that it was reasonably practicable to keep the place safe, but rather the defendant (the employers) had to discharge the legal burden of proving that it was not reasonably practicable to keep the place safe. The decision was by a bare majority, which is indicative of the problems of construing statutory provisions which may by implication reverse the burden of proof.

An earlier, and difficult, case concerned a prosecution for the offence of acquiring rationed goods without surrendering the appropriate ration coupons (*R v Putland* [1946] 1 All ER 85). The Court of Criminal Appeal held that the prosecution bore the burden of proving the acquisition of the goods and the failure to surrender the coupons.

It was against this background of apparent inconsistency in interpretation that the case of *R v Hunt* [1987] AC 352 reached the House of Lords in 1987. Hunt was charged with the unlawful possession of a controlled drug (morphine), contrary to s5 Misuse of Drugs Act 1971. The Misuse of Drugs Regulations 1973 provide that s5 does not apply to any morphine preparation containing no more than 0.2 per cent morphine. The prosecution adduced no evidence of the percentage of morphine in the substance found in Hunt's possession and the defence therefore submitted there was no case to answer. The judge refused to accept the submission and Hunt was convicted, having then changed his plea to guilty. The Court of Appeal dismissed his appeal, holding that the facts were covered by the implication in the statute and regulation that the burden of proving the substance's morphine content was on Hunt.

On appeal to the House of Lords, the decision of the Court of Appeal was reversed. Their Lordships stated that every case must depend on the construction of the particular legislation, and further stated that if there is, on construction, no clear indication as to where the burden of proof should lie, then the court may consider policy, including considerations of practicality such as the ease with which one party or the other could discharge the burden of proof (whether affirmative or negative). They further stated that it can never be readily assumed that Parliament intended a defendant to prove his innocence, so the courts should be reluctant to make such an inference from the wording of any but the clearest of statutory provisions. Especially where the statutory offence was a serious one (as in the case of Hunt's alleged unlawful possession of morphine) any ambiguity must be resolved in favour of the accused person.

The 'guidelines' of their Lordships in *R v Hunt* may be workable; if the guidelines are followed then, apart from unambiguous wording in a statute, there is virtually a presumption that the accused shall not bear a burden of proving the issue(s) referred to in the statute, and the more serious the offence charged the stronger the presumption. However, this may be in conflict with the 'policy' guideline, and in any case it pre-supposes that the courts cannot construe the statute to discover a clear indication of where the burden shall lie. In *R* v *Lambert* [2001] 3 All ER 577 the House of Lords held that a provision which imposes a legal burden of proof on the defendant must be objectively justified. It seems, therefore, that each such provision will be the subject of consideration by the courts at some stage. Although the courts may have been encouraged to seek out and apply the intentions of Parliament in a consistent way, the courts are prone to overlooking the intention of Parliament in their fervour to construe statutes linguistically. More important was the failure of the House of Lords to adopt the proposal of the 11th Report of the Criminal Law Revision Committee ([1972] Cmnd 4991) that burdens on the defence should be evidential only, both on general principles of criminal law and for the sake of clarity – clarity which will probably become increasingly elusive as conflicting guidelines in *R* v *Hunt* [1987] AC 352 are bent by the courts.

QUESTION THREE

'Throughout the web of the English criminal law one golden thread is always seen, that it is the duty of the prosecution to prove the prisoner's guilt ...' (Viscount Sankey in *Woolmington* v *DPP*).

Discuss the contemporary truth of this statement.

University of London LLB Examination
(for External Students) Law of Evidence June 1993 Q4

General Comment

This is another common question and it is easy to put your own 'stamp' upon it (and another one for jurisprudential analysis). The essay below gives a clear indication as to the writer's feelings; you, too, should develop your own views on these matters. If you think that the presumption of innocence is important, then how can you possibly approve of *R* v *Hunt* [1987] AC 352, in which the House of Lords said clearly that, in criminal statute the judges can 'imply into' the statute, as a matter of statutory construction, a reversal of the onus? It beggars belief, especially in the light of the important principle of statutory interpretation that criminal statutes should be construed in favour of the defendant. But everyone has different views, and you may take the view that defendants have been getting away with too much recently and that they shouldn't have the benefit of the doubt! The important thing is to say clearly what you think and why.

Skeleton Solution

General principle – three exceptions – express statutory exceptions – implied statutory exception – *R* v *Edwards* – s101 Magistrates Court Act 1980 – grammatical distinction and silliness of the section – *Hunt* and its relation to *R* v *Edwards* – tests in *R* v *Hunt* – Birch's arguments in *The Hunting of the Snark* – conclusion that *Hunt* a retrograde case.

Suggested Solution

It was stated in *Woolmington* v *DPP* [1935] AC 462 that the golden thread running through the criminal law was that the burden of proof remained on the prosecution to prove all elements of the offence; it can be seen that this principle embodies the general principle that a man (or woman) is innocent until proven guilty. We are thus supposed to be in a fundamentally different position in this country from the continental legal systems, where the criminal method is inquisitorial in nature.

Nevertheless, there are three exceptions to the *Woolmington* principle. In the common law, the defence must prove insanity on a balance of probabilities. As far as statute is concerned, Parliament can either expressly, or by implication, declare that a statutory enactment has shifted the burden of proof onto the defendant. Parliament has expressly done this in several areas, notably for diminished responsibility (Homicide Act 1957) and for corruption (Prevention of Corruption Act 1916). But it is the implied exception which gives rise to the most grief, mainly arising from the fact that any departure from the presumption of innocence is dangerous. It is possible that the former apparent departure from the rule is less dangerous to the presumption of innocence principle now because of the case of *R* v *Hunt* [1987] AC 352 and, since it is the most important recent and contemporary case, it would be as well to examine it.

Hunt altered the state of law as it existed – up to and including the case of *R* v *Edwards* [1975] QB 27. In *Edwards*, the Court of Appeal had tried to relieve the courts of any burden of statutory interpretation by declaring the common law for indictable offences to be the same as that within (for summary offences) s101 of the Magistrates' Court Act 1980. This provision states that the accused had the burden of proof if his allegedly offending act came within an exception to a generally prohibited act: such an exception being preceded by words such as 'exemption', 'proviso' and so on. But it was clear (and still is!) that the distinction in the provision was one of grammar only and that legislative draughtsmen did not conform to any sort of practice as to the use of these words, other than economy and elegance.

Further, the Court of Appeal in *Edwards* did not draw a substantial distinction between the element providing the definition of an offence and the element providing a defence to it. As Zuckerman points out, if we do not do so there is no substantial difference between saying 'You are forbidden to drive without a licence' or 'You may not drive unless you have a licence'.

The Court of Appeal in *Hunt* drove this sort of reasoning out the door by simply declaring that the underlying reasoning in *Edwards* was that these grammatical distinctions were only a guide to statutory interpretation, in that case a licensing statute; this made it obvious that grammar was not enough. The court should instead look to what the statute was trying to achieve (in other words, to pay attention to the normal guidelines governing the construction of statutes).

This means that the appearance of the word 'exemption' or 'exception' and so on, would not be sufficient to shift the burden. Instead, the court would have to take into consideration the fact that Parliament would not lightly have intended to shift the burden, in the light of the presumption of innocence, as well as how difficult the task would be for the defendant to 'prove' his innocence if the burden shifted. Hunt was himself charged with possession of a proscribed drug, with exceptions as to amounts being detailed in a schedule to the Act. The House of Lords held that he did not have to provide rebutting proof of the chemical composition of the particular drug.

Why? It would have been impossible for Hunt to provide proof because the drug had been taken out of his possession by the police and had already been the subject of chemical analysis by them. The prosecution had failed to bring evidence concerning the amount of morphine present and the House of Lords therefore took the view, in the light of these factors, that the relevant provision could not be read as an implied exception to the *Woolmington* v *DPP* [1935] AC 462 principle.

Birch argues (see *The Hunting of the Snark*) that the reason the presumption of innocence principles were not given great prominence in *R* v *Hunt* [1987] AC 352 was that *Hunt* was a decision about what constituted the actus reus of a particular offence of possession of a proscribed drug, rather than its mens rea. She contends that in a crime with a mental element offering a defence of 'lawful' excuse on the basis of the factors already mentioned in *Hunt*, the burden of proof is unlikely to shift. The typical s101 offence will, therefore, she says, be one which is not very serious, and lacking a mens rea requirement. If she is right, the element of defence should be independent of the definition of the offence and not too onerous for the defendant because it could easily be separated from the definition of the offence itself and the burden should not weigh too heavily on the defendant.

It is submitted that this kind of pettifogging approach lacks principle. If we are firm that, in our legal system, we have clear presumption of innocence, that must surface clearly in our law; we have a crystal clear – and famous – reaffirmation of that principle in *Woolmington*. What *Hunt* says, loud and clear, is that judges, on the basis of guidelines of statutory interpretation, can interpret a statute in a way that runs counter to that general (some would say foundational) principle of our legal system; they can find that in a criminal statute, in other words, when there are no clear words to that effect, a shift of this important and serious burden. Quite apart, too, from these considerations, there is the important interpretation principle that, for criminal statutes, ambiguities and unclarities should be resolved in favour of the defendant. I conclude, therefore, that *Hunt* was a retrograde decision when it allowed relatively flimsy reasons justifying the reversal of the burden of proof. It will be interesting to see how the courts interpret the provision contained in art 6(2) of the European Convention on Human Rights now that the Human Rights Act 1998 is in force. This provision offers scope for the decision in *Hunt* to be re-visited. In *R* v *Lambert* [2001] 3 All ER 577 the House of Lords considered whether a provision which operates to shift the legal burden of proof to the defendant is incompatible with art 6. The House held that a provision which derogates from the presumption of innocence must be objectively justified. Such a provision must be both justifiable and proportionate. Although the particular provision being considered by the House was thought by the majority to lack those characteristics, it is possible that other provisions which operate to shift the burden of proof will be thought to be objectively justified and so not in contravention of the Convention.

QUESTION FOUR

'To import the criminal standard of proof into a civil proceeding is to confuse the respective functions and needs of the criminal and civil processes.'

Discuss.

University of London LLB Examination
(for External Students) Law of Evidence June 1990 Q3

General Comment

It will be important to proceed in a logical manner and consider both criminal and civil proceedings in answering this question.

Skeleton Solution

General rule in criminal proceedings – exceptions: express statutory exceptions; implied statutory exceptions – civil proceedings: general rule in *Hornal* – exceptions: matrimonial cases and cases of extreme seriousness; *Halford* v *Brookes*.

Suggested Solution

In order to answer this question it is necessary to establish the distribution of the standard of proof in criminal proceedings. By this means it is possible to evaluate the extent to which the approach applied in such proceedings can be translated to civil proceedings.

The general rule in criminal proceedings is that the prosecution bears the legal burden in accordance with the *Woolmington* principle (*Woolmington* v *DPP* [1935] AC 462). The standard of proof on which the jury is directed is that the facts in issue must be proved beyond reasonable doubt (*Miller* v *Minister of Pensions* [1947] 2 All ER 372) or so that the jury are satisfied so that they are sure of the accused's guilt (*R* v *Summers* (1953) 36 Cr App R 14). To this general rule there are notable exceptions. The accused bears the legal burden in respect of the defence of insanity (*M'Naghten's Case* (1843) 10 Cl & Fin 200) and any statutory exception (*Woolmington*). This latter phrase incorporates both express statutory exceptions and where the exception is implied (*R* v *Hunt* [1987] AC 352, confirming the assumption of what was said in *Woolmington*).

It is relatively easy to establish express statutory exceptions from the wording of the statute but implied exceptions can be more problematical and are governed by the criteria of *R* v *Edwards* [1975] QB 27 and *R* v *Hunt*. They are where an offence is subject to exceptions, exemptions, provisos, excuses or qualification, which is the wording of s101 of the Magistrates' Court Act 1980 and declaratory of the common law (*R v Edwards* [1975] QB 27).

Where an exception to the *Woolmington* principle does apply, the standard of proof is the balance of probabilities (*R v Carr-Briant* [1943] KB 607). In other words, the jury is directed that the accused discharges the burden on him if they are satisfied that his version is more probable than not.

In translating this approach to the civil forum, the first and perhaps obvious point is that since very few civil actions are now tried with a jury, the form of the direction on the standard of proof could not appropriately be incorporated into the civil jurisdiction. In fact the tribunal in civil actions is usually the judge.

The next and more substantial point is whether there is any justification for importing a standard of proof beyond reasonable doubt as a general requirement for civil proceedings whilst at the same time leaving the current civil standard in place relative to the same matters which may be raised by one or other of the parties coinciding with the exceptions to the *Woolmington* v *DPP* [1935] AC 462 principle which exist in civil cases.

It is submitted that to provide a standard of proof beyond reasonable doubt in civil proceedings would ignore the fact that in criminal proceedings the trial is for the liberty of the individual in which the State is a party, whereas in civil proceedings the trial is of 'equals' and the stakes do not amount to a threat to liberty of either party. The development of the criminal standard of proof very much reflects these features. Moreover, it would also conflict with existing authority, in particular with *Hornal* v *Neuberger Products Ltd* [1957] 1 QB 247, which establishes that the allegation of a crime in civil proceedings attracts the civil standard of proof. A fairly recent case in which this matter was considered by the House of Lords was *Re H and Others (Minors) (Sexual Abuse: Standard of Proof)* [1996] AC 563. In that case Lord Nicholls said that: 'Where the matters in issue are facts the standard of proof required in non-criminal proceedings is the preponderance of probability, usually referred to as the balance of probability.' If the criminal standard were applied, application of a lower standard to coincide with the exceptions to *Woolmington* would have to be justified. Such justification is hard to see. Since a civil action is in a legal sense between equals for the settlement of a private dispute, it also follows that there can be no justification jurisprudentially for a lower standard of proof for insanity (if raised by the defendant) or for statutory exceptions on which the defendant seeks to rely. Yet a good deal of fuss was caused at the end of 1991 by a case decided by the High Court (QBD) – *Halford* v *Brookes* (1991) The Independent 1 October – a civil action alleging battery was brought by the mother of a murder victim against the alleged killers. The court decided that the criminal standard of proof should be adopted. Because of the serious nature of the allegations, the judge decided that the case should be conducted as if the defendants were being tried for murder in a criminal court. But the case causes problems – as a civil court it was allowed to draw adverse inferences when the defendant refused to testify, unlike in criminal cases. Also, hearsay evidence was allowed in under the Civil Evidence Act 1968 which would not have been at a criminal trial. Also, similar fact evidence would be more admissible. And, of course, there would be the usual problems of a trial within a trial when there is no jury. However, it is unlikely that this case would be followed in future for these very reasons.

There is, it is true, some other case law, particularly in the field presumptions and matrimonial proceedings, in which the criminal standard has been indicated. Examples are to be found in the old case of *Morris* v *Davies* (1837) 5 Cl & Fin 163 (presumption of validity of marriage) and authorities such as *Preston-Jones* v *Preston-Jones* [1951] AC 391 (proof of grounds for divorce). It is doubtful, however, how far these cases represent the present law, a view reinforced by the fact that that they have been largely overtaken by statutory intervention which has provided for a standard of proof on the balance of probabilities. To the extent that the degree of proof varies in civil proceedings, it is attributable to the fact that the courts require a greater weight of evidence before being satisfied on the balance of probabilities. In those cases in which the legal burden in civil cases is reversed, such as arises under s11 of the Civil Evidence Act 1968, the standard of proof is the usual civil standard and wholly consistent with the fact that civil proceedings are concerned with the settlement of disputes between private parties standing on equal terms in court.

Thus the only circumstances in which the proposition in the question would not be sound is, it is submitted, if the legal burden referred to in the question were the burden on an accused in cases where an exception to the *Woolmington* v *DPP* [1935] AC 462 principle applies. That standard is a balance of probabilities – in other words, the present civil standard.

QUESTION FIVE

What principles or policies, if any, can you detect behind judicial allocations of the legal burden of proof in criminal cases?

University of London LLB Examination
(for External Students) Law of Evidence June 1996 Q2

General Comment

The question calls for a good knowledge of Lord Sankey's rule in *Woolmington* v *DPP* [1935] AC 462 and the judicial glosses that have been put upon it subsequently, particularly with respect to implied statutory exceptions and the use of s101 Magistrates' Courts Act 1980. Some analysis of the difficulties involved in discharging a legal burden of proof is necessary to answer the question fully.

Skeleton Solution

Woolmington v *DPP* and Lord Sankey's dictum – the exceptions and the opportunity for judicial allocation of burden – s101 Magistrates' Court Act 1980: the principles and policies involved – ease or difficulty of discharging the legal burden – whether a true exception or part of the description of the offence? – applicability of s101 principles to trial on indictment.

Suggested Solution

The modern law concerning the incidence of the legal burden in criminal trials can be traced to the dictum of Lord Sankey in *Woolmington* v *DPP* [1935] AC 462, the 'golden thread' argument that, subject to insanity or statutory exception, the legal burden of proving all elements will remain throughout upon the prosecution. It might be thought from this that judicial allocation of the burden is a non-event but this is far from the case. The area that provides considerable scope for judicial views is that of implied statutory exceptions stemming from the rather broad wording of s101 Magistrates' Courts Act (MCA) 1980. The provision applies to summary trials and has the effect of placing upon a defendant the burden of proving any exception, proviso, excuse or qualification that accompanies the description of the offence in any enactment relied upon by the prosecution. The policies underlying this section are the same ones that underly *Woolmington* v *DPP* [1935] AC 462 itself, namely that for criminal liability it should never be the rule that a person is presumed to be guilty, simpliciter, until he or she can discharge a burden of proving their own innocence. In many cases it would be impossible to begin to discharge such a burden, as with a well-known liar who is accused of theft and only has his own word with which to defend himself.

Section 101 is intended to apply only to statutory offences where the prohibited situation is clearly described and the excusatory circumstance is expressly provided for. The situation is such that proving the excuse will usually be a very simple matter, such as proving the lawful authority for obstructing the highway where a person has been injured as a result, as in *Gatland* v *MPC* [1968] 2 QB 279. By contrast, the difficulties for the prosecution of discharging a burden of proof that the accused did not fit within the excusatory circumstance would be almost insuperable, usually requiring the proof of a negative. The significance of the ease or difficulty for either party in discharging the burden of proving excusatory circumstances was examined by the House of Lords in *Nimmo* v *Alexander Cowan & Sons Ltd* [1968] AC 107. The case fell very close to the line and, by a three to two majority, the House held that where the wording of the statute was not clear on the point, the court was entitled to look at the relative ease of each party in proving the excuse as well as the mischief aimed at by the Act.

One very real problem for the courts comes from the situation where it is not at all clear whether there is a separable clearly excusatory part to the provision, or whether what is written is meant to describe the definition of the actus reus itself, as was the situation in the leading case of *R* v *Hunt* [1987] AC 352. Here, the words in the Misuse of Drugs Act 1971, to the effect that the Act did not apply to preparations of less than 0.2 per cent morphine, were viewed by the House of Lords as not imposing a burden upon the accused to prove by way of defence, but as imposing a burden upon the Crown to prove as a constituent element of the actus reus. The point was made that the *Woolmington* dictum applied both to implied and express statutory exceptions. In view of the highly specialised and onerous problem of discharging the burden in *Hunt*, this is clearly based upon the *Woolmington* thinking.

In *Hunt*, the court confirmed the view of the Court of Appeal in *R v Edwards* [1975] QB 27 that the same principles should apply to trials on indictment as to summary trials by s101, and the reason for this is to give a consistency of approach. This seems to apply a fortiori where the offence is clearly a regulatory one as in *R v Alath Construction Ltd* [1990] 1 WLR 1255, a case about breach of a tree-preservation order. *Hunt* also showed that any difficulties of construction should be resolved in favour of the defendant so as to place the burden upon the prosecution. This principle was illustrated in *Westminster City Council v Croyalgrange* (1986) 83 Cr Ap R 155, where the House of Lords took the view that an exception qualified a statutory prohibition which was not, in itself, the offence charged. This allowed the court to take the position that s101 did not apply to a sex establishment licence situation and the legal burden remained upon the Crown throughout.

Chapter 5

Hearsay – General Exclusion

5.1　Introduction

5.2　Key points

5.3　Key cases and statute

5.4　Questions and suggested solutions

5.1 Introduction

Hearsay is one of the most important areas of the laws of evidence; the rule against hearsay is complex, but the rule and the many exceptions to it will always form the basis of at least one question (and frequently several) in any Evidence examination.

In this chapter the scope and application of the exclusionary rule against hearsay will be examined, together with the important common law rules which exceptionally allowed hearsay to be adduced.

In the next two chapters, admissibility by statute in civil and criminal cases respectively will be examined – only then will the full complexity of the hearsay rule emerge.

5.2 Key points

Definition of hearsay

Definitions of hearsay abound; to determine whether evidence is or is not hearsay (and therefore whether it is necessary to go any further and consider exceptions to the exclusionary rule) one should consider the purpose for which an out of court statement is tendered in evidence. If the statement is tendered as evidence of any fact (or opinion) expressed therein, then it is hearsay, ie if any out of court statement is tendered in order to invite the court to accept the truth of its content, that is hearsay. The statement may take various forms, ie it may be spoken, written, or in the form of a gesture.

Spoken or oral hearsay

A good example of this is contained in the House of Lords decision in *R* v *Blastland* [1985] 2 All ER 1095 where their Lordships upheld the decision of the trial judge to exclude as inadmissible hearsay evidence of the content of a confession made by a person other than the accused. Blastland's counsel wanted this confession statement reported to the court as evidence of its truth, ie to further Blastland's defence. It was hearsay, and because it was not covered by any recognised exception to the hearsay rule, was therefore inadmissible.

Again, in *Sparks* v *R* [1964] AC 964, a white man was charged with indecent assault on a girl aged three. Sparks's counsel wanted to call as a defence witness the girl's mother to inform the court that shortly after the incident the girl had said that a coloured boy was the assailant. This evidence was being tendered to invite the court to believe the truth of the out of court statement by the girl (who did not give direct evidence herself), and was therefore hearsay, and, again, inadmissible because not covered by a recognised exception to the rule against hearsay.

Written or documentary hearsay

The same principles apply at common law as for spoken, or oral hearsay, so again the vital issue is the purpose for which the written, or printed etc, evidence is tendered.

Gestures as hearsay

An affirmative nod or negative shake of the head may be hearsay just as the spoken or written affirmative or negative would be if tendered as an out of court 'statement'.

The ambit of the hearsay rule

If an out of court statement is tendered for a purpose other than to invite the court to accept the contents as true, then it is not hearsay. Therefore, if the fact rather than the content of the statement is what the person tendering it seeks to prove, it is not hearsay. For example, in *Ratten* v *R* [1972] AC 378 a telephone operator was permitted to give evidence that the wife of the accused had made an emergency telephone call in which she hysterically demanded the police a couple of minutes before she was fatally shot. The fact of the call contradicted Ratten's statement that his wife had made no telephone call; also the wife's hysteria tended to refute Ratten's defence that his gun went off as he was cleaning it and his wife was thus accidentally shot and died immediately. Therefore the evidence of the telephone operator was not hearsay. The case emphasises the point that the purpose for which the statement was tendered determines whether or not it is hearsay.

However, sometimes it is extremely difficult to know what that purpose is. In the case of *R* v *Kearley* [1991] Crim LR 282, there was the evidence of some police officers, who searched the defendant's house, that a number of people rang there to enquire about drugs. The court held the evidence to be admissible to prove that the defendant was the supplier of drugs. It was argued that the truth of the statements was irrelevant – what was important was the fact that the phone calls were made. However, it could be argued that the prosecution here was relying on the truth of the words said during those phone calls.

The case of *R* v *Harry* (1988) 86 Cr App R 105 concerned similar evidence which was held to be inadmissible, but the distinguishing point perhaps in this case was that the evidence was being used by one co-defendant against another. Both co-defendants were found at the same flat, but D1 wanted to use the words of the phone calls to show that it was D2 who was being asked for – hence D1 was certainly relying on the truth of the words, not just the fact that the phone calls were made.

Implied assertions

The hearsay rule applies undoubtedly to express assertions; there was some doubt as to whether implied assertions are covered by the hearsay rule. It would seem that most of the authorities (of which there is a paucity!) would support the view expressed by Lord Reid in *Myers* v *DPP* [1965] AC 1001 that implied assertions are admissible hearsay only if they come within a recognised exception to the hearsay rule. This seems to be the rationale upon which *R* v *Kearley* [1991] Crim LR 282 was decided and it should be assumed that the rule catches such matters.

Statements on tapes, films, etc

In *Taylor* v *Chief Constable of Cheshire* [1987] 1 All ER 225 a security camera in a shop made a video recording of Taylor stealing from the shop. Police officers watched the recording and identified Taylor; the recording was returned to the shopkeeper and was accidentally erased. The police officers were allowed to testify as to what they had seen on the video recording; it was not hearsay, in essence it was the same as if they had been in the shop and witnessed the incident, and then gave evidence as percipient witnesses. Similarly, a police officer may give evidence as to the reading on a radar speed meter, or the speedometer of his pursuing police vehicle, or a witness may state that an incident in issue occurred on a certain date because he looked at the newspaper he had bought or at his digital watch which displayed the date; throughout there is no element of hearsay in the evidence. In *R* v *Spiby* (1990) 91 Cr App R 186, the print-out from a machine used to monitor telephone call numbers and the length of the calls was not hearsay but real evidence because, like a speedometer, it is merely an instrument which can't contribute its own knowledge.

Admissibility of hearsay at common law

When examining hearsay admissible at common law it must be borne in mind throughout that in many instances there has been statutory intervention. Some hearsay admissible at common law in both civil and criminal cases may now be admissible by statute in either civil cases, or alternatively in criminal cases.

Informal admissions

A statement made by a party out of court, which is adverse to his interests in the case, is an informal admission and is admissible as evidence of the truth of its contents as an exception to the hearsay rule. In civil cases informal admissions are now governed by s7(1) Civil Evidence Act 1995 which supersedes the common law exception. In criminal cases informal admissions by the accused – confessions – are governed by s76 Police and Criminal Evidence Act 1984, with judicial discretion to exclude such admissible hearsay evidence being put on a statutory basis by s78 of the same Act.

Statements in public documents

Statements in most public documents are admissible at common law as evidence of the truth of their contents. The evidence was admissible as an exception to the hearsay rule because it was considered reliable and very often the official who compiled the document will have no recollection of the facts, or will have died or be unavailable or unfit to appear and give evidence in person. However, a lot of statutes now provide for the admissibility of particular classes of public documents, eg certified copies of birth certificates as evidence of a person's date of birth. In addition many statements in public documents may now be admissible in criminal cases by virtue of s24 Criminal Justice Act 1988 and in civil cases by virtue of s7(2) Civil Evidence Act 1995 which has the effect of preserving the common law on these matters.

Statements by persons since deceased

Statements by persons who have died by the time of the trial may be admissible at common law as evidence of the truth of their contents, the most common examples of which are as follows.

a) Declarations against interest

   The rationale is the same as that for admissibility of informal admissions. The declaration must be against the pecuniary or proprietary interest of the declarant; a declaration against penal interest is not admissible under this head: *Sussex Peerage Case* (1844) 11 Cl & Fin 85.

b) Declarations in the course of duty

   These are admissible in criminal proceedings – the declaration must have been made by a person acting under a duty to record some activity; the activity must have been undertaken and the declaration made sufficiently contemporaneously with the activity and with no motive to misrepresent the facts.

c) Dying declarations

   These may be admissible at the trial for the murder or manslaughter of the declarant. The statement of the victim, oral or written, as to the cause of his injuries (usually who the assailant was) must have been made when he was under a settled, hopeless, expectation of death, and had he survived he would have been a competent witness. The rationale of this exception, that the knowledge of impending death will make the declaration as reliable as a statement given in evidence under oath, is questionable. That the judge must warn the jury to treat the declaration with some caution, and should point out that the declarant was not exposed to cross-examination is indicative of the modern approach, which accepts the admissibility but is more sceptical about the weight to be attached to such declarations.

Res gestae statements

The main, and most important element of the res gestae concept is that of the admissibility of hearsay which consists of statements made with spontaneity and sufficiently contemporaneous to some relevant occurrence or some state of affairs. In *R v Callender* [1998] Crim LR 337 the Court of Appeal stated that res gestae is 'a single principle, and for evidence to come within that exception to the hearsay evidence rule it must pass the test that the trial judge is satisfied that there is no real possibility of concoction or distortion'. Though attempts are made by textbook authors to compartmentalise the different situations where res gestae statements are admissible, the categories adopted are merely sets of situations where the principle has been applied. In *Howe v Malkin* (1878) 40 LT 196 Grove J explained the rationale succinctly:

'Though you cannot give in evidence a declaration per se, yet when there is an act accompanied by a statement which is so mixed up with it as to become part of the res gestae, evidence of such a statement may be given.'

To some extent 'so mixed up' begs the question, but the following main types of statement are those which examiners favour, with the most frequently recurring one first.

a) Spontaneous and contemporaneous statements

At common law it was accepted that an occurrence could be explained by some spontaneous statement made in the heat of the moment by either a participant or a witness to the occurrence. The old cases, such as *R v Bedingfield* (1879) 14 Cox CC 341, evince the insistence of the common law on strict spontaneity and complete contemporaneity. The leading case is now *R v Andrews* [1987] AC 281 in which the House of Lords overruled *Bedingfield* as being far too strict and set out the modern criteria for admissibility.

Distortion or concoction must be safe to disregard; to ascertain that, it may be concluded that statements made because of involvement in, or the pressure of, the event will not be distorted or concocted, if they are made in conditions of approximate contemporaneity. To be sufficiently spontaneous for admissibility, the statement must have been so closely associated with the event which excited it that it can be safely inferred that the mind of the maker of the statement was still dominated by that event. Other factors which bear on the possibility of concoction or distortion must be considered by the judge, eg malice of the declarant, his sobriety at the time.

R v Andrews has relaxed the contemporaneity and spontaneity requirement, but they will still play a major role in assessing the reliability (and therefore admissibility) of such res gestae statements. In *R v Callender* [1998] Crim LR 337 the

Court of Appeal held that if there were grounds to conclude that a statement was concocted then that evidence should not be admitted under res gestae.

b) Declarations as to physical or mental condition

Statements about the contemporaneous physical or mental condition of the speaker, including his emotions, are admissible under the res gestae doctrine with the necessary inference of spontaneity. Statements as to sensations, symptoms etc are capable of admissibility under this head, but not statements as to the reason for them (but they might be admissible under another exception to the hearsay rule, eg dying declarations).

c) Statements of intention

A statement as to what the speaker intended to do is admissible as evidence of that intention on his part, but whether it is admissible as evidence of his carrying out that intention is uncertain. In *R v Wainwright* (1875) 13 Cox CC 171 a statement by a subsequent murder victim that she was going to visit the accused was inadmissible as evidence that she did so. *R v Buckley* (1873) 13 Cox CC 293 is in conflict, but the speaker was a police officer informing his superior officer of his intention to perform an act in the course of his duty, so the evidence of his intention may have been admitted as a declaration in the course of duty.

d) Statements explaining actions

The statement of the perpetrator of some act may sometimes be that of the best person to explain the proper significance of that act. Provided such a statement is made contemporaneously with the act, and by the actor as opposed to an observer, then it can be admitted as hearsay under the res gestae doctrine.

The case of *R v McCay* [1990] Crim LR 338 causes problems here. The Court of Appeal in this case held as admissible evidence given by a police officer as to the number chosen in an identification parade by the witness. The court appeared to use two possible grounds for the admissibility. First, that any identification carried out in accordance with Code D Police and Criminal Evidence Act 1984 is admissible, whether hearsay or not. This can hardly be right. Secondly, it fell within an exception to the hearsay rule, res gestae. However, this goes against authorities which suggest that it does not, eg *Teper v R* [1952] AC 480.

5.3 Key cases and statute

- *R v Andrews* [1987] AC 281
- *R v Blastland* [1986] AC 41
- *R v Kearley* [1992] 2 All ER 345
- *Ratten v R* [1972] AC 378
- Civil Evidence Act 1995, s7

5.4 Questions and suggested solutions

QUESTION ONE

Albert is charged with the murder of Betty by stabbing. Discuss the admissibility of the following.

a) Charles, walking past Albert's house, heard a woman scream 'Don't do it to me, Albert; put that knife down!'. He knocked at the door as the screams continued, got no reply, so reported to the police.

b) When the police arrived at the house, Betty staggered down the path and collapsed. Shortly before her death in hospital she recovered consciousness and said 'Albert's done for me, but I forgive him'.

c) Betty told her mother on the day of the stabbing that she intended to visit Albert.

d) When interviewed by the police, Albert stated that he was not at home on the day of the stabbing. Subsequently he retracted that statement, said he was at home but that after an argument with Betty he went out to the pub and when he returned the ambulance was departing, with the police following.

e) David, dying of cancer a month after the murder, confessed that he was the person who had stabbed Betty at Albert's house.

Written by the Author

General Comment

This problem question raises a number of different issues, all relating to common law exceptions to the rule against hearsay. Each issue should be considered as it arises.

Skeleton Solution

Examination of implied assertions and res gestae statements – exceptions to hearsay rule: dying declarations and res gestae statements – hearsay: statement of intention – corroboration: lies told by the accused – inadmissible hearsay and irrelevance.

Suggested Solution

If Charles is to relate to the court what he overheard at Albert's house, it must be relevant to the fact in issue at the trial – the murder of Betty – and must not infringe any exclusionary rule of evidence. The fact that he heard screams emanating from the house, and that they seemed to be those of a female, would be admissible if relevant, for example to prove that a female was present, and was in fear, or hysterical (*Ratten* v *R* [1972] AC 378). However, that may not be relevant if Albert is not denying the presence of a female, but rather is stating only that he was not present.

If Charles tenders in evidence the content of what was screamed, as opposed to the mere fact of the scream, then the utterance implies that Albert was holding a knife and was threatening or terrorising the female with it; it is an implied assertion that Albert was present, was wielding a knife, and was threatening a female in the house.

Therefore, Charles' evidence would be hearsay to the same extent as if the statement/utterance had been an express assertion of those facts, and thus would be inadmissible unless it came within a recognised exception to the hearsay rule (*Myers* v *DPP* [1965] AC 1001). The only exception would seem to be that of res gestae statements; if the time of the stabbing is established, and the screamed statement was sufficiently contemporaneous, and the other criteria as to spontaneity, concoction and distortion, and any relevant factors which may be given to the court have been taken into account, then Charles may report to the court not only the fact of the utterance, but its content (*R* v *Andrews* [1987] AC 281); and, of course, the fact of the continued screaming as he knocked at the door.

Betty's statement to the police may be admissible as a dying declaration, provided she was in settled hopeless expectation of death and if alive would have been a competent witness (*R* v *Pike* (1829) 3 C & P 598). (It is assumed that she is neither a child of tender years nor a person of defective intellect who would have been adjudged incompetent.) If she is Albert's wife, then she would now be both competent and compellable (Police and Criminal Evidence Act 1984, s80).) If she lost consciousness almost immediately after the last thrust of the knife and remained unconscious until she made her statement, then it could be argued by the defence counsel that she had not had enough time to reflect on her situation and thus could not make a dying declaration: *R* v *Bedingfield* (1879) 14 Cox CC 341 has not been overruled on that point, although the rest of its reasoning has been overruled by *R* v *Andrews*. However, the content of her statement would seem to suggest that she is aware of her impending death and is resigned to it. If her statement is admitted as a dying declaration, the judge must warn the jury to treat its significance with caution, and must point out to them that Betty was not subjected to cross-examination on her declaration (*Nembhard* v *R* [1982] 1 All ER 183; *Waugh* v *R* [1950] AC 203).

If Betty's statement is not admissible as a dying declaration, it may possibly be admissible as a res gestae statement dependent on the spontaneity, contemporaneity etc as stipulated in *R* v *Andrews*. If it does not meet the criteria for either a dying declaration or a res gestae statement, then it will be inadmissible hearsay.

Betty's statement to her mother is a statement of her intention. Her mother may relate this to the court as evidence of Betty's intention to visit Albert, but that is not as relevant as is whether or not she did visit him. As to the latter, it would seem that the mother's evidence would be excluded as inadmissible hearsay, as the weight of authority is against the admission of such hearsay to prove the intended act was performed (*R* v *Wainwright* (1875) 13 Cox CC 171; *R* v *Thomson* [1912] 3 KB 19; *R* v *Buckley* (1873) 13 Cox CC 293). There is conflict in the cases, and it could therefore be argued that if the interval between Betty's statement to her mother and her being stabbed at Albert's house was short, then her mother should be allowed to report the statement to the court.

Albert's retraction of his first statement and contradiction of it in his second could amount to evidence capable of corroborating prosecution evidence against him. Although in this case there is no necessity for corroboration, or a corroboration warning, nevertheless Albert's lie could be supportive of prosecution evidence unless there is some explanation for it other than one consistent with his guilt (*R* v *Lucas* [1981] QB 720). The contradictory statements about a material issue, ie his presence at the scene and time of the crime, mean that if there is a case to answer then Albert will have to elect to testify and give an innocent explanation for his lying to the police.

If David is resigned to his death and has died by the time of the trial, his statement cannot amount to a dying declaration (he is not the homicide victim!). Again, if he survives, unless in the light of his statement a decision is taken to drop the charge against Albert and instead prosecute David, David's statement cannot be reported to the court at Albert's trial as it is not a confession statement of the accused, and is therefore inadmissible hearsay (*R* v *Blastland* [1985] 2 All ER 1095 and *R* v *McGillvray* [1993] Crim LR 530). If he dies before Albert's trial, his statement is not admissible as a declaration against interest, as the declaration is not against David's proprietary or pecuniary interest, but rather against his penal interest, which does not bring it within that exception to the hearsay rule in English law (*Sussex Peerage Case* (1844) 11 Cl & Fin 85). In any event, as it is Albert, not David, who is charged with Betty's murder, an admission made by David, adverse to his interests, is not relevant to the guilt of Albert (*R* v *Blastland*).

QUESTION TWO

'Considerable relaxation of the hearsay rule has been engineered by the courts, but the decisions constitute not so much a retreat from *Myers* as a partial abandonment of the hearsay/non-hearsay analysis of evidence.' (Ashworth and Pattenden).

Discuss.

University of London LLB Examination
(for External Students) Law of Evidence June 1995 Q4

General Comment

Work logically through each of the points outlined in the skeleton solution below, ensuring that you cover each point in turn.

Skeleton Solution

Outline of what *Myers* says about the admission of hearsay – examples of analysis as real evidence – analysis as original evidence, not tendered to show truth of statements – discussion of wider view of res gestae – consideration of special view taken of certain ID evidence.

Suggested Solution

In *Myers* v *DPP* [1965] AC 1001, still a leading authority on hearsay at common law, the majority view was that there was no judicial discretion to admit even the most cogent hearsay evidence unless it fell within an established exception to the rule, and that any new extension must henceforth be a matter for Parliament. The courts have not, however, been inactive in this area since *Myers*, and this is particularly evident in the areas considered below.

Analysis as real evidence

There has been a huge increase in the amount of information produced mechanically or electronically, and much of this is tendered as a type of statement for the purpose of proving its truth so, conceptually, there are hearsay implications. In many cases the evidence given is that of someone who has observed the equipment and gives testimony of what he saw. In truth this is little more reliable than a person giving evidence of out of court statements, but the courts have consistently supported the view that if equipment has any sort of recording function then evidence of the record is real evidence not hearsay. This pre-dates *Myers* v *DPP* [1965] AC 1001 but has been much extended since that case. Examples include *The Statue of Liberty* [1968] 1 WLR 739 (film record produced by radar), *R* v *Wood* (1982) 76 Cr App R 23 (complicated computer results of spectrometer readings and calculations, far beyond a record, in stolen metal case), *Castle* v *Cross* [1984] 1 WLR 1372 (printout from intoximeter machine to show that no sample given), and *Taylor* v *Chief Constable of Cheshire* [1987] 1 All ER 225 (evidence of police who watched video record, later erased, of offence). Although the question of computer printout admissibility is largely covered by statute, the willingness to make use of the inherent reliability of such equipment does seem to influence the courts away from hearsay considerations as can be seen from *R* v *Shepherd* [1993] 1 All ER 225. The cases of *R* v *Rice* [1963] 1 QB 857 (pre-dating *Myers*) and *R* v *Lydon* [1987] Crim LR 407 show a willingness to sidestep hearsay problems by treating airline tickets and pieces of paper with writing pointing towards the persons accused as real evidence indicating circumstantial links. These cases illustrate the trend away from hearsay analysis, although many academics view this as a strained approach.

Analysis as original evidence relevant to facts in issue, not tendered to show truth of statements

In *Woodhouse* v *Hall* [1980] Crim LR 645 evidence of offers of sexual services, made to police officers by girls in a massage parlour, were held properly admitted, not to show the truth of what was said but to show that offers had been made. The limits of this approach are illustrated by *R* v *Harry* (1988) 86 Cr App R 105, where evidence of phone calls to a house involving details of enquiries about drug sales were properly excluded on the question of whether a particular person was doing the dealing. The evidence would probably have been admissible on the question of whether the house was being used for dealing, had that been in issue. Similarly, in *Ratten* v *R* [1972] AC 378, the Privy Council held that evidence of a telephone operator repeating a hysterical woman's plea to call the police was admissible to rebut a claim that no call had been made from the premises and that a fatal shooting about that time had been an accident. There was no need to examine the truth of any assertion contained in the statement.

Analysis of the evidence as part of the res gestae where the maker is dead or unavailable

The courts seem to have taken a wider view in recent time of the res gestae analysis of spontaneous statements made under the influence of startling or frightening events. *Ratten v R* [1972] AC 378 is a good example of this and, provided that the mind of the speaker is dominated by the event, and there is no real possibility of fabrication or concoction, the statement is admissible despite its obvious hearsay nature. The matter has been considerably refined and analysed in *R v Nye & Loan* (1977) 66 Cr App R 252, *R v Turnbull* [1984] Crim LR 620, and by the House of Lords in *R v Andrews* [1987] AC 281. The courts seem to have abandoned the former view, from *R v Bedingfield* (1879) 14 Cox CC 341, that statements were only admissible if they were proved to be part of the same 'transaction', a very demanding test. The test now is simply one of the dominating quality of the circumstance upon the consciousness of the speaker, so that a particularly horrific event may render a statement admissible despite a considerable time gap, as in *R v Andrews* [1987] AC 281.

Indications of a special approach towards certain ID evidence

The courts have used much ingenuity to sidestep hearsay problems where identification evidence is concerned. In *R v Osbourne; R v Virtue* [1973] 1 QB 678 evidence of two witnesses of their identification of the accused in a parade would have been completely useless without the additional evidence of a police officer as to the witnesses' actions in picking out the accused. This was clearly hearsay but no attempt was made to take the point. A similar situation occurred in *R v McCay* [1990] Crim LR 338, where the policeman's evidence was viewed as either an undefined exception to the rule or as original evidence. The cases of *R v Smith (Percy)* [1976] Crim LR 511 (sketch made by policeman to witnesses description), *R v Okorudu* [1982] Crim LR 747 (photograph of photofit), and *R v Cook* [1987] 1 All ER 1049 show that the view of the courts is that these matters and, presumably, any other means of creating an image from a witness perception, are sui generis and quite outside the hearsay rule.

It is suggested that all the above examples illustrate a determined effort by the courts to move away from an approach which relies upon a strict hearsay/non-hearsay analysis.

QUESTION THREE

'If there are to be any rules peculiar to hearsay evidence, the definition of hearsay for the purpose of such rules should include all that is presently within its ambit except implied assertions.' (Law Commission Consultation Paper No 138)

Discuss.

University of London LLB Examination
(for External Students) Law of Evidence June 1996 Q3

General Comment

There are various ways to approach a question such as this but it is necessary to bring out the distinction between express and implied assertions to see whether such distinctions justify a different, more relaxed reception for implied assertions despite their obvious hearsay component and effect. The cases cited in the Consultation Paper No 138 provide a good framework upon which to build a discussion.

Skeleton Solution

Brief definition/description of implied assertions – survey of case law development of hearsay rule as applied to implied assertions – difficulties involved in judicial analysis of whether assertion contained in evidence or not – Consultation Paper views and recommendations – conclusion.

Suggested Solution

To understand the Law Commission's views on the hearsay rule and implied assertions it is necessary to distinguish such assertions from express assertions. Words, spoken or written, or in rare cases conduct alone, may be to such effect that inferences can be drawn from them. If the inference drawn is in the form of an assertion of fact, this will be an implied assertion such as the shouted words in *Teper* v *R* [1952] AC 480 of '... your place burning and you going away from the fire' (implied assertion that shop owner was present at scene of fire), or the desperate gesturing of the dying woman in *Chandrasekera* v *R* [1937] AC 220 (sign language indicating and asserting identity of assailant).

The case law on implied assertion and hearsay is fairly voluminous and seems to stem from *Wright* v *Doe d Tatham* (1837) 7 Ad & E 313, where letters sought to be admitted to assert that the writers considered the recipient to be sane were analysed as inadmissible hearsay, through to cases such as *R* v *Harry* (1988) 86 Cr App R 105 and *R* v *Kearley* [1992] 2 All ER 345 where inferences that defendants were drug dealers were likely to have been drawn as evidence of telephone calls and personal visits by potential drug purchasers had been sought to be admitted. In *Kearley* admission of such evidence for the Crown grounded a successful appeal and defence evidence of this type was properly excluded in *R* v *Harry* (1988) 86 Cr App R 105. The House of Lords judgments in *R* v *Kearley* [1992] 2 All ER 345 reveal the very serious difficulties in rationalising and analysing such evidence at all, as the same evidence will often be able to be rationalised on a different basis altogether, such as the airline ticket in *R* v *Rice* [1963] 1 QB 857 (circumstantial real evidence) or the phone call in *Ratten* v *R* [1972] AC 378 (evidence of facts in issue – the state of affairs at the home).

It is very clear from the cases on implied assertions that the difficulties involved in considering express hearsay assertions are greatly increased when the matter becomes one of implication from absence of facts. The 'record' cases such as *R* v *Shore* (1983) 76 Cr App R 72 and *R* v *Patel* [1981] 3 All ER 94 indicate that absence of a record, where one might be expected to be found, is treated as direct evidence rather than a matter of implied assertion. This explanation is not altogether convincing and there is no doubt that these difficulties have had considerable influence on the Law Commission.

The Consultation Paper appears to be heavily influenced by the unconvincing and somewhat artificial distinctions used in the implied assertion cases, and it comes to the conclusion that any future shape of the hearsay rule ought not to include implied assertions at all, on the basis that this would prevent resort to strained judicial reasoning. The Commission has drawn support for its reasoning in the fact that many common law countries have evidence codes which expressly exclude implied assertions by defining hearsay by reference to evidence of words or acts intended by the speaker or creator to be assertive. This 'intention to assert' is suggested by the Paper as an integral and essential part of any future hearsay rule.

In conclusion, it is difficult to get away from the view that implied assertions provide enormous problems if caught by the hearsay rule, but it is also true that there are considerable possibilities for miscarriages of justice and of excessively collateral examinations if the rule does not apply to such assertions at all. The danger is of replacing long arguments on admissibility with long arguments about relevance, collateral evidence and the propriety and correctness of inferences to be drawn from such evidence. The general problems concerning hearsay outlined by Lord Reid in *Myers* v *DPP* [1965] AC 1001 were shown to be very much still relevant in *R* v *Kearley* [1992] 2 All ER 345 and are very unlikely to go away altogether, whatever comes out of the Consultation Paper. It is submitted that it would be unwise to have a new regime which does not have at least a discretionary power to catch implied assertions within some exclusionary rule, although there may be scope for extension of other discretions such as s78 Police and Criminal Evidence Act 1984 or the common law discretion to exclude highly prejudicial evidence of relatively low probative value.

QUESTION FOUR

Andrew is charged with murdering Brian. The prosecution claimed that Andrew knifed Brian outside his house because he thought that Brian was having an affair with Carol, Andrew's wife. Andrew claims that he was defending himself because Brian attacked him when Andrew told him to 'put a stop to this nonsense with Carol'. A month before he died, Brian e-mailed his brother, saying he was scared because Andrew had found out about Carol and that he, Brian, would be 'looking over his shoulder from now on'. Doreen, Brian's sister, was staying at Brian's on the night of the stabbing. She has stated to the police that she heard angry voices, amongst them Brian's voice, outside the house at the time. When the noise subsided, she went out to check and found Brian lying on the ground, bleeding, with no-one around. Brian said 'I tried to fend him off. He just went crazy'. Doreen says she won't testify because of anonymous telephone calls warning her against doing so. Sid, a detective who was pretending to be a prisoner at the time Andrew was in custody, says that he drew

Andrew into a conversation in which Andrew said 'I gave Brian a right hiding. He had it coming to him all along'.

Discuss any evidential issues arising.

University of London LLB Examination
(for External Students) Law of Evidence June 1997 Q5

General Comment

With such a situation, structuring an answer is important and one technique which suggests itself here is to deal with prosecution and defence evidence separately. Much of the question deals with the hearsay rule, but it is important to deal with other points, such as the burdens on Andrew's defence, compellability of witnesses, s23 Criminal Justice Act 1988 and ss76 and 78 Police and Criminal Evidence Act (PACE) 1984.

Skeleton Solution

Andrew's defence evidence

The burdens involved – proof that Brian was aware that Andrew knew about the affair; the e-mail, was it printed or stored? – the hearsay rule, showing state of mind – proof of the angry voices by Doreen; Doreen's unwillingness to testify; hearsay evidence.

The prosecution evidence

Proof of Brian's e-mail to show Brian's fear of Andrew – Doreen's evidence: the statement; multiple hearsay; the exceptions for spontaneous utterances; Andrews; non-hearsay statements; *Ratten* v *R* – Andrew's confession; ss76, 78 PACE 1984; breaches of Code C.

Suggested Solution

Andrew's defence evidence

Andrew is relying on self-defence and will have to discharge the evidential burden upon this matter which will be almost impossible unless he gives evidence, leaving the legal burden to rebut it upon the prosecution. An important element of his defence is that Brian was aware that Andrew knew of his wife's affair; it supports Andrew's story of a 'warning-off' approach rather than a murderous ambush. Andrew might wish to make use of the e-mail to the brother for this purpose. Brian's words are conceptually hearsay if reproduced in court for their truth, so this problem must be overcome. If the e-mail had been printed off, or was still stored on computer disc or drive, this would constitute a document within the definition applicable to criminal evidence under the Criminal Justice Act (CJA) 1988. As a first-hand hearsay document, this would be prima facie admissible under s23 CJA 1988 as meeting the requirement in s23(2)(a) of the maker being dead, but it would be subject to the exclusionary discretion in s25.

If the e-mail was not recorded or printed anywhere there would be no possibility of using s23, and the matter would have to be oral hearsay via the testimony of the brother. This would probably be admissible under the common law hearsay exception of res gestae statements showing the state of mind of the speaker as in *Neill v North Antrim Magistrates' Court* [1992] 4 All ER 846.

Andrew will almost certainly wish to get into court Doreen's evidence to the effect that she heard angry words. This is consistent with his story and he may get the advantage of this if Doreen gives prosecution evidence or her statement is allowed in by the judge (see below). If the prosecution do not use her evidence, Andrew may decide to call her and he could compel her. If she refused to give evidence, once sworn upon the point, he could possibly apply to the judge to treat her as hostile following *R v Thompson* (1976) 64 Cr App R 96 and to put her earlier statement to her under s3 Criminal Procedure Act 1865. The prosecution might object to her evidence of angry words on the ground that there is a hearsay implication. This could be met with the argument, used by the Privy Council in *Ratten v R* [1972] AC 378, that the evidence is non-hearsay evidence of 'the state of affairs' obtaining at a particular time and place, which is the issue here.

The prosecution evidence

It sounds likely that the prosecution will wish to put Brian's e-mail into evidence to show that he was already in fear of Brian. As outlined above, there should not be too many difficulties getting this in under s23 CJA 1988 if in a document, or under the common law exception if it is oral. The common law exception might be used if the court wished to exclude it in the exercise of its discretion under s23 if it was recorded. The fact that the statutory route was not open would not, of itself, bar a common law exception.

As to Doreen's evidence, the prosecution will surely wish to get Brian's last words into evidence. The defence will wish to keep them out as being inconsistent with Andrew's evidence and will try to use the hearsay rule. It should be possible to argue that this matter falls within the exception for res gestae spontaneous utterances made whilst the speaker's mind is dominated by some shocking or startling event. The leading case on this now is *R v Andrews* [1987] AC 281, and Brian seems to have been well within the state of domination of thoughts outlined by Lord Ackner. There is still the very real problem that Doreen will not testify because of fear. There has been a growing use of s23(3)(b) CJA 1988 in recent times, as in *R v Acton Justices, ex parte McMullen* (1991) 92 Cr App R 98 to admit witness statements made to the police, but there are two problems here. One is the necessity for leave under the inclusionary discretion in s26 CJA 1988 for a police investigation document, and the second is the question whether, as this is repetition of a hearsay statement via an exception, this is 'direct oral evidence by' Doreen or is it second-hand hearsay. If it is the latter, s23 will not help. The use of 'direct' seems to indicate that s23 will not help. If, by contrast, Brian's words can be seen as indicative of a state of affairs which is in issue, *Ratten v R* [1972] AC 378 is authority that this is not hearsay at all and Doreen could give 'direct' evidence of it and, consequently, her documentary evidence would fit within s23. A further possibility might be available under s24 CJA 1988.

Andrew has been tricked into making a confession at a time when he was in custody and within the protections of Code C of PACE 1984. The question here is first, whether the confession is admissible in law and, second, whether, if it is, it can be excluded as a matter of discretion. The first point is dealt with by reference to s76 PACE 1984 which shows that it will be inadmissible if shown to be obtained by oppression (s76(2)(a)) or by reason of things said or done which were likely in the circumstances to render any confession by him unreliable: s76(2)(b). It sounds very unlikely that the trickery could amount to oppression within the extended meaning of that term shown in *R v Fulling* [1987] QB 426. Trickery that does not sap the will of the doctrine is not usually sufficient: *R v Parker* (1994) 26 HLR 508. Again, with s76(2)(b), there seems nothing tending towards unreliability so probably the confession is admissible in law.

As regards exclusion by discretion, s78 PACE 1984 will allow for exclusion on the basis of the adverse effects on the fairness of the proceedings. The police action drives a coach and horses through the provisions of Code C for the questioning of suspects. This is the classic example of the 'significant and substantial' breaches of the 'verballing' provisions so disliked by the Court of Appeal in *R v Keenan* [1989] 3 WLR 1193. Such a deliberate and flagrant disregard of the Code and the worst of bad faith is almost certain to lead to the confession being excluded under s78.

QUESTION FIVE

'The rule against hearsay prohibits a witness from reporting a statement made by another person only where the purpose of adducing evidence of the statement is to establish the truth of any fact asserted in the statement.'

How far is this true of the current law relating to hearsay?

University of London LLB Examination
(for External Students) Law of Evidence June 1999 Q2

General Comment

The interpretation of this question could give rise to difficulties. It would be possible to interpret it as being about hearsay generally, but the alternative interpretation is that the question relates to implied assertions. The reference to 'any fact asserted in the statement' ought to make candidates realise that some discussion of the cases culminating in *R v Kearley* [1992] 2 All ER 345 is required.

Skeleton Solution

The scope of the rule against hearsay – application of the rule to implied assertions: *R v Kearley* – assertions made orally or in writing: *Wright v Doe d Tatham*; *Teper v R*; *Ratten* v *R* – evaluation – judgment in *R* v *Harry* – *R* v *Kearley*: views of the majority and the minority in the House of Lords – importance of *R* v *Kearley*.

Suggested Solution

The hearsay rule excludes assertions made out of court, which are tendered for the purpose of proving the truth of their content. An assertion can be made orally, in writing or by conduct. The quote which forms the substance of the question is correct in so far as it describes the application of the hearsay rule to such statements. One of the difficult questions which has arisen in relation to this rule is whether the hearsay rule applies to an implied assertion, eg an assertion from which it is possible to infer a particular fact. Implied assertions can also be made orally, in writing or by conduct. The quote supplied appears to contend that the hearsay rule does not extend to such assertions and, whilst that is a view with which some in the judiciary would agree (see, for instance, the minority view of the House of Lords in *R* v *Kearley* [1992] 2 All ER 345), the authorities suggest that the rule against hearsay does extend to assertions made orally or in writing (or by a combination of both). However, there is little authority on the issue of assertions made by conduct alone. Assertions made orally or in writing will be considered first.

The classic case in this area is *Wright* v *Doe d Tatham* (1837) 7 Ad & El 313 (although this case has been described by the editor of Cross as 'old and unsatisfactory'). One of the issues before the court was whether a testator's sanity could be inferred from the fact that others had corresponded with him as if he were sane. It was held that the actions of those who sent the letters were 'a direct and positive statement that he was sane' (per Parke B). Thus, those who sent the letters were impliedly asserting that the testator was sane. The court went on to hold that the evidence of the letters was hearsay and inadmissible.

In the more recent case of *Teper* v *R* [1952] AC 480 the accused was convicted of arson of a shop belonging to his wife. His defence was that of alibi. In order to establish that he had been in the vicinity of the shop, a policeman gave evidence that, some 25 minutes after the fire had begun, an unidentified female bystander had shouted to a motorist (who looked like the accused): 'Your place burning and you going away from the fire'. The Privy Council quashed the conviction on the ground that this assertion, which by implication contradicted Teper's defence, was inadmissible hearsay.

In *Ratten* v *R* [1972] AC 378 the Privy Council held that the evidence of the telephonist was not hearsay, but went on to consider its admissibility on the basis that the evidence did contain an element of hearsay. The obiter opinion (as subsequently understood by a majority of the House of Lords in *R* v *Kearley* [1992] 2 All ER 345) was that, in so far as it was evidence from which the jury could infer that the caller was being attacked by her husband, it was admissible as an exception to the rule against hearsay as part of the res gestae. This case was interpreted by some commentators as suggesting that a more relaxed attitude was emerging involving the exclusion of hearsay. The outcome of the case was that the statement was admitted, and the prosecution was able to rely not on the direct meaning of the words ('Get me the police'), but on the very clear implication that those words contained ('I am in fear of my husband').

There was academic support for such a trend; Cross argued that the rationale for the exclusion of hearsay applied only to the direct intentional assertion of fact and that there was no reason, be it doctrinal or concerning policy, to extend the rule to implied assertions. The trend was also in line with the rules of other jurisdictions. For example, the Federal Rules of Evidence exclude implied assertions from the ambit of the rule of hearsay.

In *R v Harry* (1988) 86 Cr App R 105 Harry and another were charged with the possession and supply of drugs. The Crown's case was that both defendants had been dealing in cocaine from the other's flat. Harry did not dispute that the flat had been used for supplying drugs, and wanted to call evidence to show that telephone calls were made to the flat asking for his co-defendant and not for him. The Court of Appeal upheld the trial judge's ruling that this evidence was hearsay, because the purpose of adducing it was to establish what the callers implied, namely that it was the co-defendant, and not Harry, who was the dealer.

R v Harry was considered and approved by a bare majority in another drugs case, *R v Kearley* and this is now the leading authority on the matter. In *R v Kearley* [1992] 2 All ER 345 the police found drugs in the defendant's flat, but in insufficient quantities to raise the inference that Kearley was a dealer. The police remained in the flat for several hours and intercepted ten telephone calls in which the callers asked to speak to the defendant and asked for drugs. Seven other people also arrived at the flat, some with money, also asking for the defendant and asking to be supplied with drugs, but at all relevant times Kearley was either absent or not within earshot. Kearley was charged with possession with intent to supply and at his trial, the officers who had taken the telephone calls or received the visitors were allowed to give evidence of these conversations. The House of Lords allowed the appeal against conviction by a majority of three to two.

The majority held that the evidence of the telephone calls established that the callers believed that they could obtain drugs from Kearley. However, the state of mind of the callers was not a fact in issue at the trial; accordingly, evidence of the requests was irrelevant and therefore inadmissible. Assuming the contrary, that the evidence was relevant, the majority went on to hold that it was inadmissible as hearsay.

Lord Bridge, one of the majority, held that the rule against hearsay extends to assertions to be implied from words spoken by a person not called as a witness in just the same way as the rule applies to words spoken by such a person. Thus, words spoken involving an implied assertion of a relevant fact are excluded by the hearsay rule, unless they can be brought within some established exception to the rule. His Lordship went on to consider whether the evidence became admissible because several requests for the supply of drugs were made. Whilst noting the probative force of the fact that a number of requests were made, Lord Bridge was unable to identify a rule allowing the admission of hearsay evidence on the ground of its probative force.

Lord Griffiths, a member of the minority, agreed that the evidence showed that the callers did believe that they could obtain drugs from Kearley. However, His Lordship then went on to consider why all the callers shared that belief, and came to the conclusion that the obvious answer was that Kearley had established a market as a drug dealer by supplying or offering to supply drugs and was thus attracting customers. There were, of course, other inferences which could be drawn from what had happened, but there are very few factual situations from which different inferences could not be drawn, and it is for the jury to decide which inference they believe they can safely draw. The relevance of the evidence was not in regard to the state of mind of the callers, but rather to prove as a fact that the callers were acting as customers or potential customers, which was a circumstance from which the jury could, if they wished, draw the inference that Kearley was trading as a drug dealer. The issue of hearsay did not arise, since the purpose of admitting the statements was not to rely on the truth of their contents.

The probative force noted by Lord Bridge was also the subject of comment by Lord Griffiths, who said that if there had been only one or two calls to the premises offering to buy drugs they would carry little weight; they could be the result of mistake or even malice. However, as the number of calls increased, so these possibilities receded until the point was reached where 'any man of sense' would be confident that any inference, other than that the defendant was a dealer, could safely be rejected. Lord Griffiths went on to comment that a judge could exercise his discretion to refuse to admit evidence where its probative value was exceeded by its prejudicial effect so that, had there been only one or two calls made, the evidence could have been excluded.

While there is authority governing the situation where a party wishes to rely on implied assertions by words, there is little authority relating to the situation where a party wishes to rely on implied assertions by conduct alone. In *Wright* v *Doe d Tatham* (1837) 7 Ad & El 313 Parke B expressed the view obiter that, where the issue of the sea worthiness of a vessel was raised, evidence relating to the conduct of a deceased captain who embarked on the vessel with his family, having first examined every part of the vessel, would be hearsay. The captain's conduct would amount to an assertion that in his opinion the vessel was seaworthy, and such a statement might be more reliable through being unintentional, and so unlikely to have been manufactured. However, Parke B regarded it as hearsay. The party adversely affected by the captain's assertion would be unable to cross-examine him as to the basis of his opinion in exactly the same way as a party adversely affected by an expressly stated opinion is disadvantaged.

However, it has also been held obiter that, in a case concerning an alleged failure by a brewer to supply a publican with good beer, evidence would be admissible that certain customers ordered the beer, tasted it, did not finish it and either left it or threw it away (per Farwell J in *Manchester Brewery Co Ltd* v *Coombs* (1901) 82 LT 347). Keane (Keane, *The Modern Law of Evidence* (5th edn, 2000)) expresses the view that the hearsay rule should not extend to cases of mere conduct from which facts may be implied, except in rare cases such as *Chandrasekera* v *R* [1937] AC 220 where there is a clear attempt to communicate non-verbally. Keane gives as reason for this view the fact that the risks of concoction or manufacture seem minimal: in the examples given in *Wright* v *Doe d Tatham* (1837) 7 Ad & El 313 and the *Manchester Brewery* case it is most unlikely that the captain and the customers were deliberately acting out roles in the hope that anybody seeing them (potential witnesses in any subsequent legal proceedings) would be deceived into thinking that the vessel was seaworthy and the beer bad.

The importance of *R* v *Kearley* [1992] 2 All ER 345 is its confirmation that implied assertions come within the hearsay rule. If what the callers said is understood to mean that Kearley is a drug dealer, and that belief is accepted as relevant, the statements by the callers remain out of court assertions by people not called as witnesses, and the hearsay rule will apply to exclude them. The majority in *R* v *Kearley* considered the argument that the rule itself is restricted to express and intentional assertions, but followed the reasoning of Parke B in *Wright* v *Doe d Tatham* and held that the rule applies to all such assertions, despite the argument that implied or unintentional assertions may be more reliable. That such an assertion may be more reliable is not determinative, because reliability is not the justification for the exclusion of hearsay evidence. Hearsay evidence is excluded because to allow it in would be to permit unfairness to the defendant, who is unable to confront and cross-examine its source.

Chapter 6

Hearsay – Statutory Admissibility in Civil Cases

6.1   Introduction

6.2   Key points

6.3   Key case and statute

6.4   Question and suggested solution

6.1 Introduction

The Civil Evidence Act 1995 (CEA 1995), which came into force on 31 January 1997, abolishes the rule against the admission of hearsay evidence in civil proceedings in England and Wales. In doing so, it gives effect to the recommendations of the Law Commission in its 1993 Report *The Hearsay Rule in Civil Proceedings* (Law Com No 216), and represents a fundamental shift of focus from admissibility to the more sensible question of reliability of evidence. The rules of court governing the provisions of the 1995 Act are set out in Civil Procedure Rules (CPR) Part 33 which came into force in 1998. These rules govern proceedings in both the High Court and the county court.

6.2 Key points

Admissibility – s1 of the 1995 Act

Section 1(1) CEA 1995 states that in civil proceedings evidence shall not be excluded on the ground that it is hearsay. Section 1(2)(b) defines hearsay as:

'... a statement made otherwise than by a person while giving oral evidence in the proceedings which is tendered as evidence of the matters stated.'

This is the standard definition used in most leading textbooks. However, the subsection continues and indicates that hearsay includes 'hearsay of whatever degree', and therefore the provisions of the Act apply whether the hearsay is first-hand (when A states what B said), second-hand (when A states what B said C had said) or multiple.

'Statement' means any representation of fact or opinion, however made: s13 CEA 1995. The Act only applies to civil proceedings which are defined as civil proceedings before any tribunal to which strict rules of evidence apply: s11 CEA 1995. Accordingly, it does not apply to the small claims court and industrial tribunals. Hearsay evidence which is admissible by virtue of other statutes is not affected by the Act.

Safeguards

The simple proposition in s1(1) CEA 1995 is subject to certain qualifications. There are two 'safeguards' built into the 1995 Act:

a) notice provisions (to prevent a party exploiting any tactical advantage in resorting to hearsay rather than direct evidence);

b) weight of hearsay evidence (to ensure that the court takes account of how probative the hearsay evidence is).

Rules of court have been made under s3 providing that where a party to civil proceedings adduces hearsay evidence of a statement made by a person who they do not call as a witness any other party may, with the leave of the court, call that witness, not as their witness, but in order to cross-examine him on his statement as if it were evidence-in-chief. This is a further aspect of the first safeguard and is designed to stop a party taking tactical advantage of the use of hearsay evidence. It is also a recognition of the sad reality that in contested litigation parties and witnesses often have an interest in being untruthful or economical with the truth. The function of cross-examination is to expose untruths.

Notice provisions

Generally

Section 2(1) CEA 1995 provides that a person wishing to adduce hearsay evidence shall:

'… give to the other party or parties to the proceedings –

(a) such notice (if any) of that fact, and

(b) on request, such particulars of or relating to the evidence as is reasonable and practicable in the circumstances for the purpose of enabling him or them to deal with any matters arising from its being hearsay.'

CPR Part 33.2(1) provides that a party intending to rely on hearsay evidence at trial complies with s2(1)(a) CEA 1995 by serving a notice on the other parties which:

a) identifies the hearsay evidence;

b) states that the party serving the notice proposes to rely on the hearsay evidence at trial;

c) gives the reason why the witness will not be called.

Under s2(2) CEA 1995 rules of court have been made specifying classes of proceedings or types to which s2(1) does not apply and as to the manner in which the notice procedure is to be undertaken (see SIs 1996/3219 and 3218). The rules are simpler than those in force under the Civil Evidence Act 1968. The parties to dispense with the provision of notice by agreement between themselves: s2(3).

However, a breach of the s2(1) duty or the rules of court passed to enshrine that duty will not render the evidence inadmissible: s2(4) CEA 1995. Rather, it will be a consideration relevant to (a) the court's exercise of its powers with respect to the course of the proceedings (eg to the granting of adjournments) and to costs; and (b) the weight to be accorded to the evidence in question.

Under the 1968 Act, the judge had to exercise his discretion to decide whether to admit hearsay evidence if the notice provisions had not been complied with and if the other party objected to its admission. Under the 1995 Act, a judge has no discretion to exclude hearsay evidence for failure to comply with any designated notice provisions – the evidence is automatically admissible. It is likely, however, that judges will make use of their power in respect of costs and adjournments, eg by penalising a late application for admission of hearsay evidence with a costs order or equally will not require an adjournment/costs where ample notice is given. The most crucial point is that failure to give notice may be taken into account by the court as a matter adversely affecting the weight to be given to the evidence, ie the evidence may be rendered valueless, despite its admission: s2(4)(b).

Weight of hearsay evidence

Section 4 CEA 1995 states that the court shall 'have regard to any circumstances from which any inference can reasonably be drawn as to the reliability or otherwise of the evidence'. Section 4(2) specifies matters the court may take into account when weighing the evidence:

a) whether it would have been reasonable and practical to have called the witness instead;

b) how contemporaneous the statement was;

c) whether it involves multiple hearsay;

d) any possible motive of the maker of the statement;

e) whether there has been any editing; and

f) whether the evidence has been adduced as hearsay in order to prevent proper evaluation of its weight.

This second safeguard is designed to ensure that hearsay evidence is only given as much weight as its probative value deserves. The list in s4(2) is not an exhaustive checklist, but the listed matters are all fairly common sense considerations.

Preservation of common law exceptions

Section 9 CEA 1968 preserved a number of exceptions to the hearsay rule. For example, published works dealing with matters of a public nature (histories, maps, dictionaries etc) were admissible as evidence of facts of a public nature stated in them. Section 7 CEA 1995 provides that the common law rule effectively preserved by s9(1) and (2)(a) CEA 1968 – admissibility of admissions adverse to a party (eg after a road accident a driver gets out of his car and says: 'I'm sorry') – is superseded by CEA 1995. Such a hearsay statement of admission adverse to a party is now subject to the notice and weight provisions of the new Act. However, the common law exceptions concerning public records and documents etc are preserved by the effect of s7(2). The common law rules on reputation/character, including reputation or family tradition as to pedigree, marriage and other matters, are preserved by s7(3) CEA 1995.

Proof of statements in documents and records

a) Section 8 CEA 1995 provides for a statement contained in a document admissible as evidence in civil proceedings to be capable of being proved by production of that document or by the production of a copy (or a copy of a copy) of it, authenticated in such way as the court might approve. This provision further confirms the death of the 'best evidence' rule.

b) Section 9 provides that business records or records of a public authority, which are substantiated as such records by an officer of the business or authority to which the records belong, may be received in evidence without further proof. Accordingly, there is no need to call a witness formally to produce documents in these categories to the court, and a lot of time and expense will be saved. However, it is still open to a party receiving such a document to challenge its authenticity and to subpoena anyone the party considers relevant to answer questions about its contents. Hearsay implications based upon an absence of an entry in records are provable by an affidavit of an officer of the authority or business to which the record belongs.

c) The Act recognises that while in general terms business records are likely to be a reliable class of evidence, there are bound to be exceptions. Section 9(5) provides a dispensing power: '… the court may direct that all or any of the … provisions [ie of s9] do not apply in relation to a particular document or record or description of documents or records'.

Computer records

The absence of any provisions relating specifically to computer records is a noteworthy feature of the CEA 1995. The 1968 Act contained provisions to ensure that the computer was operating properly at all material times before records produced by it were adduced. The provisions were very complex (doubtless explained by the fact that computer technology was still in its infancy in 1968). Under the 1995 Act, it seems that computer records will be admissible if they constitute business records or records of a public authority, but of much wider importance, the definition of 'document' in s13 may be seen to extend to almost any type of computer-generated document.

Miscellaneous matters

Hearsay evidence cannot be given of a statement made by a person who at the time of that statement was not competent as a witness: s5(1) CEA 1995. The Act does not apply to proceedings instituted before 31 January 1997 (see *Bairstow* v *Queen's Moat Houses plc* (1997) The Times 31 January).

6.3 Key case and statute

* *Bairstow* v *Queen's Moat Houses plc* (1997) The Times 31 January

* Civil Evidence Act 1995 (generally)

6.4 Question and suggested solution

A is suing B Jewellers Ltd for the loss of two rubies from a ring which A handed in to them for restyling. B Jewellers Ltd are relying on an exemption clause contained in the contract exempting them from accidental loss. A possesses a written valuation of the ring from X Valuers Ltd, dated ten years earlier, in which it is stated that the ring is worth £10,000. Unfortunately, X Valuers Ltd since went into liquidation and the valuer cannot be traced. A has also obtained a photocopy of an internal memorandum at B Jewellers Ltd which implicates C, an employee, in the theft of precious stones from jewellery handed in by customers. This memorandum had been forwarded to the company's solicitors who have refused to release it. A has further obtained a copy of an entry in the books of D Pawnbrokers Ltd which shows that C had pledged two rubies as security for a loan. The entries show that the carat weight and the refractive index of the rubies as determined by the firm's computer tally with the weight and index of A's jewels.

Advise A on the admissibility of these items as evidence and the standard of proof applicable to the assertion that C stole the rubies.

University of London LLB Examination
(for External Students) Law of Evidence June 1991 Q5

General Comment

The question requires a knowledge of the Civil Evidence Acts 1972 and 1995 and also opinion evidence, legal professional privilege and standard of proof. The points to be addressed are however fairly well compartmented and provide a framework for answering the question.

Skeleton Solution

Status of opinion evidence: application of the Civil Evidence Act 1972 and the effect of the Civil Evidence Act 1995 – notice procedure and establishment of expertise – admissibility of evidence under s7 of the 1995 Act – admissibility of business records under s9 of the 1995 Act – legal professional privilege: lawyer/client/third party – use of copies of privileged document: *Calcraft* v *Guest* and subsequent cases – discretion to exclude evidence in civil trials – admissibility of hearsay and non hearsay computer evidence; the principle in *Hornal* v *Neuberger Products*.

Suggested Solution

Issues bearing on the admissibility of the evidence are dealt with in the order in which they arise in the question.

The valuation

The fact that it is 10 years old goes to the weight to be attached to it, and not to its admissibility. It is however produced as evidence of the opinion stated on it. As it is not being given by the valuer in court, it is hearsay and the notice provisions of the Civil Evidence Act 1995 must therefore be satisfied. It must also be established to the court's satisfaction that the valuer could properly give evidence of opinion, that is, he is an expert. This is because of the effect of s3 Civil Evidence Act (CEA) 1972 on the admissibility of expert opinion evidence. The mere fact that hearsay components will not prevent admissibility does not remove other obstacles to admisibility: s14(1) CEA 1995. Opinion evidence upon a matter requiring expertise would be generally inadmissible from a non-expert as an irrelevance. This is a matter for the judge but he may take the view that the corporate nature of the valuers was some indication of the expertise and decide to admit it, particularly if there were indications that X Valuers Ltd had been in business for a period of time. Even if admitted, it would be subject to the weighing factors in s4. The leave of the Court would be needed to admit expert evidence (CPR 35).

The internal memorandum

The value of this to A is to establish B Jewellers' culpability through the employee. Its production will therefore be subject to the hearsay rule and its admissibility governed by the Civil Evidence Act (CEA) 1995.

Since the statement is self incriminatory, A falls within s7(1) which applies CEA 1995 to adverse informal admission. This means that the memorandum is admissible subject to the notice and weighing provisions.

It is possible however that A will face arguments that s7 is not applicable, because it is not self incriminating of B Jewellers, having been made (presumably) by an employee about another employee. This raises a difficult question on vicarious admissions. An answer cannot be given from the facts given, but if A is unsuccessful in contending admissibility under s7, an alternative approach is for him to use s9 of the 1995 Act.

Section 9 CEA 1995 allows for the admissibility of 'records' of a business or public authority. The requirement is that the document is 'shown' to be a record. This can be done by certification by the business, but presumably can be done by proof in the absence of a willing certifier. The intention of the Act seems to be to get away from the former rigid requirements in CEA 1968, but there could be some difficulties in showing this memorandum to be a record, although it might be put to the writer of the memorandum if that person were subpoenaed as a witness or called for cross-examination on the document under s3 CEA 1995. The memorandum will be generally admissible under s1 unless there is some separate, non-hearsay ground for exclusion. The fact that this is a photocopy of the memorandum is of no consequence as s8 allows for copies at any number of removes from the original, subject to the court's view on authentication: s8 CEA 1995.

The next problem which A will have to meet is that of legal professional privilege. On the basis that the internal memorandum can be taken as a communication of B Jewellers with their solicitors, the privilege will apply, since a legal relationship evidently existed between them and the purpose of sending the information was presumably relative to the securing of legal advice. On the other hand, it is possible for A to argue that the memorandum was a pre-existing document which has not become privileged simply because it was subsequently sent to the solicitors (*Ventouris* v *Mountain, The Italia Express* [1991] 3 All ER 472). Further, A can contend that unless written by a very senior officer of the jewellers, it is a communication between lawyer, client and third party as to which privilege will only apply if the dominant purpose of the production of the memorandum was submission to lawyers in connection with actual or contemplated litigation; *Waugh* v *British Railways Board* [1981] QB 736. If for whatever reason, legal professional privilege applies, A can nevertheless use the copy in his possession, under the principle in *Calcraft* v *Guest* [1898] 1 QB 759. He must establish authenticity if contended by B. B will also, however, be entitled to seek a pre-trial injunction: *Ashburton (Lord)* v *Pape* [1913] 2 Ch 469. But the injunctive relief can be resisted if A neither came by the copy by underhand means, nor received it as a result of an obvious mistake by B Jewellers or their advisers: *Goddard* v *Nationwide Building Society* [1986] 3 WLR 734; *Guinness Peat Properties* v *Fitzroy Robinson* [1987] 2 All ER 716.

The admissibility of the copy entry in the books of D Pawnbrokers will not depend on the way A obtained it, even if that was improperly. The courts have no discretion to exclude evidence in civil trials on the basis of the way it was obtained: *Helliwell* v *Piggott-Sims* [1980] FSR 582. The entry is useful to A in showing disposal by an employee of rubies, and it is an implied assertion of that fact. Assuming, as is probable, that it is an implied assertion to which the hearsay rule applies, the same comments as made for the memorandum (above) apply here with respect to the status of the pawnbroker's book as a business record within s9.

It is not clear whether the entry as to carat weight and refractive index is produced directly, or copied from a computer printout. No hearsay point attaches to the fact that the calculations are not subject to oral evidence. They were prepared automatically as in *The Statue of Liberty* [1968] 1 WLR 739. They are simply contained in a document. If the document can be shown to be part of the business records of the pawnbroker, there seems to be no confidentiality or privilege to be invoked here and, subject to the notice and weighing procedures, this evidence can be used.

The authenticity of the copy must also be established, this can be done in any way approved by the court: s8(1).

Finally, there is the question of the burden of proof. It now seems established that where a crime is alleged in civil proceedings, the standard of proof applicable is the civil standard of a balance of probabilities, that is, the allegation with regard to C is more probable than not: *Hornal v Neuberger Products Ltd* [1957] 1 QB 247. It has sometimes been suggested that there is a third or different standard applicable to serious allegations in civil trials (as here), but such suggestions are best treated on the basis that in deciding whether the scales have been tipped to satisfy the civil standard, the court has regard to the seriousness of the allegations.

Chapter 7

Hearsay – Statutory Admissibility in Criminal Cases

7.1   Introduction

7.2   Key points

7.3   Key cases and statute

7.4   Questions and suggested solutions

7.1 Introduction

The major statutory exceptions concern confessions (with legislation on which there has been a plethora of interpretative cases) and documentary hearsay, on which there has also been statutory activity. In criminal cases confessions constitute an important exception to the hearsay rule, and one which will remain topical for some years and always controversial.

7.2 Key points

Common law on admissibility of confessions was altered drastically by the Police and Criminal Evidence Act (PACE) 1984.

Definition

Section 82(1): '... "confession" includes any statement wholly or partly adverse to the person who made it, whether made to a person in authority or not and whether made in words or otherwise'.

Therefore a confession may be oral, written or by a gesture such as a nod of the head, and may be made to any person, not just a person in authority such as a police officer. Silence in the face of an accusation may amount, in some circumstances, to a confession.

Admissibility

As a matter of law it is governed by s76 (s77 in the case of mentally handicapped persons). If a confession is unfairly obtained yet nevertheless strictly admissible, there is a statutory discretion to exclude it given by s78, over and above the general exclusionary discretion preserved in all cases by s82(3).

Confessions are treated as inadmissible hearsay unless the prosecution proves (beyond reasonable doubt) that they were not obtained by oppression, or that they were not obtained in consequence of anything said or done which was likely to render them unreliable (s76(2)). If the defence raises the question of admissibility, that in itself is enough to put the prosecution to proof (ie the defence does not have to discharge an evidential burden). Without any representation being made by the defence the court may, of its own motion, put the prosecution to proof of reliability or absence of oppression (s76(3)). When the admissibility of a confession is challenged, by the defence or the court itself, then the issue will be decided on a voir dire – ie in the absence of the jury who, if the confession is ruled inadmissible, will hear nothing of it.

It should be noted that it may not be the prosecution which seeks to rely on a confession. In *R v Myers* [1998] AC 124 Myers and Quartey were jointly charged with murder. Myers made several confessions in circumstances involving several breaches of the Codes of Practice under PACE 1984. These confessions would have been liable to be excluded under s78 PACE 1984 and the prosecution did not seek to rely on them. The House of Lords held that Quartey was entitled to adduce evidence of the confessions made by Myers if the evidence was pertinent to Quartey's defence.

Oppression

Oppression is not defined fully in the 1984 Act. Section 76(8) gives a partial definition:

'... includes torture, inhuman or degrading treatment, and the use or threat of violence ...'

In *R v Fulling* [1987] 2 All ER 65, oppression was an issue in respect of Miss Fulling's confession: in the Court of Appeal Lord Lane CJ preferred the OED definition of 'oppression' to the partial definition in s76(8) or to any common law definition; thus, oppression in this confession context is 'the exercise of authority or power in a burdensome, harsh or wrongful manner; unjust or cruel treatment of subjects, inferiors etc; the imposition of unreasonable or unjust burdens'. So, when conduct falls short of the extreme oppression in s76(8), it would appear that there must be deliberate misconduct by the police, and that there is some subjectivity in the test for oppression, ie the strengths and weaknesses of the suspect are relevant to the issue of whether the treatment was harsh, cruel or burdensome. The fact that a suspect finds detention in a police station oppressive, however, is not sufficient for any subsequent confession to be excluded on the grounds of 'oppression' under s76 – something (much) more than that is needed.

In the case of *R v Ismail* [1990] Crim LR 109, the Court of Appeal made it clear that breaches of the Police and Criminal Evidence Act 1984 and the Codes of Practice during one interview could not be cured by a later properly conducted interview, when the confession was made. To allow such evidence would be to condone the flouting of the statute and the Codes of Practice. However, in the case of *R v Barrett* (1991) 92 Cr App R 61, the court distinguished *Ismail* in similar circumstances saying that it depended on the individual concerned and Barrett had not been affected by the breaches the way Ismail had.

Unreliability

Even the likelihood of unreliability in consequence of something said or done is enough for a confession to be inadmissible (s76(2)(b)). The laws of evidence are concerned with the reliability, but not the truth, of the confession – which seems to be a contradiction in terms, unless s76 is to be used to discipline the police or safeguard the rights of the suspect, irrespective of the guilt of the accused. However, in the case of *R v Tyrer* (1990) 90 Cr App R 446, the appellant claimed she was worried about her children and wanted to get home whilst being interviewed and that is why she confessed. She also claimed that the trial judge took into account evidence given against her which was not evidence given during the voir dire. The Court of Appeal ruled that although, strictly, s76(2)(b) does not allow the court to consider the truth of the confession, nevertheless, the issue of admissibility could not be tried in complete isolation from the background of the case, and so the confession was admitted. The cases are in conflict, presumably because of the ambivalence of the judiciary in the appellate courts, eg in *R v Alladice* [1988] Crim LR 608, although the suspect was denied his right to a solicitor, his confession was allowed in evidence because by his own admission he knew his rights and understood the cautions administered to him, therefore his confession statement was reliable despite impropriety on the part of the police. In the latter case of *R v McGovern* (1991) 92 Cr App R 228, the appellant was wrongfully denied access to a solicitor, and the Court of Appeal held that it was right to exclude her confession even though she later admitted its truth. See also *R v Chung* (1991) 92 Cr App R 314. In *R v Sat-Bhambra* [1988] Crim LR 453, the suspect was given a tranquilliser by the police doctor to steady his nerves, and therefore his subsequent confession was held unreliable despite the fact that there was no improper conduct by the police to induce the confession. In *R v Harvey* [1988] Crim LR 241, a confession was excluded as unreliable where there was no impropriety at all by the police, but the suspect, a psychopath with a low IQ, may have confessed in order to protect her lover; any unreliability was occasioned not by the words or conduct of the police but by the suspect's own mental condition. However, in the case of *R v Crampton* (1991) 92 Cr App R 369, the defendant was a heroin addict and was suffering from withdrawal symptoms when he was interviewed about the crime and confessed to it. The trial judge admitted the confession. On appeal, the Court of Appeal said the trial judge had been correct – because it was doubtful whether the mere holding of an interview when the appellant was withdrawing from the symptoms of heroin addiction was something 'done' within the meaning of s76(2)(b) Police and Criminal Evidence Act 1984. The court considered and agreed with the case of *R v Goldenberg* (1989) 88 Cr App R 285, where the defendant again was suffering from the withdrawal from drug addiction. The court there also held that this was not something 'done' within s76(2)(b) – ie the stimulus must be external to the suspect. It could therefore be argued that the decision in *Harvey* is correct because the stimulus did not come from the suspect but from a third party, ie the lover. But the case of *DPP v Blake* (1989) 89 Cr App R 179 makes it clear that the test in s76(2)(b) is objective in the sense that it is irrelevant that the police acted in perfect good faith. In *R v Fulling* [1987] 2 All ER 65, however, there was impropriety on the part of the police but the suspect's confession was held not to be unreliable despite the emotional upheaval caused within her by the police statements – the conduct of the police was considered by the Court of Appeal to be merely 'unsporting'.

So inadmissibility on the grounds of potential unreliability (s76(2)(b)), or on the grounds of oppression falling short of s76(8) as provided for in s76(2)(a), as a matter of law is the subject of a mass of, often contradictory, case law. However, even though adjudged admissible a confession may nevertheless be excluded as a matter of discretion.

Exclusionary discretion

If a confession is ruled admissible under s76, above, it may nevertheless be excluded in the discretion of the judge if it appears that in all the circumstances its admission would have such an adverse effect on the fairness of the proceedings that the court ought not to admit it (s78(1)). The case of *R v Manji* [1990] Crim LR 512 stated that a voir dire should have been used by the trial court judge to decide if a caution had been given to the defendant, and so if he should use his s78 discretion to exclude the confession.

Where a suspect was wrongly denied access to legal advice, his confession, irrespective of its admissibility under the criteria in s76, was excluded under s78 on the grounds of unfairness: *R v Samuel* [1988] 2 All ER 135. Where lies were told to a suspect and to his solicitor in order to induce a confession, it was held that the confession, despite its reliability ought to be excluded under s78 because of the unfairness of the proceedings: *R v Mason* [1987] 3 All ER 481.

If the police are in breach of the Codes of Practice issued under s66 of the Act (these Codes replacing the old Judges' Rules), then that is a matter which must be taken into account by the court (s67(11)). Breaches of the Code on the Questioning of Suspects may be sufficiently serious to constitute oppression or render the consequent confession potentially unreliable, and therefore in either situation inadmissible under the provisions of s76. If breaches of the Code are not so serious, it is then a matter of judicial discretion, under s78, as to whether a consequent confession, albeit legally admissible, is excluded. The matter is substantially one for the judge to decide according to his discretion: *R v Bailey and Smith* [1993] Crim LR 681 and *R v Smurthwaite and Gill* (1994) Cr App R 437. So it is for the judge in any particular case to decide whether there is unfairness justifying his exercise of his discretion to exclude; only if he is obviously wrong will the Court of Appeal interfere.

At common law there was throughout the criminal laws of evidence a judicial discretion to exclude evidence where its prejudicial effect outweighed its probative value, ie an exclusionary discretion which would make for a fair trial. That general discretion has been preserved by s82(3) of the 1984 Act, but to what extent that exclusionary discretion and the s78 exclusionary discretion overlap has yet to be decided by the courts, ie given there is no unfairness justifying the exclusion of a confession (s78), is it conceivable that the confession could still be excluded under s82(3)?

Facts discovered in consequence of confessions

If a confession statement is allowed in evidence, then, as regards facts discovered in consequence there is no evidentiary problem. But where the confession statement is excluded, under (s76) then, unless the defence give evidence as to how the other facts were discovered, no reference can be made to the content, or the fact, of the inadmissible confession (s76(5) and (6)).

So, although the subsequently and consequentially discovered evidence can be adduced, it cannot be linked to the accused by any reference to the inadmissible confession. But, s76(5) and (6) prohibit reference to any confession excluded under s76 – therefore if a confession is excluded under s78 in the discretion of the judge, then presumably the common law still applies and it would be acceptable for the prosecution witness to say: 'In consequence of what the accused said, I discovered X at location Y …'.

Silence as a confession

When a person is accused of having committed a crime and remains silent, then in certain circumstances that silence is capable of amounting to corroboration of other evidence against him, as has been discussed above.

Similarly, silence in the face of an out of court accusation can amount in some circumstances to adoption of the accusation as a confession. If the accused and accuser are on even terms, and it would be reasonable to expect a response, eg an indignant retort, a refutation, then silence can be left to the jury as something from which they may, in that situation, infer that the accused adopted the content of the accusation as his confession, ie tacitly accepted what was said as true: *Parkes* v *R* [1976] 1 WLR 1251. But where the accuser is a person in authority such as a police officer, then the silence of the suspect – whether cautioned or not – cannot amount to acceptance of the truth of the accusation, ie by exercising in that situation his right to silence the suspect cannot be providing evidence of guilt: *Hall* v *R* [1971] 1 WLR 298. In one case it was stated that when a suspect is questioned by a police officer in the presence of his solicitor, then his silence can amount to evidence of guilt since the parties are on even terms: *R* v *Chandler* [1976] 1 WLR 585. However, the reasoning in that case has, rightly, been criticised.

Editing confessions

A confession may be only partly adverse to the person who made it (s82(1) Police and Criminal Evidence Act 1984) and therefore may contain exculpatory as well as incriminatory material; in that case the whole confession statement must be reported – but the jury informed of the lack of evidential value of the exculpatory (ie 'self-serving') material. But if the confession includes references to the accused's previous convictions, bad character or other prejudicial matters, then that material must be excised by editing of the statement. If such editing leaves an incoherent statement, then the judge may exclude the whole statement.

If a confession statement implicates a co-accused, then the jury must be instructed that the confession is not evidence against that co-accused (that part of it is inadmissible hearsay). Alternatively, the confession statement may be edited so that the co-accused is not identified: *R v Silcott* [1987] Crim LR 765; or in exceptional cases separate trials may be ordered to avoid serious prejudice to the co-accused: *R v Lake* (1977) 64 Cr App R 172.

Documentary hearsay

Several statutes make provision for the admissibility of documentary hearsay in criminal proceedings, the most important now being the Criminal Justice Act (CJA) 1988. Sections 23–28 and Sch 2 CJA 1988 replace the provisions in the Police and Criminal Evidence Act 1984 except those in s69 relating to documents produced by computers. The overall effect is to make documentary hearsay in criminal proceedings more widely admissible.

Trade, business etc documents

Section 24 CJA 1988 is similar to s4 Civil Evidence Act 1968 regarding the pre-requisites for admissibility of documentary hearsay, but the conditions such as death, unavailability etc of the maker of the statement in the document do not apply unless the statement was prepared for the purpose of criminal proceedings or criminal investigations (s24(4)). In any event, s25 gives the criminal court a discretion to exclude such statements in the interests of justice, with mandatory considerations spelled out in s25(2). Where a statement seems to have been prepared for the purpose of criminal proceedings or investigations, then s26 stipulates that leave of the court is required before it can be adduced as hearsay evidence.

The case of *R v Cole* [1990] 2 All ER 108 explained the difference between ss25 and 26. Under s25 the court should admit the statement when the conditions laid down in ss23 and 24 are satisfied, unless it considers (looking at s25(2)) that it should be excluded. But under s26, the court should not allow the statement which satisfies the conditions in ss23 and 24 to be admitted, unless it concludes (looking at the wording of s26) that it should be admitted. In *R v McCarthy* [1998] RTR 374 the question that arose was whether documents generated by a computer were admissible under s24(1) CJA 1988. The Court of Appeal held that if the documents were computer-generated they were admissible as direct evidence and that if they were not computer-generated they had been 'supplied by a person who had, or may reasonably be supposed to have had, personal knowledge of the matters dealt with' and therefore were admissible under s24 CJA 1988.

Other documentary hearsay

Whereas s24, above, obviously covers second-hand hearsay in respect of trade or business documents (and liberalises s68 Police and Criminal Evidence Act 1984), s23 provides for the general admissibility in criminal proceedings of all first-hand hearsay in documentary form. The prerequisite for admissibility is that the maker of the statement is dead, unfit, unavailable etc (similar again to s4 Civil Evidence Act 1968), or that where the statement was made to a police officer the maker (in addition to the above disjunctive reasons), does not give evidence through fear or because he is kept out of the way (s23(3)), explained in *R* v *Acton Justices, ex parte McMullen* (1991) 92 Cr App R 98 as meaning a statement will be admissible in circumstances where someone was sought to place its maker in fear of attending court or has physically prevented him from doing so. Again, discretion to exclude (s25) and leave of the court to admit (s26) apply as in the case of s24 statements. Also, as in the case of s24 statements, Schedule 2, para 3 CJA 1988 makes provision for the weight, if any, to be attached to such hearsay statements, the court having regard to all the circumstances from which any inference can reasonably be drawn as to accuracy – similar again to the provisions in the 1968 Civil Evidence Act (s6).

Depositions and witness statements

Several statutes provide for the general admissibility (subject to restrictions and usually subject to the overriding judicial discretion to exclude) of hearsay documents.

a) Where a statement is contained in a document produced by a computer, s69 Police and Criminal Evidence Act 1984 will (pending its repeal by the Youth Justice and Criminal Evidence Act 1999, s60) have to be complied with, in addition to the provisions of the relevant section of the 1988 Act.

b) Section 102 MCA 1980 – written statements in committal proceedings.

c) Section 9 CJA 1967 – written statements in criminal proceedings other than committals.

d) Section 105 MCA 1980 – deposition of dangerously ill person, unavailable through illness or subsequent death to testify at trial.

e) Sections 42 and 43 Children and Young Persons Act (CYPA) 1963, and s103 MCA 1980 – provision made for the admissibility of depositions of children or young persons as victims of certain crimes, and witness statements of children. These sections are no longer as important as they used to be. We now have s32 Criminal Justice Act 1988 which allows for children to give evidence via a live television link during the court proceedings. The conditions are that the crime is one of a particular group – ie assault, or cruelty to persons under the age of 16 (CYPA 1963); and indecency or sexual offences under the Sexual Offences Act 1956 – s32(1)(b) and s32(2) Criminal Justice Act 1988. The trial must be a trial on indictment or an appeal to the Criminal Division of the Court of Appeal arising out of such proceedings. The section also applies to proceedings in Youth Courts, and appeals to Crown Courts from there – s32(1A) of the 1988 Act, as inserted by the 1991 Act.

The age of the child is also relevant. He or she must be under 14 if the charge is cruelty; or under 17 if a sexual offence – s55 Criminal Justice Act 1991.

The Criminal Justice Act 1991 also extends the 1988 Act by allowing video recordings of children to be shown in court – s54 of the 1991 Act inserting s32A into the 1988 Act. It applies in the same circumstances as s32 does (above). The video recording must be of an interview between an adult and the child and must relate to any matter in issue in the proceedings. However, the child must still be called to be cross-examined in court.

7.3 Key cases and statute

- *R* v *Alladice* (1988) 87 Cr App R 380

- *R* v *Fulling* [1987] 2 All ER 65

- *R* v *Samuel* [1988] 2 WLR 920

- Police and Criminal Evidence Act 1984

  - s76

  - s78

7.4 Questions and suggested solutions

QUESTION ONE

P is charged with a bank robbery of a bank in St Austell at 3.00pm. The day after the robbery, he was questioned by Inspector Q. P said that he had spent all the previous afternoon in Plymouth, 50 miles away, watching the football. Q then said, 'We have four witnesses who definitely identified you near the bank yesterday afternoon'. P replied, 'All right, maybe I was there, but I know nothing about the robbery'. In fact, only one witness, R, had identified P. After being shown a number of photographs by the police, R had pointed to the photograph of P and said 'That's probably him'. A few days later, R picked P out in an identification parade. At the trial, P claims that he was at the football match in Plymouth at 2.00pm and left at 3.00pm to attend the evening match in Manchester. He wishes to tender the stub of an airline boarding pass bearing his name, for a 3.30pm flight from Plymouth to Manchester on the day the robbery occurred. He says that he only admitted his presence in St Austell because he has an obsessive fear of being kept in custody.

Discuss any evidential issues that arise.

University of London LLB Examination
(for External Students) Law of Evidence June 1994 Q8

General Comment

A question involving issues of identification, confessions and hearsay. Understandably, some students may be confused by the somewhat esoteric geographical references (St Austell is fairly close to Plymouth, but some distance from Manchester!) and this may create difficulties. Beyond this, a manageable question which merely requires organisation to bring all the relevant issues out.

Skeleton Solution

P's admission: s82(1) Police and Criminal Evidence Act (PACE) 1984; confession; ss76, 78, 82(3) – P's initial statement: previous inconsistent statement; s4 Criminal Procedure Act 1865 – identification: from police photos: *R* v *Turnbull* – the ticket: *R* v *Rice*; but effect of *R* v *Kearley*?

Suggested Solution

This question centres around the disputed identification of P as being involved in a robbery in St Austell. Following his arrest, P makes an admission, partly as a result of dubious police practices; he later recants this, and wishes to adduce a ticket a prove that he was elsewhere on the day in question.

P's admission

The Police and Criminal Evidence Act (PACE) 1984, s82(1) provides a wide definition of a confession, as being any statement adverse to the person who made it. P's admission 'maybe I was there' is within this definition and as such either the defence or the judge may require the prosecution to prove beyond reasonable doubt that the 'confession' was not obtained by oppression or in consequence of anything said or done which was likely to render the confession unreliable (s76 PACE 1984).

Oppression does not seem likely on the given facts, but it could be argued that the confession is unreliable because P says he only admitted his presence in St Austell because of his obsessive fear of being held in custody.

However, following *R* v *Goldenberg* (1989) 88 Cr App R 285, this is unlikely to provide a ground of appeal since it is not external to the accused. The defence could still argue that the confession should be excluded under s78 (unfairness) or s82(3) (the common law), in the judge's discretion, and in this regard there exists a further ground, namely P is told that four witnesses definitely identified him, whereas in fact only one possibly identified him. This would appear to be unfair within the meaning of s78 and thus the defence could seek to convince the judge to exclude this confession in the exercise of his discretion (*R* v *Alladice* [1988] Crim LR 608).

P's other statement

P initially said he had spent the entire day in Plymouth. At trial, he claims to have flown to Manchester in the afternoon of that day. His original statement is inconsistent with the version he puts forward at trial. The original statement is not a confession, and therefore need not be tested under s76 PACE 1984. It may be put to P in cross-examination, and if he denies it, it may be proved, under s4 Criminal Procedure Act 1865.

The previous statement does not go to truth but merely goes to the credibility of P, and the judge should warn the jury of this (*R* v *Askew* [1981] Crim LR 398).

Identification

R identifies P initially from police photographs (and subsequently in an identification parade). It must be stressed that the fact that the initial identification was from police photographs must not be disclosed to the jury (*R* v *Wainwright* (1925) 19 Cr App R 52), the obvious risk being that the jury may take a bad view of the defendant if they know that he is already on police records.

Since the prosecution case rests on this identification, the *Turnbull* warning must be given to the jury (*R* v *Turnbull* [1977] QB 224). They should be told of the special need for caution in identification cases, and why there is this need. Their attention should be drawn to the circumstances of the identification (lighting, length of observation, distance etc), and they should be told to look for supporting evidence (which need not be corroboration in the strict sense). The judge should identify the evidence in the case which is capable of supporting the identification.

On the given facts, the only piece of evidence which is capable of supporting R's identification is P's alibi, if the jury reject it.

The judge must take care in directing the jury as to the use they may make of this. If the jury reject P's alibi, they must be told that this does not of itself mean that he was where the identifying witness (R) says he was. Defendants can raise false alibis for any number of reasons and the judge must tell the jury that it is only when they are satisfied that the sole reason is to deceive them, that the falsity of the alibi can support the identification.

Further, following *R* v *Goodway* [1993] 4 All ER 894 it would seem that a *Lucas* direction (*R* v *Lucas* [1981] QB 720) should be given in these circumstances (ie, the lie, to support the identification, must be deliberate, relating to a material issue and motivated by a realisation of guilt and a fear of the truth).

Having said this, the judge must make it clear that, having considered the special need for caution, the jury can safely assess the evidence without any supporting evidence. If the quality of the identification is good, the judge may leave the issue to the jury; but if the quality of the identification is poor, then if there is no supporting evidence, the judge should withdraw the issue and direct an acquittal (*R* v *Flemming* (1987) 86 Cr App R 32).

The ticket

P wishes to support his trial alibi by means of an airline ticket stub bearing his name and indicating that he flew to Manchester at 3.30pm on the day in question.

This is clearly a piece of hearsay, especially in the light of *R* v *Kearley* [1992] 2 All ER 345. It is an out of court statement from which it is possible to infer that P was on that flight. As hearsay it is submitted it should be inadmissible. Despite this logical reasoning, the present state of the law appears to make this evidence admissible. In *R* v *Rice* [1963] 1 QB 857, a case with a similar factual basis, it was held that a ticket would be admissible since it would seem logical that the person whose name appears on the ticket had actually used it. Hence, it would seem that the ticket will be admissible in P's defence.

QUESTION TWO

Mike is charged with the murder of Andrew by running him over in his car. Andrew had been having an affair with Mike's wife, Barbie. Mike tells the police that Andrew stepped off the pavement in front of Mike's car and that 'hitting Andrew was unavoidable'. Two days before he died, Andrew wrote on his computer that he was afraid because Mike had discovered the affair Andrew was having with Barbie and that he 'would have to watch where he stepped' from now on. This message was recorded in a file. On the day Andrew died, Xenophanes, a passing preacher, heard an unidentified woman near the spot where the accident occurred say, pointing to Andrew's lifeless form, 'That man stood no chance; the driver meant to run him down'. Barbie has stated that Mike told her about six hours after Andrew died that Andrew had been involved in an accident, adding that 'Andrew deserved it'. Mike does not wish to give evidence at his trial but he does wish to call two social workers who will give evidence that Barbie is suffering from a mental disorder which causes anti-social behaviour and that he, Mike, has a timid personality and is unlikely to behave aggressively.

Advise the prosecution on any evidential issues arising.

University of London LLB Examination
(for External Students) Law of Evidence June 1995 Q7

General Comment

The question requires consideration of the hearsay rule and exceptions, particularly those relating to states of mind and res gestae, as well as the use of expert and non-expert opinion evidence.

Skeleton Solution

Admission of evidence to show Andrew's state of mind, if relevant to the issues – admission of first hand hearsay by s23 Criminal Justice Act 1988 – res gestae exception for Xenophanes – Barbie's evidence of Mike's call: hearsay implications – use of the social workers as expert witnesses – admissibility of good character – significance of Mike's refusal to testify.

Suggested Solution

Mike's defence is one of unavoidable accident, so the real issue in the case is that of intention. It could be highly relevant to this issue if there is some evidence that Andrew had some apprehension of the danger to himself. In *Subramaniam* v *Public Prosecutor* [1956] 1 WLR 965 the Privy Council held that defence evidence of threats was wrongly excluded as the evidence concerned the state of mind of the defendant which was in issue, irrespective of the truth of the statements. Similarly, in *Ratten* v *R* [1972] AC 378 a jury was correctly directed that a fearful state of mind could be inferred from a distressed woman's voice regardless of what she said or its truth. The significance here is that the apprehension is, in some way, connected to the affair and Andrew.

The message is on a computer file and can be retrieved, presumably by printout. This raises the question whether the 'computer' is a simple word processor or something more sophisticated. Section 23 Criminal Justice Act (CJA) 1988 certainly allows admissibility for first-hand documentary hearsay where the maker is dead as evidence of any fact to which the maker would have been allowed to testify, if alive. This is subject to s69 Police and Criminal Evidence Act (PACE) 1984 which covers computer records. Mike could certainly have testified as to his state of mind so there seems to be no problem here. If the instrument was a simple word processor it is probable that s69 would not need to be complied with, according to the Court of Appeal obiter in *R* v *Blackburn* (1992) The Times 1 December, because of the proliferation of such equipment.

Xenophanes heard an unidentified woman say that the driver meant to run Andrew down. Much depends here upon how long after the incident this woman spoke. If almost immediately afterwards, it might be admissible as a spontaneous declaration made under the impress of the event, even though she could not be identified according to dicta in *Teper* v *R* [1952] AC 480. The longer the gap, the less chance of true spontaneity and the greater the chance for distortion or concoction as in *R* v *Gibson* (1887) 18 QBD 537.

Barbie's statement that Mike told her about the accident six hours afterwards, and the additional 'he deserved it', can be treated in several different ways. It clearly is hearsay if repeated to show its truth. It might be used to show the state of the maker's mind or emotional condition, or to shed light on his intentions, previous or prospective, irrespective of the truth of what was said. In *R* v *Hagan* (1873) 12 Cox CC 357 a person's out of court statement was admitted to show his dislike of his child, and *R* v *Fletcher* [1917] 1 Ch 339 shows that there may be admissibility to show both past and future intention. The problem here is that the statement points more towards dislike than intention, but may evidence motive. The statement might be used to show Mike's awareness of the death at that time if it were in issue (*Thomas* v *Connell* (1828) 4 M &

W 267). Barbie could give evidence that Mike actually spoke to her at that time without offending the hearsay rule.

Mike wishes not to give evidence but to use two social workers to give evidence of Barbie's mental disorder and his own personality. Any testimony of any witness can be challenged as to credibility on grounds of mental disorder affecting its reliability (*Toohey* v *MPC* [1965] AC 595). This needs to be done by an expert witness in the particular field because the matter is outside the experience of judge and jury. The social workers will not be able to shed light upon Barbie's mental condition as affecting her credibility, which is the issue. Anti-social behaviour may affect truthfulness, but on the authority of *R* v *Turner* [1975] QB 834 the social workers will not be allowed to give expert evidence on her mental condition. Mike's behavioural characteristics are an issue here, and in *R* v *Bryant; R* v *Oxley* [1979] QB 108 it was held that evidence of disposition or character which tended to show that the accused was not the type of person likely to commit the offence charged was admissible. This was confirmed in *R* v *Vye* [1993] Crim LR 604 and, in principle, evidence on this point by these witnesses seems admissible whether as expert or as non-expert witnesses to Mike's good character. If the latter, it will need to avoid evidence of specific acts to avoid falling foul of *R* v *Rowton* (1865) 34 LJMC 57, but it will be evidence going both to credit and to the main issues. It will need to relate to the period proximate to the running down (*R* v *Swendsen* (1702) 14 How St Tr 559). If Mike does not give evidence, his silence will allow prosecution comment and invite proper inferences to be drawn by the jury, as well as requiring the judge to direct as to the significance of the silence (s35 Criminal Justice and Public Order Act 1994 and *R* v *Martinez-Tobon* [1994] 2 All ER 90).

QUESTION THREE

Knowing of their previous convictions for dishonesty, Inspector H invites K and L to the police station to help with enquiries into a burglary. K demands a solicitor but is told that he will have to wait. K is then questioned for four hours without a break and, finally, K says 'I don't know why you bother; I'm used to this; what can you police do about it?'. In reply, H says, 'If you tell us about it now we probably won't do much about it; we just want to clear the matter up'. As he does this, he loosens his tie and begins to roll up his sleeves. Thinking that H may be about to strike him, K blurts out 'OK I did it; the loot is at L's garage but L made me do it; he threatened me with a gun if I didn't go along with him'. K is then formally cautioned and charged with the burglary. The police then search L's place and discover the stolen property. Meanwhile, L, who was frightened to begin with, has become very agitated by having been left in a cell on his own for two hours. H begins questioning him by saying that the stolen goods had been found in L's garden shed. L then admits to the burglary.

Advise K and L.

University of London LLB Examination
(for External Students) Law of Evidence June 1993 Q6

General Comment

Confessions questions are relatively straightforward, posing none of the conceptual difficulties of hearsay. Prepare these questions bearing in mind the chronological pattern of so many examination questions: the invitation to the police station, the refusal of a solicitor, the interrogation, the admission, the finding of the stolen property. Remember to have up your sleeve a reasonable knowledge of the Codes of Practice, a prepared discussion of the meaning and rationale of 'oppression', of the differences between s76(2)(a) and (b) Police and Criminal Evidence Act (PACE) 1984, and of the uses of discretion under ss78 and 82(3). You should also be well aware of how s76(4) and (5) work (and show how the law derived from *R* v *Warwickshall* (1783) 1 Leach 263).

Skeleton Solution

H's invitation – relationship between the 1995 Codes of Practice and the Police and Criminal Evidence Act 1984 – K: refusal of solicitor; questioning without break oppression (*R* v *Fulling*) or s76(2)(b)?; inducement; perceived assault; confession with exculpatory part (*R* v *Sharp*) – L: subjective oppression?

Suggested Solution

The police are always entitled to ask someone to come to the police station to 'help them with their enquiries'; it is only when they have grounds to suspect such a person of an offence that they should caution and arrest. It is clear that such grounds could not be those of K and L having previous convictions since the reasoning of the similar facts rules tells us that. Nevertheless, those people who are so assisting the police have, according to the Codes of Practice, the same 'absolute' rights as those who have been arrested (s58 says that a person arrested is entitled to a solicitor) and so there has been a breach of the Code when H refuses access to a solicitor (on the other hand, K should have left instead of putting up with 'You'll have to wait'; it is clear that those not taken into custody have a right to leave whenever they want).

The Codes are not law, however; this is discussed in ss66 and 67 Police and Criminal Evidence Act (PACE) 1984. They are evidence that can be put into court and this means that breaches by the police are evidence from which the judge can conclude (in the voir dire) whether there has been 'oppression', or a cause of unreliability of any confession, or whether he should exercise his discretion to exclude evidence under ss78 and 82(3).

In addition to the refusal of access, what other breaches of the Code are there? Four hours' continuous interrogation breaches the requirement that those questioned be given short breaks every two hours; H's reply to K's rhetorical question about what the police can do, that the police won't 'probably' do much comes close to breaching the Code's requirement that police only say what they will do in response to a direct question and, in any case, appears to be a lie.

But these do not look like serious enough breaches to warrant 'oppression' (the advantage to which, to a defendant, is that, however reliable the induced confession is, it must be rejected). 'Oppression' refers to 'harsh, burdensome and wrongful behaviour' and even then, that is a common law, widened, interpretation of the words of s76(8) which refer to torture and criminal assaults. The facts are too ambiguous here to say whether H intended or was reckless as to assaulting K as in *R v Venna* [1976] QB 421 (but recklessness cannot be ruled out; in which case there would be an assault and, therefore, oppression). One argument could be explored here. Although commentators like to say that, because of *R v Fulling* [1987] QB 426, the definition of 'oppression' is objective, that is, independent of the subjective qualities of impressionability on a weak person, there is an argument that subjective qualities of the suspect can affect whether there is oppression whenever a policemen acts 'wrongfully' (the definition in *R v Fulling* [1987] QB 426) by exploiting the suspect's weakness. In other words, had H known that K was the sort of person who would weaken despite these relatively minor breaches of the Code, arguably the confession should be rejected however reliable it seemed.

However, there are easier ways to do it. This must be a situation where there is a reasonable doubt (because that is all that is necessary: s76(2)(b)) that K's confession has been rendered unreliable from things said and done. Section 76(2)(b) clearly covers the case where the suspect has weakened and, whether or not H committed an assault, it is relevant for this paragraph that K thought that H had assaulted him. Even if this argument is not accepted, K's confession has an exculpatory element which, if accepted by a jury, would provide him with the defence of duress (see *R v Hudson* [1971] 2 QB 202, for example). In fairness to the defendant and ignoring, so it seems, the hearsay rule (see *Myers v DPP* [1965] AC 1001, *R v Sharp* [1988] 1 All ER 65) permits the exculpatory part to go before the jury, although the Court of Appeal in that case made it clear that the jury should be warned that the exculpatory part of the judgment should be given less weight as it could be self-serving. Incidentally, there is an argument that there is no breach of the common law rules on hearsay; s82(1) defines a 'confession' as a statement which 'includes' an admission – 'partly adverse' – and this would allow K's whole statement, which includes the exculpatory part, because another part of that one statement is an admission.

What is the position with L? He hasn't asked for a solicitor; on the other hand, the police should have informed him of his right to have one, or a friend, present. L could have left; but it is not always easy at a police station to do this and he possibly has no idea of what rights he has. If he has become excessively agitated in the cell (although it is not such a long time) this could, in theory, have had the effect of rendering his confession unreliable; but what evidence is there otherwise that it is unreliable? The stolen goods were, after all, found at his place. On being confronted with them, he blurts out immediately his involvement in the offence. It is unlikely, therefore, that his confession will be rejected.

QUESTION FOUR

Sykes is charged with the murder of Nancy by stabbing. Oliver is prepared to testify that Nancy telephoned him and shouted: 'Come quickly, Sykes is threatening to kill me …', the phone then going dead. Oliver raced to Nancy's house and found her lying in a pool of blood. She whispered: 'You're too late, he's done for me' and lapsed into unconsciousness. A doctor arrived, briefly examined Nancy, covered her with a blanket and accompanied her in an ambulance. The ambulance collided with a lorry and the totally charred bodies of the ambulance's occupants were recovered from the burnt out wreckage.

Oliver finds Sykes and tells him he will kill him unless he comes to the police station. Sykes is dragged to the station by Oliver; as Oliver lunges at him and punches him in the face Sykes shouts to the police officers who are present: 'Get him off me for God's sake! I killed her; the knife's down the drain outside her house'. A knife is found there, wiped clean of blood and prints.

Advise the prosecution on the evidentiary problems, given that Sykes refused to write out or sign any subsequent statement.

Written by the Author

General Comment

A number of exceptions to the rule against hearsay require discussion. A good knowledge of case law is needed for a good answer.

Skeleton Solution

Res gestae statement: dying declaration; competence – statement by conduct – causation in murder; alternative verdicts – confessions: reliability; oppression; admissibility; voir dire – facts discovered in consequence of confessions.

Suggested Solution

Oliver may be allowed to report not only the fact but also the content of the phoned statement as a res gestae statement. If it was contemporaneous, approximately, with the stabbing and was sufficiently spontaneous to enable the court safely to ignore the possibility of concoction or distortion, and any other factors such as malice on Nancy's part are taken into account, then the judge can admit the content of the call as a res gestae statement (*R v Andrews* [1987] AC 281). Its admissibility is determined by the judge, who will advise the jury on factors affecting the weight they may attach to it.

The fact that Nancy was shouting or was hysterical can be stated by Oliver (*Ratten v R* [1972] AC 378) and is relevant to the spontaneity issue. As regards contemporaneity, this depends on how much time elapsed between the phone call and Oliver's reaching Nancy's side, since there will be no medical evidence available to pinpoint the time of the stabbing, nor very probably its severity. Given that the stabbing and the phone call were approximately contemporaneous, that is sufficient to satisfy the court as to that element of admissibility of the res gestae statement. Given also that Oliver found Nancy within a short time (say ten minutes) of the phone call, then her second statement could also be admissible. Such a lapse of time, coupled with questions to elicit the res gestae statement, has been accepted by the court (*R v Andrews* [1987] AC 281 and *R v Turnbull* [1984] Crim LR 620). The other major issue for the court is whether Nancy's second statement is mere narration or whether her mind is still dominated by the drama of the event – the prosecution must persuade the court of the latter for the statement to be admitted.

If the second statement is not admissible under the res gestae doctrine, it may be admissible as a dying declaration. Nancy's statement certainly implies that she entertains no hope of survival, but she must be in settled hopeless expectation of death (*R v Perry* [1909] 2 KB 697) and therefore must have had sufficient time for reflection (*R v Bedingfield* (1879) 14 Cox CC 341). In addition, had she survived she must have been a competent witness (*R v Pike* (1829) 3 C & P 598); even if she is Sykes' wife she would nevertheless be competent (s80(1)(a) Police and Criminal Evidence Act (PACE) 1984). Nancy's declaration does not in itself state expressly the cause of her injuries, but in conjunction with her earlier exclamation it is very relevant to their cause.

The prosecution will want Oliver to testify as to what he saw the doctor do, arguing that he would be giving evidence, as a percipient witness, of an act performed by the doctor. The defence contention would be that the doctor's covering Nancy is an implied assertion by him that Nancy is already dead, and that implied assertions, just like express assertions, constitute inadmissible hearsay unless they come within a recognised exception to the hearsay rule.

There is a paucity of authorities on implied assertions (see Lord Bridge in *R v Blastland* [1985] 2 All ER 1095 and *Cross on Evidence* (8th edition, 1995), but the reason for the law's suspicion of them is the danger of concoction by the observed doctor. There seems to be little doubt that the doctor would have no motive to fabricate evidence for the observers, therefore Oliver should be allowed to state what he perceived and the jury draw their own inferences. In the unlikely event that Oliver cannot give this evidence, there may be no acceptable evidence of causation and therefore Sykes could not be convicted of murder; he could nevertheless, if the prosecution can prove his specific intent to kill Nancy when he stabbed her, be found guilty of attempted murder as an alternative verdict (s6 Criminal Law Act 1967).

Sykes' confession is damning if it is admissible. However, it may well be excluded under s76 Police and Criminal Evidence Act 1984, given the likelihood of its unreliability in consequence of Oliver's conduct (s76(2)(b) PACE 1984). An alternative or additional reason for the confession's inadmissibility is oppression by Oliver, which would lead to exclusion of the confession (s76(2)(a) PACE 1984). Lord Lane CJ, giving the judgment of the Court of Appeal in *R v Fulling* [1987] QB 426 defined 'oppression' in this context, and his definition implies that the conduct must be that of a person in authority such as a police officer. However, he was dealing with conduct falling short of violence or threats of violence, and a partial definition of violence in the Police and Criminal Evidence Act 1984 has not been affected. Section 76(8) states that 'oppression' includes torture, inhuman or degrading treatment, and the use or threat of violence', and there is no requirement that this sort of conduct must be that of a person in authority. So, unless the prosecution can prove beyond reasonable doubt that, despite Oliver's words and conduct the confession was not made in consequence of oppression and is not likely to be unreliable, the judge (on a voir dire) will rule Sykes' confession statement inadmissible, and the jury will therefore be unaware that it was made.

If the confession is excluded under s76, then no reference can be made to it by the prosecution in order to link Sykes to the knife found in the drain, ie a police officer will not be permitted to testify: 'In consequence of what the accused said I went to the drain outside the house of the deceased and found a knife …' (s76(5) and (6) PACE 1984). Therefore, unless the knife is Sykes's or unless there is some other admissible evidence to link it to Sykes it is inadmissible real evidence because it has no apparent relevance; relevance cannot be given to it by any reference to the fact of, let alone the content of, a confession statement excluded under s76.

QUESTION FIVE

Able was taking his daughters, Baker aged seven and Charlie aged 11, for a walk when a car horn sounded behind them. Able looked behind him and saw that a green Mercedes car had left the road and was approaching them at high speed across the wide grass verge. He pushed his daughters to one side and was run down by the car; although conscious he could not get to his feet. He saw the car stop, a man alight and chase Baker (Charlie had jumped behind a hedge); the man indecently assaulted Baker, got back in the car and drove off.

A police patrol car arrived at the scene, and both Baker and Able gave the registration number of the car as C454 VKV; Charles said the car was green. From this information Douglas was traced as the car owner, was interviewed by the police but refused to comment. He has been charged with indecent assault and reckless driving. Able, Baker and Charlie have made written statements, but Able is paralysed as a result of the incident and cannot attend court; Baker is still in shock and having to give evidence could damage her mental health.

Advise the prosecution.

Written by the Author

General Comment

There are several aspects of the rule against hearsay which arise in this question. A good overall subject knowledge is required and the issues should be addressed chronologically.

Skeleton Solution

Hearsay: exceptions to exclusionary rule – applicability of statutory exce̅
pre-trial – corroboration: sexual offences; identification; children of tender ye̅
competence of children – silence of accused: evidential value.

Suggested Solution

If the police officer(s) in the patrol car are to repeat what A, B and C said to them, the only purpose is to invite the court to believe the truth of what is repeated, therefore that is hearsay and will be inadmissible unless it falls within a recognised exception to the hearsay rule (*Myers* v *DPP* [1965] AC 1001). If A and B do not testify, then the same applies if a witness wishes to read their statements to the court. Therefore, unless there are common law or statutory provisions which permit this hearsay evidence in criminal proceedings it cannot be adduced.

If a doctor certifies that A is dangerously ill and is unlikely to recover, then a magistrate may take A's deposition out of court, and provided Douglas's lawyer was given notice of this and the opportunity to cross-examine A, then if A is, by the time of the trial, dead or so ill that it is unlikely that he will ever be able to travel to court or give evidence, his written statement can be read to the court (s105 Magistrates' Courts Act 1980 and s6 Criminal Law Amendment Act 1867 (an offence is indictable even though it may be tried summarily)). If any of these conditions do not obtain, eg A is not certified as dangerously ill, then his written statement may still be given in evidence if 'by reason of his bodily or mental condition' he is 'unfit to attend as a witness' (s23(1) and (2)(a) Criminal Justice Act 1988). If A's condition does not come within either of these categories, then his statement, as a 's9 statement' is unlikely to be admitted, since the defence must be served with a copy and will doubtless give written notice of objection (s9 Criminal Justice Act (CJA) 1967).

In the case of B's statement, if a doctor certifies that her attendance in court would involve serious danger to her life or health (including mental health), then a magistrate may take her deposition out of court, since she is under 17 and indecent assault is an offence contrary to the Sexual Offences Act 1956 (s42 Children and Young Persons Act 1963). But Douglas's lawyer must be given notice of the taking of the deposition and the opportunity to cross-examine (s43 Children and Young Persons Act 1933). If there is no such 'serious danger' to her mental health, but rather in her shocked state she has an abject fear of a court appearance, then it is conceivable, subject to how s23 Criminal Justice Act 1988 is construed, her statement would still be admissible in evidence as would the deposition. Section 23(1)(ii) and (3)(b) provide for the admissibility of such written statements if 'the person who made it does not give oral evidence through fear …'. This was inserted in the 1988 Act to cater for witnesses to terrorist activities who might fear for their lives, but on a literal construction could cover our situation.

One drawback, if in the case of A's and/or B's statement resort has to be made to s23 CJA 1988, is that leave of the court is required before the statement can be admitted, and the court must have regard to all relevant circumstances, including in particular any risk of unfairness to the accused (s25 Criminal Justice Act 1988). Alternatively a video recording of an interview with Baker could be used, under s32A of the Criminal Justice Act 1988 (as inserted by the Criminal Justice Act 1991), which could be played back to the court to replace Baker's testimony. However, she would still need to appear in court for cross-examination. Alternatively, a live TV link could be used under s32 as she is under 14. However, there may be problems with the fact that only one of the offences Douglas is charged with (indecent assault) allows for s32 and s32A to come into play.

If A and B could not recollect the car number by the time they gave their written statements and therefore the number does not appear in those statements, then a police officer tendering in evidence their oral statements would be attempting to give hearsay evidence. If he wrote down the number at the time in his notebook, and A and B verified the entry as correct, then the officer could refresh his memory from the notebook and so could A and/or B if giving evidence (*Jones* v *Metcalfe* [1967] 1 WLR 1286; *R* v *McLean* (1968) 52 Cr App R 80 and see *R* v *Eleftheriou* [1993] Crim LR 947). If A and B do not give direct evidence, the officer could nevertheless, with leave of the court, give the particulars in his notebook as a 'statement in a document' under s24 CJA 1988 if A and B are unfit to attend or given the lapse of time cannot be expected to have any recollection of the number (s24(1) and (4)).

Charlie (C) may have relevant evidence to offer as to the identity of the assailant etc, and the fact that she is aged only 11 does not in itself necessitate corroboration or a corroboration warning (s34(2) CJA 1988). The former requirements for corroboration warnings with respect to child or sexual complainant witnesses have now gone and the matter of jury directions as to supporting evidence in both of these situations is very much a question of the judge's direction. If A saw not only the assailant but also the incident, there is more corroborative evidence. As regards the identity of the assailant, the evidence of one witness may be sufficient for the court to be satisfied, but supportive evidence (even though it does not amount to 'corroboration' as defined in evidence) is highly desirable where the accused was not previously known, sighting not very good etc – per the guidelines in *R* v *Turnbull* [1977] QB 224. Even though A, B and C identify Douglas, the judge should still caution the jury, where the identification is disputed by the defence, on the general unreliability of visual identification evidence of this sort.

Douglas's refusal to comment when interviewed will amount to a road traffic offence if he refuses to state who was driving the car at the time, given that, presumably, he is the registered owner. But his silence when accused of committing the offences cannot amount to corroboration when his accuser is a police officer (*R* v *Whitehead* [1929] 1 KB 99; *R* v *Keeling* [1942] 1 All ER 507) nor can it in those circumstances amount to an adoption by him of the accusation as his confession, because he has a right to remain silent of which he should have been reminded (*Hall* v *R* [1971] 1 All ER 322). This must, however, be viewed in the light of *R* v *Chandler* [1976] 3 All ER 105 on the point of accused and accuser speaking on 'even terms' and the very considerable statutory inroads made upon this so-called 'right to silence' by s34 Criminal Justice and Public Order Act 1994.

Chapter 8
Character Evidence

8.1   **Introduction**

8.2   **Key points**

8.3   **Key cases and statute**

8.4   **Questions and suggested solutions**

8.1 Introduction

Character evidence, especially that of the accused and its admissibility in the course of the trial, is one of the most difficult areas of evidence, but one with which all students must be conversant as it will appear in almost every examination paper on Evidence. For example, there is often, in problem questions, a statement that a person has previous convictions; that should immediately alert the examinee to the fact that the bad character of that person (usually the accused) will require discussion. Any witness in criminal or civil proceedings is liable to be cross-examined as to character, including previous convictions, to destroy or damage his credibility as a witness; the one exception is the accused who elects to testify – that witness is given protection from such gratuitous cross-examination, except where he has discarded that protection or where evidence of his previous bad character has become relevant to his guilt on the charge he faces.

Although, therefore, evidence of the bad character of the accused is the major area of concern, something must be said, briefly, of character of parties in civil cases and of character of witnesses in civil and criminal cases.

You should be aware that para 4 of Sch 7 Youth Justice and Criminal Evidence Act 1999 has renumbered the provisions of s1 Criminal Evidence Act 1898. The result is that s1(e) becomes s1(2), and s1(f) becomes s1(3). It seems that the intention was to tidy up a statute which has been much amended, but the result has been a certain amount of confusion as practitioners, academics and students have adjusted to the changes.

8.2 Key points

Parties to a civil action

Dependent on what issues are raised in the statements of case in civil cases, the character of a party may be in issue – 'character' here referring to general reputation, disposition and particular conduct. A prime example is an action in defamation; if the defendant pleads justification of his assertion that the plaintiff is a rapist, then evidence of a rape conviction of the plaintiff can be adduced by the defendant; as regards damages in defamation the general reputation of the plaintiff is in issue, to assess the injury done to it.

Where evidence of disposition is admissible as character evidence to show that a party has a propensity to a particular kind of misconduct, because it is sufficiently relevant to the facts in issue, that evidence is known as 'similar fact evidence' and is dealt with in Chapter 9 (in both civil and criminal proceedings).

Witnesses in civil and criminal proceedings

All witnesses, whether or not parties, may be cross-examined as to credibility. The answers of the witnesses to such questions in cross-examination are almost invariably final, ie evidence cannot be adduced to contradict the answers, as the issue is a collateral one. However, one major exception is where the witness denies the commission by him of a criminal offence, in which event the appropriate conviction can be proved by the cross-examiner. For example, in the case of *R v Edwards* [1991] NLJ 91, the Court of Appeal held that police officers could be cross-examined about relevant criminal offences or disciplinary charges found proved against them, but could not be questioned about any previous misbehaviour not yet adjudicated upon.

The accused

Good character

As a general rule at common law the accused may adduce evidence of his good character despite the general prohibition on the prosecution's adducing evidence of his bad character – but evidence of bad character may be given to rebut the accused's evidence of his good character (see below).

The evidential value of evidence of good character is unclear; in *R v Bryant; R v Oxley* [1979] QB 108 it was held that such evidence goes not just to the credibility of the accused but also to his guilt or innocence. But in *R v Levy* [1987] Crim LR 48 it was held that where there are two co-accused, one of good character and one bad, the good character of one goes only to credibility not unlikelihood of offending – otherwise the bad character of the other would give rise to an inference that he was likely to have committed the offence, which would be unacceptable!

It is not always clear whether a defendant is in fact of good character. In *R v Martin* [2000] Crim LR 615 the Court of Appeal held that the fact that a defendant had admitted a criminal offence and been cautioned in respect of it was not something that could or should be ignored, but was a matter for the trial judge to have regard to in exercising the discretion in giving a good character direction.

The appropriate direction for situations where the defendant has given good character evidence is confirmed in *R v Wren* [1993] Crim LR 952 which confirmed the earlier case of *R v Vye* [1993] Crim LR 604. *R v Vye* is now seen to be the leading case and the guidelines given by the Court of Appeal show that a 'first limb' direction, ie that good character supports the credibility of the accused as witness, should be given in every case where it is appropriate. A 'second limb' direction, ie that good character may shed light on the probability of guilt, should be given whether or not the accused testifies. This has clarified the law considerably. See also *R v Cain* [1994] 2 All ER 398 CA on the question of multiple defendants, some of good character, some of bad. See also *R v Aziz* [1995] 3 All ER 149 HL on the judicial discretions where character is mixed or questionable. In *R v Garrod* [1997] Crim LR 445 CA, the Court of Appeal held *Vye* requires that a first limb direction be given (a) if the accused testifies and (b) if the accused does not testify but relies on exculpatory statements (ie pre-trial answers or statements made to the police or others). It is clear from *Aziz* that 'pre-trial answers or statements' means 'mixed' statements. Thus where the accused did not give evidence but relied on wholly exculpatory answers given in interview prior to the trial he was not entitled to a 'first limb' direction.

In *R v Miah* [1997] Crim LR 351 the trial judge told the jury that they were 'entitled' to take good character into account. The Court of Appeal held that there was no obligation for a judge to use a particular form of words, but that judges might be well-advised to use another form of words so that it was not suggested to the jury that they had a choice whether or not to take the evidence of good character into account.

Bad character

At common law, evidence of the bad character of the accused may be given by the prosecution if it is admissible similar fact evidence (see Chapter 9); it may also be given to rebut evidence given by the defence of the accused's good character. Such rebutting evidence will usually be as to the general bad reputation of the accused, but evidence of previous convictions has been admitted under the common law: *R v Redd* [1923] 1 KB 104; *R v Winfield* [1939] 4 All ER 164.

Section 1 Criminal Evidence Act 1898 deals with cross-examination of the accused as to his bad character, and therefore it applies only when the accused elects to testify for the defence. Otherwise, the common law rules apply.

The 1898 Act made the accused competent for the first time, and the legislators compromised between treating the accused exactly the same as any other witness and making him immune from cross-examination; the result was to give the accused protection (often called a shield) from cross-examination as to character, but protection which may be lost in circumstances set out in the provisos to s1(3) of the Act. The provisions in s1(2) and (3) should be known verbatim by every Evidence student who hopes to do justice to examination questions on character.

Relationship between s1(2) and s1(3)

Section 1(2) permits cross-examination of the accused even though it tends to incriminate him as to the offence charged, and in that context allows 'any question'. Section 1(3) prohibits questions in cross-examination which tend to show that the accused has committed or been convicted of any other offence. There is thus apparent conflict between s1(2) and (3), because a question tending to show the accused has committed or been convicted of some other offence may well also tend to incriminate him as to the offence charged – such a question is apparently allowed by s1(2) but prohibited by s1(3). After several conflicting decisions, the House of Lords ruled (by a bare majority) in *Jones* v *DPP* [1962] AC 635 that s1(2) must be read subject to s1(3). The majority also ruled that 'show' in s1(3) means reveal or disclose to the jury for the first time, so if the jury is already aware of the bad character of the accused, the prohibition in s1(3) does not apply. The ruling in *Jones* v *DPP* was used by the Court of Appeal in *R* v *Anderson* [1988] 2 All ER 549, but the principles were not merely followed but extended, to the disadvantage of the accused who testifies: see discussion in [1988] Crim LR 298.

Exceptions to the s1(3) prohibition

a) Section 1(3)(i) allows cross-examination of the accused on similar fact evidence which is admissible as proof of his guilt. However, only where the similar fact evidence shows the commission or conviction of an offence (not other misconduct or previous charges which did not result in convictions) is cross-examination under s1(3)(i) allowed as to the bad character of the accused.

b) Section 1(3)(ii) contains two exceptions (the two 'limbs'). The first is where the defence has attempted to establish the good character of the accused; the second where the defence involves imputations on the character of the prosecutor or prosecution witnesses.

Under the first limb, 'character' includes both general reputation and disposition: *R* v *Samuel* (1956) 40 Cr App R 8. Evidence of good character can go not merely to the credibility of the accused as a witness, but also to his innocence: *R* v *Bryant; R* v *Oxley* [1979] QB 108. Yet the cross-examination under the first limb goes directly to credibility – any bearing on the guilt of the accused is the subject of controversy: *Maxwell* v *DPP* [1935] AC 309; *R* v *Samuel*. The better view would seem to be that the purpose of cross-examination is to discredit the accused as a witness, not to prove his guilt by disclosing prior convictions.

It is important that in this context the character of the accused is not divisible; if the accused puts any good aspect of his character forward then he may be cross-examined on his character, not just the aspect on which he relies: *R* v *Winfield* [1939] 4 All ER 164; *Stirland* v *DPP* [1944] AC 315.

Under the second limb of s1(3)(ii), the accused may be liable to cross-examination as to his bad character if imputations have been cast on the character of the prosecutor or prosecution witnesses or the deceased victim (this last having been added by s31 Criminal Justice and Public Order Act 1994, which inserts at the end of s1(3)(ii) the words 'the deceased victim of the alleged crime'). For the 'shield' to be lost under this limb, there must be something more than an emphatic denial of guilt – but it can be difficult to draw the line between a robust denial and an imputation on the character of a witness: compare, and reconcile *R v Nelson* (1978) 68 Cr App R 12 and *R v Tanner* (1977) 66 Cr App R 66. The second limb can be brought into play by implied, as well as express, imputations on the character of prosecution witnesses. (NB: it must be an imputation cast on the character of someone called as a witness for the prosecution; if the accused attacks the character of a person not called as a witness, the shield is not lost under the second limb: *R v Lee* [1976] 1 WLR 71.)

Even if casting imputations is necessary as a part of the defence case, nevertheless the shield is dropped: *Selvey v DPP* [1970] AC 304; *R v Bishop* [1975] QB 274. See also the case of *R v Lasseur* [1991] Crim LR 53 – the defendant suggested to an accomplice that he was only giving evidence against him so as to get a more lenient sentence. The Court of Appeal held that the shield had been dropped.

One very important point, made in *R v Turner* [1944] KB 463, and approved in *Selvey v DPP*, is that where consent is in issue in a rape trial the accused can allege consent by the complainant (and even gross indecency on her part) without losing his shield, the reasoning being that a defence of consent is merely a denial that an element of the offence has been proved and thus is not an imputation. Section 41(1) Youth Justice and Criminal Evidence Act 1999 provides that where a person is charged with a sexual offence, then, except with the leave of the court, no evidence may be adduced, by or on behalf of the accused at trial, about any sexual behaviour of the complainant.

It is not clear how far cross-examination under s1(3)(ii) should extend to the factual details of the offences in question. In *R v Davison-Jenkins* [1997] Crim LR 816 CA the accused was charged with shoplifting and was treated as having put her character in issue. She was then cross-examined on the detail of her previous convictions, one of which related to the shoplifting of clothes and cosmetics. The Court of Appeal held that the cross-examination on the detail of these convictions was improper. However, it was also held that, since the purpose of cross-examination was to impugn her credibility, that could have been achieved by confining the cross-examination to her three previous convictions for other forms of dishonesty.

c) Under s1(3)(iii) an accused is liable to cross-examination as to bad character by a person charged in the same proceedings when he gives evidence against that person. It is not necessary that he attacks the person's character, only that he gives evidence that supports the prosecution's case against him.

In *Murdoch v Taylor* [1965] AC 574, the House of Lords stated that the determinant is whether, objectively, the evidence undermines the other's defence or strengthens the case against him – regardless of whether this was intended. A denial of involvement by one accused, or evidence from him which appears to be in conflict with evidence given by the other, may, dependent on the particular facts, amount to evidence under s1(3)(iii): *R v Varley* (1982) 75 Cr App R 242.

Under s1(3)(iii) the co-accused can cross-examine the accused who loses his shield as of right, ie leave of the judge is not required and the judge cannot restrict the scope of the cross-examination, the effect of which is to attack credibility, not to go to the issue of guilt.

Judicial discretion in cross-examination

The discretion of the judge to refuse the prosecution leave to cross-examine the accused as to his character was given the ultimate seal of approval in *Selvey v DPP* [1970] AC 304.

The judge must ensure a fair trial, and even where bad character of the accused goes to credibility rather than guilt, it would prejudice a fair trial if, for example, the accused had a bad record with many previous convictions, or one conviction for a very grave crime and the instant charge was relatively minor and/or the imputation on the prosecution witness was relatively slight. Alternatively, there may be a number of charges against the accused and an attack was made on the character of a prosecution witness to one charge only. Again, the greater the similarity of the previous convictions to the instant charge the greater the prejudice to the accused if they are all revealed. Finally, an allegation that a prosecution witness was mistaken may, objectively, amount to a necessary imputation of fabrication of evidence. Guidelines for the exercise of judicial discretion were laid down in *R v Britzman; R v Hall* [1983] 1 All ER 369, and a detailed summary of the current law is given in the judgment of Neill LJ in the Court of Appeal in *R v Owen* (1986) 83 Cr App R 100. An important guideline case in this area is *R v McLeod* [1994] 3 All ER 254 CA concerning judicial control and discretion in situations where the earlier offences are similar in type or detail to the offence charged.

8.3 Key cases and statute

- *Murdoch v Taylor* [1965] AC 574

- *R v Britzman; R v Hall* [1983] 1 All ER 369

- *R v Vye* [1993] Crim LR 604

- *Selvey v DPP* [1970] AC 304

- *Stirland v DPP* [1944] AC 315

- Criminal Evidence Act 1898, s1

8.4 Questions and suggested solutions

QUESTION ONE

Edgar is charged with raping Fiona in her flat after an office party. Fiona says that for some hours after the rape she was too shocked to do anything, but that when her flatmate, Greta, returned home next morning at about 10.00am she told Greta that she had been raped by Edgar. Greta went abroad before she could be interviewed by the police, and she cannot now be traced. Edgar's defence is that Fiona consented. He says that he met her in a wine bar at about 10.00pm. He had never seen her before, but she came up to him and said: 'It's boring here. Why not come back to my place and we can have some sex?'. Edgar wishes to call Hugo, who was present at Fiona's office party earlier that evening. Hugo says that Fiona had come up to him and said: 'This is so dull! Lets get out of here and have some sex!'. Hugo says that he declined the invitation. Edgar also wishes to call John, who says that he had sex with Fiona at her invitation, though he knew her only by sight, during the week before the party.

Discuss the evidential matters arising.

University of London LLB Examination
(for External Students) Law of Evidence June 2000 Q6

General Comment

This question raises a number of issues and, once again, a chronological approach should result in a logically structured answer and guard against inadvertent omissions.

Skeleton Solution

Recent complaint: effect of admission of this evidence; *R* v *Islam*; 'the first opportunity'; *R* v *Osborne*; Greta's absence; *R* v *White*; s23 Criminal Justice Act 1988 – Edgar's evidence: consider hearsay; *Subramaniam* v *Public Prosecutor*; *Woodhouse* v *Hall* – effect of including the words as part of the defence on Edgar's 'shield' – effect of Youth Justice and Criminal Evidence Act 1999: *R* v *Hinds and Butler* – effect of asserting consent as a defence: *Selvey* v *DPP*.

Suggested Solution

The first issue to arise in this scenario concerns Fiona's complaint to Greta. The general rule is that a witness may not be asked about previous consistent statements in examination-in-chief, and the rule extends to prevent other witnesses from giving evidence of such a statement. If this rule were to apply, it would prevent Fiona and Greta (were she to be produced to give evidence) from giving evidence as to the statement. However, there are a number of exceptions to the general rule, including one which relates to complaints in sexual cases. In cases of rape (and other sexual offences) where the complainant made a voluntary complaint shortly after the alleged offence, the person to whom the complaint was made may give evidence of the particulars of that complaint in order to show the consistency of that conduct with the complainant's evidence and, in cases such as the present scenario where consent is in issue, to negative consent. In *R v Islam* (1999) 1 Cr App R 22 the Court of Appeal held that where evidence is given of such a complaint, it is essential that the judge gives the jury a direction to the effect that the complaint is not evidence of the facts complained of, but may be of assistance in assessing the veracity of the complainant.

A complaint is only admissible if it is 'made at the first opportunity after the offence which reasonably offers itself' (per Ridley J, *R v Osborne* [1905] 1 KB 551). This is a question of fact and degree which will have to be decided by the trial judge, and issues such as whether Fiona had a flatmate other than Greta who was at home on the night of the alleged rape and available to talk to Fiona will be important. In *R v Hedges* (1909) 3 Cr App R 262 a complaint made one week after the offence was admitted, so the delay between the alleged incident and Fiona's complaint to Greta will not of itself determine the admissibility of the complaint.

The more difficult issue for the prosecution concerns the fact that Greta has not made a statement to the police and cannot now be traced. In *R v White* (1999) 1 Cr App R 153 the Court of Appeal held that if the person to whom the complaint was made does not give evidence, the complainant's own evidence that she made a complaint cannot assist either in proving her consistency or negativing consent because, without independent confirmation, her own evidence that she complained is of no assistance to the jury when they are considering whether she should be believed. Greta's absence from the jurisdiction would be grounds for adducing her evidence in the form of a hearsay statement under s23 Criminal Justice Act 1988, but the fact that she made no witness statement is fatal to this course of action. If she cannot now be traced and produced as a witness, her evidence of the complaint may not ever come in front of the court and the evidence of Fiona's consistency will be lost.

The second issue concerns Edgar's evidence that Fiona said certain words to him. The first point to note here is the application of *Subramaniam v Public Prosecutor* [1956] 1 WLR 965 and *Woodhouse v Hall* [1980] Crim LR 645 with the result that her words will not be caught by the prohibition against hearsay evidence, since Edgar would not seek to assert that the words spoken were true (it being no part of his defence that the party was boring or even that Fiona was sincere in her invitation). Edgar's purpose in repeating the words would simply be to show that the words were spoken, whether they were true or not. The relevance of the words is the effect that they had on Edgar and his state of mind when they returned to Fiona's flat. If the assertion that the words were spoken is to be part of the defence, it is possible that the judge will allow cross-examination of Edgar under s1(3)(ii) Criminal Evidence Act 1898 on the basis that this amounts to an imputation of character so far as Fiona is concerned.

Edgar wants to rely on evidence from Hugo and John. The first question that must be considered here concerns the relevance of this evidence. It seems that the evidence could be relevant either to Fiona's credibility and/or to Edgar's defence of consent.

Assuming that the evidence is relevant, the next issue that arises concerns whether the judge will allow the evidence to be adduced or put to Fiona. Section 41(1) Youth Justice and Criminal Evidence Act 1999 provides that where a person is charged with a sexual offence, then, except with the leave of the court, no evidence may be adduced by or on behalf of the accused at trial, about any sexual behaviour of the complainant. This provision could also apply to questions being asked of Fiona in cross-examination.

'Sexual behaviour' is defined in s42(1) and includes any sexual behaviour or other sexual experience whether or not involving any accused or other person. The first question to arise concerns whether Fiona's verbal advances to Hugo come within that definition. The phrase 'sexual experience' appeared in the Sexual Offences (Amendment) Act 1976 replaced by the 1999 Act and was sufficiently widely defined in *R v Hinds; R v Butler* [1993] Crim LR 111 to include a conversation which the complainant had had with the defendants prior to the alleged rape. It seems that the verbal advances could come within the phrase 'sexual behaviour' and that the intercourse with John certainly comes within that phrase. Assuming that that is the case, Edgar will require the court's leave in order to adduce the evidence. If the evidence is adduced, counsel for Edgar will have a duty to put it to Fiona.

Leave will not be granted unless the court is satisfied both that the evidence comes within one of the specified cases set out in subss3 or 5 of s41, and that a refusal of leave might render the jury's conclusion unsafe (s41(2)).

So far as the evidence from Hugo is concerned, the court may not give leave unless it is satisfied that Fiona's behaviour towards Hugo was so similar to her behaviour towards Edgar that the similarity cannot reasonably be explained as a coincidence (s41(3)(c)(ii)). There is also a requirement that the two events must have taken place 'at or about the same time'. The original Bill imposed a rigid 24-hour framework in this provision, but the Act contains no such time limit, although the period is unlikely to be significantly wider. Since Hugo will say that Fiona made advances to him earlier on the same evening as the alleged rape, it seems that this requirement will be satisfied.

So far as the evidence from John is concerned, Edgar could try to rely on the provision discussed above (s41(3)(c)(ii)) on the basis of the similarities (Fiona invited a man to have sex with her, and the two were not previously well-known to each other). However, it is possible that the judge would hold that such similarities as exist are insufficient to come within that provision so that Edgar would have to rely instead on s41(3)(b). That provision enables the judge to allow evidence or questioning where the evidence or questions relate to the issue of consent, and the sexual behaviour of the complainant to which the evidence or question relates is alleged to have taken place at or on about the same time as the event which is the subject matter of the charge against the accused. The difficulty which Edgar could face under either subss(3)(b) or (c) is the requirement that the behaviour must have taken place at or on about the same time as the alleged rape. John will say that he had intercourse with Fiona the week before the alleged rape, and it is possible that the judge will hold that an event which took place the week before did not take place at or on about the same time as the alleged rape.

The effect of s41(4) is that leave will not be given (because the evidence will not be regarded as relating to a relevant issue) if it appears to the court reasonable to assume that the purpose (or main purpose) for which the evidence is to be adduced is to establish material for impugning the credibility of Fiona as a witness.

If the judge is satisfied that the events (the advances to Hugo and the intercourse with John) each relate to a relevant issue, and that each took place at or on about the same time as the alleged rape, and that there is the requisite degree of similarity between the advances allegedly made to Hugo and those said to have been made to Edgar, he will consider whether to allow the evidence to be given; the test to be applied here is whether a refusal of leave might make the conclusion of the jury unsafe (s41(2)(b)). This requirement is met if the judge concludes that there might be such a risk; there is no requirement that the risk be probable or even likely. It seems that Hugo's evidence may be allowed. The difficulty with John's evidence relates to the delay between the incident which he would give evidence of and the alleged rape.

Edgar's defence is consent and it should be noted that this defence will not, in itself, lead to a loss of the shield protecting Edgar from cross-examination as to his previous character under s1(3)(ii) Criminal Evidence Act 1989 (*Selvey* v *DPP* [1970] AC 304). However, it may very well be the case that Edgar's fall back position will be that, if the jury are satisfied beyond a reasonable doubt that Fiona did not in fact consent to intercourse, he nevertheless had a mistaken belief that she was consenting. If this is the case, then evidence from Hugo and John will be allowed if the judge is satisfied that a refusal of leave might have the result of making the conclusion of the jury unsafe (in other words, s41(2)(b) is then the only condition to be met; s41(3) does not apply). A crucial question would then be whether Edgar knew of the incidents involving Hugo and John prior to the alleged rape and, if so, whether that knowledge was relevant to his belief that Fiona was consenting.

QUESTION TWO

Ludwig and Bertrand are charged with maliciously wounding Freddy. Thomas is charged with assisting Ludwig and Bertrand by doing an act with intent to impede their apprehension.

Freddy testifies that he was attacked by Ludwig and Bertrand at a public lavatory one night and that one or other stabbed him. Inspector Bentham testifies that when he visited Thomas to enquire of Ludwig and Bertrand's whereabouts Thomas informed him, falsely, that they had gone to Italy. Ludwig, who is conducting his own defence, testifies that Freddy struck the first blow and claims that he hit back in self-defence. He says that he has no idea how Freddy sustained a stab wound. He adds that Freddy has a disposition towards violence. Bertrand testifies in his defence that he and Ludwig had made up their minds to assault Freddy, but says that Freddy's injury must have occurred when he slipped and fell coming towards them. When asked by counsel for the Crown whether he had a knife with him that night Bertrand refuses to answer. Thomas claims that during a short conversation with Inspector Bentham he said that he had no idea of Ludwig and Bertrand's whereabouts.

Ludwig has previous convictions for assault and theft. Bertrand has a previous conviction for perjury. The prosecution can prove that the perjury consisted of giving false testimony providing an alibi for friends charged with offences, and furthermore that Thomas was acquitted of perjury on another occasion in respect of a similar allegation.

Advise Ludwig, Bertrand and Thomas.

University of London LLB Examination
(for External Students) Law of Evidence June 1995 Q8

General Comment

This question concerns the circumstances in which a defendant's shield against reference to his previous convictions and character may be lost by the working of the Criminal Evidence Act 1898, and the extent to which judicial discretion operates on this point.

Skeleton Solution

Criminal Evidence Act 1898: Ludwig's potential imputations on Freddy – Bertrand's evidence against Ludwig and judicial discretion in this situation – Bertrand's silence about the knife – Thomas's and Inspector Bentham's evidence: s1(3)(ii) – examination on acquittals – significance of lies: *R v Lucas*.

Suggested Solution

Ludwig testifies that he merely defended himself against Freddy's attack and has no idea about the injury, but states that Freddy has a violent disposition. Ludwig's convictions, if brought out, may damage his case. The matter is governed by s1 Criminal Evidence Act (CEA) 1898 and he does have a shield againt such evidence, but it may be lost in the three ways provided by the section. Here, s1(3)(iii) is in issue, that is that the nature of his defence involves imputations on the character of the prosecutor or prosecution witnesses. If there was an unavoidable implication that Freddy was lying, this would cause the shield to be lost, but it is possible in these circumstances that Ludwig is only giving his view of a confused situation, perhaps in a badly lit fracas. *R v Britzman; R v Hall* [1983] 1 All ER 369 indicates that the judge should exercise his discretion in favour of the accused in these circumstances. Ludwig goes further, though, in dealing with Freddy's violent disposition. The fact that this is a necessary part of his defence will not prevent loss of the shield (*Selvey v DPP* [1970] AC 304), but it does look more like a vigorous denial of the offence so as not to lose the shield, as in *R v Rouse* [1904] 1 KB 184.

If the shield is lost, any cross-examination can only be as to credibility (*Maxwell v DPP* [1935] AC 309 and *R v Watts* [1983] 3 All ER 101). The trial judge is, in any case, more likely to exercise his discretion in favour of an unrepresented defendant and he should warn of the danger in appropriate circumstances (*Selvey v DPP* [1970] AC 304).

Bertrand has a previous conviction for perjury and will not want this to come out. He makes no imputation about Freddy, but he does give evidence against Ludwig when speaking about the plan to assault Freddy. Any evidence which supports the prosecution case in a material respect, or which undermines the defence of the co-accused, will activate s1(3)(iii) (*R v Varley* [1982] 2 All ER 519), whether in cross-examination or in-chief. There is a direct conflict between the two and once it is decided that evidence has been given against Ludwig by Bertrand the judge will have no discretion to prevent Ludwig examining him (*Murdoch v Taylor* [1965] AC 574), although he will have discretion as regards examination by the Crown (*R v Seigley* (1911) 6 Cr App R 106).

Bertrand's refusal to answer about the knife may now be the subject of comment by the prosecution, and the judge may invite the jury to draw proper inferences (s35 Criminal Justice and Public Order Act 1994). This will be of great significance if Bertrand loses his shield. Although the evidence of the conviction should only go to credibility, there is a danger here of the judge failing to direct the jury that Bertrand's silence may have other explanations than that he must have had a knife. There is a possibility of a misdirection here.

Thomas's evidence is completely at odds with the Inspector's and creates a clear implication that the Inspector is fabricating his version (unless there was some problem such as excessive noise or a hearing defect) so Thomas is likely to lose his shield under s1(3)(ii): *R v Tanner* (1977) 66 Cr App R 66 shows that this will be so no matter how the point is worded. Thomas's previous trial finished in acquittal. The subsection is worded with respect to offences 'committed', 'convicted' and 'charged' but it seems unlikely that it is permissible to examine as to acquittals (*Maxwell v DPP* [1935] AC 309), although there may be a possibility that the circumstances of such an acquittal might be looked at if there is a possibility of bringing the matter within s1(2) in respect of similar fact evidence. Such a situation was seen *R v Ollis* [1900] 2 QB 758 and *R v Shellaker* [1914] 1 KB 464. If Thomas does not give evidence, his bad character will not be admissible as he would not be 'called as a witness' (*R v Butterwasser* [1948] 1 KB 4).

The judge will be obliged to give a *R v Lucas* [1981] QB 720 warning as to the significance of Thomas's lies. The Court of Appeal in *R v Goodway* [1993] 4 All ER 894 made it clear that in all cases where the accused's lies may be relied upon to support the prosecution evidence, such a warning is mandatory.

QUESTION THREE

Joe and Kevin are charged with the burglary of Lolita's house and Mervin is charged with handling a gold bracelet stolen in the burglary. Lolita testifies at trial that two men entered her bedroom one night. One, whom she identifies as Joe, held her down while the other, who was wearing a stocking over his face, ransacked her drawers. When they had gone, she called the police. Noel, a police officer, testifies that while driving to Lolita's house, he gave chase to two men who had acted suspiciously on seeing the police car. He stopped one, who was Kevin. Kevin had a stocking in his hand, and admitted the burglary. Noel also testifies that he found Lolita's bracelet when he later went to Mervin's jewellery shop. Joe testifies that on the night of the burglary he was in another town, attending Alcoholics Anonymous. He says he has 'never seen Mervin in his life'. Joe has two convictions, one for a bank robbery and another for taking ruby rings in a burglary. Kevin testifies that he tried to evade Noel because he'd 'had cops on him before'. Kevin says that when he was arrested he said [he] 'hadn't done anything', when accused of burglary. Kevin has been convicted for indecent assaults on young children and for tax evasion. Mervin testifies that he bought the bracelet from Joe, who had told him he was selling for his wife. In fact, Mervin had already told the police that he'd bought the bracelet from a 'man in the street'. Mervin's interview with the police is excluded by the trial judge because it contravened the Code of Practice.

Discuss the cross-examination of Joe, Kevin and Mervin.

University of London LLB Examination
(for External Students) Law of Evidence June 1997 Q8

General Comment

A fairly complex interplay of the rules on cross-examination, the question calls for careful planning if clarity is to be achieved. One approach is to take each witness separately, list the matters upon which they could be cross-examined and deal with any rules governing each evidential point as it arises. Remember that cross-examination can extend to matters in issue even though not dealt with in-chief as well as to credit.

Skeleton Solution

Joe

Matters raised by his evidence: the alibi; his statement about Mervin; the collateral evidence rule – other matters: matters arising from Lolita's evidence; Mervin's evidence about Joe; his convictions; s1(3) Criminal Evidence Act 1898; Joe's evidence 'against' Mervin.

Kevin

Matters raised by his evidence: his suspicious actions; trouble with the police; s1(3) Criminal Evidence Act 1898; *Jones* v *DPP* – other matters: matters arising from Noel's evidence; matters arising from Lolita's evidence; his convictions; s1(3) Criminal Evidence Act 1898; his earlier confession.

Mervin

Matters raised by his evidence: his evidence 'against' Joe; s1(3)(iii) Criminal Evidence

Act 1898; cross-examination by Joe and by the prosecution – other matters: matters arising from Noel's evidence; Mervin's earlier inconsistent statement to the police – possible assertion of good character by Mervin: s1(3)(ii) Criminal Evidence Act 1898.

Suggested Solution

Joe

The prosecution may wish to cross examine Joe about various matters raised by his examination-in-chief. They may quite properly ask him about any facts in issue, of which one will be his alibi, to seek to strengthen the prosecution case or to weaken the defence evidence. They will also be permitted to ask questions about his acquaintance with Mervin as being in issue. The prosecution may also, within limits, ask questions about Joe's credibility. The questioning on credit will also be limited (by the rule of finality of answers to collateral questions) to exceptional matters as set out in *Attorney-General* v *Hitchcock* (1847) 1 Exch 91.

Joe may be asked about other matters such as arise from Lolita's or Mervin's evidence. He might properly be asked about the events in Lolita's bedroom and the circumstances of her identification; also about Mervin's version of Joe's participation. Mervin would have been able to repeat Joe's explanation, despite its hearsay nature, on the basis of it being a 'confession' within s82(1) Police and Criminal Evidence Act (PACE) 1984. There is nothing 'collateral' about these matters and, similarly, he could be asked about matters raised by Noel's evidence. Clearly, prolonged questioning about these matters runs the risk of becoming collateral or even irrelevant if it goes too far.

The prosecution may also wish to ask questions about Joe's previous convictions. The questioning will be governed by s1(3) Criminal Evidence Act (CEA) 1898. This will only permit questioning if the offences were relevant to prove the instant charge within the similar fact doctrine (s1(3)(i)), which seems doubtful here, or if Joe has lost his shield under s1(3)(ii) or (iii). There are no indications that Joe has crossed the line on either of the two situations set out in s1(3)(ii). If he had, the questioning would have been governed by the guidelines set out by the Court of Appeal in *R* v *McLeod* [1994] 3 All ER 254. The primary purpose of this questioning is as to credibility and the jury must be told this, but this will not necessarily prevent questioning about offences similar to that charged as in *R* v *Powell* [1986] 1 All ER 193. Joe might, however, have 'given evidence against' Mervin by undermining his defence: *Murdoch* v *Taylor* [1965] AC 574. This would cause loss of shield under s1(3)(iii) against cross-examination by counsel for Mervin and, by leave of the judge, the prosecution. Again the questioning goes to credibility: *Murdoch* v *Taylor*.

Kevin

Similarly, Kevin may be properly cross-examined about issues raised by his own evidence, and about the confession made upon being detained by Noel, subject to there being no ss76 or 78 PACE 1984 problems attaching to it. This will probably have been already introduced into evidence by Noel under s76 and Kevin may be asked about it, despite the collateral evidence rule, as a previous inconsistent oral statement within the requirements of s4 Criminal Procedure Act 1865. This would not, in any case, be a collateral issue, but instead, clearly 'relative to the subject matter of the indictment' within s4.

Kevin's evidence of having been in trouble with the police has probably removed his protection under s1(3)(ii) or (iii) under the view taken by the House of Lords in *Jones* v *DPP* [1962] AC 635, whereby any loss of shield is caused by the accused revealing his own convictions. Even if this were not the case, Kevin is clearly making an imputation that Noel has fabricated his confession; no other view can be taken of the matter following *R* v *Britzman*; *R* v *Hall* [1983] 1 All ER 369, so the shield would inevitably be lost. The questioning, as before, would be about credit and be governed by *R* v *McLeod*. Kevin could properly be asked about any matter raised by Noel's evidence of suspicious actions and the stocking or about Lolita's evidence concerning the stocking and, presumably, about the stocking itself.

Mervin

Mervin can be cross-examined about his own evidence by the prosecution. He has also very clearly 'given evidence against' Joe within s1(3)(iii), both strengthening the prosecution case and weakening Joe's defence within the guidelines in *Murdoch* v *Taylor* [1965] AC 574, and this would cost him his shield against examination on the discreditable matters set out in s1(3) by counsel for Joe, or, with leave of the judge, by the prosecution. We are not told of anything particularly discreditable in Mervin's past but Joe's counsel will need to ask, if he can, about Mervin's earlier excluded statement. This does not need any shield to be lost because an accused may, as of right, examine a co-accused about an inadmissible confession which is relevant to the defence of the accused, provided that the judge directs the jury that the statement is not to be used as evidence of its maker's guilt: *R* v *Rowson* [1985] 2 All ER 539. This right applies only to cross-examination on behalf of an accused not the prosecution.

It is very unlikely that the judge, having excluded the earlier statement as inadmissible, would now allow prosecution cross-examination about it simply to attack credibility. The Court of Appeal in *R* v *Treacy* [1944] 2 All ER 229 held this to be completely impermissible. Mervin could properly be examined about matters arising from Noel's evidence other than the earlier statement.

It sounds possible here that Mervin (if he has no convictions) might be tempted to put his good character into evidence to get the advantage of a *R* v *Vye* [1993] Crim LR 604 direction. The prosecution would be able to cross-examine on this because of a loss of shield under s1(3)(ii) as could counsel for Joe, presumably by leave of the judge; possibly even counsel for Kevin, again, by leave.

QUESTION FOUR

'It is a useful working hypothesis … that good law is both simple and produces a result that is sensible, predictable, and readily intelligible.' (*Re Leyland DAF Ltd* [1994] 1 BCLC 264, per Henry LJ.)

Discuss the operation of s1(3)(iii) [formerly s1(f)(iii)] of the Criminal Evidence Act 1898 in the light of this statement.

University of London LLB Examination
(for External Students) Law of Evidence June 2000 Q4

General Comment

In order to write a straightforward answer to this question, a knowledge of cases such as *R v Varley* [1982] 2 All ER 519 and *R v Kirkpatrick* [1998] Crim LR 63 is required. The Consultation Paper (No 141) produced by the Law Commission in 1998 makes a number of criticisms of the law and a better answer would demonstrate a knowledge of these criticisms and include some evaluation. Note that this suggested solution is written on the basis that the provisions of the Youth Justice and Criminal Evidence Act 1999 are fully in force.

Skeleton Solution

Subsections 1(3)(ii) and 1(3)(iii) Criminal Evidence Act 1898 – the 'shield' – 'persons charged with the same offence' – judgment in *Murdoch v Taylor*; *R v Varley* – meaning given to 'evidence against': *R v Ellis*; *MPC v Hills* – direct contradiction: *R v Hatton* – Consultation Paper (No 141): criticisms and recommendations.

Suggested Solution

Until s1 Criminal Evidence Act 1898 came into force, the defendant in criminal proceedings was not a competent witness in his own defence. Under the scheme contained in the Act, the defendant is made a competent (but not compellable) witness. If the defendant elects to give evidence, he is liable to cross-examination, and the immunity which would otherwise save him from being required to answer questions which would tend to incriminate him as to the offence currently charged is removed by s2. Section 3 of the Act provides the defendant with some protection against being asked questions concerning his previous character. This protection is commonly referred to as the 'shield'. However, by virtue of subss1(3)(ii) and 1(3)(iii) of the Act the defendant may lose the shield as a consequence of the content of his defence, or the manner in which that defence is run. This question concerns the operation of s1(3)(iii) which applies where the defendant has 'given evidence against any person charged in the same proceedings'.

The section originally referred to other persons 'charged with the same offence'. This wording gave rise to problems and was changed in 1979 by the Criminal Evidence Act 1979 to include all co-accused, irrespective of the offences with which they are charged.

The House of Lords considered various aspects of this provision in *Murdoch* v *Taylor* [1965] AC 574. In *R* v *Varley* [1982] 2 All ER 519 the Court of Appeal later expanded and restated these conclusions, deriving a number of 'established principles'.

The meaning of 'evidence against'

The term 'evidence against' means evidence which supports the prosecution case in a material respect or which undermines the defence of the co-accused. The test to be applied is objective and it is the effect of the evidence on the minds of the members of the jury which is significant, rather than the intention of the defendant.

'Evidence against a co-defendant' means evidence which supports the prosecution's case in a material respect or which undermines the defence of the co-defendant. There is no requirement that both of these propositions are met, although in many cases that will be so. It has been held that the prosecution case is supported in a material respect so that a defendant gives evidence against a co-defendant where he gives evidence which shows that the co-defendant committed one or more elements of the offence charged. Accordingly, the provision was satisfied in *R* v *Ellis* [1910] 2 KB 746 by evidence that the co-defendant was in possession of stolen goods and in *Metropolitan Police Commissioner* v *Hills* [1980] AC 26 by evidence suggesting that the co-defendant drove dangerously, the charge under consideration being that of causing death by dangerous driving. The case law also shows that the defendant will undermine the defence of a co-defendant where the effect of the evidence is that it is made less likely that the co-defendant will be acquitted (*R* v *Bruce* [1975] 1 WLR 1252). Accordingly, the provision was satisfied in *R* v *Varley* [1982] 2 All ER 519 by evidence in which the defendant denied evidence given by his co-defendant to the effect that he had exerted duress on his co-defendant, and in *R* v *McGuirk* (1963) 48 Cr App R 75 by evidence in which the defendant claimed he had nothing to do with a fraudulent document which his co-defendant had said he had duped his co-defendant into signing.

The construction to be given to the phrase 'evidence against' seems to be clear, but it appears to be easier to state than to apply. It is arguable that any contradiction or inconsistency with a defence advanced on behalf of a co-defendant is sufficient to activate the provision in s1(3)(iii). However, the Court of Appeal has rejected this argument in cases such as *Varley* and *R* v *Kirkpatrick* [1998] Crim LR 63 so that it is clear that what has been described as 'inconvenience' to the co-defendant's defence or inconsistency with it will not, by itself, be sufficient to activate the provision. It is the effect of the evidence which is significant, and the provision will be triggered if the effect of the evidence is that the defence of the co-defendant is undermined.

Similarly, evidence which amounts to a mere denial of participation in a joint venture will not, of itself, activate s1(3)(iii) (see *Varley*). Again, the court will have to consider the effect of the evidence. For instance, where there are only two defendants alleged to have been involved in the venture, if the effect of the denial is to lead to the conclusion that if this defendant did not participate then it must have been the other who did, the provision will be triggered (*R* v *Crawford* [1998] 1 Cr App R 338).

However, whilst a mere denial of complicity in a joint venture will not be sufficient to activate the provision, a defendant whose view of the joint venture is directly contradicted by evidence of the joint venture given by a co-defendant may be able to assert that that contradiction amounts to 'evidence against' him. The contradiction referred to must amount to more than a mere inconvenience or inconsistency, because of the decisions in *R v Varley* [1982] 2 All ER 519 and *R v Kirkpatrick* [1998] Crim LR 63. In *R v Hatton* (1977) 64 Cr App R 88, there were three co-defendants, Hatton, Ripley and Hildon. The prosecution alleged that the three defendants had gone to a scrap metal site and had taken metal dishonestly in accordance with a pre-arranged plan. Hildon gave evidence denying the existence of such a plan, and said that he had met the others at the site by chance. Hatton gave evidence that all three of them had gone to the site in order to collect scrap metal which had been purchased by his stepbrother. Thus there was a direct contradiction between Hildon's view of the joint venture and that put forward by Hatton which amounted to more than a contradiction. If Hatton's account was believed, then Hildon's defence was destroyed. The Court held that Hatton had supported a material part of the prosecution's case which Hildon had denied, namely that Hildon had set out for the site with Hatton and Ripley to collect scrap for Hatton's stepbrother, and he had contradicted Hildon's evidence that he had only joined them later on the site. That evidence of Hatton, if believed, brought Hildon into a plan (albeit honest) to collect scrap, and although it provided Hildon with another defence, it not merely undermined his credit but on balance did more to undermine his defence than to undermine the prosecution's case. Indeed it supported the prosecution's case in a material respect, that there was a plan to take scrap from the site, and thereby rendered Hildon's conviction more likely and reduced his chances of acquittal. Accordingly, the Court held that s1(3)(iii) had been activated and the trial judge had been correct to allow Hildon to cross-examine Hatton.

The judge's discretion

Under s1(3)(ii) there are two questions for the judge to decide. The first is whether, as a matter of law, the relevant provision has been activated, and the second is whether he should exercise his discretion to refuse to allow cross-examination under the subsection. Under s1(3)(iii) the judge has no discretion to disallow cross-examination by a co-defendant, once he is satisfied that the provision is activated (see *R v Varley* [1982] 2 All ER 519). It has been held that the prosecution is not in the same position as a co-defendant in this regard, so that the judge has a discretion as to whether to allow cross-examination by the prosecution once s1(3)(iii) is triggered (*R v Lovett* [1973] 1 WLR 241).

Relevance of cross-examination

Cross-examination under s1(3)(iii) is relevant to the credibility of the co-defendant and not to his guilt (*R v Stannard* [1965] 2 QB 1). The judge should include a direction to the jury in his summing up on this point, but a failure to do so will not necessarily be fatal to any conviction (*R v Hoggins* [1967] 1 WLR 1233).

The provision contained in s1(3)(iii) is deceptively easy to state and rather more difficult to apply. Since what is significant is the effect of the evidence, and this can be determined only by reference to the facts of each individual case, it is not easy to extrapolate principles which are not contradictory and which are capable of general application.

Criticisms of the current law

In its Consultation Paper (No 141) in 1998, the Law Commission made a number of criticisms of the current law. Considering the whole of s1(3) the Commission observed that bad character evidence generally may be of less use in assessing a witness's truthfulness than has previously been assumed; and the bad character evidence that will be treated as most relevant to a defendant's truthfulness will be that which shows a disposition to behave in the manner now alleged.

So far as s1(3)(iii) is concerned, the major criticism made by the Law Commission related to the fact that the trial judge has no discretion to disallow cross-examination by a co-defendant once the provision is activated. The Commission noted a number of possible explanations for this rule. For instance, in *Murdoch v Taylor* [1965] AC 574, Lord Donovan expressed the view that nothing should be done to impede a defendant in the conduct of his or her defence. An alternative explanation is that the judge must not be seen to be 'picking and choosing' between defendants, since the 'fairness' they show to one may produce an appearance of unfairness to another (Munday, R 'The Wider Permutations of s1(f) of the Criminal Evidence Act 1898' (1987) 7 LS 137).

The Law Commission expressed the view that the undiscriminating nature of s1(3)(iii) prevents any consideration by the court of whether the rationale of the provision justifies the admission of an accused's criminal record, in whole or in part. It could, for instance, be the case that a co-defendant's record may do little or nothing to inform the court as to whether or not his evidence should be believed on this occasion.

The Commission was also concerned that a jury may be particularly prone to imply the 'forbidden chain of reasoning' in relation to evidence adduced under cross-examination under s1(3)(iii) which links propensity and guilt.

The Commission also noted the potential that exists for the court to be misled where the operation of s1(3)(iii) deprives one co-defendant of the shield, whilst exposing another to cross-examination.

Recommendation

The Law Commission proposed that the trial judge should have a discretion to refuse to allow cross-examination under s1(3)(iii) and that a defendant should not lose the shield as a result of evidence concerning the facts of the charge, but should only be at risk of losing the shield where he gave evidence relating to matters other than the facts of the incident giving rise to the present charge, and included reference in that evidence to other discreditable conduct by his co-defendant. This proposal would enable a defendant to give evidence as to his defence on the present charge without fear of losing his shield. However, a defendant who chose to do more than merely put forward his defence and included reference to a co-defendant's bad character would be at risk of losing his shield. The existence of a discretion would avoid the risk of unfairness.

QUESTION FIVE

Oliver is charged with theft of a bottle of whisky from a supermarket. During examination-in-chief he says that he put the bottle in his own plastic bag because he was afraid that it might crush other items in the store's wire basket, which he was also carrying. He says that at the checkout he produced the goods from the wire basket for payment, but forgot to produce the bottle from the plastic bag. He says that the reason for this was that he was worried about a speech that he was going to make at the meeting of a local society for the relief of homeless people. He adds that he has been a member of this society for several years. When cross-examined, he says that the store detective's evidence that he looked to right and left before putting the whisky in his own bag is 'all lies'. Oliver has a previous conviction for theft of a bottle of whisky from a supermarket and a conviction for indecent assault on a woman.

Discuss the evidential matters arising.

University of London LLB Examination
(for External Students) Law of Evidence June 2000 Q8

General Comment

This is a straightforward question concerning the effect of evidence given by the defendant. Consideration of the significant difference between a strong denial and evidence amounting to an imputation is called for. Consideration of the judge's discretion is also relevant. Note that this suggested solution is written on the basis that the provisions of the Youth Justice and Criminal Evidence Act 1999 are fully in force.

Skeleton Solution

Explanation of the shield protecting Oliver from cross-examination: s1(3) Criminal Evidence Act 1898 – evidence of the defendant's good character: *R* v *Ferguson*; *R* v *Baker* – relevance of cross-examination under s1(3)(ii) – relevance of the two previous convictions: *R* v *Marsh* – Rehabilitation of Offenders Act 1974: are the convictions 'spent'? – imputations: *R* v *Levy* – guidelines in *R* v *Britzman*; *R* v *Hall* – exercise of discretion: *Selvey* v *DPP* – similarity of previous conviction: *R* v *Powell*.

Suggested Solution

Section 1 Criminal Evidence Act (CEA) 1898 made the defendant a competent witness for his own defence. In this scenario, Oliver has chosen to give evidence on his own behalf and accordingly will be liable to cross-examination by the prosecution. He will not be able to claim the privilege against self-incrimination in respect of the offence charged, since this privilege is removed by s1(2) of the Act. However, s1(3) of the Act provides Oliver with a 'shield' protecting him from cross-examination about his previous convictions. The prohibition exists to prevent the introduction by the prosecution of prejudicial material which could mislead the jury into reasoning that, because the accused has a criminal record, he is likely also to have committed the offence with which he is currently charged. However, the shield provided by s1(3) may be lost in certain circumstances, which are set out in subss(i), (ii) and (iii). The question that arises in this scenario is whether the consequence of Oliver's answers in examination-in-chief is that questions about his former convictions will be allowed by the trial judge.

Oliver's explanation for his forgetfulness will be considered first. If the judge takes the view that what Oliver says amounts to evidence of his own good character, then he would be entitled to allow questioning as to the former convictions under s1(3)(ii) CEA 1898. The effect of that subsection is that the shield may be lost where the accused has given evidence of his own good character. The question of whether the accused has put his character in issue by giving evidence of good character is a matter of law for the judge to determine, and so counsel for the prosecution will have to seek the leave of the court before cross-examining on the previous convictions. In *R v Ferguson* (1909) 2 Cr App R 250 the accused was held to have activated this provision by giving evidence that he was a religious man who had attended church services for a number of years. In *R v Baker* (1912) 7 Cr App R 252 the accused put his character in issue by giving evidence that he had earned an honest living for a number of years, and the same result occured in *R v Coulman* (1927) 20 Cr App R 106 when the accused gave evidence that he was a married man and in regular employment. Applying all these cases, it seems that the judge is likely to hold that Oliver has put his character in issue by his references to active membership of the local society for the relief of the homeless. If the proposed cross-examination is relevant, it would then follow that cross-examination as to the previous convictions is permissible as a matter of law. Cross-examination under this first part of s1(3)(ii) goes to credit (*R v Samuel* (1956) 40 Cr App R 8) and, at most, has only an indirect bearing on the likelihood that Oliver has committed the offence charged. A failure to direct the jury that cross-examination is relevant to credit, and not to guilt, is a good ground of appeal (*R v Inder* (1977) 67 Cr App R 143) and so the judge should tell the jury that the questioning goes only to credit and that they should not consider that it shows a propensity to commit the offence they are considering (*R v McLeod* [1994] 3 All ER 254).

Turning to the two previous convictions, it is apparent that the first relates to a dishonesty offence and, that being the case, it seems that the relevance to Oliver's credibility is made out. However, the judge has a discretion to exclude questioning permissible as a matter of law under s1(3)(ii) (*R v Marsh* [1994] Crim LR 52), and it is arguable that the similarity of the earlier offence to the offence currently charged is such that the judge should not allow questioning as to the earlier offence, since the risk is that the jury might decide that the fact that Oliver has committed a similar offence in the past indicates that he is disposed to have committed this offence. In *R v Powell* [1985] 1

WLR 1364 and *R v McLeod* [1994] 3 All ER 254 the Court of Appeal held that the fact that an earlier offence is similar to that currently charged is a matter for the judge to take into account when exercising his discretion, but does not oblige him to disallow the questioning. In *McLeod*, the Court held that similarity alone will not make questioning improper, so it may well be that the trial judge will allow questioning as to this conviction. However, if the questioning is allowed, it should not be prolonged or extensive, because such questioning could divert the jury from the principal issue in front of them, namely the guilt of Oliver on the present charge (*McLeod*).

The second previous conviction relates to an offence of an entirely different nature and one in which there is no element of dishonesty. This last point may be significant, since the defence may argue that an offence of this nature has no bearing on the issue of credibility, so that questioning as to this previous conviction would be merely prejudicial. In *R v Watts* [1983] 3 All ER 101 the Court of Appeal held that convictions for indecent assaults, not being offences which involve dishonesty, were at best of 'slight' probative value in relation to the credibility of the accused.

The question does not state the sentences imposed for the previous offences and it is possible that the offences will be 'spent' under the terms of the Rehabilitation of Offenders Act 1974. This Act establishes a tariff under which offences become spent after a certain period of time, the period of time being determined by reference to the sentence imposed, so that, for instance, a conditional discharge becomes spent after one year. Section 4(1) of the Act forbids the questioning of a 'rehabilitated' person about 'spent' convictions. Section 7(2)(a) provides that s4(1) does not apply to criminal proceedings, but in a *Practice Direction* issued by the Lord Chief Justice in June 1975 (*Practice Direction* [1975] 1 WLR 1065) it is recommended that in criminal cases no reference should be made to a spent conviction if it can reasonably be avoided, and no reference should be made in open court to a spent conviction without the authority of the judge, and such authority should only be given if the interests of justice so require. Accordingly, if Oliver's previous convictions are spent, the judge will have to consider whether the interests of justice require that they are the subject of cross-examination. If the judge takes that view that this test is satisfied and allows cross-examination as to spent convictions, it may very well be the case that the cross-examination will be of little evidential weight.

If the convictions are not spent, it seems likely that the judge will allow cross-examination under s1(3)(ii), and in those circumstances it may be to the advantage of the defence to introduce evidence of these convictions in examination-in-chief. This course of action will enable Oliver's counsel to manage the disclosure of the information so as to present Oliver in the best possible light, and will also avoid the impression being given to the jury that Oliver was less than frank in his examination-in-chief.

In addition to (probably) putting his character in issue, Oliver asserts that the store detective has told lies in the course of his evidence. The consequence of this evidence may be that Oliver will be deemed to have cast imputations on the character of a witness for the prosecution (the store detective) so that the second part of s1(3)(ii) is activated. The second part of s1(3)(ii) would allow the prosecution to question Oliver about his previous convictions, subject to the judge's discretion to exclude the questioning.

The first question to be determined concerns whether Oliver has made imputations. In the case law, a distinction is made between cases in which the defence involves mere assertions of innocence or emphatic denials of guilt (no imputation), and cases in which the defence involves attacks on the veracity of the prosecution or a witness for the prosecution (see, for example, *R v Clark* [1955] 2 QB 469). In *R v Levy* (1966) 50 Cr App R 238 the Court of Appeal held that each case will fall to be determined on its own facts and, possibly as a consequence of this approach, the cases are not all easy to reconcile. In *R v Rouse* [1904] 1 KB 184 the Court held that when the defendant called the prosecutor a liar he was merely denying his guilt in emphatic terms so that no imputation was made and the shield was not lost. However, in *R v Rappolt* (1911) 6 Cr App R 156, the defendant lost his shield as a result of describing a witness for the prosecution as a 'horrible liar'. Applying these cases, it seems that Oliver's case is closer to *Rouse* than to *Rappolt,* but more recently guidance as to when a judge should grant leave to the prosecution to cross-examine under s1(3)(ii) has been given in the Court of Appeal in the case of *R v Britzman; R v Hall* [1983] 1 All ER 369. According to these guidelines, the judge should exercise his discretion against the prosecution if Oliver's evidence amounts to nothing more than a denial, however emphatic or offensively made, of an act or even a short series of acts amounting to one incident. However, the discretion should be exercised in favour of the prosecution if the evidence amounts to a denial of evidence of a long period of detailed observation.

Applying these guidelines, it seems that Oliver's evidence is closer to the first category than the second, but clearly it is possible that the judge could decide that the questioning should be allowed. If the judge is minded to allow the cross-examination then he should consider whether there is a possibility of mistake, misunderstanding or confusion. If there is such a possibility, the questioning should not be allowed (*R v Britzman; R v Hall* [1983] 1 All ER 369) and in considering this issue the judge should make allowance for the strains of giving evidence and the exaggerated use of language that the Court noted can result from such strain or lack of education or mental stability. The questioning should only be allowed if the jury will necessarily have to consider whether the store detective has fabricated evidence.

Finally, the Court in *Britzman* commented that there will be no need for the prosecution to rely on s1(3)(ii) where the evidence against a defendant is overwhelming, so the strength of the prosecution case against Oliver will be an important matter for the trial judge to consider.

If the judge decides that Oliver has cast imputations on the store detective through his evidence, he will then have to consider whether to exercise his discretion to disallow questioning under s1(3)(ii). Principles governing the exercise of the discretion were established in *Selvey v DPP* [1970] AC 304 and set out again by Ackner LJ in *R v Burke*

(1985) 82 Cr App R 156. According to these guidelines, the judge must weigh the prejudicial effect of the questions against the damage done by the attack on the store detective, and must generally exercise his discretion in such a way as to ensure that the trial is fair to the prosecution, as well as to the defence. Lord Ackner LJ noted in *R v Burke* (1985) 82 Cr App R 156 that there must be cases in which questioning becomes technically admissible as a result of imputations, but the evidence of character thereby admissible is so gravely prejudicial to the accused that it should not be allowed, but it does not seem that the present case comes within that exceptional category. It seems that Oliver's case comes within the 'ordinary and normal case' which Lord Ackner went on to describe in which the attack on the credit of a witness for the prosecution means that it is only fair that the jury should be informed of the defendant's previous convictions. Accordingly, the judge may very well take the view that the jury are entitled to know of Oliver's previous convictions, since this information will enable them to decide whether the store detective or Oliver is the witness more worthy of belief.

R v Powell [1985] 1 WLR 1364 and *R v McLeod* [1994] 3 All ER 254 apply to proposed lines of questioning under the second part of s1(3)(ii) so that the similarity of the current offence and the first conviction, and the fact that the second previous offence is not an offence of dishonesty, will be relevant matters for the trial judge to consider when exercising his discretion.

The comments made above concerning the application of the Rehabilitation of Offenders Act 1974 are also relevant here. Questioning under the first part of s1(3)(ii) goes to credibility; questioning under the second part of this provision is to the same effect, and the judge should direct the jury accordingly (*R v Jenkins* (1945) 31 Cr App R 1). Where questioning has been allowed under the second part of s1(3)(ii) the judge should give the jury the propensity warning required by *R v McLeod* [1994] 3 All ER 254 and a failure to do so will constitute a good ground for appeal (*R v Inder* (1977) 67 Cr App R 143).

Chapter 9
Similar Fact Evidence

9.1 **Introduction**

9.2 **Key points**

9.3 **Key cases and statute**

9.4 **Questions and suggested solutions**

9.1 Introduction

When evidence of the misconduct of the accused is admitted in the form of previous convictions, its relevance is generally to the credibility of the accused as a witness. This admissibility of convictions etc as evidence of bad character at common law and under the Criminal Evidence Act 1898 was dealt with in Chapter 8, where it was stated that evidence of bad character could sometimes be admitted as similar fact evidence – ie to prove the guilt of the accused on the instant charge. Usually it is not permissible for the prosecution to lead evidence of the propensity of the accused towards misconduct (whether or not criminal), or of specific misconduct by him, since this would be prejudicial and thus prevent a fair trial.

However, exceptionally, evidence of misconduct, for example the details of how the accused misbehaved, not purely the fact of conviction (there may not have been one) may be admissible as 'similar fact evidence', ie to tend to show that the accused, given the similar fact evidence, committed the crime with which he is charged. In the main the topic centres on this issue, but similar fact evidence is sometimes admissible in civil cases, and is occasionally admissible in criminal cases by statute when certain crimes are charged.

9.2 Key points

In *Makin* v *Attorney-General for New South Wales* [1894] AC 57, Lord Herschell LC made a pronouncement on similar fact evidence which has been referred to on innumerable occasions. In effect, he stated that, if evidence of other misconduct of the accused did no more than show a general disposition to commit crime or a particular crime, then such evidence is inadmissible; but if the evidence goes further than that, and is 'relevant to an issue before the jury', then it may be admissible. This relevance to an issue before the jury led to attempts being made to categorise circumstances where the evidence was admissible, eg to rebut a defence; to show design; to prove a system; to prove 'guilty relations'; as identification of the accused. This elaborate and complex systemisation did not help to clarify the law on similar fact evidence, and is to some extent responsible for the confusion which still prevails, despite the attempt by the House of Lords to move away from categories of relevance to degrees of relevance in *DPP v Boardman* [1975] AC 421. In other words, their lordships concentrated on the striking similarity between the conduct of the accused alleged in the instant case and that of which the prosecution seek to adduce similar fact evidence.

However, in the cases since *Boardman* there is evidence of some disquiet with the application of the test of 'striking similarity' to the exclusion of all other tests for admissibility; in *Boardman* itself it is considered that the standard of striking similarity was set somewhat low. Two Court of Appeal decisions soon after *Boardman* evinced the difficulties which the striking similarity test was to cause; on almost identical facts the court admitted evidence of similar facts to prove guilt in one case and rejected it in the other: *R v Johannsen* (1977) 65 Cr App R 101; *R v Novac* (1976) 65 Cr App R 107.

Post-*Boardman*, cases have also confirmed that similar fact evidence is admissible not only if strikingly similar to the fact of the offence with which the accused is charged but also if strikingly similar to the circumstances in which the offence was committed, eg *R v Scarrott* [1978] QB 1016. Further, it has been held that such evidence of circumstances does not need to show the actual commission of the evidence, providing it goes beyond merely proving a propensity to commit that type of crime, or crime generally: *R v Barrington* [1981] 1 WLR 419; *R v Butler* (1987) 84 Cr App R 12; *R v Tricoglus* (1976) 65 Cr App R 16. But the problem still remains of the difficulty, to the point of impossibility, in formulating a test of striking similarity, and evidence has been admitted by apparently applying a standard lower than that in *Boardman* itself – see eg *R v Seaman* (1978) 67 Cr App R 234.

In the case of *R v Brookes* (1991) 92 Cr App R 36, the defendant was charged with sexual offences against three of his daughters. The Court of Appeal held that it was not enough for the facts to be similar, they must tell the court something useful. The court must enquire into what the evidence was being used to prove, and whether that evidence was then probative of that fact. In this case, the similarity alleged was the common coin of evidence in the case of father-daughter incest, and there was a real risk that the daughters had colluded. Therefore, separate trials were ordered.

Where, as in *Boardman*, the similar fact evidence consists of testimony by another witness or witnesses as to conduct of the accused on other occasions similar to that alleged by a prosecution witness or witnesses on the occasion giving rise to the charge, then the court must satisfy itself that there has been no collusion between the witnesses and therefore no question of concoction: *R v Barrington*.

Similar fact evidence continues to be admitted post-*Boardman* to rebut a defence raised or which is reasonably open to the accused (this pre-emptive adducing of the evidence by the prosecution being permitted to avoid a successful defence submission of 'no case to answer'). In *R v Lunt* (1987) 85 Cr App R 241 evidence of other misconduct by the accused was admissible to rebut a defence of innocent association; in *R* v *Anderson* [1988] 2 All ER 549 evidence was admitted to prove how implausible was the defence which the accused raised. 'Striking similarity' was not the test applied, but rather the positive probative value of the evidence.

See now also the case of *R* v *Carrington* [1990] Crim LR 330, where the function of the similar fact evidence was to show the defendant's intent in relation to the charge of threatening to kill the victim, the similar fact evidence being a threat made in a similar (but not strikingly similar) way to the victim a few months before.

Consider also the important House of Lords' decision in *R* v *P* (1991) 93 Cr App R 267. Here the House of Lords held that it had been correct to admit evidence that the defendant (a father) had similarly abused children of the family other than the complainant, in the absence of collusion, despite the absence of 'striking similarities'. The essential feature, the House of Lords said, of the evidence which was to be admitted was that its probative force in support of the allegation that the defendant committed a crime was sufficiently great to make it correct to admit the evidence, notwithstanding that it was prejudicial to the defendant. Probative force can be achieved by striking similarity, but there are other means. Here, the evidence of the girls described a prolonged course of conduct by the accused, including threats, use of force, and payment for abortions. This, the court felt, gave strong probative force to the evidence of each of the girls. The important question here was not who had committed these crimes, but had they been committed at all. 'Striking similarity' is more concerned with identifying the assailant when the fact that the crime has taken place is not in issue.

A particularly important decision followed in *R* v *Hepburn* (also reported as *R* v *H*) [1995] 2 All ER 865 HL, where their Lordships decided, on a majority decision, that the possibility of collusive witnesses was not, as formerly, a question of admissibility for the judge. By contrast, it was to be a question of weight for the jury. It is submitted that the combined effect of *R* v *P* and *R* v *H* in cases where identification is not in issue but the possibility of collusion exists, may well produce surprising results. This matter may, perhaps, be back with their Lordships in the not-too-distant future.

Where a defendant is charged with two or more offences and similar fact evidence is adduced to support his identification in relation to the later offence, the jury should be directed to consider first whether they were sure the accused had committed the first offence (see *R* v *Gurney* [1994] Crim LR 116). However, the jury should be told to consider the defendant's guilt as regards the first offence in isolation – ie without consideration of the other offences before his guilt as regards the first offence can be used as similar fact evidence with the other offences. Common sense? But what about the coincidence theory? – ie if the accused is said to have committed several different but similar offences by several independent witnesses, he must have committed the offences otherwise those witnesses would not have all told the same story against him.

In *R* v *Z* [2000] 3 All ER 385 the defendant had previously been acquitted on charges of rape when he had relied on the defence of consent. The prosecution wished to rely on evidence of the previous complaints to negate the defence of consent or belief as to consent. The issue that arose was accordingly whether evidence of previous acquittals could be adduced as evidence to establish guilt of a current offence. The House of Lords held that the evidence of the earlier complaints was relevant as similar fact evidence and was not inadmissible, because it showed that the defendant was in fact guilty of the earlier offences for which he had been acquitted. However, the House went on to state that admissibility of the evidence was subject to the trial judge's discretion, weighing its prejudicial effect against its probative value, and under s78 Police and Criminal Evidence Act 1984.

It seems, therefore, that generally the prosecution may adduce similar fact evidence in chief if it shows some unique linking characteristic or is of sufficiently striking similarity to be positively probative of guilt. But, similar fact evidence would appear to be admissible despite lacking that degree of striking similarity, dependent on the particular facts in issue, for example to rebut a defence raised, to prove opportunity, identity etc where any of these is in issue, or where the probative force outweighs the prejudicial value.

Arguably, in the general run of cases, the judge has a discretion to exclude similar fact evidence if its prejudicial effect will outweigh its probative value; given these two factors should be weighed by the judge in deciding admissibility, it seems that there is no scope for discretionary exclusion – but the courts continue to recognise its existence. In *R v Butler* (1987) 84 Cr App R 12, it was stated that where the similar fact evidence constitutes the commission by the accused of other offences there is greater prejudicial effect, which is relevant to the exercise of the judge's discretion.

Two important statutory provisions in criminal cases are:

a) s27(3) Theft Act 1968: allows the prosecution to prove mens rea on the part of the handler of stolen goods by evidence which shows a general propensity to dishonesty; judicial discretion to exclude this evidence in the interests of a fair trial of the accused is recognised without argument: *R v Perry* [1984] Crim LR 680;

b) s1(2) Official Secrets Act 1911: allows evidence of disposition of the accused to prove that his purpose was prejudicial to the safety or interests of the state.

In civil proceedings, similar fact evidence is admitted more easily than in criminal proceedings, because the civil courts are not concerned with the fair trial of an accused and therefore prejudicial effect and probative value do not have to be weighed.

In *Mood Music Publishing Co Ltd* v *De Wolfe Publishing Ltd* [1976] 1 Ch 119, similar fact evidence was admitted even though some of it had been obtained by the plaintiff's setting a trap for the defendant; that was not considered oppressive or unfair to the defendant, who had had notice of the plaintiff's intention to adduce the evidence during the course of the pre-trial procedure.

9.3 Key cases and statute

- *DPP* v *Boardman* [1975] AC 421

- *Makin* v *Attorney-General for New South Wales* [1894] AC 57

- *R* v *Hepburn* [1995] 2 AC 596

- *R* v *P* [1991] 2 AC 447

- *R* v *Z* [1990] 3 WLR 940

- Police and Criminal Evidence Act 1984, s78

9.4 Questions and suggested solutions

QUESTION ONE

To what extent is evidence of a defendant's disposition admissible in criminal cases?

University of London LLB Examination
(for External Students) Law of Evidence June 2000 Q3

General Comment

The classic account of similar fact evidence used to be that evidence which amounted to no more than evidence of disposition was inadmissible. But this account is difficult to reconcile with cases such as *R* v *Straffen* [1952] 2 QB 911, *DPP* v *Kilbourne* [1973] AC 729 and *R* v *Butler* (1987) 84 Cr App R 12. A good knowledge of these cases will be required for this question. In addition, the developing line of cases relating to possession of incriminating items is relevant, as is the trend to admit 'background evidence'.

Skeleton Solution

The general rule as expressed in *Makin* v *Attorney-General for New South Wales* – explanations for the rule advanced in *DPP* v *Boardman* – evidence of propensity admitted in cases such as *R* v *Straffen* and *DPP* v *Kilbourne* – possession of incriminating items: *Thompson* v *R*; *R* v *Groves*; *R* v *Peters* – 'background evidence: *R* v *Sawoniuk*.

Suggested Solution

The classic formulation of circumstances in which similar fact evidence may be admitted is that given by Lord Herschell in *Makin* v *Attorney-General for New South Wales* [1894] AC 57, which has been cited with approval by the House of Lords in *DPP* v *Boardman* [1975] AC 421. According to this statement of the law, evidence which amounts to no more than evidence of disposition is not admissible.

In *Boardman*, Lord Hailsham said that there are two explanations for this rule. First, the evidence is irrelevant, since no matter how many times the accused is shown to have committed previous offences, nothing in the fact of that offending shows that the accused committed the offence presently charged. A good illustration of this is *R v Neale* (1977) 65 Cr App R 304 in which two defendants, Neale and Burr, were charged with arson and manslaughter following the death of an inmate at a hostel for boys in a fire which had been deliberately started. Neale said at first that he had been in bed and woke to find that the hostel was on fire, but later said that he had been with Burr when Burr started the fire. Neale wished to adduce evidence to show that Burr had started fires on five previous occasions. The only question for the judge to consider was whether the evidence was relevant. Since Neale and Burr were co-defendants, the judge had no discretionary power to exclude the evidence because of its prejudicial effect upon Burr, and Neale would be entitled to adduce the evidence if it were relevant. The trial judge decided that the evidence was not relevant and the Court of Appeal held that this decision was correct, since the fact that Burr had a propensity to start fires had no bearing on the issue of whether Neale had been with him or had participated on this particular occasion. In addition, the evidence was no more than evidence of propensity and there was nothing to show that the man with the propensity committed the offence on this occasion.

The second explanation for the rule advanced by Lord Hailsham in *DPP v Boardman* [1975] AC 421 is that, even if evidence of propensity is logically probative, it is so prejudicial that the prejudice outweighs any probative value by undermining the integrity of the presumption of innocence and the burden of proof.

Lord Hailsham said that both explanations were correct. Where there is nothing to connect the accused with a particular offence except bad character or similar crimes committed in the past, the evidence has no probative value and is consequently rejected. Where there is some evidence connecting the accused with the crime, evidence that the defendant has committed similar offences in the past is inadmissible because of its prejudicial effect.

This account of *Makin v Attorney-General for New South Wales* [1894] AC 57 apparently means that mere evidence of propensity is not admissible. However, in some cases evidence of propensity has been admitted. One such case was *R v Straffen* [1952] 2 QB 911, in which what Lord Simon described as a 'most unusual murder' took place. A young girl was found strangled. There had been no attempt to assault her sexually or to hide the body. The accused had previously been convicted of two murders which shared these features. He had escaped from Broadmoor and was in the vicinity at the time of the third murder. In *DPP v Kilbourne* [1973] AC 729, Lord Simon explained that although it was possible that the third murder had been committed by someone else and that an 'ultra-cautious jury' might still have acquitted Straffen, it would have been absurd for the law to have prevented the evidence of the other murders being put before the jury, although it was simply evidence to show that Straffen was a man likely to commit a murder of that particular kind. Lord Simon explained that the reason for the exclusionary rule is not that the law regards such evidence as inherently irrelevant, but because it is believed that if it were generally admitted jurors would, in many cases, think that it was more relevant than it was – its prejudicial effect would outweigh its probative value. However, there are cases in which evidence of disposition becomes admissible, because to refuse to admit it would be an 'affront to common sense'.

In *R v Butler* (1987) 84 Cr App R 12, the accused was charged with rape and indecent assault. He denied all the allegations and raised the issue of identification. His former girlfriend was permitted to give evidence of her sexual experiences with him on the basis that there were eight points of striking similarity between the practices she described and those described by the two complainants. The trial judge held that the probative value of the evidence was very strong and the Court of Appeal commented that where, as here, the 'similar fact' evidence does not amount to evidence of the commission of an offence, the prejudicial effect of allowing the evidence is likely to be small.

So the position appears to be as follows: if the evidence of disposition does no more than raise or strengthen a suspicion that the accused committed the offence with which he is charged, it is inadmissible under the similar fact rule. However, the evidence becomes admissible if it would point so strongly to his guilt that only an ultra-cautious jury, if they accepted it as true, would acquit in the face of it.

There have been a number of cases in which evidence relating to the possession of incriminating articles has been allowed in under the 'similar fact' rule. In *Thompson v R* [1918] AC 221, the prosecution was permitted to adduce evidence that the accused had powder puffs in his possession at the time of his arrest, and that a search of his rooms resulted in the discovery of photographs of naked boys. Thompson raised the defence of mistaken identity and the House of Lords held that the evidence had been correctly allowed in on the basis that it showed that both the offender and the accused shared an 'abnormal propensity', and accordingly tended to identify the accused as the offender. *Thompson* has been interpreted to mean that sexual offences against men or boys form a special category, with the consequence that evidence of an accused's homosexuality, or of his homosexual activity on other occasions, is admissible to prove his commission of the offence charged. This interpretation was decisively rejected by the House of Lords in *DPP v Boardman* [1975] AC 421 but the decision in *Thompson* may be interpreted using Lord Simon's formulation of an 'affront to common sense'. If Thompson was the victim of a mistaken identification, it would be an enormous coincidence that the man who was pointed out to the police by the complainants had arrived at the time and place previously arranged between the complainants, and the offender happened also to be a homosexual and interested in young boys. The evidence that was adduced in *Thompson* was evidence of propensity but its relevance was that it made it very unlikely that the defendant was telling the truth.

The same result was obtained in *R v Groves* [1998] Crim LR 200 in which the defendant was charged with an offence relating to the importation of drugs. The defendant was present when an illegally imported consignment of cannabis was delivered to one of his friends. When he was searched, the defendant was found to be in possession of certain quantities of drugs, and a search of his property led to the discovery of larger quantities of drugs. His defence was one of innocent association (he had merely been having a drink with a friend when the drugs were delivered to the friend), and he claimed that he was looking after the drugs found at his property for a friend. The prosecution was allowed to adduce evidence relating to the discovery of drugs at his property. The Court of Appeal held that the trial judge had been correct to allow this evidence, since it was relevant to the defence of innocent association. The question was whether the direct evidence (the defendant's presence at the scene when the imported drugs were delivered to a friend of the defendant at a meeting at which the defendant was present) and the indirect evidence (the discovery of the drugs at the defendant's property) were inexplicable on the basis of coincidence. In this case, the defendant had not claimed to have no knowledge or involvement with drugs. On the contrary, he was in possession of drugs for personal use and, on his own account, was prepared to look after a larger quantity of drugs for someone else. It seems apparent, therefore, that the defendant mixed with people involved with drugs, and it must be questionable whether, in those circumstances, his innocent presence on an occasion when delivery of a consignment of drugs was made really was an affront to common sense in the way described by Lord Simon.

In several cases concerning drugs offences, the Court of Appeal has held that evidence of possession of drugs is relevant to charges involving other drugs. For instance, in *R v Sokialiosis* [1993] Crim LR 872 the defendant was charged with importing a Class A drug and said in interview that he was not a drug dealer, and that neither did he take drugs. He claimed that the drugs which formed the subject matter of the charge had been planted on him. A search of his property led to the discovery of a quantity of cocaine in a holdall belonging to the defendant. The Court of Appeal held that the trial judge had been correct to allow the prosecution to adduce evidence relating to the discovery of the cocaine, since the discovery of the cocaine was relevant to the defendant's answers in interview, and the judge had correctly weighed the prejudicial effect of the evidence against its probative value. Evidence of the finding of the cocaine was evidence of propensity but, as in *Thompson v R* [1918] AC 221, its relevance was that it made it less likely that the defendant was telling the truth.

A similar case is that of *R v Peters* (1995) 2 Cr App R 77 in which the defendant was charged with an offence relating to importation of a Class B drug. He denied all knowledge of the imported drugs. A search of the defendant's home address led to the discovery of small quantities of cannabis (a Class C drug) and drug-related equipment. The Court of Appeal held that evidence relating to these discoveries had properly been admitted, since the jury were entitled to consider the coincidence of an accused, who denied knowledge of drugs being imported, having possession of other drugs in the United Kingdom. Evidence of the defendant's disposition was relevant here to his credibility.

Cases such as *Sokialiosis* and *Peters* demonstrate that evidence of the defendant's bad disposition may be relevant to his credibility. However, if the defendant is of good character, evidence of his disposition may also be relevant, both to the likelihood that he committed the offence charged and to his credibility. Where the defendant is of good character the judge is required to direct the jury that character is relevant to guilt, in that a person of good character is less likely to have committed the offence charged (*R* v *Vye* [1993] Crim LR 604). In addition, if the defendant's credibility is in issue, the judge should direct the jury that good character is relevant to credibility.

Evidence of disposition may be admitted other than as 'similar fact' evidence. In *R* v *Sawoniuk* [2000] Crim LR 506 the Court of Appeal held that evidence of acts of violence which did not form the subject matter of a count in the proceedings was admissible on the basis that it was relevant and probative, and was admissible even if it disclosed the commission of other criminal offences.

QUESTION TWO

'Despite the vast bulk of authority to which the subject has given rise, the law remains complex and uncertain in many respects.'

Do you agree with this assessment of the present state of the law relating to similar fact evidence?

University of London LLB Examination
(for External Students) Law of Evidence June 1999 Q4

General Comment

The nature of this question is quite clear but a good knowledge of the leading cases is required. A discussion of the requirement for a high degree of relevance, sufficient to outweigh prejudicial effect, is necessary and it should be made clear that *DPP* v *Boardman* [1975] AC 421 did not make 'striking similarity' the sole test of admissibility. Some discussion of the prejudice to the defendant should be included.

Skeleton Solution

Lord Herschell's propositions in *Makin* – the 'ticket of admission' approach – the judgment in *DPP* v *Boardman* – probative force and prejudicial effect – 'striking similarity' as a means of obtaining probative force – difficulty of applying *DPP* v *Boardman* – *R* v *P* – the importance of probative force – consideration of whether it is just to admit the evidence – interpretation of *R* v *P* by the Court of Appeal.

Suggested Solution

The starting point for a discussion of the law relating to similar fact evidence is *Makin* v *Attorney-General for New South Wales* [1894] AC 57. In that case the defendants were charged with murder. They had taken custody of a child from its mother, saying that they would adopt it and care for it in return for a small payment of money. The prosecution sought to adduce evidence from other mothers that the defendants had taken babies from them on the same basis. The prosecution also sought to rely on the fact that the bodies of thirteen babies had been found in the gardens of three houses formerly occupied by the defendants. The relevance of this prosecution evidence was that it tended to rebut any defence of accident or natural causes.

The defendants were convicted and Lord Herschell gave judgment on the appeal in the Privy Council. The judgment contains two propositions, as shown below.

a) Evidence which relates merely to the defendant's disposition is inadmissible.

b) However, it does not follow that evidence which tends to show the commission of other crimes by the accused is therefore inadmissible. Such evidence is admissible where it is relevant to an issue in front of the jury. Relevancy may be derived from the fact that the evidence tends to show that the acts said to constitute the offence were accidental or designed, or from the fact that the evidence rebuts a defence which would otherwise be open to the accused.

The first proposition excludes evidence which shows, or tends to show, no more than that the accused has a disposition to commit crimes in general or to commit the sort of offence with which he is now charged. Zuckerman (Zuckerman, *The Principles of Criminal Evidence* (1989)) describes this exclusionary rule as a statement of an ideal, that the accused should be charged only for the offence in question. An example of the operation of this principle is provided by *R v B (RA)* (1997) 2 Cr App R 88. The defendant was charged with indecently assaulting his two grandsons. His defence was a denial, and he suggested that the boys had been encouraged to invent the allegations by their mother. The Court of Appeal held that the trial judge had erred when he admitted in evidence homosexual pornographic magazines found in the defendant's possession, and his answers to police questions about his sexual proclivities; the evidence proved propensity and no more. The argument that propensity renders it more likely that the accused committed the offence presently charged was described by Lord Hailsham in *DPP v Boardman* [1975] AC 421 as a 'forbidden chain of reasoning'.

The second proposition allows the admission of evidence which is relevant to an issue in front of the jury, even though that evidence also shows, or tends to show, that the defendant has committed offences other than the one with which he is now charged. Zuckerman describes this inclusionary rule as a statement of reality; it is not always possible to achieve the ideal reflected in the exclusionary rule.

One of the difficulties associated with the interpretation of the second proposition developed because of the way Lord Herschell expressed the rule. The formulation of the rule encouraged courts and advocates to develop categories or types of relevance for which similar fact evidence might be relevant. This led to what Lord Hoffman (Hoffman LJ, 'Similar Facts After *Boardman*' (1975) 91 LQR 193) later described as the 'ticket of admission' approach. If the evidence could be said to be relevant to a specific issue, such as 'system', 'identity' or 'innocent association', it became admissible on the basis that it was either outside the scope of the exclusionary rule or was an exception to it. This led to much technical and complex case law concerning questions such as: how many acts make a 'system', or when does the defendant raise the defence of innocent association? Where a ticket of admission could be identified, evidence which was highly prejudicial but of little relevance could justifiably be admitted. As a result, the courts developed a requirement that admissibility remained subject to a discretion to exclude evidence where the prejudicial effect was outweighed by the probative value. The decision on admissibility accordingly had two stages: the judge had first to determine whether the case fell within an established category of relevance; if it did, he then had to consider whether he should exercise the discretion to exclude it nevertheless.

In *DPP* v *Boardman* [1975] AC 421 Lord Wilberforce noted that the defendant's denial of the incidents in question did not fit easily within any of the established categories. However, the House of Lords unanimously held that the admission of similar fact evidence did not depend on whether the evidence fitted into one of the categories recognised under the second proposition in *Makin* v *Attorney-General for New South Wales* [1894] AC 57. The Lords agreed that the test was one of relevance, and a high degree of relevance was required. Lord Wilberforce said that the 'basic principle must be that the admission of similar fact evidence … is exceptional and requires a strong degree of probative force'.

The Lords agreed that the probative force of the evidence must be weighed against its prejudicial effect, and it should only be allowed if it would not be unfair to the defendant to allow it to be submitted. One way in which sufficient probative force can be demonstrated is by showing a 'striking similarity' with the evidence in the case.

The status of *Makin* was unclear following the decision in *DPP* v *Boardman* [1975] AC 421. The rules had been cited with approval by three of the Law Lords but none of the Law Lords purported to apply them directly to the case, and in the years between 1975 and 1991 most of the reported decisions of the Court of Appeal applied the test of admissibility as stated in *Boardman*, but in some cases, *Makin* was cited as the authority for the decision on admissibility.

Keane (Keane, *The Modern Law of Evidence* (5th edn, 2000)) comments that although the principles enunciated in *Boardman* are reasonably easy to state, their application 'has not been without difficulty'. Two lines of authority developed on the interpretation of *Boardman* itself. In one group of cases, striking similarity was interpreted as requiring unusual or peculiar features of similarity sufficient to amount to a 'hallmark or signature' of the defendant. If the similarities relied upon could be described as common for the type of crime involved ('the stock in trade of the seducer of small boys') the high degree of relevance required was not demonstrated and the evidence would not be admitted (*R* v *Inder* (1977) 67 Cr App R 143). In the second group of cases, the standard required was stated as 'positive probative value' (*R* v *Scarrott* [1978] QB 1016). Evidence would be admissible only if it went beyond showing a tendency to commit offences generally, or a particular type of offence, by having some feature which provided a link to the offence charged.

The question of the admissibility of similar fact evidence reached the House of Lords again in *R* v *P* (1991) 93 Cr App R 267 in which the defendant was charged with rape and incest, the complainants being his two daughters. The trial judge refused the defence application for separate trials in relation to each daughter, and also held that the similarities in the evidence of the girls was sufficient to make the evidence of each girl admissible on the count relating to the other. The Court of Appeal quashed the conviction on the basis that the similarities (the use of force and threats to dominate each girl and payment for abortions) did not amount to more than the 'stock in trade' of an incestuous father, so that the evidence lacked the quality of striking similarity that was required. The House of Lords restored the convictions on the basis that it was not appropriate to single out striking similarity as an essential feature in every case involving the use of the evidence of one victim on a charge relating to another victim. Lord Mackay said that the principle was whether the probative force of the evidence was sufficiently great to make it just to admit the evidence, notwithstanding the prejudicial effect of the evidence in tending to show that the defendant had committed another offence. The other members of the House of Lords agreed with Lord Mackay, and the Court of Appeal cases requiring striking similarity beyond the 'stock in trade' were overruled.

The required probative value may be derived from striking similarities, but striking similarity is not a requirement except in cases where the identity of the defendant is in issue. Lord Mackay explained that what was significant was the 'relationship' between the evidence of the victims. This relationship may take many forms, including striking similarity in the manner in which the offence is committed. However, other factors, such as time and circumstances other than the manner in which the offence is committed, may also give rise to a sufficient relationship justifying the reception of the evidence.

In *R* v *P* (1991) 93 Cr App R 267 identity was not an issue and Lord Mackay appeared to lay down a special requirement for cases in which similar fact evidence was tendered in proof of identity. The Court of Appeal has subsequently interpreted this to mean that in cases where identity is in issue, if there is no other evidence in the case, something akin to a signature or fingerprint may be necessary (*R* v *Whartin* [1998] Crim LR 668). The degree of similarity required will vary according to the other evidence in the case.

The view that *R* v *P* has extended the limits of admissibility for similar fact evidence where identity is not in issue is arguable, and has been accepted by the Court of Appeal in subsequent cases such as *R* v *Simpson* (1993) 99 Cr App R 48. *R* v *P* has been the subject of adverse comment; for instance Tapper (Tapper, 'The Erosion of *Boardman* v *DPP*' (1995) 146 NLJ 1223) argues that the effect of *R* v *P* is to erode the protection afforded to the accused by *DPP* v *Boardman* [1975] AC 421 in all cases, including those in which identity is an issue.

Similar fact evidence is often an important part of the prosecution case because of the support provided to what may otherwise be an evidentially weak case. It is clear from the cases that relevant evidence should be admitted. Relevance can be demonstrated through a process of deductive reasoning; the concepts of probative value and prejudicial effect are not susceptible to such a process, and in the absence of guidelines governing the admissibility of similar fact evidence, it is often impossible to predict whether the trial judge will admit such evidence. If the trial judge has correctly addressed his mind to the considerations of probative force and prejudicial effect, the Court of Appeal is unlikely to interfere with the judge's decision as to whether the evidence is admissible.

QUESTION THREE

L is charged with the murder of her elderly aunt, M. M was found dead at her home having died of asphyxia from a plastic bag which had been placed over her head. L, who visited M regularly, says that M had been ill and depressed for a long time and had expressed suicidal thoughts. She says that it is very likely that M had committed suicide. L's elderly father, N, whom L had been looking after for some time before, had died a year ago in similar circumstances. Further, L subscribes to an organisation, known at the 'The Dying Light', whose members advocate the legalisation of euthanasia, and L is found to have in her possession a book published by 'The Dying Light' in which various methods of carrying out euthanasia are described, including causing death by placing plastic bags over peoples' heads. In this book, passages relating to this method of killing are underlined in red ink. Further, O, who works in the same office as L, says that when O's mother had been suffering from a terminal illness three years ago, L had urged her to 'give her an overdose and end her suffering'.

Advise L.

University of London LLB Examination
(for External Students) Law of Evidence June 1994 Q7

General Comment

This is a question in which the issues are fairly easy to isolate.

A brief explanation of the basis of admissibility of similar fact evidence is useful, but since this is a problem question, such discussion should be kept fairly short. Each item of evidence can be subjected to the same basic test of 'probative value' but a sound knowledge of the relevant case law is required to fully explain the side issues which arise – without this, any answer to this question would be rather too short!

Skeleton Solution

Isolate issues: evidence of father's death; book; O's evidence – brief explanation of basis of similar fact evidence admissibility: probative value (*R v P*); applicable in any case (no 'categories of relevance') – father's death: probative value/striking similarity; nature of defence raised; does the absence of charge/conviction re father's death lead to bar to admissibility of similar fact evidence? *Noor Mohamed* v *R* – book: probative value;

'incriminating article': *Thompson* – O's evidence: hearsay or original evidence; probative value; circumstances surrounding offence as opposed to actual commission of the offence.

Suggested Solution

The issues raised in this question involve the topic of similar fact evidence, that is to say, evidence of other 'similar' acts, admissible to prove the guilt of the defendant.

There are three items of evidence which should be discussed:

a) evidence of the death of N (L's father) in 'similar' circumstances, whilst in L's care;

b) evidence of L's membership of 'The Dying Light', a pro-euthanasia organisation, and in particular the book found in her possession, with underlined passages;

c) O's evidence of the advice given to her by L (suggesting the 'mercy killing' of O's mother).

Before considering each of these issues, it is useful to consider the basis for the admissibility of similar fact evidence. In exceptional circumstances, the defendant's guilt may be proved by adducing evidence of disposition. Such evidence is termed 'similar fact evidence'.

It must be stressed that such evidence is only admissible in exceptional circumstances. The reason for this severely restricted admissibility is that whilst evidence of disposition is clearly relevant, juries may often attach greater weight to similar fact evidence than it perhaps deserves. Hence, more often than not, probative value is exceeded by prejudicial effect.

However, when evidence is 'so very relevant that to exclude it would be an affront to common sense', then it may be admitted: per Lord Cross in *DPP* v *Boardman* [1975] AC 421. This does make it clear that in order for similar fact evidence to be admissible it must be highly relevant – would it be an affront to common sense to exclude it?

The test of admissibility can therefore be defined simply – it is a test of probative value: *R* v *P* [1991] 2 AC 447. This 'probative value' can be supplied in many ways – it was thought that striking similarity was required but *R* v *P* has confirmed that this requirement is only necessary in cases involving identity, where evidence is given by another victim of the alleged offender. Nor is the principle of similar fact evidence only applicable in certain types of case. It is potentially admissible in any type of case, categories of relevance having been rejected: *Harris* v *DPP* [1952] AC 694.

It is now necessary to consider each of the items of evidence arising in this case, to determine whether any of them may be admissible as similar fact evidence.

a) *Evidence of the death of L's father (N) in similar circumstances whilst in L's care.*

As stated above, 'categories of relevance' have been abandoned, hence there is no limit to the type of case in which similar fact evidence may be admissible. That having been said, the nature of the defence raised (one of these so called 'categories of relevance') can nevertheless be of importance.

As explained above, the test for the admissibility of similar fact evidence is probative value: *R* v *P* [1991] 2 AC 447. This may, but need not, be provided by striking similarity. Striking similarity requires some 'unusual feature' – perhaps, for example, a Red Indian headdress worn during the commission of the offence: *DPP* v *Boardman* [1975] AC 421.

Can it be said that there is such striking similarity between M and N's death? It is certainly arguable, but plastic bags on heads are not quite in the 'Red Indian headdress' league of similarity!

In assessing the relevance (and hence the probative value) of an item of similar fact evidence, the defence raised becomes an important factor. In deciding whether evidence of other conduct is sufficiently relevant to an issue in the case it is necessary to take account of the defence, otherwise the issue may not be clear enough (Criminal Law Revision Committee 11th report (Cmnd 4991) para 81). Hence, similar fact evidence may be admissible to show the implausibility of a defence: *R* v *Anderson* [1988] 2 All ER 549. The fact that L has sought to explain M's death as suicide is thus of great importance in deciding the probative value of the similar fact evidence.

It will be observed that L has not been charged or convicted of any offence relating to N's death. This, however, is no bar to the admissibility of the similar fact evidence The evidence will be admissible even if the jury might not accept that the event ever occurred, so long as they might conclude as a possibility,that it occurred: *Harris* v *DPP* [1952] AC 694.

To conclude, in advising L with regard to the admissibility of this evidence the case of *Noor Mohamed* v *R* [1949] AC 182 is instructive. Factually, it is similar to L's case (evidence of a previous killing which could have been (but was not proved to be) caused by the defendant), this evidence was held to be inadmissible. In that case, Lord du Parcq said that evidence which is impressive merely because it shows a person to be more likely (from his character) to have committed the offence, being otherwise of no real substance, is inadmissible.

On this basis, it is submitted that evidence of N's death is likely to be insufficiently relevant, and hence more prejudicial than probative – the jury would almost certainly attach too great a weight to this evidence.

b) *The incriminating book found in L's possession (and L's membership of 'The Dying Light')*

Again, one must assess the probative value of this evidence.

As stated in *R* v *P*, striking similarity is not the only means of providing probative value. Here, there is evidence of L's possession of an incriminating article. Obviously there is no 'striking similarity' between possession of a book and the commission of the alleged murder, but the book may still be admissible under the similar fact doctrine. Articles which could have been used in the commission of the offence (but which are not proved to be) can still identify the accused as the offender: *Thompson* v *R* [1918] AC 221.

Again, the defence raised will be of importance in assessing the relevance (probative value) of the articles: *R* v *Reading* [1966] 1 WLR 836.

Clearly, if the evidence merely shows L's disposition (ie that she favours euthanasia) it will not be enough, but if it goes beyond this it may suffice: *R* v *Taylor* (1923) 17 Cr App R 109.

Here, the underlining of certain passages relating to a particular style of killing may take this evidence beyond merely showing disposition and hence, it is submitted, the book itself may be admissible. Mere evidence of her membership of the organisation is unlikely to go beyond simple disposition, and hence is less likely to be admissible.

c) *O's evidence*

First, this is clearly an out-of-court statement. Problems of hearsay, however, do not arise – the purpose of adducing this statement is not to prove the truth of its contents, but merely to show that the statement was made. It is, therefore, original evidence: *R* v *Chapman* [1969] 2 QB 436.

As similar fact evidence, is this evidence admissible? The test is that of probative value (*R* v *P* (1991) 93 Cr App R 267) and, as stated above, the defence raised remains an important factor in deciding admissibility. This evidence amounts to evidence of L counselling or procuring an offence. (However, even if the similar fact evidence does not disclose the commission of an offence, it may still be admissible if the similar facts are inexplicable on the basis of coincidence and are of probative value: *R* v *Rodley* [1913] 3 KB 468.) Further, it need not be merely the actual commission of the offence which is similar. Similar fact evidence can be admissible if the circumstances surrounding the offences are similar: *R* v *Barrington* [1981] 1 WLR 419.

According to O, L merely suggested the killing; further, the method suggested is different. Whilst, potentially, it may be argued that these amount to 'surrounding circumstances' within *Barrington*, it is submitted that O's evidence would lack the necessary probative value, and does not go significantly beyond mere evidence of disposition.

In conclusion, of the items of evidence available, it is submitted that only the book may bear sufficient probative value to go beyond mere evidence of disposition. It is arguably an 'affront to common sense' to exclude this, given the underlined passages and the nature of the defence raised.

QUESTION FOUR

'The job of court and jury is to see whether the suspect has committed the particular offence.' (Llewellyn)

Have recent developments in relation to similar fact evidence made this objective more likely to be achieved?

University of London LLB Examination
(for External Students) Law of Evidence June 1996 Q4

General Comment

It is necessary here to analyse the recent Court of Appeal and House of Lords cases to see whether the general change of emphasis in similar fact evidence cases, particularly sexual assaults, away from questions of admissibility and more towards weight of evidence, has made sustainable and safe convictions more likely or less so. An important consideration is the effect upon the judges' power to hold a voir dire and to give adequate and understandable directions to the jury.

Skeleton Solution

Recent cases and their implications; striking similarity; collusion and distortion – independence of evidence – judges' power to admit or to exclude evidence – considerations that might alter the balance between prosecution and defence – other changes in the law of evidence bearing upon the matter – conclusion.

Suggested Solution

Some of the most recent developments in the areas of similar fact evidence have been concerned with the area of sexual offences against multiple victims, usually children, where the question of cross-admissibility of their evidence under the similar fact evidence rationale has been in issue. *R* v *P* (1991) 93 Cr App R 267 started the ball rolling with the view of the House of Lords that 'striking similarity' of evidence was not an indispensable precondition for admissibility except where identity is in issue, and that probative force was what should be looked for in such cases. This decision has considerable implications for a general widening of admissibility but, by itself, might not have had too radical an effect. The obvious problem for a judge moves from the relatively straightforward matter of a voir dire argument about admissibility to the truly formidable task of directing the jury as to the true relationship and significance of the different witnesses' evidence. It is certainly not clear that this will achieve the objective set out in Llewellyn's proposition, and it may well do the opposite. A consequence that follows this wider admissibility, as surely as night follows day, is that of the possibility for accidental or deliberate collusion between witnesses in this type of case. The real point in issue here is whether the question is one of admissibility, or whether it is one of weight and so for the jury. The point is far from easy and has given the Court of Appeal considerable food for thought in cases such as *R* v *Ananthanarayanan* (1994) 98 Cr App R 1, *R* v *Ryder* [1994] 2 All ER 859, *R* v *W* [1994] 2 All ER 872 and, most recently, both the Court of Appeal and the House of Lords considered the matter in *R* v *H* [1995] 2 AC 596. In the earlier cases, the view of the Court of Appeal was, generally, that the matter was one for the judge on a question of admissibility. There was an abrupt (and not very well explained) change of tack in *R* v *H* [1995] 2 AC 596 by the Court of Appeal, to the view that the question of collusion went to probative value and was for the jury to decide rather than the judge on admissibility. The House of Lords confirmed this view by a majority decision and the thrust of the Lord Chancellor's judgment seems to be that collusion is, generally, not a matter to be considered at the stage of deciding admissibility, apart from the most exceptional cases.

This judgment has enormous implications for the judge and jury alike. If a judge believes himself bound to admit evidence in the face of quite strong evidence of possible collusion or accidental contamination, as can easily have occurred in familial situations, his difficulties in directing the jury as to the appropriate weight to attach to evidence are likely to become insuperable. The jury is likely to ask itself why the judge admitted the evidence at all, or might jump to the opposite conclusion and disregard the collusion point altogether. It is hard to escape the conclusion that a jury will find itself in very great difficulties in such cases and take the safe course of acquittal.

It may well be that one result of *R* v *H* is that more prosecutions are commenced and, paradoxically, a greater number of acquittals or successful appeals result. The point that seems to have come out of the case is that the 'independent' quality of similar fact evidence that has figured so prominently in its development seems to have been relegated to an altogether lower scale of importance. There is certainly an impression to be gained from the judgment that other recent changes in the law of evidence, such as the abrogation of formal corroboration warnings, have also been seen to abrogate the need for support between those witnesses who were formerly subject to such warnings. It is submitted that this may well have caused a significant departure from guiding principles developed over a long period and in a much wider context than multiple juvenile sexual complaint cases, which will be likely to require the House of Lords to revisit this area in the not too distant future. A possible basis for a further House of Lords appeal might be the distinction, picked up by Lord Mustill in *R* v *H*, of the difference in thinking and approach between those cases where collusion of a deliberate type might have occurred and those altogether different situations where accidental contamination or a particular pattern of questions has occurred. Another possible side effect of the cases since *R* v *P* (1991) 93 Cr App R 267 is some resurgence of the 'special' treatment of certain types of sexual offence so condemned in *DPP* v *Boardman* [1975] AC 421.

QUESTION FIVE

To what extent have recent similar fact cases clarified the law?

> University of London LLB Examination
> (for External Students) Law of Evidence June 1997 Q3

General Comment

Few areas of common law have seen such diversity of views among the higher appellate judges as the development of the similar fact evidence doctrine. The recent judgments in the House of Lords have achieved a clarity of sorts, but they may, paradoxically, have created greater difficulties for those least able to cope with the complexities involved: the jurors. There should be some limited exposition of the pre and post *DPP* v *Boardman* [1975] AC 421 law, a review of the important House of Lords decisions since *R* v *P* (1991) 93 Cr App R 267, and some attempt at a firm conclusion about clarification one way or the other (either view is quite supportable).

Skeleton Solution

Development of the similar fact evidence doctrine: *Makin*; *Boardman*; application of *Boardman* – *R* v *P*: significance of the judgment – *R* v *H*: significance of the judgment – other cases since *R* v *P* – cumulative effect of cases – conclusion.

Suggested Solution

Very few other areas of the law of evidence have exercised the minds of the appellate judges to the extent of cases concerning similar fact evidence. This type of evidence, inevitably highly prejudicial, is always seen as being in tension with the judicial discretion to exclude evidence, the prejudicial effect of which outweighs its probative value. The nature of such evidence is that, once admitted, it usually convicts. Such is the caution that courts have exercised with similar fact evidence that very lengthy judicial analysis has been given to it on a frequent basis over, at least, the last century or so. Similar fact evidence may be described as evidence indicating a disposition to act in a certain way on occasions other than the circumstance for which a person is being tried. Such evidence, normally inadmissible, as dangerously prejudicial but irrelevant, is admissible, by way of exception, where it has true relevance to the instant charge. The relevance can be shown in an infinite variety of ways, but relevance or probative value (which is the same thing) there must be, sufficient to outweigh prejudice.

The origins of the modern view can be seen in Lord Herschell's seminal speech in *Makin* v *Attorney-General for New South Wales* [1894] AC 57 which formulated the general rule of exclusion of similar fact evidence and went on to postulate a general exception allowing admissibility on the basis of relevance to the issues in the case. He, perhaps unfortunately, went on to give examples of such relevance, such as rebutting defences claimed or questions of accident. The tendency after *Makin* was to try to bring evidence within various categories of exception which, so it was argued, were expressly or impliedly admissible by Lord Herschell's speech. The problem was that the cases subsequent to *Makin* developed ever more technical distinctions, often based upon the defences relied upon or the explanations given by the accused as a rationale for admissibility. This rationale of relevance based upon defences fairly available, as distinct from defences actually relied upon, means that similar fact evidence can be led in evidence-in-chief by the prosecution: *Harris* v *DPP* [1952] AC 694.

The doctrine received a good deal of consideration and some very welcome clarification in *DPP* v *Boardman* [1975] AC 421. The main benefit of the judgments in *Boardman* is the general disavowal of a principle of admissibility based upon established categories of situation. The only real principle justifying admissibility of such dangerously prejudicial evidence is probative value; in *Boardman*'s case, arising from the 'striking similarity' of the different witness accounts. Such probative value may arise not from striking similarity at all, but from something as mundane as the unlikelihood of coincidence in the stories told by completely unconnected witnesses. The judges in *DPP v Boardman* [1975] AC 421 do seem to rely quite heavily on the inexplicability of such evidence on grounds of coincidence. The problem with *Boardman* is that it does tend to emphasise the 'striking similarity' or 'special feature' rationale and to obscure the fact that probative force can come from other directions. One of the difficulties that arose in cases over the next few years was the unwillingness to admit into evidence behaviour which was said to be 'no more than the stock-in trade' of certain types of offender (as in *R v Inder* (1977) 67 Cr App R 143 and *R v Novac* (1976) 65 Cr App R 107) and, indeed, in the Court of Appeal in *R v P* (1991) 93 Cr App R 267.

A considerable shift of emphasis could be seen when *R v P* was decided by the House of Lords. Dealing with the particular situation of the cross-admissibility of the evidence of the alleged two victims of incest, it being devoid of unusual features (beyond the incest itself), the House of Lords stated, as a general principle, that in cases where there was no issue as to identity of the offender, there was no requirement to look for special features or 'striking similarity'. This is quite a monumental change, and all that needs to be looked for is 'probative force'. This has been used to link offences of robbery in *R v Laidman; R v Agnew* [1992] Crim LR 428 without any special features at all, and seems to have been extended, with frightening effect, to the possession of quite small sums of money (£135) as evidence of drug dealing, along with a mobile phone and some plastic bags as evidence of the paraphernalia of drug dealing, in *R v Wilkinson; R v Fraser* (1997) Trans Ref: 9700349W2, 9700870W2, 7 August 1997, although the Court of Appeal indicated that to admit such a small cash sum into evidence was 'at the limit' of the judge's discretion.

A further considerable change of thinking came about as illustrated in *R v H* [1995] 2 AC 596, where the House of Lords departed from earlier views by holding that the similar fact evidence from two alleged victims of sexual offences where there was, at least, a risk of collusion, should be admitted on the assumption that the witnesses are truthful and the question of collusion be left to the jury as going to weight rather than admissibility. This is absolutely contrary to the earlier position which would generally have kept the evidence out because of the dangers of such evidence.

Other cases have shown a greater willingness to treat similar fact evidence as being something that juries can deal with in a relatively structured and analytical way. In *R v Christou* [1996] 2 All ER 927 the House of Lords confirmed that the question of severing the counts on sexual offences which are similar to each other, but where the evidence is not cross-admissible between the different offences, so as to ensure separate trials, is purely one for the discretion of the trial judge. If he decides not to sever, he must (simply!) ensure that the jury understand the position on the significance of the evidence on each count and keep the matters separate.

It seems as if the cumulative effect of *R* v *P* (1991) 93 Cr App R 267, *R* v *H* [1995] 2 AC 596 and *R* v *Christou* [1996] 2 All ER 927 is such that, in other than identification situations, most of the safeguards of the last 100 years or so have been jettisoned and the position for the person standing accused of the most mundane types of offence, possibly even in situations where witness collusion is a possibility, will be one of enormous difficulty in keeping out evidence having overwhelming potential for prejudice.

The conclusion to be drawn seems to be that either the earlier courts were right about the dangers of this evidence or the modern judges are right about its relative safety. Both cannot be right. It may be said that the effect of recent similar fact cases has clarified the law by distinguishing between cases where identification is in issue (where something akin to a 'signature' must be present to justify the admissibility) and non-identification cases where much less will suffice. It may also be said that leaving collusion to a jury may have simplified matters. Whether a jury in such a situation would find the law clearer is greatly to be doubted; time alone will tell.

Chapter 10
Privilege

10.1   Introduction

10.2   Key points

10.3   Key cases and statutes

10.4   Questions and suggested solutions

10.1 Introduction

As with public policy in Chapter 13, privilege is an area where relevant evidence is capable of admissibility but is excluded (or may be excluded) by some extrinsic rule which denies the court the benefit of that evidence. One bald distinction between public interest immunity and privilege is that in the case of the latter the person in whom the privilege vests may waive it and thus allow the court to hear the evidence, whereas in the case of the former the decision as to disclosure of the evidence is for the court, not the witness or party. Further, evidence which is privileged may nevertheless be put before the court in some circumstances in secondary as opposed to primary form, but if evidence is the subject of public interest immunity, then the immunity cannot be circumvented by adducing secondary evidence. In this area the law is continually developing, particularly in regard to journalistic, or media, privilege.

10.2 Key points

There are four main heads under which privilege falls to be considered, ie self-incrimination privilege; legal professional privilege; 'without prejudice' communications; and journalistic privilege. This fourth head highlights the blurring of the distinction between privilege and public policy which often occurs when there is a claim for non-disclosure of evidence. In all cases of privilege, however, what must be borne in mind is that although a witness is both competent and compellable, to testify does not mean to answer every question put – privilege may be claimed, and if claimed successfully no inferences may be drawn from the refusal to answer questions.

Self-incrimination privilege

Any witness may refuse to answer a question (in examination-in-chief or in cross-examination) if the answer would tend to expose him to a criminal charge, penalty or, in criminal proceedings only, a forfeiture. It is for the court to decide whether there is a likelihood of any such consequence: *British Steel Corporation* v *Granada Television Ltd* [1982] AC 1096. Self-incrimination includes incrimination of one's spouse, but whether it includes incrimination of one's employer, principal etc has not been decided: *Rio Tinto Zinc Corporation* v *Westinghouse Electric Corporation* [1978] AC 547. Without doubt an out of court admission by a servant etc is not capable of amounting at common law to an admission against the interest of the employer: *Burr* v *Ware RDC* [1939] 2 All ER 688, therefore it would seem to follow that until there is some statutory intervention a servant cannot claim a right not to answer a question tending to incriminate his employer, because such a question should not be put – but this reasoning cannot be employed to agents of principals, directors of companies etc.

If a witness is wrongly compelled to answer a question where the answer tends to expose him to criminal proceedings, then the answer is treated as an inadmissible confession. The privilege is not available to an accused in respect of the charge he faces, whether the question be put in cross-examination during the trial or on the voir dire – but the accused who testifies can refuse to answer questions where the answer would tend to expose him to other criminal proceedings. The privilege has been under some attack in civil actions, see Lord Templeman in *AT & T Istel* v *Tully* [1992] 3 All ER 523 at 530, and in *V* v *C* (2001) The Times 1 November the Court of Appeal held that the privilege did not give rise to a defence in civil proceedings, nor did it give rise to a right not to plead a defence in civil proceedings.

Legal professional privilege

This covers both communications between lawyer and client regarding legal advice, and communications between client and/or lawyer and other persons where the 'dominant purpose' is to seek advice, opinion etc preparatory to contemplated or pending legal proceedings. In *Ventouris* v *Mountain, The Italia Express* [1991] 3 All ER 472 the Court of Appeal held that legal professional privilege could not attach to original documents which did not come into existence for the purposes of the litigation, but were already in existence before litigation was contemplated or commenced.

Lawyer-client communications

These are privileged (the privilege is in the client, who may therefore waive it) whether or not proceedings are pending, provided the purpose was to obtain, or give legal advice. Other communications made between lawyer and client, although not specifically seeking or giving legal advice, are similarly protected from disclosure, given they are part of the ongoing relationship: *Balabel* v *Air India* [1988] 2 All ER 246. The lawyer need not be a solicitor or barrister, ie could be an unqualified employee, or in matters relating to conveyancing could be a licensed conveyancer: s33 Administration of Justice Act 1985.

The privilege does not attach to communications made to assist the client to commit crimes or to defraud, whether or not the lawyer is aware of the client's motive for seeking advice: *R* v *Cox and Railton* (1884) 14 QBD 153. But a distinction must be drawn between communications made to facilitate, or assist in, commission of crime or tort giving rise to the instant proceedings (no privilege) and those which relate to other wrongdoing even though relevant in the instant proceedings: *R* v *Crown Court at Snaresbrook, ex parte DPP* [1988] 1 All ER 315. Also, for the purpose of s10 of the Police and Criminal Evidence Act 1984, if items are held for the furtherance of some criminal purpose it is irrelevant whether the person holding the items is aware of the criminal purpose or not: *Francis & Francis* v *Central Criminal Court* [1988] 3 All ER 775. No privilege attaches, per *R* v *Cox and Railton* (1884) 14 QBD 153. The definition of 'furthering a criminal purpose' is restricted to some extent so that it does not extend to every unlawful scheme; for example, it does not apply to a conveyance carried out without consideration designed to defeat creditors – *Re Konigsberg* [1989] 3 All ER 289. In order to determine whether documents fall within s10(2) Police and Criminal Evidence Act 1984, the court has the power to inspect the documents – *R* v *Governor of Pentonville Prison, ex parte Osman* [1989] 3 All ER 701.

Legal professional privilege will not usually apply to communications, otherwise privileged, the production of which can assist in the defence of an accused person: *R* v *Barton* [1973] 1 WLR 115. But the court must consider the conflicting interests of respecting legal professional confidences and promoting the proper administration of justice: *R* v *Ataou* [1988] 2 All ER 321.

Where privilege attaches to a communication it attaches to the original only. If the communication falls into the hands of a third party who makes a copy, or if an oral communication is overheard, then a witness may give that secondary evidence of the communication: *Calcraft* v *Guest* [1898] 1 QB 759; *R* v *Tompkins* (1977) 67 Cr App R 181.

Where the party in whom the privilege vests is aware of the fact that the other party intends to adduce secondary evidence he may seek an injunction restraining the disclosure of the privileged information, and it is immaterial whether the other party obtained the material by some unfair means or fortuitously: *Ashburton (Lord)* v *Pape* [1913] 2 Ch 469; *Guinness Peat Properties* v *Fitzroy Robinson* [1987] 2 All ER 716. The case of *Webster* v *James Chapman* [1989] 3 All ER 939 said that where protection of confidential information was sought the court was required to exercise its discretion by balancing the legitimate interests of the plaintiff in seeking to keep the confidential information suppressed, and the legitimate interests of the defendant in seeking to make use of it. In carrying out that balancing exercise the circumstances in which the information came into the hands of the defendant, the issues in the action, the relevance of the document and whether the document would in one way or another have to be disclosed, were all highly relevant. In *Derby & Co Ltd* v *Weldon (No 8)* [1990] 3 All ER 762, the court held that where privileged documents came into the hands of the other side inadvertently, and the other side must have realised a mistake had been made, the court had the power to intervene and order the other side to return all copies of the privileged documents and to grant an injunction to stop them using the information contained in or derived from documents. An injunction is an equitable remedy and therefore discretionary; it has been held that where privileged documents were filched in the courtroom they could not be used: *ITC Film Distributors Ltd* v *Video Exchange Ltd* [1982] Ch 431. It has also been held that no injunction will be granted to restrain the prosecution from adducing secondary evidence of privileged communications which have inadvertently fallen into their possession: *Butler* v *Board of Trade* [1971] Ch 680.

The person in whom the privilege vests, ie the client, may waive the privilege; an express waiver results in the lawyer having to answer any questions put to him about the communications in question. Alternatively, the client may, when testifying, impliedly waive the privilege by giving evidence about the content of such communications. Similarly, where a plaintiff alleged a letter had been deliberately concealed from him by his former solicitors (M and O), he was held to have waived the legal professional privilege in respect of documents going to the issues in that case. The plaintiff K had brought proceedings against W, his solicitor subsequent to M and O, who in turn sought discovery of documents (papers and letters which had passed between the plaintiff and his former solicitors M and O in previous related proceedings) and pleaded limitation. Discovery of these documents was crucial to the limitation issue, as the plaintiff claimed that he was not aware, and could not with due diligence have been aware earlier of the letter giving rise to the current proceedings. By claiming that the letter in question had been deliberately concealed from him, the plaintiff had waived the privilege in respect of solicitor/client material relating to that issue: *Kershaw* v *Whelan* [1996] 1 WLR 358.

The client may also impliedly waive privilege by including a privileged document in the list exchanged between parties. If this has happened, the court should then conduct a balancing exercise to see whether or not the other side should be allowed to use this document (*Webster* v *James Chapman* [1989] 3 All ER 939); but, if the other side must have realised the mistake, the court should order the return of the document and grant an injunction to stop the use of the information (*Derby & Co Ltd* v *Weldon (No 8)* [1990] 3 All ER 762).

Communications with third parties

Similar principles apply to those applicable to lawyer-client communications. However, for privilege to attach, communications with third parties must have been made in contemplation of litigation, eg seeking expert's opinion. There may be several purposes to be served by lawyer or client communicating with a third party, but if the communication is to be privileged under this head, the dominant purpose must be preparation for anticipated litigation: *Waugh* v *British Railways Board* [1981] 1 QB 736; *Peach* v *Commissioner of Police for the Metropolis* [1986] 2 All ER 129.

In *Re L (A Minor) (Police Investigation: Privilege)* [1997] AC 16, the House of Lords held that litigation privilege is a component of the courts' adversarial procedure, and therefore has no application in proceedings under Part IV Children Act 1989, which are investigative and non-adversarial in nature. Accordingly, the House of Lords ordered disclosure to police of an expert report prepared for the mother.

Without prejudice communications

Because one of the major objectives of civil procedure is settlement without resort to litigation, parties to a prospective or potential civil suit, and their lawyers, must be able to negotiate and make offers of settlement or compromise without the fear of such communications being admitted in evidence against them – as admissions of liability – if the attempts at settlement fail and litigation ensues. To remove such fear of disclosure in court if negotiations break down, privilege attaches to such 'without prejudice' communications.

This privilege is in many respects more valuable than legal professional privilege:

a) it is a joint privilege of both the parties, and their lawyers;

b) waiver must be by both parties to be effective;

c) the communication cannot be proved by secondary evidence.

Communications do not necessarily have to be headed 'without prejudice' for the privilege to attach; conversely the phrase 'without prejudice' on a communication does not automatically vest privilege in it – ultimately any dispute as to privilege will be resolved by the court: *South Shropshire District Council* v *Amos* [1987] 1 All ER 340; *Buckinghamshire County Council* v *Moran* [1989] 3 WLR 152.

A privilege similar to that attaching to such 'without prejudice' communications attaches (by analogy) to communications made in the course of attempts at matrimonial reconciliation. These may be communications between the spouses, or communications between spouse and conciliator. The conciliator may be someone such as a marriage guidance counsellor, probation officer, priest, doctor or any other individual who is invited to assist in reconciliation: *Theodoropoulas* v *Theodoropoulas* [1964] P 311; *Mole* v *Mole* [1951] P 21 and see Lord Simon's statement regarding the public policy underlying this privilege in *D* v *NSPCC* [1978] AC 171 at p236.

Journalistic privilege

Sometimes dealt with as part of public interest immunity, but it may be waived by the journalist who decides to disclose his sources, therefore, although to some extent 'straddling' public policy and private privilege, it seems to be correctly placed in the latter area of non-disclosure.

A journalist may decline to answer questions which would result in disclosure of his source of information contained in a publication – but this privilege is not without restriction. There are conflicting interests, viz:

a) freedom of the press, and the public's right to know;

b) interests of administration of justice; prevention of crime;

c) efficient functioning of the press if sources are open to disclosure and therefore may dry up (drawing an analogy with police and their sources).

Section 10 Contempt of Court Act 1981 recognises that sources of information may be privileged, unless disclosure is necessary 'in the interests of justice or national security or for the prevention of disorder or crime'.

Where disclosure is sought, the burden of proving that it is necessary for one of the four specified reasons is on the party seeking such disclosure: *Secretary of State for Defence* v *Guardian Newspapers* [1984] 3 All ER 601. As regards the definition of 'necessary in the interests of justice', in the case of *X Ltd* v *Morgan Grampian Ltd* [1990] 2 WLR 1000 the House of Lords said it should not just mean administration of justice in legal proceedings. It should mean that persons should be enabled to exercise important legal rights and to protect themselves from serious legal wrongs whether or not court proceedings will be necessary to do this. In *Goodwin* v *UK* (1996) 22 EHRR 123, the European Court of Human Rights held that the order requiring the journalist to reveal his source of information and the fine imposed for his refusal to do so in *X Ltd* v *Morgan Grampian Ltd* breached the right of freedom of expression as contained in art 10 European Convention on Human Rights. The Court noted that such orders might be justified if necessity could be convincingly established but found it had not been in the instant case.

In *Camelot Group plc* v *Centaur Communications Ltd* [1999] QB 124 CA the facts were similar to those in the *Morgan Grampian Ltd* litigation. An order for the delivery up of documents was upheld where compliance would necessarily reveal the source. There was no threat of further disclosure of confidential information, since an injunction had been granted, but there was a continuing threat of damage in that there was unease and suspicion among the plaintiff's employees which inhibited good working relationships, and there was clearly a risk that an employee who had proved untrustworthy in one regard might be untrustworthy in a different respect and reveal other confidential information. The court said that in making its judgment a court should give great weight to any relevant judgment of the European Court of Human Rights. This decision is difficult to reconcile with that of the European Court in *Goodwin*.

As regards 'prevention of crime' as a reason for disclosure of the source of information, the party seeking disclosure does not need to specify any particular crime which will be prevented, but merely satisfy the court that disclosure is necessary to prevent criminal activity generally – which substantially erodes the privilege: *Re an Inquiry under the Company Securities (Insider Dealing) Act 1985* [1988] 1 All ER 203. However, there must be sufficient evidence to satisfy the court that disclosure is necessary for the prevention of crime: *X* v *Y* [1988] 2 All ER 648, otherwise, if the burden of proof is not discharged by the party seeking disclosure, the privilege of the journalist prevails.

10.3 Key cases and statutes

- *Calcraft* v *Guest* [1898] 1 QB 759

- *L (A Minor) (Police Investigation: Privilege), Re* [1996] AC 16

- *Waugh* v *British Railways Board* [1980] AC 521

- *X Ltd* v *Morgan Grampian Ltd* [1990] 2 WLR 1000

- Contempt of Court Act 1981, s10

- Police and Criminal Evidence Act 1984, s10

10.4 Questions and suggested solutions

QUESTION ONE

'Because the extent of rules of privilege is to deprive the tribunal of relevant evidence, powerful arguments are required to justify their existence.' (Cross)

What are the 'powerful arguments' which justify legal professional privilege and 'without prejudice' privilege? Are they convincing?

University of London LLB Examination
(for External Students) Law of Evidence June 1995 Q3

General Comment

It is necessary here to deal with the limits of each type of privilege, illustrating to what extent the privilege attaches and who has the privilege. This will show just what is denied to the tribunal, and to what extent this can be overcome in other ways. The answer should conclude by looking at the advantages to the parties and the legal system generally provided by the privileges.

Skeleton Solution

Legal professional privilege: describe its scope with emphasis on the narrowness of application, illegality exception, etc – describe ways of using overlapping evidence, secondary evidence, etc – give arguments justifying legal professional privilege, and extend these to without prejudice privilege – conclude by illustrating overwhelming advantages of having the privileges, protection of parties, preventing unnecessary and oppressive litigation.

Suggested Solution

Legal professional privilege may be described as that privilege against disclosure that the law provides to certain communications between client and lawyer, and between either of them and third parties. Communications between client and lawyer are privileged in so far as they concern the obtaining, giving and receiving of legal advice. Whether or not litigation is contemplated or proceeding, such communications are privileged against disclosure (*Wheeler* v *Le Marchant* (1881) 17 Ch D 675). This extends to oral, as well as written, communications and the essence of it is that the communication must be intended to be confidential so that no privilege attaches if the presence of others or the context indicates non-confidentiality.

The case law shows many unsuccesful attempts to raise privilege, often in quite unusual circumstances. In *Re Konigsberg* [1989] 3 All ER 289 an attempt was made by a wife to prevent disclosure of an affidavit made by a solicitor who formerly acted for wife and husband. The affidavit had been sworn for the purposes of the husband's trustee in bankruptcy, and privilege was refused because the trustee, effectively, stood in the husband's shoes as the owner of the privilege, jointly with the wife, joint clients not being entitled to maintain the privilege against each other or to waive the benefit of privilege for the other.

The other form of legal professional privilege concerns communications between a client or his lawyer and third parties in circumstances where the dominant purpose of the communication is pending or contemplated litigation (*Waugh v British Railways Board* [1980] AC 521). This dominant purpose requirement is fairly strictly observed and has defeated many claims of privilege, such as in *Waugh* itself and *Neilson v Laugharne* [1981] 1 QB 736, although in the latter case other privilege was available. Nevertheless, the privilege can extend to in-house communications as in *Waugh* and *Alfred Crompton Amusement Machines Ltd v Customs and Excise Commissioners (No 2)* [1974] AC 405. The whole point of the privilege is that it protects the privacy of the confidential and vulnerable parts of the client-lawyer communication, and other communications as necessary, in a litigation situation, such as *R v R* [1994] 4 All ER 260 where the evidence of an expert defence witness on DNA was held to be a proper subject for privilege. The privilege does not protect materials which did not come into existence for a privileged purpose as in *Harmony Shipping Co v Saudi Europe Line* [1979] 1 WLR 1380, where an original unprivileged document was supplied to a handwriting expert within the context of privileged correspon-dence by one party. He was allowed to give his opinion in examination by the other side; in effect there was an overlap between evidence that he could properly give and matters protected by his own client's privilege.

The privilege cannot be abused by a client knowingly entering into communication with his lawyer as part of a fraud or a design involving clear illegality (*R v Cox and Railton* (1884) 14 QBD 153). Copies of privileged documents which come into the possession of the other party without impropriety appear to be completely admissible as secondary evidence on the authority of *Calcraft v Guest* [1898] 1 QB 759, although it may be possible to injunct this before the admission (*Ashburton (Lord) v Pape* [1913] 2 Ch 469). The privilege is that of the client, and the obvious rationale of the privilege is to secure the candour about admissions and concessions that can only come about in confidential communication. If such matters were open to discovery they would undoubtedly lead to great difficulties in preparing cases and might well influence the judgment of the tribunal itself. This latter point is highlighted by 'without prejudice' correspondence and its growing use. Such correspondence, in which matters of negotiation or attempts to settle are discussed, is of the greatest value in preventing unnecessary litigation. The essence of the privilege is that, regardless of whether the correspondence is headed 'without prejudice' or not, provided that there is a clear understanding that this is an attempt to settle, the correspondence is not to be further used if it is unsuccessful in achieving settlement out of court. This clearly removes the constraints imposed by the possibility of the correspondence appearing before a court and of inferences being drawn. The maximum of flexibility has been introduced by the widespread acceptance and use of the Calderbank letter (*Calderbank* v *C* [1976] Fam 98), which expressly retains the right to refer to the correspondence on the limited question of costs. Such letters are a vital tool where payments into court are not appropriate or possible. They can be examined by the court to determine the question whether an agreement has actually been concluded (*Tomlin* v *Standard Telephone and Cables Ltd* [1969] 1 WLR 1378), the privilege having ended when the need for it ended. On balance, the range of relevant evidence denied to the courts by legal professional privilege that cannot be obtained by other means is surprisingly small. The relevant evidence that is kept from the courts by 'without prejudice' correspondence is considerable, but is often rendered unnecessary, along with the litigation of the question, by reason of the settlements reached. The arguments for both types of privilege are thoroughly convincing and justify the retention of both.

QUESTION TWO

'The law relating to privilege is in need of substantial reform.'

Discuss.

University of London LLB Examination
(for External Students) Law of Evidence June 1989 Q7

General Comment

This question is open to interpretation and it will be necessary to set the parameters of the answer in the opening paragraph. It will also be important to define terms.

Skeleton Solution

Private privilege generally, and distinctive nature of public interest immunity – exclusion of evidence under three main heads: self-incrimination privilege; legal professional privilege; 'without prejudice' communications – arguments for reform of the law.

Suggested Solution

For evidence to be admissible it must firstly be legally relevant to the issue before the court and, given that high degree of relevance, it must not infringe any of the exclusionary rules which, for varying reasons, forbid the admission of evidence or permit a party or witness to refuse to give evidence on some issue. Evidence which is relevant may be excluded by the laws of Evidence where public policy so dictates – ie the concept of 'public interest immunity' – or, alternatively, a party or a witness may be permitted to claim a privilege whereby he is not compelled to give evidence despite its relevance and reliability because there are recognised extrinsic factors which outweigh the public interest in the court's being apprised of all relevant facts in order to reach the proper conclusion.

The basic difference between 'public interest immunity' and 'privilege' is that in the case of the former the courts decide as a matter of law (and policy) whether the evidence, albeit relevant, must be excluded, in the case of the latter the party or witness may claim the privilege (in which case the court will decide on the issue of exclusion) or may waive any potential privilege, thus relieving the court of the duty to deliberate and to adjudicate on disclosure.

The successful claiming of privilege means that the court must decide the issue before it without the benefit of all the relevant facts; this, however, is fairly commonplace in the adversarial or accusatorial system in English courts where a number of exclusionary rules deprive the court of the entirety of relevant material (the hearsay rule in criminal cases is a prime example).

One general, but important, point to bear in mind is that where a person whether witness or party claims privilege, no inferences adverse to that person can be drawn (*Wentworth* v *Lloyd* (1864) 10 HL Cas 589).

There are three main heads of privilege.

Self-incrimination privilege

This is based on the law's encouragement of witnesses to testify without fear of being forced to choose between incriminating themselves and committing perjury and, more importantly perhaps, on the unwillingness of the law to force any person (whether a witness or a party in civil or criminal proceedings) to give evidence which will be self-incriminatory (*Blunt* v *Park Lane Hotel* [1942] 2 KB 253). It is for the judge to decide whether there is a real as opposed to fanciful risk of criminal proceedings if the question is answered by the witness (*R* v *Boyes* (1861) 30 LJQB 301). If the evidence against the witness is already so strong that proceedings will be taken whether or not the witness answers the question, then any claim of privilege will fail (*Rio Tinto Zinc Corporation* v *Westinghouse Electric Corporation* [1978] AC 547).

If a witness is wrongly denied the self-incrimination privilege and thus compelled to answer the question, his response, in any subsequent criminal proceedings against him, is on the same footing as an inadmissible confession and therefore cannot be used (*R* v *Garbett* (1847) 1 Den CC 236). This, however, is not a great safeguard since the response will be an admission of guilt of that crime. Therefore, although that response cannot be used in subsequent proceedings, it alerts the police to the fact that the witness committed that offence and a subsequent interview could well elicit an admissible confession which could be used without any reference to the earlier proceedings or the denial of the self-incrimination privilege. Apart from that weakness, value judgments must be made when the privilege is claimed, ie is there a real likelihood of subsequent criminal proceedings? Are those proceedings, should they be instituted, for an offence the triviality of which is outweighed by the need to have the relevant evidence put before the court in the instant case? Given the wide margin for error by the judge, either the repugnance of enforced self-incrimination or the proper administration of justice by the admission of relevant evidence should be the one determinant. Additionally there is alarming uncertainty as to whether the privilege can be claimed by directors, agents or employees of a corporate body on behalf of the corporate body (*Rio Tinto Zinc Corporation* v *Westinghouse Electric Corporation* [1978] AC 547).

Finally, the privilege can be claimed in respect of the witness' spouse, but perhaps incongruously in 1989, not in respect of a co-habitant or 'common law' spouse.

Legal professional privilege

This privilege covers two sorts of communications: (a) communications between client and legal adviser for the purpose of obtaining or giving legal advice; and (b) those between client or lawyer and third parties (eg experts) where the dominant purpose is preparing for contemplated or imminent legal proceedings. The rationale of this privilege is said to be that the lawyer-client relationship would be unworkable if communications were liable to compulsory disclosure by the courts (*Waugh* v *British Railways Board* [1980] AC 521).

As regards lawyer-client communications under (a) above they are privileged from disclosure even though there was no prospect of litigation, provided the purpose was requesting or giving legal advice. Provided there was no question of the advice being sought or given to facilitate fraud (*R* v *Cox and Railton* (1884) 14 QBD 153 but see *R* v *Crown Court at Snaresbrook, ex parte DPP* [1988] 1 All ER 315), the communication will not be disclosed in court unless the client waives the privilege. But the privilege will be overriden by the public interest in avoiding the conviction of an innocent accused person. In *R* v *Barton* [1973] 1 WLR 115 it was held that no privilege attached to lawyer-client communications where their production in court could help the defence of an accused person. Obviously there is in this situation a degree of conjecture on the part of the judge in resolving the conflict between legal professional privilege and public policy regarding the administration of justice. The problem of resolution of these conflicting interests is highlighted in the case of *R* v *Ataou* [1988] QB 798 (where the judge did not even avert his mind to the competing interest!).

As distinct from matters of public interest immunity or 'without prejudice' communications, when legal professional privilege attaches to original documents or conversations, then these communications may be proved by secondary evidence (*Calcraft* v *Guest* [1898] 1 QB 759). Therefore, overheard privileged conversations, duplicates of privileged documents etc may be admitted in court whether this secondary evidence has been obtained fortuitously or by some wrongful act. Where the possession of the secondary evidence becomes known to the party in whom the privilege vests, then an injunction may be obtained to prevent its disclosure, but an injunction is discretionary (*Ashburton (Lord)* v *Pape* [1913] 2 Ch 469; *Calcraft* v *Guest*) and whatever the circumstances is not retroactive (*ITC Film Distributors Ltd* v *Video Exchange*

Ltd [1982] Ch 431). The case of *Derby & Co Ltd* v *Weldon (No 8)* [1990] 3 All ER 762 suggests that where a privileged document falls into the hands of the other side by mistake, and that side must have realised the mistake, the court should exercise its discretion to prevent the information being used by that side.

An illogical distinction has been made between privileged documents stolen inside the court and those stolen elsewhere – secondary evidence of the former is not admissible; secondary evidence of the latter is admissible, subject to a speedy application for an injunction (*ITC Film Distributors Ltd* v *Video Exchange Ltd*).

A further illogicality is the distinction made in *Butler* v *Board of Trade* [1971] Ch 680 where it was held that in the case of a prosecution there can be no question of an injunction prohibiting the adducing of secondary evidence of privileged material. It was stated that public policy dictated that decision but it has since been quite strongly criticised (in *Goddard* v *Nationwide Building Society* [1986] 3 WLR 734).

Again, therefore, in the realm of legal professional privilege there abound incongruities and anomalies. Reform is long overdue to clarify the extent to which legal professional privilege attaches to primary and secondary communications in both civil and criminal proceedings. So much uncertainty and irreconcilability has been created by appellate court decisions that it may require the intervention of Parliament to clarify the law.

'Without prejudice' communications

Where attempts are being made by parties to settle their differences without litigation, then public policy dictates that there should be joint privilege attaching to such negotiations, ie they cannot be disclosed in subsequent litigation unless both parties agree (*La Roche* v *Armstrong* [1922] 1 KB 485; *Rush & Tompkins* v *GLC* [1988] 3 WLR 939). Unlike the illogicality in legal professional privilege, secondary evidence of the communication is not admissible because the rationale of the privilege is to encourage uninhibited negotiation, settlement, and avoidance of litigation.

The fact that the phrase 'without prejudice' is not specifically used is immaterial provided a genuine attempt was being made to settle a dispute (*Chocoladefabriken Lindt* v *The Nestlé Co Ltd* [1978] RPC 287). Conversely, merely heading a document or communication 'without privilege' does not ipso facto render it privileged; it is for the court to determine whether it amounted to a genuine attempt to resolve a dispute without resort to litigation (*South Shropshire District Council* v *Amos* [1987] 1 All ER 340).

In this area of attempted settlements which also covers genuine attempts at matrimonial reconciliation (see *D* v *NSPCC* [1978] AC 171) the content of communications may be protected from disclosure, for sound reasons of public policy in civil law where one of the major objectives is the settlement of disputes without recourse to litigation. In this area also there is less need for reform of the law than in the other two areas of privilege discussed.

QUESTION THREE

'The rationale of legal professional privilege is inseparable from the adversarial system of litigation which would become unworkable if no document could ever be kept from an opponent.' (Cross)

Discuss.

University of London LLB Examination
(for External Students) Law of Evidence June 1994 Q2

General Comment

Legal professional privilege is a fairly discrete topic. However, to answer this question fully, it is obvious that the student requires knowledge of the adversarial/inquisitorial systems (although no great detail is needed!). Again, knowledge of possible alternative means of preventing disclosure (public interest immunity?) will be useful. Above all, the importance of the privilege within the context of the adversarial system, and generally, should be discussed.

Skeleton Solution

Brief explanation of adversarial (inquisitorial) system – brief explanation of the privilege (lawyer/client/third party) – the exceptions to the privilege – discussion: is the privilege still of importance, having considered the established exceptions?; are there other means of preventing disclosure; eg, public interest immunity?; are there other reasons for the importance of the privilege?

Suggested Solution

Clearly, it is in a party's interests to have all relevant facts which support his or her case before the court. However, in almost every case there will be a number of facts which may detract from a party's case, and which a party will therefore not wish to be disclosed. Legal professional privilege provides parties with a method of restricting the disclosure of communications of such facts.

As the quotation suggests, legal professional privilege (henceforward 'LPP') can be seen to be of greater importance in an adversarial system (where parties pit their evidence and arguments against each other), than in an inquisitorial system where the judge has the investigative role of sifting through the evidence. In the former system, the competitive atmosphere encourages parties to 'keep their cards close to their chest'.

Before considering whether the adversarial system would be unworkable without LPP it is useful to consider, in brief, what it entails. LPP acts to prevent disclosure of two types of communication:

a) communications between lawyer and client: as long as the communication is for the purposes of the giving or receiving of legal advice, it is covered (*Greenhough* v *Gaskell* (1833) 1 MY & K 98);

b) communications by either lawyer or client with third parties: such communications are privileged only if their dominant purpose is for use in anticipated or pending litigation (*Waugh* v *British Railways Board* [1980] AC 521).

Is the adversarial system unworkable without LPP? This question is usefully addressed by considering the exceptions to the privilege.

LPP covers communications not facts. Thus, instructions to and from a lawyer are covered. But if a pre-existing document is shown to a lawyer it can be argued that the contents of this document are not subject to privilege (*Brown* v *Foster* (1857) 1 H & N 738). Equally, evidence perceived by a lawyer about the client (eg his mental state) is not privileged since it is a fact not a communication (*Jones* v *Godrich* (1845) 5 Moo PCC 16).

The privilege is that of the client, not the lawyer; hence it may be waived by the client at any time (but not by the lawyer, who must assert it at all times). Once waived, the privilege is lost and cannot then be re-asserted by the client or the lawyer (*Lillicrap* v *Nalder & Sons* [1993] 1 All ER 724).

Legal advice sought to facilitate the commission of crime is *not* privileged (*R* v *Cox and Railton* (1884) 14 QBD 153). This applies whether or not the lawyer is aware of the purpose of the advice; however if the lawyer merely responds by warning the client that the conduct may lead to a prosecution, then the privilege remains intact (*Butler* v *Board of Trade* [1971] Ch 680).

Evidence to prove innocence is not privileged – this is because the privilege gives way to the public interest in the avoidance of conviction of the innocent. Thus, if documents help to further the defence of an accused, no privilege will attach to them (*R* v *Barton* [1973] 1 WLR 115).

Legal professional privilege permits certain parties to refuse to give evidence (ie client/lawyer/certain third parties). If documents fall into the hands of persons other than the above, these persons may produce (indeed may be compelled to produce) the documents (*Calcraft* v *Guest* (1898) 1 QB 759). This is true even if the documents are obtained by improper means (*R* v *Tompkins* (1977) 67 Cr App R 181) (although subject of course to other rules of Evidence). However, injunctions may be granted against a party holding secondary evidence of documents if they have not as yet been used in litigation (*Ashburton (Lord)* v *Pape* [1913] 2 Ch 469).

In civil actions, the court will order a party to serve on the other parties any witness statement of the oral evidence which the party serving the statement intends to rely on in relation to any issues of fact to be decided at the trial (CPR 32.4(2)). If a witness statement is not served in respect of an intended witness within the time specified by the court, then the witness may not be called to give oral evidence unless the court gives permission (CPR 32.10). This in effect removes the privilege in civil proceedings with regard to facts contained in communications, which the party wishes to adduce at trial via oral testimony.

Litigation privilege is a component of the courts' adversarial procedure, which has no application in proceedings under Part IV Children Act 1989, which are investigative and non-adversarial in nature: *Re L (A Minor) (Police Investigation: Privilege)* [1997] AC 16 HL (order for disclosure to police of expert report prepared for mother).

From the above, it is clear that exceptions to LPP do exist. However, and particularly in the criminal sphere, these exceptions cannot be said to be so far-reaching as to have emasculated LPP.

As long as general confidentiality remains unprotected by the law of public interest immunity (*D v NSPCC* [1978] AC 171), LPP remains of great importance in a legal system under which parties are posited as adversaries. However, it is submitted that the true importance of LPP is not confined to adversarial systems of litigation. It's real importance lies in the fact that it encourages parties to state facts within their knowledge to their legal representatives, with fullness and honesty, without fear of being compelled to disclose them at a later date (per Lord Wilberforce in *Waugh v British Railways Board* [1980] AC 521). Without this assurance, it is submitted, any system of litigation becomes unworkable.

QUESTION FOUR

Mrs Windfall is suing the Rest in Peace Hospital Company (RIPH) for negligently causing the death of her husband during an operation in which the drug Happydreams had been administered by Dr Corpsemaker, one of the hospital's doctors, to Mr Windfall. Consider the issues in the law of evidence relating to the following items of evidence.

a) A research paper by Dr Ironlegs, in which he warns of the danger of administering Happydreams where a patient's heart rate is above a particular level. The paper is published in the medical journal 'Bones and Skeletons'. Dr Ironlegs is unavailable to give evidence in the case.

b) Two computerised documents produced by advanced computers at St Lucifer's hospital and St Juda's hospital recording the effects of administering Happydreams to two patients during an operation. The computer had controlled the administration of the drug during each operation according to a programme fed into it by research scientists. In each case the computer recorded the amount of the drug fed into the patient and the resultant change in heart rate.

c) The record of a disciplinary enquiry against Dr Corpsemaker in which the hospital's Board had found him guilty of negligence. The report had been forwarded to RIPH's internal lawyers in the event that the hospital was sued or prosecuted, and the hospital have refused to give discovery of the document.

d) The conviction of Corpsemaker for recklessly causing death on a previous occasion at another hospital.

Adapted from University of London LLB Examination
(for External Students) Law of Evidence June 1987 Q6

General Comment

A range of issues arise in this question, suggesting that it will be difficult to answer unless the candidate has a good knowledge of evidence as a cohesive subject area. As always, issues should be addressed chronologically.

Skeleton Solution

a) Relevance of article – documentary hearsay – s1 Civil Evidence Act 1995 – notice procedure.

b) Legal professional privilege – dominant purpose test.

c) Relevance – similar fact evidence.

d) Relevance to vicarious liability of hospital.

Suggested Solution

It is not known on what basis the Rest in Peace Hospital is being sued in negligence. It is most likely that the claim depends upon proof of the negligence of Dr Corpsemaker, for which the hospital is vicariously liable, although part (d) indicates that there may be a claim that the hospital was primarily liable for employing Dr Corpsemaker at all.

a) *The research paper*

The research paper could be of relevance in one of two ways, either because Dr Corpsemaker did not read it and therefore acted negligently or because he did not act according to its advice. In either case it would be necessary to prove that what it said was correct. If it is alleged that Dr Corpsemaker was negligent in not reading it then the question arises whether that caused any damage because if, in fact, the article was nonsense and would properly have been ignored then his failure to read it would not have caused any damage. If, on the other hand, the allegation is that Dr Corpsemaker, although having read it, should have followed the advice of the article then the question arises whether he acted with due care by not checking Mr Windfall's blood pressure first.

In civil actions hearsay statements are made admissible by the Civil Evidence Act (CEA) 1995, subject to ss5 and 6(2) of the Act. Section 13 of the Act defines 'statement' as 'any representation of fact or opinion however made.' Accordingly, the fact that opinion evidence is presented as hearsay will not usually affect its admissibility. Notice should be served of the intention to rely on the article in accordance with CPR Part 33.2(1) which provides that a party intending to rely on hearsay evidence at trial complies with s2(1)(a) Civil Evidence Act 1995 by serving a notice on the other parties which:

i)   identifies the hearsay evidence;

ii) states that the party serving the notice proposes to rely on the hearsay evidence at trial;

iii) gives the reason why the witness will not be called.

Failure to give this notice would not affect the admissibility of the evidence (s1 CEA 1995) but would be a matter to which the court could have regard when considering the weight to be attached to the evidence (s4 CEA 1995).

To an extent the article may contain restatements of research of people other than Dr Ironlegs. If it did then statements in it about that other research would be inadmissible because Dr Ironlegs would not be able to give direct oral evidence of their truth (*The Ymnos* [1981] 1 Lloyd's Rep 550).

b) *The computer print-outs*

There is a question of the relevance of the evidence of what happened to two other patients. It is not necessarily the case that what happened to them would always happen to a patient to whom Happydreams is administered. In the absence of any further information on the matter it will be assumed that this evidence is relevant.

The statement upon which Mrs Windfall will wish to rely is the statement about the change in heart rate occurring after the administration of Happydreams. No hearsay point arises because the statement is not subject to oral evidence. It was prepared automatically as in the case *The Statute of Liberty* [1968] 1 WLR 739.

c) *The disciplinary report*

The hospital would be entitled to refuse to disclose the report if the dominant purpose of compiling it was for the furtherance of pending or contemplated litigation (*Waugh* v *British Railways Board* [1980] AC 521). It appears that this was not so, and that the dominant purpose was for disciplinary purposes within the hospital itself. A party cannot protect a report simply by passing it to his lawyers, it is the purpose for which it is compiled which counts for the purposes of privilege and not the purpose to which it is put after it is compiled (*Neilson* v *Laugharne* [1981] 1 QB 736; *Guinness Peat Properties* v *Fitzroy Robinson* [1987] 2 All ER 716; *Ventouris* v *Mountain, The Italia Express* [1991] 3 All ER 472).

d) *Dr Corpsemaker's conviction*

Unless the conviction of Dr Corpsemaker for causing death at the other hospital shows that he acted negligently on this occasion it would not be admissible. The admissibility of similar fact evidence in civil cases is more easily achieved than in criminal cases, but it is still necessary for it to be probative of the issue on which it is adduced (*Mood Music Publishing Co Ltd* v *De Wolfe Publishing Ltd* [1976] 1 All ER

463). As far as can be gathered from the information given, there is nothing about the conviction which proves negligence in relation to Mr Windfall.

Evidence of the conviction could be relevant not in relation to whether Dr Corpsemaker was negligent in treating Mr Windfall, but in relation to whether the hospital was negligent in employing Dr Corpsemaker in the first place. The liability of the hospital in such a claim would be primary not vicarious. In the absence of any information about the way in which Dr Corpsemaker killed the other patient it cannot be said whether the hospital was negligent in employing him to administer Happydreams to Mr Windfall.

QUESTION FIVE

Half-Life Radiation plc, is collaborating with the Chemistry department of Faustus University. Together they are developing methods of producing chemical and radiated rain clouds for use by the Ministry of Defence. Particularly under investigation is the possibility of irradiating water with the use of small pellets of uranium. Harold, a lecturer in philosophy, who is investigating the moral status of such work, receives a massive overdose of radiation when he finds a batch of these pellets which have been carelessly left unprotected. He brings a negligence action against Half-Life Radiation plc, but the defendants refuse to disclose a report made by a special committee consisting of members of the Law and Chemistry departments of Faustus University. This committee had been created by the university after there had been a radiation leakage some years earlier. The terms of the Committee were 'to investigate the causes of accidents at Faustus'. Harold persuades his sister, Irene, who works for Half-Life Radiation plc, to give him a computer file of this report for him, saying that he needs it for his research. This file is clearly marked 'Confidential'. Harold finds that it contains summaries of statements made by staff involved in the accident and the conclusions of the committee. Harold seeks to have this document admitted in evidence.

Advise Half-Life Radiation plc.

University of London LLB Examination
(for External Students) Law of Evidence June 1997 Q7

General Comment

The question requires an overview of the various types of privilege and immunity that can attach to sensitive communications and of how, and by whom, the protections can be invoked. The aspects of the report connected with hearsay and computer recording, as well as its opinion nature, should be dealt with. The use of secondary evidence should be discussed.

Skeleton Solution

Note the legal protections suggested by the question and the persons who could invoke them.

a) Legal professional privilege and the University/Half-Life Radiation plc.

b) The privilege against self-incrimination and the University/Half-Life Radiation plc.

c) Public interest immunity: Half-Life Radiation plc, the University, the Ministry of Defence and the court.

d) Confidentiality and Irene.

Secondary evidence: the rule in *Calcraft* v *Guest* [1898] 1 QB 759, injunction – the hearsay and opinion aspects of the evidence – Civil Evidence Act 1995, discovery and notice, computer evidence.

Suggested Solution

The evidence of the copy report raises several possibilities of privilege and immunity of such evidence which might give the opportunity to the various persons in the question to object to the use of the report in evidence and its consequent publication. It is assumed that Half-Life plc and the University are partners in joint enterprise.

a) *Half-Life Radiation plc/the University and legal professional privilege*

The fact that the special committee consists in part of lawyers suggests that providing a legal advice component might be a normal part of its remit despite the narrow nature of its terms of undertaking. Communications between lawyer and client for the purpose of giving and receiving legal advice are protected, in the hands of the lawyer and client, by legal professional privilege. This will extend to in-house lawyers: *Alfred Crompton Amusement Machines Ltd* v *Customs and Excise Commissioners (No 2)* [1974] AC 405. This would be likely to cover any views of the lawyers in the report. The privilege also extends to communications with third parties (such as the scientists on the committee) where the dominant purpose of the communication is actual or contemplated litigation: *Waugh* v *British Railways Board* [1980] AC 521. It is a question of fact whether this is the dominant purpose here but, even if it is not, the protected part of the report may well prevent disclosure of the whole unless some severance is properly available: *Re Sarah C Getty Trust* [1985] 2 All ER 809. Half-Life and the University could invoke this privilege for themselves and against the committee members; the question against others is discussed below.

b) *Half-Life Radiation plc/the University and the privilege against self-incrimination*

There is a long-established principle that no-one is bound to answer questions if, in the opinion of the judge, to do so would expose him to criminal charge or penalty: *Blunt* v *Park Lane Hotel* [1942] 2 KB 253. Although rather disapproved of in the civil context by the House of Lords in *AT & T Istel* v *Tully* [1992] 3 All ER 523, exposure to prosecution under the health and safety at work or nuclear radiation legislation would allow the University to argue against producing or answering questions about the report, but would probably not be enough to justify injunctions against its use. The other problem with this is that the University cannot refuse to answer problems which incriminate its staff and vice versa. The privilege is only against self-incrimination: *Tate Access Floors Inc* v *Boswell* [1990] 3 All ER 303.

c) *Public interest immunity: Half-Life Radiation plc, the University, the Ministry of Defence and the court*

There is a very wide range of matters where evidence may be withheld from disclosure on the basis that to do so would harm various public interests to an extent sufficient to outweigh the public interest in the administration of justice. Interests of national defence carry very great weight in this regard (*Duncan* v *Cammell Laird & Co Ltd* [1942] AC 624), but the courts, since the House of Lords judgments in *Conway* v *Rimmer* [1968] AC 910, have taken the view that very few documents are of such a class of importance as to be beyond, at least, scrutiny by the judges to see whether the claim to non-disclosure is justified on public interest grounds. It does seem to be the case that public interest immunity certificates signed by ministers of the Crown are fairly conclusive of the question where matters of national security are concerned: *Balfour* v *Foreign and Commonwealth Office* [1994] 2 All ER 588. This privilege could be invoked by any person in possession of the report and should be taken by the judge at his own instance if others fail to do so: *Duncan* v *Cammell Laird & Co Ltd.*

d) *Irene and the 'confidential' file*

Confidentiality is not by itself a sufficient ground to protect material against disclosure but it is still a very important matter. Section 10 Contempt of Court Act 1981 shows that national security is sufficient to outweigh confidentiality of sources. In our situation confidentiality, national security and public interest all go hand in hand to keep this report from disclosure at the instance of Irene or anyone else in the question. The one person who could not keep it from disclosure, if he wished to do so, would be Harold himself where disclosure was sought to identify the source of the leak: *Secretary of State for Defence* v *Guardian Newspapers* [1984] 3 All ER 601.

The mere fact that legal professional privilege covered the report would not prevent the use of secondary evidence in the hands of another (*Calcraft* v *Guest* [1898] 1 QB 759) but, as a general rule, injunctions and orders for delivering up of the file would usually be available to the owner of the privilege, the University: *Ashburton (Lord)* v *Pape* [1913] 2 Ch 469.

Even if there were no difficulties with privilege or immunity, questions might be raised about the hearsay rule and the opinion aspects of the report (assuming that there are opinions expressed). The fact that these are opinions of experts as distinct from laypersons would tend towards their admissibility about issues requiring the need for such expertise: *Folkes* v *Chadd & Ors* (1782) 3 Doug 157. The hearsay problem is removed, as a question of admissibility by s1(1) Civil Evidence Act (CEA) 1995, but the main problem is that compliance must be made with CPR Part 33 requiring the court to consider the question of disclosure, thus preventing any ambush by Harold.

The inevitable result of all of this is that all questions of the admissibility of the report and its privileged or immune status are likely to need resolution at an interlocutory stage. One question which has now been much simplified by s13 CEA 1995 is the assimilation of the treatment of computer-stored or computer-generated documents to that of any other documents compared to the earlier cumbersome treatment of computer documents by s5 Civil Evidence Act 1968. No special problems will attach to the report because of its computer-stored quality.

Chapter 11

Evidence Illegally or Unfairly Obtained

11.1   **Introduction**

11.2   **Key points**

11.3   **Key cases and statute**

11.4   **Questions and suggested solutions**

11.1 Introduction

If evidence has been obtained by some criminal or tortious or other unlawful act (eg in breach of contract) or by some unfair or improper means which is not in breach of the law (eg trickery, bribery), then at common law such evidence would usually be admissible if it was relevant to the facts in issue before the court.

11.2 Key points

The first question to be asked is whether the evidence is admissible as a matter of law; if that is answered in the affirmative, the question is then whether the judge ought, in his discretion, to exclude it.

Admissibility in law

The common law position prevails, ie 'It matters not how you get it; if you steal it even, it would be admissible in evidence' (per Crompton J in *R* v *Leatham* (1861) 8 Cox CC 498, 501). There are two exceptions to this.

a) If evidence consists of a confession which has been obtained in consequence of some inducement, or by oppression (s76 Police and Criminal Evidence Act (PACE) 1984).

b) If the evidence of one party is filched in court by the other party – as this would probably amount to a contempt of court (*ITC Film Distributors Ltd* v *Video Exchange Ltd* [1982] Ch 431).

Discretion to exclude

Civil cases

Since the Civil Procedure Rules (CPR) 1999 came into force in 1999, the civil courts have had the power to exclude evidence which could be relevant (see Civil Procedure Rules (CPR hereafter); CPR 32.1 and *Grobbelaar v Sun Newspapers Ltd* (1999) The Times 12 August).

Criminal cases

a) Common law discretion

In criminal cases there has been evidence of ambivalence by the courts in the exercise, and control, of discretion to exclude. The conflict is between admitting all relevant, admissible evidence to ensure that those who are guilty of crime are convicted, and the view that to admit such improperly obtained evidence condones and even encourages the improprieties of (usually) the police. This conflict was discussed at length in the House of Lords in *R v Sang* [1980] AC 402, but there was still a substantial amount of uncertainty. *R v Sang* was authority for the overriding discretion to exclude evidence which is more prejudicial than probative, but apart from that denied the existence of any exclusionary discretion (confessions apart) unless, apparently, the evidence was obtained by oppression, or improperly obtained from the suspect after the commission of the offence.

This uncertainty remained until an attempt was made by Parliament to clarify matters.

b) Statutory discretion

Section 78(1) Police and Criminal Evidence Act (PACE) 1984 provides:

> 'In any proceedings the court may refuse to allow evidence on which the prosecution proposes to rely to be given if it appears to the court that, having regard to all the circumstances, including the circumstances in which the evidence was obtained, the admission of the evidence would have such an adverse effect on the fairness of the proceedings that the court ought not to admit it.'

It has been held that s78 PACE 1984 applies to all evidence including evidence of identification (*R v Quinn* [1990] Crim LR 581) and confessions (*R v Mason* [1987] 3 All ER 481). The courts have been much more prepared to exercise their exclusionary discretion since s78 became operative in 1986, and have given due weight to breaches by the police of the Codes of Practice issued under s66 of the Act.

Although the discretion to exclude is being more widely exercised, it is not clear for what reason evidence is being excluded under s78 PACE 1984 – some cases imply that the rationale is that of discouraging police misconduct (eg *R v Mason*, above; *Matto v Crown Court at Wolverhampton* [1987] RTR 337; *R v Alladice* (1988) 87 Cr App R 380), others that it is protecting the civil rights of the suspect in police custody (eg *R v Samuel* [1988] 2 WLR 920; *R v Smurthwaite and Gill* (1994) 98 Cr App R 437). There is, however, some doubt whether s78 PACE 1984 affects the so-called defence of entrapment. In *R v Sang*, the House of Lords said entrapment is no defence, and that cannot be changed by any evidential discretion. But the case of *R v Gill and Ranuana* [1989] Crim LR 358 suggests otherwise.

If the exclusion is to discipline the police, then only where they wilfully abuse their powers should the discretion be exercised; if the exclusion is to protect the suspects' rights then the bona fides of the police are irrelevant. In the case of *R v Quinn* [1990] Crim LR 581, the cases of *R v Walsh* [1989] Crim LR 822 and *R v Keenan* [1989] 3 WLR 1193 were approved to suggest that where there is a significant and substantial breach of a Code of Practice, this could result in the exclusion of the evidence obtained, even in the absence of bad faith: also see *R v Okafor* [1994] 3 All ER 741 and *R v Christou* [1992] 4 All ER 559.

In *R v Chalkley and Jeffries* [1998] 2 All ER 155, the Court of Appeal said obiter that s78 PACE 1984 did not entitle a court to exclude evidence simply as a mark of disapproval of the way in which the evidence was obtained unless the admission of the evidence resulted in unfairness. Auld LJ, giving the judgment of the court, added that s78 PACE 1984 was not intended to widen the common law rule as enunciated in *R v Sang* [1980] AC 402, HL, in that, save in the case of admissions, confessions and evidence obtained from the accused after the commission of the offence, there is no discretion to exclude evidence unless its quality was or might have been affected by the way in which it was obtained. This is inconsistent with the comments made by Lord Taylor CJ in *R v Smurthwaite* (above). In *Mohammed (Allie) v The State* [1999] 2 AC 111, the Privy Council stated that a breach of a suspect's constitutional right was a cogent factor militating in favour of the exclusion of a confession and that it would generally not be right to admit a confession where the police had deliberately frustrated such a right. In *R v Shannon* [2001] 1 WLR 51 the Court of Appeal reiterated that, while there is no substantive defence of entrapment in English law, the fact that evidence has been obtained by entrapment is a relevant factor for the judge to take into account when considering his discretion under s78 PACE 1984. However, the Court also confirmed that the judge's main focus of attention had to be upon the procedural fairness of the proceedings, the nature and reliability of the prosecution evidence and the extent and fairness of the opportunity allowed to a defendant to deal with the evidence which the prosecution sought to adduce. The ultimate consideration was not whether the evidence had been obtained by entrapment, or even illegally, but whether the trial itself was fair. A key consideration for the judge was whether the defendant had been 'enticed' into committing an offence. Even if it was the case that the defendant was enticed, that was not in itself sufficient to require exclusion. The defence relied on the decision of the European Court of Human Rights (ECHR) in *Teixeira de Castro v Portugal* (1998) 28 EHRR 101 and argued that in cases of incitement or instigation by an agent provocateur, the court should not entertain a prosecution at all, regardless of the question of whether the trial as a whole can be a fair one in the procedural sense. The Court rejected that argument, commenting that *Teixeira* should not be read in that way. The full effect of the Human Rights Act 1998 remains to be seen, but Lord Woolf has commented that if the defendant cannot succeed by relying upon s78 PACE 1984, he would not be able to succeed by relying on the provisions of either art 6 (the right to a fair trial) or art 8 (*R v Sanghera* [2001] Crim LR 480).

In *R* v *Samuel* [1988] 2 WLR 920 CA Hodgson J said that, because of the infinite variety of circumstances, it was undesirable to attempt any general guidance as to how the judge's discretion under s78 PACE 1984 or his inherent powers should be exercised. However, in that case the Court unhesitatingly rejected a submission that the power under s78 PACE 1984 could not be exercised in the absence of impropriety, although the propriety or otherwise of the way in which the evidence was obtained is something to which the court is specifically enjoined to take into account. So it is clear that each case has to be decided on its own facts (see also *R* v *Parris* (1989) 89 Cr App R 68 at 72, CA and *R* v *Jelen and Katz* (1989) 90 Cr App R 456 CA. 'This is not an apt field for hard case law and well founded distinctions between cases': per Auld J in *Jelen and Katz*, at p465). In *R* v *Shannon*, the Court agreed that it would be difficult and undesirable to attempt to establish guidelines for the exercise of the judge's discretion under s78 PACE 1984 since the circumstances and situations in which any test may fall to be applied are multifarious: it is therefore important that the broad and unqualified discretion contained in s78 PACE 1984 should not be constrained or standardised.

c) Co-defendants

While it is clear that a judge in a criminal trial has a discretion to refuse to admit a piece of otherwise relevant and admissible evidence on which the prosecution intends to rely if he concludes that its prejudicial effect outweighs its probative value, *Lobban* v *R* [1995] 1 WLR 877 established that a judge has no discretion on that basis to exclude at the request of one co-defendant, in a joint trial, evidence tendered by another co-defendant, or to edit a co-defendant's statement on which the co-defendant wanted to rely. A defendant has an absolute right, subject to considerations of relevance, to present his case asserting his innocence as he thinks fit. The court recognised that in joint trials there is a real risk of prejudice to co-defendants where evidence is admitted which is admissible against one defendant but not against the others, and suggested that a possible remedy in such situations was for an application to be made for separate trials. If separate trials are not ordered then it is crucial that the trial judge gives the jury a direction in the terms given on this occasion.

In *R* v *Latif* [1996] 1 All ER 353 it was suggested that, as an alternative to excluding evidence under s78 PACE 1984, the court might stay proceedings as an abuse of process. Giving judgment in the House of Lords, Lord Steyn noted that 'The principles applicable to the court's jurisdiction to stay criminal proceedings, and the power to exclude evidence under s78 of the Police and Criminal Evidence Act 1984 in a case such as the present, are not the same. Nevertheless, there is a considerable overlap.' According to Lord Steyn, in deciding this question the judge must weigh in the balance the public interest in ensuring that those charged with grave crimes should be tried and the competing public interest in not conveying the impression that the court will adopt the approach that the end justifies any means. On the facts in *Latif* the House unanimously held that although a customs officer had acted illegally, the public interest did not require that the proceedings should be stayed. In *R v Chalkley and Jeffries* [1998] 2 All ER 155 the Court of Appeal noted that the determination of the fairness or otherwise of admitting evidence under s78 PACE 1984 was distinct from the exercise of discretion in determining whether to stay criminal proceedings as an abuse of process. The approach suggested in *Latif* was not followed in *R v Mullen* [1999] 2 Cr App R 143 in which the Court of Appeal preferred a rather broader approach to the exercise of the court's discretion on the question of abuse of process.

In *Attorney-General's Reference (No 3 of 2000): R v Looseley* [2001] 4 All ER 897, Lord Nicholls said that two remedies have developed as a response to entrapment. These remedies are: (i) exclusion of the evidence under s78 PACE 1984, (ii) ordering a stay of the proceedings. His Lordship went on to observe that these responses have developed despite the fact that entrapment is not a substantive defence. The two remedies are alternatives but His Lordship stated that a court should normally order a stay of proceedings rather than excluding the evidence under s78 PACE 1984. In many cases the practical effect of the two responses will be the same in that the prosecution will be unable to continue. However, Lord Nicholls took the view that a stay of the proceedings is the more appropriate remedy, since a prosecution founded on entrapment would be an abuse of the court's process to such an extent that the court would not allow the prosecutorial arm of the state to behave in that manner.

In making these observations, Lord Nicholls also pointed out that, although ordering a stay might have the effect of disciplining the police, that would not be the court's objective. The objective of the court would be the avoidance of an improper prosecution based on evidence obtained through entrapment.

d) Right to silence

The accused's right to silence was radically altered by the Criminal Justice and Public Order Act (CJPOA) 1994. Basically, s34 says that from the time the accused is under caution until he is charged, failure to answer a question which he reasonably could have been expected to answer is evidence from which a court may draw appropriate conclusions. Section 35 says the same, but the period relates to the court stage and the failure to give evidence there may lead to the court drawing appropriate conclusions. A *Practice Direction* has been given on the Crown Court satisfying itself that a defendant was aware of the opportunity to give evidence and the effect of his deciding not to do so: *Practice Direction (Crown Court: Evidence: Advice to Defendant)* [1995] 2 All ER 499. In the subsequent case of *R v Cowan* [1995] 4 All ER 939, the Court of Appeal highlighted five essential elements of a trial judge's direction to a jury under s35 CJPOA 1994. The trial judge must make it clear to the jury that:

i) the burden of proof remained on the prosecution throughout, and what that required standard was;

ii) the defendant was entitled to remain silent;

iii) an inference from a failure to give evidence could not on its own prove guilt;

iv) the jury had to be satisfied that the prosecution had established a case to answer before drawing any inferences from silence; and

v) if the jury concluded that the silence could only sensibly be attributed to the defendant having no answer, or none that would stand up to cross-examination, they could draw an adverse inference.

Lord Taylor CJ stressed that the right to silence had not been abolished, and that no one could be convicted solely because of their silence. It was also emphasised that s35 applied to all cases and was not (as contended by the defence) restricted to exceptional ones, and that the Court of Appeal would not lightly interfere with a trial judge's exercise of discretion in directing a jury on the issue, provided that the correct formula was followed.

11.3 Key cases and statute

* *Attorney-General's Reference (No 3 of 2000): R* v *Looseley* [2001] 4 All ER 897

* *Mohammed (Allie)* v *The State* [1999] 2 AC 111

* *R* v *Chalkley and Jeffries* [1998] 2 All ER 155

* *R* v *Sanghera* [2001] Crim LR 480

* *R* v *Shannon* [2001] 1 WLR 51

* Police and Criminal Evidence Act 1984

    * s76 – admissibility as a matter of law

    * s78 – creates a discretion to exclude evidence

11.4 Questions and suggested solutions

QUESTION ONE

Is it possible to generalise about the ways in which the courts have applied s78(1) of the Police and Criminal Evidence Act 1984?

University of London LLB Examination
(for External Students) Law of Evidence June 1999 Q1

General Comment

This is a fairly standard question on the application of s78(1) of the Police and Criminal Evidence Act (PACE) 1984. Candidates should avoid the tendency to 'write all they know' and should pay attention to the particular form which the question takes. What is required is the description of the general principles underlying and informing the application of this section.

Skeleton Solution

Relevance of evidence as a sufficient condition – *R* v *Leatham* – use of illegal means to obtain evidence – common law: *R* v *Sang* – statute: s78 PACE 1984 – importance of the circumstances in which the evidence was obtained: *R* v *Khan (Sultan)* – effect of breaches of the Codes of Practice: *R* v *Mason* – bad faith on the part of the police: *R* v *Alladice* – 'fairness of the proceedings' – impact on people other than the defendant: *R* v *Smurthwaite and Gill* – position of the Court of Appeal on guidelines for the application of s78: *R* v *Samuel*.

Suggested Solution

Where evidence has been obtained illegally there are two opposing views which may be taken. One view is that relevant evidence should be admitted, regardless of how it was obtained, since to do otherwise could result in the most cogent evidence being excluded with the result that a court might reach an unjust decision. The opposing view is informed by the concern that allowing the use of such evidence would encourage the use of illegal means to procure relevant evidence, and consequently is to the effect that illegally obtained evidence should not be admitted because of the way in which it has been obtained. The modern law of evidence has been described as a compromise between these two views (Keane, *The Modern Law of Evidence* (5th edn, 2000)). Generally speaking, the law reflects the first view in relation to admissibility, so that the famous dicta in *R* v *Leatham* (1861) 8 Cox CC 498 ('It matters not how you get it. If you steal it even, it would be admissible in evidence.') remains correct. However, this position on admissibility is tempered by an ability on the part of the judge to exclude evidence in the exercise of his discretion. This discretion exists both at common law (*R* v *Sang* [1980] AC 402) and under statute (s78 of the Police and Criminal Evidence Act (PACE) 1984) and the common law discretion is preserved by s82(3) of PACE 1984. At common law, the court is concerned not with the way in which the evidence was obtained, but with the way in which the prosecution propose to use the evidence at trial. Thus, a judge cannot refuse to admit relevant evidence because of the way in which it was obtained, except in the case of admissions, confessions and other evidence obtained from the accused after the commission of the offence (*R* v *Sang* [1980] AC 402). Under statute the court is also concerned with the fairness of the proceedings, so that the test to be applied is whether the admission of the evidence would have such an adverse effect on the fairness of the proceedings that the court ought not admit it (s78 PACE 1984). However, s78 expressly directs the attention of the judge to 'all the circumstances, including the circumstances in which the evidence was obtained', so that it is clear that a judge is entitled to take into account any illegality or impropriety attaching to the acquisition of the evidence when deciding whether to exercise the discretion to exclude.

Although illegality or impropriety is a relevant consideration when a judge is considering whether to exercise the discretion to exclude evidence under s78, the fact that evidence was obtained in such circumstances will not, of itself, result in the exclusion of the evidence. In *R v Khan (Sultan)* [1977] AC 558 the House of Lords held that the trial judge had not been wrong when he declined to exclude a tape recording which was the only evidence against the accused and which implicated him in the importation of heroin. The tape recording had been obtained by the police through the use of an electronic listening device, which had been attached to the outside of a house without the knowledge or consent of the owner. At trial, the prosecution conceded that this constituted a civil trespass, and that some damage had been caused to the property by the installation of the device. The police had failed to comply with the Interception of Communications Act 1985, although they had followed the relevant Home Office guidelines. The House of Lords held that, nevertheless, the evidence obtained as a result was admissible, and Lord Nolan emphasised that this remained the case where evidence was obtained improperly or even illegally. So it seems that the first general principle applying to the interpretation of s78 is that the courts will not use the section to exclude improperly or illegally obtained evidence merely because of the way in which it has been obtained.

Many of the cases which have reached the Court of Appeal concerning the use of the discretion under s78 concern breaches of Code C of PACE 1984 (which governs the treatment of detained persons) and also breaches of the provisions of PACE 1984 concerning the right of access to a solicitor (s58 PACE 1984). However, it is clear that the mere fact that one of these provisions has been breached will not alone determine the admissibility of evidence thereby obtained, and furthermore evidence may be excluded where there has been no breach of the relevant provisions. Thus, it can be said that the second general principle which emerges from the case law is that the courts will not use s78 to exclude evidence in order to discipline the police. The section requires that the discretion to exclude should be exercised where the admission of the evidence would have such an adverse effect on the fairness of the proceedings that it ought not to be admitted. So the focus of consideration is the effect of admitting the evidence, rather than the effect of excluding it. In *R v Mason* [1988] 1 WLR 139 the police deliberately misled the suspect (and his solicitor) regarding the strength of the evidence against the suspect, and consequently obtained a confession from the suspect. The Court of Appeal held that the judge had been wrong to refuse to exclude the confession under s78. However, Lord Justice Watkins emphasised that the evidence should have been excluded not in order to discipline the police, but in the interests of the defendant's right to a fair trial. Similarly, in *R v Chalkley and Jeffries* [1998] 2 All ER 155 Lord Justice Auld stressed that the critical test under s78 is whether any impropriety affects the fairness of the proceedings; the judge is not entitled to exclude evidence in order to demonstrate his disapproval of the way in which the evidence was obtained.

Another identifiable theme running through the case law concerns the effect of bad faith on the part of the police. In *R v Alladice* (1988) 87 Cr App R 380, for instance, the defendant was improperly refused access to a solicitor (a right guaranteed by s58 of

PACE 1984). The Court of Appeal held that the trial judge had not been wrong to refuse to exclude the evidence in that case, but that courts would have little difficulty in excluding evidence where there had been bad faith on the part of the police. However, the contrary does not follow, and good faith on the part of the police will not guarantee the admissibility of evidence.

The cases discussed so far have been considered from the perspective of fairness to the accused. However, the Court of Appeal has pointed out, on more than one occasion, that the phrase 'fairness of the proceedings' involves a consideration of fairness to the public, as well as fairness to the accused. In *R v Smurthwaite and Gill* (1994) 98 Cr App R 437 the defendant was convicted of soliciting to murder. The person solicited was an undercover police officer, and the defendant appealed against his conviction on the ground that the trial judge should have excluded the police officer's evidence. Lord Taylor CJ held that the fact that evidence has been obtained by entrapment, or by agent provocateur, or by the use of a trick, does not in itself require the judge to exclude it. The question for the judge to consider is whether, in all the circumstances, the obtaining of the evidence in one of those ways would have an adverse effect as described in s78. Lord Taylor went on to give a non-exhaustive list of relevant factors to be considered, which included whether or not the accused had been enticed into committing an offence which he would not otherwise have committed. In *R v Christou* [1996] 2 All ER 927 the accused were filmed disposing of stolen goods in a jewellery shop staffed by undercover officers. It was held that the trial judge had not been wrong to refuse to exclude the evidence obtained, as the defendants had not been enticed into committing offences which they would otherwise have not committed. Whereas the trick in *R v Mason* [1988] 1 WLR 139 resulted in unfairness, the trick in *R v Christou* [1996] 2 All ER 927 did not. As can be seen, it is not the case that every trick which results in evidence against the accused automatically causes unfairness, and the issue of good and bad faith referred to above will be relevant in this context.

In *R v Samuel* [1988] 2 WLR 920 the Court of Appeal held that the infinite variety of circumstances was such that it was undesirable to attempt any general guidance as to how the judge's discretion under s78, or his inherent powers, should be exercised. In *R v Parris* (1989) 89 Cr App R 68 at 72 the Lord Chief Justice reiterated that each case has to be determined on its own facts, and that a breach of PACE 1984 or one of the Codes will not necessarily result in the exclusion of evidence. Despite this judicial reluctance to establish guidelines for the exercise of the discretion, the case law establishes the general principles discussed above.

QUESTION TWO

Martin, a bank manager, is shot and killed during a robbery of the bank. Inspector Pecksniff arrests and cautions Tom after receiving information that Tom was involved in the robbery. At the police station, Pecksniff refuses Tom's request for a solicitor on the ground that granting the request immediately will lead to the alerting of Tom's accomplice. He then questions Tom for long periods over the next 24 hours. Eventually,

Tom agrees to make a statement. He admits that he and Gamp carried out the robbery but claims that the gun was carried by Gamp and that he, Tom, did not know it was loaded.

Pecksniff then goes to Gamp's flat. Because no-one answers the doorbell, he decides to break in. A search of the flat reveals money from the robbery and a gun bearing fingerprints later identified as Tom's. Gamp is arrested later that day. In an interview with Pecksniff, Gamp refuses to answer any questions about the robbery or the presence of the gun and money in his house. The defence have now discovered that Pecksniff's notebook records a statement by Gamp at the end of the interview in which he admits taking part in the robbery. Gamp has never been shown the notebook.

Advise Tom and Gamp.

University of London LLB Examination
(for External Students) Law of Evidence June 1995 Q5

General Comment

The question requires an overview of the law upon improperly obtained evidence and other evidence obtained as a consequence. It is necessary to look briefly at aspects of the Police and Criminal Evidence Act (PACE) 1984 and the Codes of Conduct and also at the Criminal Justice and Public Order Act (CJPOA) 1994, and to apply these to the many issues raised.

Skeleton Solution

Treatment of Tom on arrest – refusal of access to lawyer: prolonged questioning; breaches of Code C – Tom's statement: ss76 and 78 PACE 1984 – use of statement by police – methods employed at Gamp's flat – Gamp's off-the-record statement: Code C and verballing – Gamp's refusal to answer questions – evidence of accomplices.

Suggested Solution

Pecksniff, in arresting and taking Tom into custody, has moved the matter within the scope of the Police and Criminal Evidence Act (PACE) 1984 and Code C. Tom is refused a solicitor because Pecksniff believes that this will lead to an accomplice being alerted. Unless Tom has asked for a particular solicitor, whom Pecksniff has good reason to suspect as likely to do such a thing, there may be a breach of Code C6 and Annex B. Section 58 PACE 1984 provides for access to a solicitor, but s58(8) will give Pecksniff the right to delay access in the circumstances of a 'serious arrestable offence', which this is (s116).

In *R v Silcott; R v Braithwaite; R v Raghip* (1991) The Times 9 December the Court of Appeal held that, to deny access under s58(8), the officer must reasonably suspect that the particular solicitor, if allowed consultation, would thereafter commit a criminal offence – nothing less suffices because of the fundamental nature of the right. Tom is questioned for prolonged periods over 24 hours before agreeing to make a statement. It sounds as if there have been further breaches of the Codes during this period, and it can be said with some certainty that Tom's statement and confession will have to be considered in the light of ss76 and 78 PACE 1984. Tom may be able to rely upon both limbs of s76 to have his statement excluded: s76(2)(a) in respect of the oppression (*R v Beales* [1991] Crim LR 118); and s76(2)(b) in consequence of things said or done which would render any confession made by him unreliable. This would require the prosecution to prove, to the criminal standard, that the statement was not so obtained, a considerable problem here.

Tom should also be able to rely upon s78 for the court's discretion to exclude on the grounds of adverse effect upon the fairness of the proceedings caused by significant and substantial breaches of s58 and the Codes (*R v Alladice* [1988] Crim LR 608). Section 78 expressly requires consideration of the circumstances in which evidence is obtained, and most of the cases under s78 illustrate willingness to exclude statements obtained by serious breaches of the Codes.

Pecksniff then uses the information to go in search of Gamp. Section 76(4)(a) confirms the common law rule from *R v Warwickshall* (1783) 1 Leach 263 that the admissibility of evidence as a result of a confession is not affected by the inadmissibility of the confession, provided the the confession is not referred to in evidence (s76(5)). Pecksniff breaks in because no one is there to let him in. This matter is governed by s17 PACE 1984 and Code B and it does sound as if there may have been breaches of both, unless Pecksniff believes Gamp to have been on the premises so that he could claim to enter for the purpose of arrest (s17(2)(a)). It is hard to see what unfairness to the proceedings can follow from this because the same results would follow if the search was under warrant, this seems to be the effect of the judgment in *R v Wright* [1994] Crim LR 55 which concerned s18. The common law position on this was that the evidence would undoubtedly have been admissible (*Kuruma v R* [1955] AC 197, *Jeffery v Black* [1978] QB 490). There was no trickery practised as in *R v Mason* [1988] 1 WLR 139.

When Gamp is arrested and interviewed he refuses to answer questions, but according to Pecksniff made a confession at the end. Gamp has never seen the notebook. In *R v Scott* [1991] Crim LR 56 the Court of Appeal considered the admission of a note made in similar circumstances, which was not signed by the accused or put to him, and it was said that it was 'hard to conceive a clearer breach of Code C'. The philosophy behind the Code, of preventing 'verballing', will either exclude this statement or found an appeal, if admitted. As to Gamp's silence, either outside or inside court, since *R v Martinez-Tobon* [1994] 2 All ER 90 it seems that the judge will be positively required to direct the jury as to its significance – in effect not to attach excessive significance to it. The effect of ss35 and 168 Criminal Justice and Public Order Act (CJPOA) 1994 will allow prosecution comment and proper inferences to be drawn, particularly where some explanation would be a reasonable expectation. Section 34 applies this to the silence on interview.

Any evidence given by Tom or Gamp which implicates the other in the same offence will almost certainly require some sort of direction to the effect that the witness may have a purpose of his own to serve as in *R v Prater* [1960] 2 QB 464. The requirement for formal accomplice corroboration warnings has been abrogated by s32 CJPOA 1994, but care is needed as shown by *R v Cheema* [1994] 1 All ER 639. This may not be necessary with regard to the shooting incident if it is clear that one or the other, but not both, must have committed the offence (*R v Whitaker* (1977) 63 Cr App R 193).

QUESTION THREE

Several antique shops had been burgled within a ten mile radius of Marlborough. One day in January DC Pierrepoint visited Quentin, a man with a long record of burglaries, and asked him to come down to the police station to help the police with their inquiries. Quentin agreed. When they arrived, Pierrepoint left Quentin to wait for several hours in a room without light or heating. At the end of that time Quentin asked to see a solicitor. Pierrepoint agreed to find one. Ten minutes later he falsely told Quentin that none was available. He then said that he was ready to start asking questions. Quentin was an alcoholic and had by then been without a drink for so long that he was beginning to feel sick. He wanted to get the interview over as soon as possible and so agreed to do so without a solicitor. In the course of the interview he confessed to taking part in one of the burglaries but denied the rest. He told Pierrepoint that he would find the stolen property from the burglary in which he had taken part hidden under the floorboards of an empty house nearby. The police searched the house and the property was found where Quentin had said it would be.

Discuss the evidential issues arising.

University of London LLB Examination
(for External Students) Law of Evidence June 1996 Q7

General Comment

This question requires consideration of PACE 1984 and the Codes of Practice made thereunder, the effect of breaches of the Codes upon confessions and other evidence obtained in consequence and the discretions available to the court to exclude such evidence.

Skeleton Solution

Discussion of the circumstances of Quentin's presence at the police station – Quentin's treatment while at the station – cautions – access to legal advice – s76 PACE 1984 and the confession – s78 PACE 1984 – the stolen property and its value as evidence.

Suggested Solution

Quentin appears to have gone to the police station voluntarily and much will depend upon the way in which he was treated and the extent to which the Police and Criminal Evidence Act (PACE) 1984 Code C, for the detention, treatment and questioning of persons by the police, has been complied with. There is no mention of any caution being given to Quentin in accordance with ss10 and 16 of Code C. This should have been given, at the latest, when DC Pierrepoint said that he was ready to commence questioning, according to the guidelines in *R v Osbourne; R v Virtue* [1973] 1 QB 678. Assuming that Quentin had not been arrested, he should have been told at the time that he was cautioned that he was not under arrest or obliged to stay but that he could have free legal advice and the right to speak by telephone to a solicitor if he so wished: s3.15 Code C.

Leaving Quentin in a room in January without heat or light seems to indicate that Quentin was not told that he was free to leave, but insufficient information is available to know whether he had been induced by trickery to believe that he was being detained. However, Quentin has a long history of involvement with the police and is unlikely to have been mistaken as to his rights. If he was there voluntarily, the failure to provide for his comforts, while reprehensible and unsatisfactory, is not really a breach which might indicate behaviour calculated to sap the will of a person such as would constitute 'oppression' at common law, so as to trigger s76(2)(a) PACE 1984 or, indeed, the exclusionary discretions in ss78 or 82(3) PACE 1984.

DC Pierrepoint's lie concerning the non-availability of a solicitor would be a very serious breach of s58 PACE 1984 and s6 Code C if Quentin was under detention. The question seems to indicate that he was not detained but that the intention was to question him before he had access to legal advice and that this was achieved by trickery. Guidance Note C: 1A describes this as an absolute right to legal advice. If it can be shown that this trickery has been practiced in association with a manipulation of the circumstances surrounding Quentin's treatment which is designed to outflank the protection offered by the Codes, the court may very well take the view that the bad faith of the police affects the fairness of the proceedings as a whole, sufficient to trigger the exclusionary discretions under s78 PACE 1984 as in *R v Mason* [1987] 3 All ER 481 and *Matto v Crown Court at Wolverhampton* [1987] RTR 337.

The effect of Quentin's alcoholic condition on his willingness to make a confession might or might not have been known to DC Pierrepoint. If this condition was known to him, the holding of an interview at such a vulnerable time could well be within 'anything said or done' which could render any confession made by Quentin in those circumstances unreliable, so as to trigger s76(2)(b) PACE 1984. This would put the burden of proving that the confession was not unreliable upon the prosecution, but *R v Crampton* [1991] Crim LR 277 seems to show that DC Pierrepoint would have had to know of Quentin's condition to trigger this consequence. However, the physical and mental state of Quentin at the time is part of the 'circumstances existing at the time' and will be relevant to the matter: *R v McGovern* (1991) 92 Cr App R 228 and *R v Silcott; R v Braithwaite; R v Raghip* (1991) The Times 9 December. The confession to one burglary but denials of the rest, a 'mixed' statement, will not prevent this being a confession within s82(1) PACE 1984.

All things considered, it seems likely that there is a strong possibility that this confession will eventually be excluded, but because Quentin has enabled the police to find the stolen goods the question becomes one of what use, evidentually, the prosecution can make of this. The evidence of the finding of the stolen property at the empty house is certainly admissible by the effect of s76(4)(a) PACE 1984, reflecting the common law in *R v Warwickshall* (1783) 1 Leach 263, but the fact that it was discovered by means of an inadmissible statement by Quentin cannot be revealed to the court because ss76(5) and (6) prevent admissibility into evidence of that link: *Lam Chi-ming v R* [1991] 3 All ER 173.

QUESTION FOUR

Are there sufficient controls over the use of illegally obtained evidence other than confession evidence?

University of London LLB Examination
(for External Students) Law of Evidence June 1997 Q1

General Comment

The modern case law on the judicial discretion to exclude relevant criminal evidence tends to obscure the fact that a very large number of cases every year involve arguments about the exclusion of non-confession evidence such as bodily samples, real evidence and evidence of acts by an accused which, although short of a confession, is evidence capable of supporting the case against him. Some discussion of the scope of ss78, 76(4), (5) and 82(3) PACE 1984 and the common law discretion is called for.

Skeleton Solution

The main problems areas for non-confession evidence: bodily samples; unauthorised searches of persons or premises; evidence obtained by trickery or deception – control of the use of intimate samples – control of the use of real evidence obtained – control of the use of other evidence, including identifications – scope and relationship of the judicial discretions involved – conclusions.

Suggested Solution

The years since the enactment of PACE 1984 have seen a vast increase in the number and diversity of cases involving the judicial discretion to exclude relevant evidence in criminal trials. Because of the very wide meaning given to 'confession' by s82(1) PACE 1984 and the common law, the large preponderance of cases dealing with confessions tends to obscure the importance of providing proper judicial control of other types of evidence. No less serious than confession evidence for an accused is the adducing by the prosecution of evidence of intimate bodily samples, items of real evidence or evidence of other activities by the accused, not consisting in a confession, which was, in each case, improperly or illegally obtained.

The question of the evidential use of intimate bodily samples is governed by ss62 and 65 PACE 1984. The most important point is that such samples may only be taken from a person in police detention by consent: s62(1)(b) PACE 1984. Since the advent of DNA testing, the probative value of such evidence may be very high. This will naturally increase the pressure to obtain such samples by improper means where consent is withheld, although scientific advances may allow for much greater significance and specificity to be given to non-intimate samples which are more easily obtained and can, in the circumstances set out in s63 PACE 1984, be obtained without consent. The case of *R v Apicella* [1986] Crim LR 238 shows that the Court of Appeal were unwilling to equate an intimate sample, taken in custody and without consent, with an oral confession; they upheld the judge's decision not to exclude it.

The problem with a decision such as *Apicella* is that it raises a temptation to abuse the opportunities for medical or dental treatment of a detained person, which occur as a routine matter, to obtain a non-consensual sample. It would be simplicity itself to obtain blood or month impressions from an emergency dental treatment. Although *Apicella* may have achieved a just result, it is hoped that the courts will do more than pay lip-service to the requirement for consent, in that it is a vital constitutional safeguard for detainees. *R v Nathaniel* [1995] 2 Cr App R 565 showed a much more principled approach to ss62 and 64(3B) PACE 1984.

Many difficulties have arisen concerning evidence of substances or objects obtained as the result of unauthorised searches of premises or persons. There is clearly a tension involved here between the general admissibility of illegally obtained evidence, as explained by Crompton J in *R v Leatham* (1861) 8 Cox CC 498, and the protections given by Codes A and B of PACE 1984. The position of the accused is safeguarded only by the exclusionary discretions of the judge. The nature of these discretions is considered below but, if the test of 'fairness of the proceedings' (s78 PACE 1984) is applied, it really does appear as if even quite serious breaches of the Codes will be overlooked by the courts provided that the means of obtaining the evidence does not, in itself, throw doubts upon its cogency. This much can be seen from cases such as *Jeffrey v Black* [1978] QB 490 (a pre-PACE 1984 case), *R v Stewart; R v Schofield* [1995] 3 All ER 159 and *R v Wright* [1994] Crim LR 55. This seems to confirm the pre-PACE 1984 distinction set out in *R v Sang* [1980] AC 402 between evidence obtained from a suspect after detention and other evidence concerning the discretion to exclude. Since PACE 1984 there is a discretion concerning such evidence which was not there at all before, according to *Sang*, but its exercise is fairly exceptional. This discretion is probably a sufficient control bearing in mind that 'fairness' means even-handedness to both sides.

Certain other types of non-confession evidence cause problems occasionally, such as identifications obtained in breach of Code D of PACE 1984, or tricking suspects into entering the jurisdiction from outside, where it is easier to obtain evidence against them (as in *R v Latif* [1996] 1 All ER 353). Generally, this type of approach does not involve actual illegality by the police and the test of 'fairness of the proceedings' and the prejudice to the accused is a sensible yardstick to use; it seems reasonable to use a judicial exclusionary discretion where no illegality has been practised by the police. It can be argued that this should not be the case where the time-honoured recourse is had to the use of agents provocateurs to actually procure the commission of crime – but it is still English law that this will not provide a defence. It will be rare that the police will go so far into entrapment of persons as to become true agents provocateurs, in the sense used in *R v Sang* [1980] AC 402, but, as matters stand, evidence obtained by the police agents will continue to be admissible in law, subject only to the discretion to exclude according to *R v Smurthwaite and Gill* (1994) 98 Cr App R 437.

The principal judicial discretions in the above areas are the powers to exclude under ss78 and 82(3) PACE 1984 which retain the common law discretions. It seems that the current judicial view is that s78 PACE 1984 is at least as wide as the common law discretion as stated in *R v Sang* so, for present purposes, the paramount requirement is a fair balance between the two sides. Only time and the case law will determine whether this is a sufficiency of control in such a broad range of matters, but it seems that the courts are maintaining their consistent approach of general admissibility of evidence regardless of dubious methods of acquisition. This is allied to an exclusionary discretion of great width but which must be governed by balancing the interests of the parties. The House of Lords examined the scope of s78 PACE 1984, the common law discretion and art 8 of the European Convention and their interrelationship in *R v Khan (Sultan)* [1997] AC 558. Lord Nolan took the view that an apparent breach of art 8 may be relevant to the exercise of the discretion under s78 PACE 1984, but would not be determinative of the issue. The Court of Appeal has since held that the criteria contained in art 6 relating to the fairness of a trial were the same criteria that would be applied in considering an application to exclude evidence under s78 PACE 1984.

QUESTION FIVE

After a knife fight at a club, the police question everyone present. After this, and as a result, Ewan, Fred and George are arrested and charged with wounding with intent. During this initial questioning, Ewan makes a couple of admissions. The police search him at the police station, before his solicitor arrives, and they find that he has a number of pills. The police ask him what these are, and Ewan admits that they are 'a controlled drug'. Fred barely speaks English. The police hold him for nine hours while they obtain an interpreter. They then interview him and, in due course, he admits that he was involved in the fight. As a result of what Fred says, a bloody knife is found in a garden next door to the club. George is of very low intelligence, but the police are not aware of this, and George looks up to Ewan and Fred as his superiors. The police tell George that Ewan and Fred have admitted to being in the fight and, on hearing this, George admits that he himself took part and, further, played the major role. All three were offered access to a solicitor as soon as they reached the station, but only Ewan accepted the offer.

Discuss any evidential issues arising.

University of London LLB Examination
(for External Students) Law of Evidence June 1997 Q6

General Comment

Students attempting this type of question should be prepared to show some knowledge of Code C PACE 1984 and the problems attached to evidence obtained by the police directly from the accused. A detailed knowledge of confessions and ss76 and 78 PACE 1984 is called for, as well as a good answer structure showing the interrelationship of the various items of evidence but, at the same time, keeping the evidential points on each accused separate.

Skeleton Solution

Ewan

The admissions made under initial question – were cautions required? – the search, the pills and Ewan's answer.

Fred

The reason for his arrest – the delay and use of interpreter – his confession – the offer of legal advice – the evidential use of the knife: ss76(4) and (5) PACE 1984.

George

Sections 76 and 77 PACE 1984 – the means of obtaining the confession: s78 PACE 1984– the offer of access to legal advice – the interrelationship of the evidence.

Suggested Solution

Ewan

Ewan has made some admissions during initial questioning, presumably without caution. Generally a statement wholly or partly adverse to him will be within the Police and Criminal Evidence Act (PACE) 1984 definition of a confession (s82(1) PACE 1984) and be admissible against him subject to s76 PACE 1984. It sounds likely that 'initial questioning' would not imply oppression within s76(2)(a) PACE 1984, and there are no indications that the admissions were obtained in consequence of things 'said or done' tending towards unreliability of the statements: s76(2)(b) PACE 1984. As a matter of law, the confessions are likely to be admissible. A point that should be considered is whether, after a serious crime in a (perhaps small) club with, perhaps, few persons present, everyone present might be considered a suspect so that questioning only takes place under caution. Section 10.1 of Code C states that a person whom there are grounds to suspect of an offence must be cautioned before questioning if his answers are to be given in evidence. This is a basic and fundamentally important right of a suspect, and failure to give a caution at the appropriate time is a justification for the discretionary exclusion of the answers to police questions: *R* v *Hunt* [1992] Crim LR 582.

The police search Ewan after the arrest, find pills and obtain what might be a damaging admission. Ewan should have been cautioned under s10.3 Code C but, assuming that he was, this fresh turn of events may well constitute an 'interview' within s11.1A about a completely different offence and, again, a fresh caution should be given before questioning (s11.2A). Thus, as before, there may be a problem in using his answer against him. There is no requirement under Part 4 of Code C for the solicitor to be present during this search which seems to be authorised within s4.1. The only problem with using Ewan's answer about the drug against him may be the lack of proper cautioning and the s78 PACE 1984 discretion.

Fred

As Fred barely speaks English, it begs the question as to why he was arrested in the first place. What reasonable grounds of suspicion were there? Evidence in the form of a confession obtained as a result of wrongful arrest would be likely to fall within s76(2)(a) PACE 1984 as obtained by oppression and thus be inadmissible in law regardless of the truth of the confession. The offer of legal advice on arriving at the station would be of no use to Fred as he would be unlikely to have understood it. Unless the offer were repeated through an interpreter, Fred has been denied another of his most fundamental rights, that of legal advice, under s58 PACE 1984 and Part 6 of Code C. This confession is almost certain to fall foul of both limbs of s76(2) PACE 1984, as well as the discretion to exclude under s78 PACE 1984: *R* v *Samuel* [1988] 2 All ER 135.

The delay in obtaining an interpreter would not be significant, provided that his conditions of detention fell reasonably within Part 8 of Code C and the use of the interpreter seems to show the police attempting compliance with Part 13 of the Code. The real problem is that the confession by Fred is almost certain to be excluded as explained above. Nevertheless, his confession has led to the discovery of the knife. This knife has two evidential aspects. The first is that it may carry upon it traces of its user – blood, prints etc – or of its provenance, ie the evidence of someone who recalled selling this particular knife to someone. There would be no problems about this because the mere fact that it was found as the result of an inadmissible confession would not render it inadmissible as evidence: s76(4)(a) PACE 1984. The second aspect would be to show that it was found as the result of a confession by Fred, ie linking him to it. This is completely impermissible except by Fred's own evidence: s76(5) PACE 1984.

George

George has made a confession after hearing that the other two have confessed. There are several problems about this. The first is that if George is mentally handicapped, his understanding of the need for a solicitor would be defective. He would have needed to be interviewed in the presence of an 'independent person' or 'appropriate adult' and, if not, a special warning will have to be given to the jury under s77 PACE 1984: Annex C, Code C. The police handling of this matter is probably well within 'oppression' for the purposes of s76 PACE 1984. Even if not inadmissible by s76 PACE 1984, it is almost certain to fall foul of s78 PACE 1984: *R v Silcott* [1987] Crim LR 765.

The offer of access to legal advice to the three suspects at the arrival at the station would, effectively, only have been offered to Ewan. The other pair were simply, rather cynically, denied the right. This will, almost by itself, deny their evidence to the prosecution.

The interrelationship between the evidence is that the confessions, where admissible, are evidence only against their maker, not against the others: *Lobban* v *R* [1995] 1 WLR 877. The only applicable exception to that principle is if there is a common design or conspiracy involved in the offence(s). Here the confessions, if relating to acts in the furtherance of the conspiracy, are admissible against other members: *R v Blake and Tye* (1844) 6 QB 126. The knife, of course, may be evidence against any of them.

Chapter 12

Opinion Evidence

12.1   Introduction

12.2   Key points

12.3   Key cases and statutes

12.4   Questions and suggested solutions

12.1 Introduction

Opinion evidence is perhaps the most straightforward topic in the laws of evidence, in that there is not a great deal of complexity or incongruity in the principles involved. There have been relatively recent statutory changes in criminal proceedings which have made hearsay opinion evidence generally admissible. Judgments in previous proceedings are capable of being regarded as the opinion of that court, and therefore will be covered in this chapter.

12.2 Key points

General rule

General rule is that opinion evidence, whether given as direct testimony or hearsay, is inadmissible as proof of the belief held – subject to three exceptions.

General reputation

Where direct evidence is unavailable on some matter of public concern, that matter may be proved by evidence of general reputation, eg pedigree or marriage (decreasing in importance as public records are more available and their content admissible as an exception to the hearsay rule) identifying a reference to a person, eg that a defamatory statement was accepted by the public in general as referring to the plaintiff; proving character, whether good or bad; evidence of reputation in these instances is admissible in civil cases by virtue of s7 Civil Evidence Act 1995, thus obviating the need for the notice procedure under the rules issued under s2. One final example of general reputation is the public's opinion on some matter, such as information from a survey admissible in cases involving trademarks, passing off etc: *Sodastream* v *Thorn Cascade* [1982] RPC 459.

Expert opinion evidence

The court must be satisfied as to the competence of a witness to testify as an expert, whether by recognised qualification, and/or expertise gained by experience. Such a person's evidence is essential to assist the court not only to understand specialised facts but to form correct opinions and draw the correct inferences from those facts, or general facts. A medical orderly was held not to be an expert for the purposes of a prosecution against the defendant for assault occasioning actual bodily harm: *R* v *Inch* (1990) 91 Cr App R 51. A person who is competent as an expert witness is also compellable as such: *Harmony Shipping Co* v *Saudi Europe Line* [1979] 1 WLR 1380.

However, in *Brown* v *Bennett (Witness Summons)* (2000) The Times 2 November the court held that a litigant who had agreed to pay an expert witness should not be permitted to avoid paying the fee by issuing a witness summons. Only in exceptional circumstances should such a summons not be set aside.

The expert evidence may be subjected to cross-examination, including cross-examination going to credit, and may be contradicted by other, usually expert, evidence, but otherwise the expert is regarded as an independent witness whose opinion evidence has substantial probative value: *R* v *Lanfear* [1968] 2 QB 77.

Expert opinion evidence is not admissible on subject matter of which the lay opinion of the court is just as valid: *R* v *Turner* [1975] QB 834, and also the case of *R* v *Weightman* (1991) Cr App R 291, where the Court of Appeal held that a psychiatrist's evidence was inadmissible where the purpose was to tell a jury how a person who was not suffering from mental disorder might react to the stresses and strains of life. The area which has given rise to most forensic and academic discussion is that of a person's state of mind. In *R* v *Loughran* [1999] Crim LR 404 the defendant was convicted of rape and robbery. At the time of the offences, he had been suffering from a medical condition which his expert said might have made him anxious and insecure, and that this might have affected his dealings with women in the way he described in his evidence. It was not asserted that there was any organic or psychiatric link between the defendant's medical condition and his claimed inability to commit the crime at the relevant time. In those circumstances, the Court of Appeal held that the expert evidence was inadmissible, as it amounted to no more than an opinion on which, given the defendant's evidence of those matters, the jury were in as good a position as the expert to assess without the need for expert guidance. The conviction was, however, quashed on another ground. If the issue arises in relation to the reliability of the witness's evidence, then medical opinion evidence is admissible: *Toohey* v *MPC* [1965] AC 595. But if the issue is the state of mind of the accused at the time the offence was committed, then several cases highlight the difficulties the courts face. If there is no question of mental disorder, and the issue is purely the mens rea of the accused, then that is within the competence and experience of the court and therefore expert opinion evidence of a psychiatrist is not admissible because it is not necessary: *R* v *Chard* (1971) 56 Cr App R 268. However, where there is a question of mental disorder or similar conditions outside the usual experience of the court, then expert opinion evidence of psychiatrists is admissible because necessary, eg insanity, automatism, diminished responsibility. In *R v Smith* [1979] 1 WLR 1445, the opinion evidence of a psychiatrist was admitted to rebut a defence of automatism on a charge of murder; *R v Turner* [1975] QB 834. In the case of *R v Toner* (1991) 93 Cr App R 382 medical evidence was admitted which related to hypoglycaemia and its possible effect upon intent (mens rea). The court could see no difference between this and medical evidence admitted as to the effect of a drug on intent. If no such medical evidence is allowed, the court said, the jury would be deprived of assistance in a field where their ordinary experience did not enable them to judge for themselves. In *R v Rimmer & Beech* [1983] Crim LR 250, expert opinion evidence relating to mental state was inadmissible because in effect it was tendered to prove the veracity of the statement made by the accused in his defence and thus would have tended to usurp the function of the court. These decisions are perhaps reconcilable with *Toohey v MPC* [1965] AC 595. But in *Lowery v R* [1974] AC 85, the opinion evidence of a psychiatrist as to the tendency of one of the two co-accused to murder for pleasure, the admissibility of which was naturally challenged by the other co-accused, was held to have been properly admitted to assist the jury to make a decision as to the veracity of the two co-accused! The decision in *Lowery* did not receive the approval of the Court of Appeal in *Turner*, but the former is a Privy Council decision, which should, and no doubt in due course will, be overruled by the House of Lords.

The common law rule prohibiting expert opinion evidence on the ultimate issue has been abrogated in civil trials by s3 Civil Evidence Act 1972 which provides for the admissibility of expert evidence on any 'relevant matter', stated in s3(3) to include 'an issue in the proceedings in question'. In criminal trials the issue of diminished responsibility on a charge of murder can be, and often is, the subject of expert opinion evidence – and often the expert will be asked the question: 'Do you think the accused was suffering from diminished responsibility?', despite the fact that that constitutes the ultimate issue in deciding guilt of murder or manslaughter. Lord Parker CJ gave this as an example of the inroads into the common law prohibition in criminal trials: see *DPP v A and BC Chewing Gum* [1968] 1 QB 159 at p164. It is generally accepted that the principle in s3 Civil Evidence Act 1972 now applies also in criminal cases subject to the discretion of the judge to exclude such evidence where the expert witness would be effectively usurping the function of the jury.

Where the expert bases his opinion on facts, he cannot thus make those facts evidence unless he has first-hand knowledge of them (*R v Abadom* [1983] 1 All ER 364) and in any situation where the expert is giving opinion evidence with an underlying factual basis, then those facts must be proved by admissible evidence of the expert himself as a witness of fact, or of some other competent witness. To save time and costs in calling the assistants of expert witnesses, counsel should maximise the use of admissions or written statements to prove facts on which the expert's opinion is based: *R v Jackson* [1996] 2 Cr App R 420. The proper time to fill such 'evidential gaps' was after the first reading of the expert's statement.

An expert witness must approach his task seriously and any expert witness who does not should not be surprised if the court strongly censures him, or even refuses to hear his evidence. The duties and responsibilities of expert witnesses in civil cases were clearly spelt out by Cresswell J in *National Justice Compania Naviera SA v Prudential Assurance Co Ltd (The Ikarian Reefer)* [1995] 1 Lloyd's Rep 455. Despite this important clarification for expert witnesses of their role, there are still not infrequent instances of expert witnesses falling well short of what is required of them. See also *Autospin (Oil Seals) Ltd v Beehive Spinning (A Firm)* (1995) The Times 9 August.

Expert opinion hearsay evidence is admissible in civil cases under the Civil Evidence Act 1972. In criminal cases hearsay was restricted to statements of facts until s30 Criminal Justice Act 1988 provided for the admissibility of expert reports as hearsay, with leave of the court.

Disclosure of expert evidence pre-trial in criminal proceedings was provided for under s81 Police and Criminal Evidence Act 1984, under which Crown Courts Rules could be issued. Under the Act, the Crown Court (Advance Notice of Expert Evidence) Rules 1987 require that, following committal for trial, if either prosecution or defence proposes to adduce expert evidence of fact or opinion at the trial, then the other party must be furnished with that detailed expert evidence as soon as practicable. If a party fails to furnish details as required, then the expert evidence can only be adduced with leave of the court.

This requirement of disclosure has existed for some time in civil proceedings. The relevant rules of court are contained in CPR Part 35 which applies in both the High Court and the county court. CPR Part 35.4 states that 'no party may call an expert or put in evidence an expert's report without the court's permission'. The court may direct that a single expert is to be instructed (Practice Directions 28 and 29). If a single expert is not to be used, the court may direct that expert's reports are to be exchanged prior to the trial (simultaneoulsly or sequentially). The court may also require the experts to hold discussions in order to identify the issues in the proceedings and, where possible, reach agreement on an issue (CPR Part 35.12).

R v Clare; R v Peach [1995] 2 Cr App R 333 is a good illustration of the law of Evidence having to evolve in order to keep pace with technological developments. It seems to sanction a new category of witness – the 'expert ad hoc' – who can give opinion evidence after becoming qualified to do so by virtue of sustained study of one given matter. The case concerned intensive frame by frame study of video evidence and comparison with still photos, by a police constable, and the conclusions he drew from that study. It is likely, however, that the mantle of an expert ad hoc will not be bestowed too readily, and it will be necessary to show considerable application by the purported expert ad hoc to convince the court to allow his/her evidence.

Non-expert opinion evidence

Section 3(2) Civil Evidence Act 1972 provides for opinion evidence of non-expert witnesses to be admissible to convey to the civil court relevant facts perceived by them as evidence of what they perceived. It is considered that this sub-section restates the common law, and is therefore applicable also to criminal proceedings. Admissibility is confined to areas of general experience and competence of the lay person, for example evidence as to identity of a person or document etc; evidence as to physical or mental condition of a person, eg that a person had been drinking heavily, but not that he was so drunk as to be unfit to drive through drink: *R v Davies* [1962] 1 WLR 1111; evidence as to the speed of a motor vehicle (but see Chapter 3 as to corroboration), or as to age or value other than in relation to antiques when expert opinion evidence is essential. In the case of *R v Simbodyal* (1991) The Times 10 October the Court of Appeal made it clear that a judge would be vulnerable to proper criticism if he appeared to be acting as a handwriting expert by comparing the notes himself.

Judgments in previous proceedings

A judgment in any proceedings is in the nature of specialised opinion – ie the opinion of the court as to whether a party has discharged the general burden of proof to the appropriate standard.

At common law the rule in *Hollington v Hewthorn* [1943] KB 587 stipulated that a previous judgment was inadmissible in subsequent civil proceedings as evidence of the facts on which it was based. The rule has been held to apply in subsequent criminal proceedings: *R v Spinks* [1982] 1 All ER 587. As regards conviction in earlier criminal proceedings of the defendant in subsequent civil proceedings, s11 Civil Evidence Act 1968 not only makes the fact of the conviction admissible but renders it conclusive of the commission of that relevant offence unless the contrary is proved. It is the fact of conviction which is crucial, not the sentence, and therefore even if a pardon is given the conviction still subsists: *R v Foster* [1984] 3 WLR 401. The burden of proof on the civil defendant seeking to prove 'the contrary' when a conviction is proved against him is to the civil standard; ie proof on a balance of probabilities, which, given the standard of proof in his earlier prosecution, will be an uphill task: *Hunter v Chief Constable of the West Midlands* [1981] 3 All ER 727. A claimant in civil proceedings must include in his statement of case a statement of his intention to rely on s11 Civil Evidence Act 1968, together with the particulars of the conviction and the issue in the civil proceedings to which the conviction is relevant (Practice Direction to CPR 16 (para 10.1)).

In s12 Civil Evidence Act 1968 there is a similar provision in relation to previous findings in matrimonial proceedings of adultery or paternity – the adultery or paternity shall be treated as conclusively proved unless the contrary is proved. (Again, the standard, as with s11 convictions, is the civil standard of balance of probabilities.)

In criminal proceedings, where proof of guilt of a person (including the accused) is admissible because relevant to an issue in those criminal proceedings, then the conviction of that person can be proved under s74 Police and Criminal Evidence Act 1984, and he shall then be taken to have committed the offence unless the contrary is proved. A relevant issue in criminal proceedings for handling is whether the goods were stolen, which may be shown by proof under s74 of conviction of the thief. The

Court of Appeal has stated that s74 should be used sparingly, particularly in the case of joint trials for eg conspiracy, and should not be used where the evidence implicates the accused: *R* v *Robertson; R* v *Golder* [1987] 3 All ER 231. Problems arise under s74(1) and (2) where two or more defendants have been jointly charged, and one or more pleads guilty, leaving the other pleading not guilty. If it is alleged that the remaining defendant was very closely linked with what are now previous convictions of the other people, the jury is likely to infer that this defendant is guilty also. In such cases, the judge could exclude the convictions under s78 Police and Criminal Evidence Act 1984, if the prosecution counsel intended to rely on the convictions of the other(s) not merely to prevent mystification of the jury, but as evidence of the guilt of the appellant – *R* v *Kempster* (1990) 90 Cr App R 14; *R* v *Mattison* [1990] Crim LR 117.

In *R* v *Boysen* [1991] Crim LR 274 the Court of Appeal said that in order to admit evidence of a co-accused's conviction (including a plea of guilty) it was necessary to observe the following principles:

a) the conviction must be clearly relevant to an issue in the case;

b) s74 should be sparingly used;

c) the judge should consider the question of fairness under s78 of the Act and whether the probative value of the conviction outweighs the probative value of fairness;

d) the judge must direct the jury clearly as to the issues to which the conviction is not relevant and also why the evidence is before them and to what issue it is directed.

These conditions were satisfied in *R* v *Stewart* [1999] Crim LR 746, although the Court of Appeal commented in that case that s74 should be used 'sparingly'. Where a person has a legal burden of disproving the commission of an offence by virtue of s74, the standard is the civil one only.

12.3 Key cases and statutes

- *DPP* v *A & BC Chewing Gum Ltd* [1968] 1 QB 159

- *Lowery* v *R* [1974] AC 85

- *National Justice Compania Naviera SA* v *Prudential Assurance Co Ltd (The Ikarian Reefer)* [1995] 1 Lloyd's Rep 455

- *R* v *Abadom* [1983] 1 WLR 126

- *R* v *Turner* [1944] 1 KB 463

- Civil Evidence Act 1972, s3

- Criminal Justice Act 1988, s30

12.4 Questions and suggested solutions

QUESTION ONE

'The existing law on expert evidence prevents psychiatrists and psychologists from playing a more extensive role in criminal trials, and thereby denies factfinders' valuable help on difficult issues.'

Discuss.

University of London LLB Examination
(for External Students) Law of Evidence June 2000 Q1

General Comment

This is a straightforward question concerning the use of psychologists and psychiatrists in criminal trials. A short explanation of the rationale for the exclusion of opinion evidence will lead naturally to a more detailed consideration of the exception relating to expert opinion evidence. It will be relevant to consider the importance of the state of mind of the defendant (whether deemed normal or abnormal) and the approach of the court to the issues of the reliability of confessions and the mens rea of the defendant.

Skeleton Solution

The general rule – exceptions to the rule – the importance of the state of mind of the defendant, whether normal or abnormal: *R v Masih* – matters within the everyday experience of the tribunal of fact: *R v Turner* – the reliability of a confession: *R v Walker*; *R v Weightman* – conclusion.

Suggested Solution

The general rule is that a witness is not permitted to give evidence of his opinion, but should confine his evidence to reporting what he perceived with his senses. This exclusionary rule is justified by reference to the role of the tribunal of fact, whose function it is to draw inferences and form opinions. If a witness is permitted to give evidence of his opinion, the role of the tribunal of fact is usurped.

There are, of course, exceptions to the general rule and the exception raised by the question relates to the opinion evidence of experts. Experts are permitted to give evidence of opinion where the court is in need of assistance. Some matters, for instance those of a technical or scientific nature, will clearly be outside the experience of the tribunal of fact, and expert evidence will be admitted on such matters. Since the tribunal of fact will already have experience of the reactions and perceptions of a person whose mental state is not abnormal, in general no assistance from an expert will be required where it is not contended that the accused was mentally abnormal at the time of the offence. So, for instance, a court might require assistance when contemplating the effect of provocation upon a person whose mental state at the time was abnormal. Such assistance will not, however, be required where the person experiencing the provocation was not mentally abnormal, since the experience of provocation will be within the ordinary experience of the tribunal of fact. Thus in *R v Chard* (1971) 56 Cr App R 268 the Court of Appeal held that the trial judge had been correct when he excluded evidence relating to the intention of the accused at the relevant time because, there being no issue of mental abnormality raised, the jury were able to judge for themselves the accused's state of mind at the time of the killing on the basis of their own everyday experience of life. Had the issue of insanity or diminished responsibility been raised, the jury would have required assistance, these states of mind being outside their everyday experience.

The courts have on occasion taken what appears to be a rather inflexible view of the demarcation between normal and abnormal states of mind. In *R v Masih* [1986] Crim LR 395 the defendant had an intelligence quotient of 72, just above the level of subnormality. The Court of Appeal held that evidence relating to his intelligence, appreciation of his situation and state of mind had been properly excluded, since he did not come within the category of 'mental defective'. The Court held that evidence on such issues would be admissible where the defendant came within that category (ie had an intelligence quotient of 69 or less), provided that the evidence is confined to an assessment of the defendant's intelligence and an assessment of any relevant abnormal characteristics. The assumption in this case that there is a clear dividing line between normality and abnormality has been criticised (for instance by commentators such as Mackay (Mackay, 'Excluding Expert Evidence: A Tale of Ordinary Folk and Common Experience' [1991] Crim LR 800)), and in *R v Silcott* [1987] Crim LR 765 Hodgson J commented that it seemed 'somewhat artificial' to draw a strict line at 69/70. The result of the decision in *Masih* excludes evidence from psychiatrists and psychologists in cases of 'borderline abnormality'. Such evidence could be both valuable and helpful, but one justification for its exclusion is that these qualities could be overly important in the eyes of members of the jury so that they would accord it inappropriate weight. The result could be trial by expert rather than trial by jury. The existence of this risk has been recognised by the courts and is reflected in the requirement that a trial judge should direct the jury that they are not bound to accept an expert opinion, and that matters of fact are for the jury alone to decide (*R v Stockwell* (1993) 92 Cr App R 260).

The prospect of trial by experts is also the justification for the rule that no witness may testify as to the 'ultimate issue' (ie the very issue between the parties). This common law rule has been abrogated in civil proceedings by the Civil Evidence Act 1972, although technically it still operates in criminal proceedings. In *DPP v A & BC Chewing Gum Ltd* [1968] 1 QB 159 Lord Parker CJ observed that more and more inroads have been made into the rule, so that it is now honoured more in its breach than in its observance.

The courts will also generally refuse to admit expert evidence on the issue of an accused's credibility or on the question of whether he was likely to have been provoked. The justification for excluding such evidence is, again, that such matters are within the everyday competence and experience of the jury. In *R v Turner* [1975] QB 834 the defendant was charged with murder and raised the issue of provocation. The trial judge refused to allow the defence to call a psychiatrist to give evidence as to the credibility of the defendant, and as to whether he was likely to have been provoked. The defendant was convicted and the Court of Appeal held that the evidence was rightly excluded on the basis that the jury did not need, and should not have been offered, the evidence of a psychiatrist to help them to decide whether the defendant's evidence was truthful. When the matter was appealed, counsel for the defence relied on an earlier decision in which the Privy Council had approved the admission of the evidence of a psychologist on the issue of credibility (*Lowery* v *R* [1974] AC 85). The Court distinguished this case, saying that it had been decided on 'its special facts', and went on to hold that it was no authority for the proposition that in all cases psychologists and psychiatrists can be called to prove the probability of the truthfulness of the accused. The ratio decidendi of *Lowery* v *R* [1974] AC 85 is unclear, although a number of factors can be identified in that case which were not present in *R* v *Turner* [1975] QB 834. In *Lowery*, Lowery and a co-defendant, King, were charged with the murder of a girl in circumstances where the facts were such that the murder must have been committed by one or other of them, or by both of them acting in concert. At trial, each sought to blame the other and Lowery put his character in issue. The trial judge allowed King to call a psychologist to give evidence that King was immature, emotionally shallow and likely to be dominated by a more aggressive man, and that Lowery had a strong aggressive drive with weak controls. The psychologist had examined both defendants. One justification for the admission of this evidence was that the psychologist's evidence was admissible for King, as co-accused, in rebuttal of Lowery's claim to good character. Another justification for the admission of the evidence was that the jury needed assistance in order to resolve the question of which defendant had the more aggressive personality, as this was a question which they could not determine from their own experience. Neither circumstance offers any support for the proposition that the case is authority for the admission of expert evidence on the issue of credibility generally. Indeed, in *Turner* Lord Justice Lawton said that a rule allowing the admission of such evidence would be likely to lead to the development of trial by psychiatrists rather than trial by jury and magistrates, a prospect which he described as unattractive.

Evidence concerning the credibility of the accused is accordingly generally inadmissible. However, the evidence of a psychologist or psychiatrist is admissible in a voir dire on the issue of the reliability of a confession. In *R* v *Walker* [1998] Crim LR 211 the defendant contended that her confession should be excluded under s76(2)(b) Police and Criminal Evidence Act (PACE) 1984 and she was allowed to call a psychiatrist at the voir dire to give evidence that she suffered from a severe personality disorder such that her confession might be unreliable. The Court of Appeal held that the evidence was rightly admitted, and also held that the admissibility of such evidence was not limited to cases of 'mental impairment' or 'impairment of intelligence or social functioning'. The Court arrived at this conclusion because of the construction of s76(2)(b) and the reference to the 'circumstances existing at the time', which is wide enough to include the defendant's mental state, whether or not that was abnormal.

Although the expert evidence of a psychiatrist is admissible on the issue of the reliability of a confession at the voir dire, this evidence is not admissible before the jury. In *R v Weightman* (1991) 92 Cr App R 291 the central issue at trial was whether confessions which the defendant admitted having made were reliable. The defence wished to call evidence from a psychiatrist who would say that the defendant was histrionic, theatrical and likely to say things to draw attention to herself. The trial judge refused to admit the evidence on the ground that to allow scientific or medical evidence by an expert in a case where there was no suggestion that the appellant suffered from mental illness or was below normal intelligence was a usurpation of the functions of the jury. This ruling was upheld by the Court of Appeal.

Decisions such as *R v Weightman* (1991) 92 Cr App R 291 and *R v Masih* [1986] Crim LR 395 can be criticised on the basis that they place too much emphasis on what may be an arbitrary distinction between that which is regarded as 'normal' and that which is regarded as 'abnormal'. In addition, the ability of the jury to assess the impact of abnormal circumstances and stresses on 'normal' individuals may not be as great as the decisions suppose. The relatively restrictive approach taken in *R v Turner* [1975] QB 834 may result in the exclusion of what might be valuable expert opinion evidence, and the only exception to this conclusion concerns hearings which are governed by s76(2)(b) PACE 1984.

QUESTION TWO

Potbelly is charged with causing the death of Cleopatra by reckless driving.

The driver of the car which caused Cleopatra's death did not stop and Potbelly's defence is an alibi.

Advise on the admissibility of the following.

a) PC Bojak says he got to the scene to find Cleopatra lying on the road, and she said, 'It was a red Ferrari ... doing eighty.' She then died. Potbelly has a red Ferrari.

b) PC Bodie says he was at an identification parade when Doyle identified Potbelly as the driver but Doyle has now gone abroad.

c) Evidence of a psychiatrist, Quincy, who has examined Potbelly, that Potbelly is highly disturbed, an individual who is capable of behaving in a manner calculated to injure people around him.

d) A 'parking ticket' issued by a traffic warden to the owner of a Ferrari bearing the same number as Potbelly's car. The ticket had been found near the scene of the accident.

Adapted from University of London LLB Examination
(for External Students) Law of Evidence June 1983 Q6

General Comment

The structure for the answer to this question is contained in the question itself. Each issue is compartmentalised and should be considered in turn, as it arises.

Skeleton Solution

a) Hearsay: dying declaration; res gestae – non-expert evidence as to speed.

b) Previous inconsistent statement: exception with identification – hearsay rule: exception to rule.

c) Expert opinion evidence – admissibility – competence of jury to decide for itself.

d) Inadmissible hearsay – *R* v *Rice* versus *R* v *Lydon* – traffic warden as witness in court.

Suggested Solution

a) In cases of murder or manslaughter, a dying declaration by the victim, under a settled and hopeless expectation of death, is admissible as to the cause and circumstances of the death (*R* v *Woodcock* (1789) 1 Leach 500). This exception to the rule against hearsay appears to be confined to the two offences mentioned (see *R* v *Hutchinson* (1822) 2 B & C 608n and *R* v *Newton and Carpenter* (1859) 1 F & F 641) but arguably extends to cover all cases where the death is the subject of the charge and accordingly could apply in the instant case of causing death by reckless driving. Alternatively, it should be argued that Cleopatra's statement formed part of the res gestae. The judge must be satisfied that the statement was so clearly made in circumstances of spontaneity or involvement in the event that the possibility of concoction or fabrication can be disregarded (*Ratten* v *R* [1972] AC 378; *R* v *Andrews* [1987] AC 281). If Cleopatra's statement is admissible, it is evidence of the truth of the facts contained in it. Part of her statement relates to the speed of the car. Non-expert opinion evidence as to speed is admissible being regarded as a matter within ordinary human experience, and in this case corroboration is not imperative, as the offence is not one of exceeding a speed limit.

b) At common law, former consistent statements are generally inadmissible. One recognised exception is evidence of prior identification admissible both by the identifying witness and by other witnesses who saw the identification being made (unless the evidence contradicts the evidence of the identifying witness). Thus in *R* v *Osbourne; R* v *Virtue* [1973] 1 QB 678 where the identifying witness was unable to remember having picked anyone out of the ID parade, the Court of Appeal held that a police officer, who saw the identification being made, could testify as to the person identified. The court held the same in the case of *R* v *McCay* [1990] Crim LR 338. On one view these cases should be confined to their facts. On a wider view it may be argued that since the evidence was not admitted as an exception to the rule on prior consistent statements (there was no evidence of identification in court with which the police officer's evidence could be consistent), it was admitted as an exception to the hearsay rule, ie to prove the truth of an out of court statement by conduct. Accepting this argument, PC Bodie may give evidence of Doyle's identification of Potbelly. However, in *R v Osbourne; R v Virtue* [1973] 1 QB 678, the court made no reference to the hearsay problem, and the case has been much criticised on this basis. In *R v McCay* [1990] Crim LR 338, the court seemed to believe it fell within the res gestae exception, but this goes against old authority. Furthermore, in *Sparks v R* [1964] AC 964, Lord Morris held that there is no rule which permits the giving of hearsay evidence merely because it relates to identity, and that for hearsay to be admissible it must come within a recognised exception.

c) Expert opinion evidence is admissible on subjects demanding special knowledge and competence where in its absence the court would be unable to reach a proper conclusion (*Folkes v Chadd & Ors* (1782) 3 Doug 157; also *R v Weightman* (1991) 92 Cr App R 291). However, such evidence is inadmissible if the lay opinion of the tribunal of fact is equally valid on the subject in question. Thus if Quincey's evidence is designed to show Potbelly intended the offence, and there is no question of mental illness, the matter is properly regarded to be within the competence of the jury (*R v Chard* (1971) 56 Cr App R 268). In *R v Toner* (1991) 93 Cr App R 382 mental illness had been caused, it seems, by the hypoglycaemia, and so expert medical evidence was admissible as regards its effect on intent. By contrast, matters of insanity are regarded as proper subjects of expert opinion evidence. In the case of *Lowery v R* [1974] AC 85 the Privy Council allowed one co-defendant to adduce psychiatric evidence to show that the other was of a character and disposition likely to have committed the offence. However, in that case, it was clear from all the circumstances that one or other or both of the co-defendants must have committed the offence. It is submitted that *Lowery* be confined to its own facts given the judgment in *R v Turner* [1975] QB 834. In the instant, case, the evidence is not only inadmissible character evidence but also outside the boundaries of admissible expert opinion evidence.

d) The parking ticket is prima facie inadmissible hearsay, being a statement, in writing, made by a person outside court, and tendered for the purpose of proving the facts contained in it, ie that Potbelly's car was within the vicinity of the accident on the day in question (presumably). By analogy with *R v Rice* [1963] 1 QB 857, a much criticised case, it could be argued that the parking ticket, like the airline ticket bearing a traveller's name, is admissible evidence that a car with the same number as Potbelly's was within the vicinity of the accident. It is submitted that *Rice* should not be followed: *R v Lydon* [1987] Crim LR 407. Although it was held in that case that the ticket did not speak its contents, the ticket was valueless as a piece of real evidence without regard to the truth of its contents. To allow a ticket in evidence so that an inference can be drawn as to the truth of its contents is, in effect, to do what is prohibited by the rule against hearsay. One practical solution, in the instant case, would be to call as a witness the traffic warden in question who could refresh his or her memory by reference to the parking ticket. It may be safely assumed that the statements in the ticket were made by the warden and were contemporaneous to the events to which they related.

QUESTION THREE

Caligula is charged with procuring Livilla, a severely subnormal woman, to have unlawful sexual intercourse with a number of men contrary to s9 of the Sexual Offences Act, knowing that she was severely subnormal. The Crown wish to put the following items of evidence at his trial.

a) A certificate of the Director of St Mary's Mental Health Institute that Livilla was an inmate of the Institute and that she was severely subnormal.

b) The evidence of her mother that Livilla was incapable of reading and writing and was subnormal.

c) The evidence of Phoebe, another subnormal girl, that she had been asked by Caligula to come to a party where she could 'earn lots of money from rich businessmen'.

> Adapted from University of London LLB Examination
> (for External Students) Law of Evidence June 1984 Q5

General Comment

The range of issues raised in this question demonstrates the cohesive nature of the law of evidence and the difficulties faced by the student wishing to 'question spot'.

Skeleton Solution

a) Hearsay – documentary hearsay – s23 Criminal Justice Act 1988 – expert opinion.

b) Opinion evidence – outside experience of jury – subnormality – incompetence with reading and writing.

c) Competence – evidence of previous bad character of accused – probative value and prejudicial effect.

Suggested Solution

a) It is for the prosecution to prove every element of the offence charged. In this case that includes proving that Livilla was subnormal. The certificate of the Director of St Mary's Mental Health Institute seems a sensible way of proving her subnormality, but since it is by no means certain that Caligula will accept the certificate the law requires the Director himself to give evidence in person. The hearsay rule will prima facie exclude the certificate but it could be admitted under the provisions of s23 Criminal Justice Act 1988, given that one of the requirements in s23(2) is satisfied, and the court gives leave, having considered the factors in s25. If the certificate contains elements of expert opinion as to severe subnormality, this is admissible as hearsay under s30, again with leave of the court, and subject to the conditions in s30(3).

b) Opinion evidence is only admissible in a criminal case if the jury is not in a position to decide an issue without hearing someone else's opinion – in other words if the matter on which opinion evidence is given is outside the normal experience and knowledge of the jury (see *R v Turner* [1975] QB 834 and *R v Weightman* (1991) 92 Cr App R 291, where the court would not allow in psychiatrist's evidence about a person's reaction to stress and strains of life, where there was no mental illness, although she may have an abnormal personality. But subnormality and abnormality are two different things).

The mother's opinion on the issue of subnormality is inadmissible. A lay witness is not allowed to give his or her opinion on an issue which is an issue for the jury. It is for the jury to decide whether Livilla is subnormal, not for her mother, and so her opinion on this matter is inadmissible. She is not an expert, as far as we know, and so her opinion is of no assistance and is inadmissible (*M'Naghten's Case* (1843) 10 Cl & Fin 200).

The mother's evidence of Livilla's inability to read and write would be admissible. This is not opinion evidence, but is evidence of facts perceived by the mother. We can assume that she had seen and knows her daughter well enough to know whether she can read and write and would not be giving an opinion, but would be stating a fact which she herself has seen. It is possible, though it seems unlikely, that the mother was only saying her daughter could not read and write because she was in the Institute and had not perceived these facts for herself. If that is the case, her evidence on the matter would be inadmissible.

The prosecution could try to rely on the case of *R v Davies* [1962] 3 All ER 97 where the Courts Martial Appeal Court held that a witness to a motor accident could give evidence that in his opinion a driver had taken drink. Provided he also stated the grounds on which he comes to the conclusion, such a statement is quite proper. The Crown could argue that the mother could give evidence of what she perceived, using the term 'subnormal' to describe her daughter's behaviour. It is submitted though, that the *Davies* case should not be stretched so as to allow such evidence, because the mother could give evidence of what she saw of her daughter's condition without needing to use the word 'subnormal' to describe Livilla accurately and clearly.

c) The evidence of Phoebe will not be at all admissible unless the judge is satisfied that she is a competent witness. A person who is mentally ill may give evidence if the judge is satisfied that he or she understands the oath and is able to give evidence without the mental illness making it impossible for the witness to recall events (*R v Hill* (1851) 2 Den 254). Even if Phoebe is competent, her evidence is unlikely to be ruled admissible. Evidence of previous misconduct of the accused is inadmissible as evidence of his guilt unless it is so probative of guilt that this probative value outweighs its prejudicial effect. This test, laid down in *DPP* v *Boardman* [1975] AC 421, means that the evidence of Phoebe must prove Caligula's guilt on the charge with regard to Livilla, to such an extent that the jury will not be acting unfairly to the accused if they jump to the conclusion that because he made such an offer to Phoebe, so he must have done to Livilla.

There seems to be nothing particularly strange about the offence charged which could be seen to make it strikingly similar to the offer made to Phoebe. Both 'victims' are mentally subnormal, but that of itself does not show such an underlying link or unity or system to make the evidence of Phoebe positively probative that the offence charged was committed. But following the case of *R* v *P* (1991) 93 Cr App R 267 what matters more is what is in issue – identification, or the crime itself?

QUESTION FOUR

Albert, Charles and Douglas are charged with armed robbery of a sub-post office and murder of the postmaster. Discuss the admissibility of the following:

a) medical evidence in the form of a psychiatrist's report in support of Albert's defence of diminished responsibility;

b) Charles having testified that he was unaware that Albert was armed, and had he known would not have been involved, psychiatric evidence that Charles is of a passive disposition and that psychopaths, such as Albert appears to be, are prone to violence and to lying;

c) evidence of Hinton, a priest, that Douglas is a regular churchgoer and a pillar of society who could not possibly commit any crime at all, let alone a grave crime of violence;

d) previous convictions of Charles and Douglas for armed robberies of sub-post offices.

Written by the Author

General Comment

The issues raised in the question concern both opinion evidence and character evidence. A good knowledge of both areas will be required.

Skeleton Solution

Expert opinion evidence: ultimate issue; hearsay; admissibility – expert opinion: factual basis; pure hypothesis; competence of jury; s1(3)(iii) Criminal Evidence Act 1898 – character evidence: status of character witness; evidence of general reputation, and evidence in rebuttal at common law and under s1(3)(ii) Criminal Evidence Act 1898 – similar fact evidence.

Suggested Solution

If Albert's plea is diminished responsibility, then he is admitting that he unlawfully killed the postmaster but running a defence which if successful will lead to his conviction for manslaughter rather than murder. The burden of proving diminished responsibility must be discharged by Albert – discharge of an evidential burden will not suffice (s2(2) Homicide Act 1957). As diminished responsibility bears on mental disorder of the accused, expert opinion evidence is admissible given that this is a matter not within the realm of the ordinary juryman's competence and experience (eg *R v Smith* [1979] 1 WLR 1445). Given that the psychiatrist examined and questioned Albert and from that factual basis formed his opinion that Albert suffered from diminished responsibility, the evidence is admissible as expert opinion testimony of the psychiatrist (*R v Bradshaw* (1986) 82 Cr App R 79). Where the medical evidence with diminished responsibility is unequivocal and uncontradicted, the trial judge should direct the jury to accept it if there are no other circumstances to consider. Where, however, such other circumstances exist, the aforesaid medical evidence should be assessed in the light of those other circumstances – *R v Sanders* (1991) 93 Cr App R 245. If the underlying facts are not proved by admissible evidence – which can be percipient evidence of the psychiatrist or some other witness – then the opinion, formed on inadmissible hearsay rather than facts, would be inadmissible (*R v Bradshaw* and *R v Abadom* [1983] 1 All ER 364).

The Crown Court (Advance Notice of Expert Evidence) Rules 1987, issued under s81 Police and Criminal Evidence Act 1984, require reciprocal disclosure of expert evidence prior to a trial on indictment. Albert's counsel should therefore disclose to the prosecution, as soon as practicable after Albert's committal for trial (Rule 3), the expert evidence which the defence intend to adduce. Failure to comply is not fatal, but admissibility is then in the discretion of the trial judge (Rule 5). Given that Albert's counsel wishes to adduce a psychiatrist's report, although this is hearsay, it is now admissible subject to the Advance Notice Rules above, with leave of the court (s30 Criminal Justice Act (CJA) 1988) if the psychiatrist is not to be called to give oral evidence. In deciding whether to grant leave to the report's being admitted in evidence without the psychiatrist attending as a witness, the court must have regard to factors such as the contents of the report and any unfairness to the accused (s30(3) CJA 1988).

On the facts of this murder trial, the diminished responsibility of Albert is going to be an 'ultimate issue'. The common law rule prohibiting opinion evidence on the ultimate issue has been repealed in civil cases (s3 Civil Evidence Act (CEA) 1972), and it is considered that it no longer applies in criminal cases (*DPP v A & BC Chewing Gum Ltd* [1968] 1 QB 159). Given the nature of the expert opinion evidence to be adduced, and its relevance to the ultimate issue, it is highly probable that the psychiatrist will have to attend and give oral testimony, being subjected to cross-examination. As he is a competent witness, he is compellable (*Harmony Shipping Co* v *Saudi Europe Line* [1979] 1 WLR 1380).

The psychiatric evidence as to Charles's 'passive disposition' is of dubious admissibility, as such passivity (not bearing on mental disorder) is within the jury's sphere of competence and therefore expert evidence is unnecessary in helping them to form their own opinion (*R* v *Turner* [1975] QB 834 and *R* v *Weightman* (1991) 92 Cr App R 291). The opinion as to Albert's propensity to violence and mendacity appears to be pure hypothesis from the wording of the question – 'such as Albert appears to be' etc – and as such would be inadmissible. If there is factual evidence of Albert's psychopathy, then expert opinion evidence may be admissible as to the common traits of psychopaths, but contradictory opinion evidence could then be adduced on what in itself is, or should not be, an issue lending itself to expert opinion evidence. In *Lowery* v *R* [1974] AC 85 opinion evidence of an expert was admitted apparently to tend to prove the veracity of one of two co-accused, but the decision was criticised in *Turner*, and the admissibility of the opinion of the psychiatrist in the case now under review appears to be less supportable than that in *Lowery*.

Charles's testimony would tend to undermine a defence by Albert of alibi or that he was unarmed etc, thereby causing Charles to lose his shield under s1(3)(iii) CEA 1898 and giving Albert's counsel the right to cross-examine Charles on his previous convictions (*Murdoch* v *Taylor* [1965] AC 574). But, given that Albert's defence is in essence that he was present, committed homicide with mens rea for murder but because of his arrested or retarded development etc ought to be convicted of manslaughter, Charles's testimony does not undermine that defence, is not favourable to the prosecution and is not therefore 'evidence against any other person charged in the same proceedings'. Therefore Charles's evidence should not result in his previous convictions being revealed in cross-examination.

Douglas's calling a character witness to state what Hinton said amounts to his adducing evidence of his good character, not just of general reputation but of specific acts and disposition. Such evidence is strictly inadmissible (*R* v *Rowton* (1865) 34 LJMC 57; *R* v *Redgrave* (1981) 74 Cr App R 10). However, if evidence of good character is adduced on behalf of the accused, then the prosecution may lead evidence of bad character in rebuttal but this must be merely evidence of bad reputation, not specific acts or convictions or disposition etc. However, if Douglas elects to testify after Hinton has given this evidence, then with leave of the judge the prosecutor may cross-examine Douglas on his previous convictions, not to prove his guilt but to attack his credibility (s1(3)(ii) CEA 1898).

In the case of both Charles and Douglas, their previous armed robberies may bear such a striking similarity to the one which is the subject of the instant charge that the circumstances of those robberies (not purely the previous convictions) may be given in evidence by the prosecutor to prove their guilt, under the doctrine of similar fact evidence (*DPP* v *Boardman* [1975] AC 421). Whether there is such a similarity or any other kind of probative relationship is a question of law for the judge who must weigh the probative value against the prejudicial effect.

Chapter 13

Public Policy

13.1   Introduction

13.2   Key points

13.3   Key cases and statute

13.4   Questions and suggested solutions

13.1   Introduction

There have been substantial developments in the past decade in this area of evidence, with the courts having to resolve the conflict between the public interest in the proper administration of justice and the public, or national, interest in safeguarding national security and related matters of state and the efficient functioning of the public service. Where the former interest prevails, then there will be full disclosure of all relevant evidence (eg at pre-trial discovery stage of civil litigation). Where the latter prevails, then the protected or sensitive information will be withheld from the court (ie excluded because of 'public interest immunity').

13.2   Key points

Historical background and development

In *Duncan* v *Cammell Laird* [1942] AC 624 the House of Lords held that the jury had no discretion to order disclosure of documents when a Minister certified that they should be withheld in the interests of national security or the efficient functioning of the public service. The decision was followed despite criticism of the rigidity of the rule and the fact that exclusion on the grounds of public interest immunity was in the hands of the Executive and could easily be abused. In *Conway* v *Rimmer* [1968] AC 910 the House of Lords reviewed its earlier decision and decided that where there is a claim of public interest immunity, the decision whether to exclude is ultimately that of the judiciary, not the executive. There were some reservations as to the position of 'class' documents, eg Cabinet papers, but in subsequent cases it was stated that, whatever the nature of the document, whatever the reason given for non-disclosure, the judges (if appropriate after private scrutiny of the documents) will decide whether public interest immunity shall obtain: *Burmah Oil* v *Bank of England* [1980] AC 1090; *Air Canada* v *Secretary of State for Trade (No 2)* [1983] 2 AC 394.

Extent of public interest immunity

The extent of non-disclosure on the grounds of public interest immunity was discussed at length, and with some conflicting opinions, in *D v NSPCC* [1978] AC 171, where their Lordships accepted that the list of categories of public interest is not closed – but its development will be by extending its ambit by reference to pre-existing, judicially recognised, public interests. In that case their Lordships, by reference to the long-established public interest in excluding the identity of police informers, extended the scope of public interest immunity to the NSPCC in regard to its efficient functioning being dependent, like the police, on information imparted in confidence.

Existing, recognised categories

These can be summarised as follows.

a) State security

Duncan v *Cammell Laird* [1942] AC 624 exemplifies this.

b) International relations

The public policy element figures strongly in sensitive areas of English foreign policy, such as territorial disputes with other countries: *Buttes Gas and Oil* v *Hammer (No 3)* [1981] 1 QB 223.

c) Detection and prevention of crime

The public interest in withholding evidence which would identify police informants has been recognised since, at the latest, 1794 (*R* v *Hardy* (1794) 24 State Trials 199). (Consider the analogy in *D v NSPCC*.) The public interest is obviously not only in the detection of crime but also in its prevention, consequently it is not only the identity of informants which will be withheld but also methods used by police such as surveillance tactics and locations used, and sophisticated forensic methodology *R* v *Rankine* [1986] 2 All ER 566; *R* v *Brown and Daley* (1988) 87 Cr App R 52; *R* v *Johnson* [1989] 1 All ER 121. Where disclosure is requested by the defence to assist in establishing the innocence of the accused, then the judge must consider whether non-disclosure on this ground of public interest immunity will lead to injustice to the accused: *R* v *Brown and Daley* and *R* v *Johnson*. In the case of *R* v *Agar* (1990) 90 Cr App R 318, the defence counsel argued that the police informant had caused the defendant to arrive whilst they were searching the informant's house for drugs, and that the drugs were planted on the defendant by the police. On appeal, it was held that although there was a clear and well-established rule that the identity of police informants should be kept secret, there was even stronger public interest here in allowing the appellant to put forward a tenable case in its best light.

In *McNally* v *Chief Constable of Greater Manchester Police* (2002) The Times 6 March the Court of Appeal observed that United Kingdom case law had moved away from the approach to public interest in non-disclosure stated by Lord Diplock in *D v NSPCC*

[1978] AC 171. The Court held that the decision in *Powell v Chief Constable of North Wales* (2000) The Times 11 February was applicable so that in civil proceedings, it would only be in exceptional circumstances that the public interest in preserving a police informant's anonymity would be waived.

In *R v Keane* (1994) 99 Cr App R 1 the Court of Appeal approved the description of the approach to be adopted by the court in *Governor of Brixton Prison, ex parte Osman* (1991) 93 Cr App R 202; 'a judge is balancing on the one hand the desirability of preserving the public interest in the absence of disclosure against on the other hand the interests of justice'. In *Osman*, the Court went on to note that 'where the interests of justice arise in a criminal case touching and concerning liberty … the weight to be attached to the interest of justice is plainly very great indeed.' These cases were approved in *R v Menga and Marshalleck* [1998] Crim LR 58 in which Leggatt LJ refers to the obligation to provide adequate material to the relevant parties in good time. Statutory duties and procedures for disclosure in cases involving events after 1 April 1997 are contained in the Criminal Procedure and Investigation Act 1996.

d) Efficient functioning of public service

This extends not just to government departments, but to the police, to local government and to other bodies (eg NSPCC – *D v NSPCC*; Gaming Board – *Rogers v Home Secretary* [1973] AC 388). In the case of the police, in the case of *Sharples v Halford* [1992] 3 All ER 624, it was held that police disciplinary files were the subject of public interest immunity. The trend is to restrict this head of public interest immunity to bodies performing a statutory function, and to restrain a proliferation of agencies claiming the immunity merely on the grounds of confidentiality or candour: *Science Research Council* v *Nassé* [1980] AC 1028, per Lord Scarman at p1087.

e) Confidentiality

Confidentiality of some communication or relationship is not in itself a reason for non-disclosure, but it is often a vital factor in a claim of public interest immunity. Often where confidentiality in respect of sources of information is an issue, there is a blurring of the distinction between public policy and private privilege (see Chapter 10). In *British Steel Corporation v Granada TV* [1982] AC 1096 the House of Lords recognised that in deciding whether to order the disclosure of the identity of an informant and thus to induce a breach of confidentiality, the courts do have some discretion – but obviously it is very much the function of the person receiving the information which is the crucial factor, eg a police officer as opposed to a journalist.

In the case of *Brown v Matthews* [1990] 2 All ER 155, the Court of Appeal held that a court welfare report did not fall within that category of documents which in the public interest could not be disclosed except for the purposes for which it came into existence. Instead, the court may give leave for the report to be used in other proceedings if, after evaluating and balancing the confidentiality of the report against the need for the contents of the report to be put into evidence if there was to be a fair trial, the court decided that in this particular case, the interests of justice required the reports to be released. In other words, the Court Welfare Officer's report could be disclosed at the discretion of the court which had ordered the report.

It was also held in the case of *W* v *Edgell* [1990] 2 WLR 471, that a psychiatrist's report was not protected against disclosure.

Although a journalist who refuses to disclose his source of information is often said to be claiming journalistic, or media, privilege, the use of the word 'privilege' is almost as misleading as when public interest immunity was referred to as 'Crown privilege'. However, one distinction made between public policy and private privilege is that of waiver. If a matter is accepted as being the subject of public interest immunity, then it is not permissible for a witness to waive that 'right' to withhold evidence; but in the realm of privilege a witness may claim the privilege or may decide to waive the privilege and apprise the court of the evidence or the source of the information. In the case of journalistic privilege, s10 Contempt of Court Act 1981, governs the protection from disclosure of sources of information; on balance, this is an area of privilege rather than of public interest immunity, so is dealt with in Chapter 10.

13.3 Key cases and statute

- *Burmah Oil* v *Bank of England* [1980] AC 1090
- *D* v *NSPCC* [1978] AC 171
- *Duncan* v *Cammell Laird* [1942] AC 624
- *McNally* v *Chief Constable of Greater Manchester Police* (2002) The Times 6 March
- Contempt of Court Act 1981, s10

13.4 Questions and suggested solutions

QUESTION ONE

'It is universally recognised that ... there are two kinds of public interest which may clash. There is the public interest that harm shall not be done to the nation or the public service by disclosure of certain documents, and there is the public interest that the administration of justice is to be done.' (Lord Reid in *Conway* v *Rimmer*)

Discuss critically the principles upon which the courts attempt to resolve this conflict.

University of London LLB Examination
(for External Students) Law of Evidence June 1992 Q1

General Comment

This question requires a discussion of the principles which govern the court's examination of claims of 'public interest'. You should examine the criteria which the courts use when faced with an assertion of 'public interest'.

Skeleton Solution

Types of public interest – national security – investigation of crime – confidential/ personal statements – *Duncan* v *Cammell Laird & Co* criteria – *Conway* v *Rimmer* criteria – public interest versus proper administration of justice – contents claim versus class claim.

Suggested Solution

A claim or assertion of 'public interest' is often raised in order to prevent disclosure of documents which would otherwise have to be disclosed. The courts, when faced with a claim of 'public interest' immunity from disclosure, have to perform a balancing act between the interests of the state in non-disclosure of potentially damaging documents and the proper administration of justice which requires the production of documents which a party has in its possession, custody or power which relate to an issue in dispute between the parties to litigation.

Privilege from the duty to disclose documents is a right which a party has. However, that party must assert its right to withhold a document from disclosure. Refusing to disclose a document on the grounds of public interest immunity or public policy is a duty as well as a right (as stated by Lord Simon in the case of *Rogers* v *Home Secretary* [1973] AC 388). The court must protect documents which are privileged or immune from disclosure because of the 'public interest' and it is also under a duty to ensure that such documents are not disclosed.

The case of *Duncan* v *Cammell Laird* [1942] AC 624 was one of the first cases which dealt with the vexed problem of 'public interest' immunity. It concerned the sinking of the submarine Thetis.

Thirty-nine lives were lost when the Thetis sank. The plaintiffs sued Cammel Laird in negligence (Cammel Laird built the Thetis). The plaintiffs sought discovery of the contract between the defendant and the Government for the construction of the Thetis. The Board of Admiralty objected to the production of the contract on the grounds of public interest. The court upheld the Admiralty's objection.

Lord Simon, who gave the leading judgment in the case, held that where a government minister objects to the disclosure of documents on the grounds that the disclosure would damage, for example, the country's defence, the court could not go beyond that objection. Such objection would bind the courts. It was clear from Lord Simon's judgment that the Executive would be able to determine what types of documents were privileged from production. In effect the court subverted its power of enquiry to the Executive.

The ruling in *Duncan* v *Cammell Laird* [1942] AC 624 was criticised on many occasions. Devlin J in the case of *Ellis* v *Home Office* [1953] 2 QB 135 expressed considerable dissatisfaction with the ruling in *Duncan*. Devlin J was concerned with the most worrying aspect of the effect of *Duncan*, that justice would not be seen to be done. Devlin's worries were addressed by the House of Lords in the case of *Conway* v *Rimmer* [1968] AC 910.

In *Conway* v *Rimmer* [1968] AC 910 the House of Lords cast considerable doubt on the reasoning behind the decision in *Duncan* v *Cammell Laird* [1942] AC 624. It was held that the question whether evidence should be withheld from disclosure on the grounds of public interest was a question for the court only. The House decided that a government minister's decision was not binding on the courts. Although great weight would be placed on a minister's opinion the final decision was for the courts.

The House of Lords specifically addressed the question of 'class' and 'contents' claims in relation to public interest immunity. It was held that documents which are alleged to be immune from disclosure because of the class which they fall in would be examined fully and they would not be privileged from production just because they fall within a specified class. The House criticised the argument that whole classes of documents should be withheld just because it might inhibit freedom of expression within public service. In relation to 'contents' claims the court said that it would be rare to order disclosure of such a document, the argument being that they were protected from disclosure because their contents would be damaging. In 'class' claims the real question for the court will be whether withholding of such documents would be really necessary for the functioning of the public service.

The underlying reasoning in *Conway* was that ultimately the decision whether a document should be disclosed lies with the court and not the executive. This reasoning was followed in *Burmah Oil* v *Bank of England* [1980] AC 1090 where it was held that no class of document would ever be absolutely immune from production. In the case of *Air Canada* v *Secretary of State for Trade (No 2)* [1983] 2 AC 394 the House of Lords re-asserted that disclosure of high level government documents could be ordered. The question for the court in the *Air Canada* case was whether the documents were helpful evidentially. It seems that the court will only withhold such documents if they cannot assist the proceedings. Lord Fraser expressed the view that even Cabinet minutes are not immune from disclosure. However, he did state that they were entitled to the highest protection.

It is quite clear from the authorities that it is not only government bodies or authorities which are entitled to rely on public interest for withholding documents. In the case of *D* v *NSPCC* [1978] AC 171 the House of Lords rejected the plaintiff's application for discovery of documents which could prove the identity of an NSPCC informant. The House acknowledged the importance of the NSPCC's work and the public interest in allowing the free, unimpeded flow of information. Lord Hailsham accepted that the categories of public interest are not closed.

The main categories of public interest are as follows.

a) National security, diplomatic relations and international comity.

b) Information for the detection of crime.

c) Confidential and personal statements.

It is well established that information and documents can be withheld on the grounds of national security; diplomatic relations and international comity. The reasoning behind this is that the public interest requires the promotion of these matters. Furthermore, the public interest requires that police informers be protected; the public has a vested interest in the supply of information which can assist in the detection of crime. For example, a witness cannot be asked to name a police informer: see *R* v *Taroy* (1794) 24 State Tr 199. However, if a defendant can show that disclosure of an informer's name can assist in establishing innocence then disclosure will be allowed: see *R* v *Hennessey* (1978) 68 Cr App R 419.

In relation to confidential relationships, disclosure will not be ordered as it can threaten the very existence of the confidential relationship. Such relationships include that as between priest and parishioner, doctor and patient and journalist and source. The leading case on this matter is *Science Research Council* v *Nassé* [1980] AC 1028 where it was held that the important test is whether discovery is necessary for disposing fairly of the proceedings. If it is necessary then the court will order discovery but the court will consider whether there are other means by which the evidence can be disclosed.

Accordingly, when issues of public interest arise, the court performs a 'balancing act' between the public interest in keeping documents disclosed and the public interest in justice being done and being seen to be done. By retaining a power to review claims of public interest the court can ensure that claims are tested in accordance with law and legal principles. One of the most alarming aspects of the decision in *Duncan* v *Cammell Laird* [1942] AC 624 was that the Executive could usurp the function of the courts. However, the result of *Conway* v *Rimmer* [1968] AC 910 is that, in principle, the Executive's powers have been curtailed and the courts have ensured that its pre-eminence in such matters is asserted.

QUESTION TWO

'Exclusion of evidence on the ground of public policy as a matter of law has only one thing in common with the exclusion of evidence which is illegally obtained as a matter of discretion: the absence of any coherent policy rationale underlying the case law.'

Discuss.

University of London LLB Examination
(for External Students) Law of Evidence June 1987 Q3

General Comment

A critical account of the development of case law is required here, necessitating a good knowledge of case law. It is important to avoid an overly descriptive approach and to focus on the question set.

Skeleton Solution

Categories of case covered by public policy: state secrets; minor state secrets; identity of police informants; identity of other informants – exclusion of evidence under s78 Police and Criminal Evidence Act 1984: disciplinary and reliability approach of courts – public interest in protection of civil liberties.

Suggested Solution

The exclusion of evidence on the ground of public policy is sometimes referred to as Crown privilege, public interest privilege or public interest immunity. Evidence will be excluded on grounds of public policy as a matter of law where it is deemed not to be in the public interest to allow it to be given. The privilege arises in relation to four different types or sources of information: (a) state secrets; (b) minor state interests; (c) identity of informants to the police; and (d) identity of other informants.

State secrets comprise, in general terms, matters involving the armed forces and the intelligence services. The courts have always been reluctant to allow any information to be given where the government has indicated that it should be kept secret. The policy behind this is that it is not for the courts but for government to take decisions about defence of the realm, which includes decisions about how much information should be made public of military and intelligence operations. The equation of the public interest with the interests of the government of the day is always criticised by the party of opposition, but once that party takes over in government it is quite content to use the equation in its own interest.

There are certain classes of document which the courts used to say are always privileged, for example cabinet minutes (*Conway* v *Rimmer* [1968] AC 910), but the tendency today is to examine each claim for immunity on its merits: *Burmah Oil* v *Bank of England* [1980] AC 1090. Where state secrets are involved the courts will not allow their repetition in court save in the most exceptional circumstances (*Burmah Oil* v *Bank of England* [1980] AC 1090; *Air Canada* v *Secretary of State for Trade (No 2)* [1983] 2 AC 394). The court will have received a certificate from a minister or senior civil servant setting out the reason why immunity is claimed and will hear the other party's outline reasons why the document should be disclosed and a balance must be struck. Either the nature of the information or its source will be a good enough reason for non-disclosure in a state secrets case, or if the court is in some doubt about whether the information really is a secret then it may have a look at the document to see for itself, although it is reluctant to use this right.

The protection of minor state interests can be cited as a reason for withholding documents and these include matters of the internal operation of government departments. In such cases the court will rarely say that the information in the documents is of a type which should not be disclosed but may justify immunity by citing the type of document as being a type which should not be disclosed. It is usually where third parties have given the information in confidence that the court will uphold a claim to immunity (*Alfred Crompton Amusement Machines Ltd* v *Customs and Excise Commissioners (No 2)* [1974] AC 405), but in the absence of involvement of innocent third parties there is no reluctance to order disclosure even where the government has said it is contrary to the public interest, provided that the nature of the document or of the information is such that the court is able to say that it cannot harm the nation's interests to order disclosure. There are cases which suggest that many internal government reports can be withheld (*Re Joseph Hargreaves Ltd* [1900] 1 Ch 347; *Ellis* v *Home Office* [1953] 2 QB 135; *Broome* v *Broome* [1955] P 190) but their authority is doubted by Cross, and since the court will now always balance the public interest in keeping them secret against the public interest in allowing a party full access to documents he needs in litigation (*Ellis* v *Home Office*), they cannot be treated as authoritative.

It is a cardinal rule that the police do not have to disclose the identity of informants. This rule has stood since well before *Marks* v *Beyfus* (1890) 25 QBD 494 and cannot be challenged now, save in the most exceptional circumstances, for example in the case of *R* v *Agar* (1990) 90 Cr App R 318. The Court of Appeal has shown on a further three occasions that it is prepared to investigate whether the withholding of the informant's identity is in the public interest (*Neilson* v *Laugharne* [1981] 1 QB 736; *Hehir* v *Commissioner of Police for the Metropolis* [1982] 1 WLR 715; *Peach* v *Commissioner of Police for the Metropolis* [1986] QB 1064).

Two reasons have been given for this rule, firstly that sources of information may dry up and secondly that information given to the police is given in confidence and the confidence should be respected. There is, it seems, little evidence to support the first reason; but the second is persuasive. Today the court will attempt to balance the public interests cited above, but when deciding the strength of the public interest in keeping the information secret it will take into account the desirability of retaining confidence.

Informing public bodies other than the police of certain types of wrongdoing is likely to be done in confidence in the same way as information give to the police is given in confidence, but the rule appears to be that there can be no privilege arising out of confidentiality alone. Public interest immunity can arise where the recipient of the information has a statutory function to perform, but not otherwise (*D* v *NSPCC* [1978] AC 171). The apparent justification is that the scope of public interest immunity must be limited and that there can be no public interest in maintaining secrecy unless the purpose of giving the information is to start investigations.

It is clear that the courts will always try to balance the public interest in keeping matters secret against the public interest in allowing a litigant access to all information which he may need in litigation. The different types of information and the different sources from which it may come mean that different factors will be weighed when the balancing operation is done. In the case of *Brown* v *Matthews* [1990] 2 All ER 155, the public interest in keeping a court welfare report secret was said to have to be weighed against the need for the contents of the report to be put into evidence if there was to be a fair trial. Nevertheless, it is also clear that until 1979 the balancing operation was not universally recognised and there are many cases giving different reasons for upholding or rejecting a claim of public interest immunity.

The exclusion of evidence obtained by illegal means is a matter for the discretion of the court under s78 Police and Criminal Evidence Act 1984. Prior to the enactment of that statutory discretion the courts had built up a complex body of law from which it was clear that a discretion existed in some circumstances but far from clear what those circumstances were. The rationale lying behind the exclusion of interest obtained by illegal means has never been clearly explained. In cases on the exclusionary discretion under s78, the accent has been on the 'unfairness' of admitting evidence improperly obtained, but the courts vacillate between a 'disciplinary' and 'reliability' approach (*R v Mason* [1987] 3 All ER 481; *R v Alladice* [1988] Crim LR 608; *DPP v Marshall* [1988] 3 All ER 683 and *R v Quinn* [1990] Crim LR 581). Illegally, or improperly, obtained evidence (other than confessions) is admissible under English law; whether it will be excluded in any particular case depends on whether admissibility would result in unfairness, and/or whether the prejudicial effect of the evidence outweighs its probative value – but this is a matter of discretion rather than law.

One thing which is now clear about the exclusion of evidence obtained illegally is that the courts adopt the balancing operation applicable to claims of public interest immunity; they balance the public interest in using relevant probative evidence against the public interest in the protection of civil liberties (*R v Samuel* [1988] 2 All ER 135). Indeed it is important to note that once evidence has been obtained illegally, there is a discretion and not a duty to exclude it, and this, of course, differs from the position in true cases of public interest immunity where exclusion is a matter of law not discretion once the criteria for exclusion have been laid down.

QUESTION THREE

'The categories of public interest are not closed and must alter from time to time whether by restriction or extension as social conditions and social legislation develop.' (Lord Hailsham in *D v NSPCC*.)

Discuss in relation to the law of evidence.

University of London LLB Examination
(for External Students) Law of Evidence June 1993 Q2

General Comment

This is a wide open question which appears with some frequency. Here is chance to make some interesting jurisprudential statements about the relationship between policy and principle and/or the role of the judiciary in restraining self-interested decisions by government bodies (jurisprudence is not confined to jurisprudence!). It is important to give the history of the idea, arising from what was formerly known as

'Crown privilege' and then proceeding through *Duncan* v *Cammell Laird* [1942] AC 624 and *Conway* v *Rimmer* [1968] AC 910; from then on it is over to you: the extensions are fairly easily noted (eg to the NSPCC) but the rationale, not easy to extract from the cases, is not.

Skeleton Solution

Meaning of 'Crown privilege' – *Duncan* v *Cammell Laird* – the 'balancing act of the judge' – *D* v *NSPCC* and *Conway* v *Rimmer* – the idea of the minister's certificate in the light of the overall public interest – the subsequent developments (*Air Canada*, and others) – the special extension in relation to crime – subsequent analogous bodies – the confidentiality category of 'the public interest'.

Suggested Solution

Public interest privilege was originally termed 'Crown privilege' and was defined as having been the absolute right of the Crown to object to producing documents in court on the ground that it would be against the public interest to do so. The claim, made in an affidavit by a minister of the Crown, would prevent the court from looking at those documents; that principle was firmly established in *Duncan* v *Cammell Laird* [1942] AC 624. Today, the phrase is regarded as a misleading misnomer (see, for example, Lord Simon in *R* v *Lewes JJ* [1973] AC 388) and although a minister of the Crown is often the most appropriate person to assert the public interest, it is open to any interested person to raise the question; indeed, the trial judge himself may raise it. In *D* v *NSPCC* [1978] AC 171, for example, Lord Simon concluded that the state could not be restricted to the Crown and the departments of central government but included the whole organisation of all the legal institutions concerned with civil rule and government. Formerly, it was considered that only the organs of central government could assert the privilege. In *D* v *NSPCC*, for example, it was extended to the National Society for the Prevention of Cruelty to Children.

If a party to litigation claims that certain documents are privileged from disclosure on the grounds of public policy, the court must hold the balance between that public interest and the public interest in the disclosure of the documents to ensure the proper administration of justice. This test was adopted in *Conway* v *Rimmer* [1968] AC 910, where the House of Lords rejected their previous ruling in *Duncan* v *Cammell Laird* that the minister's certificate was conclusive and binding on the court. Although there is an argument that a minister is better placed to assess the public interest, there is also an argument about abuse of power (ever more important these days); ministers could assess (even unconsciously) the public interest to be that which equated with the party or government in power. *Conway* v *Rimmer* represented a welcome reform by ending the possibility of ministerial misuse of power by requests for immunity in cases where the alleged public interest was barely discernible yet non-disclosure of the documents could have resulted in a partial or complete denial of justice to the parties.

The judge may, therefore, now question ministerial assertions that documents be withheld and may balance against this the importance of the documents to the litigation and justice, and the importance of the litigation to the parties, provided that the party seeking disclosure has shown that the information is likely to help his own case or damage his adversary's in the sense that there is a reasonable probability, not a mere speculative belief, that it will do so (see, for example, *Air Canada* v *Secretary of State for Trade (No 2)* [1983] 1 All ER 910). That this method of judging a claim of privilege on the grounds of public policy represents a fair balance between the competing public interests may be shown by contrasting *Burmah Oil* v *Bank of England* [1980] AC 1090 and *Williams* v *Home Office* [1981] 1 All ER 1151. In the former case, an inspection of documents relating to the formulation of government economic policy, it was held that they contained nothing of sufficient evidential value to order their disclosure. By contrast, in *Williams*, a case involving the rights of the citizen and the liberty of the subject, on inspection of the documents, disclosure was ordered. The public interest in justice prevailed over the fact that disclosure could lead to ill-informed criticism of the Home Office.

It should be noted that there is a more inflexible rule in relation to information for the detection of crime. The rule, subject to few exceptions, is that in public prosecutions, and in civil proceedings arising from them, no questions may be asked and no evidence given, which would reveal the identity of an informant whose information led to the prosecution (*Marks* v *Beyfus* (1890) 25 QBD 494). The realistic and sensible basis for this rule is the danger that if disclosure were permitted, informants would be deterred from coming forward to help the police for fear of reprisal. This rule has been extended, by way of analogy, to persons supplying information to other bodies (see, for example, *R* v *Lewes JJ* [1973] AC 388, *D* v *NSPCC* [1978] AC 171, *Alfred Crompton Amusement Machines Ltd* v *Customs and Excise Commissioners (No 2)* [1974] AC 405).

In each of these cases, the decision against disclosure was based upon the danger of the sources drying up (which would in turn lead to an impairment of the efficiency of those parts of the public service in question, ie, the Gaming Board, the NSPCC and the Inland Revenue). The fact that such information is given in confidence is not in itself sufficient to create public interest immunity, but it is a material factor to be taken into account in deciding the privilege claim. It is for this reason that the above cases may be legitimately reconciled with the other confidentially cases (for example, *Science Research Council* v *Nassé* [1980] AC 1028 and *British Steel Corporation* v *Granada Television Ltd* [1982] AC 1096). In *R* v *Agar* (1990) 90 Cr App R 318, it was made clear, however, that the public interest in keeping the identity of an informant a secret had to be balanced against the public interest in seeing that a defendant is well able to defend his case in criminal proceedings. It is clear that the immunity of the press from revealing its sources of information should be regarded as being in the public interest, given its importance for the democratic nature of our institutions (see *On Liberty* by John Stuart Mill, for example), even more so than the efficient functioning of the public service, and that the freedom of the press depends upon immunity.

QUESTION FOUR

'Confidentiality is not a separate head of privilege, but it may be a very material consideration to bear in mind when privilege is claimed on the ground of public interest.' (Lord Cross in *Alfred Crompton Amusement Machines Ltd* v *Commissioners of Customs and Excise (No 2)*.)

Discuss.

University of London LLB Examination
(for External Students) Law of Evidence June 1990 Q2

General Comment

A good answer to this question will focus on the area raised by the question. It is important to avoid the temptation to write 'everything I know about privilege' and to tailor what is written to the question.

Skeleton Solution

Balance of interests with public interest immunity – 'high' grade to 'low' grade documents: confidentiality less relevant – confidentiality more relevant with public agencies, and police informants – journalistic privilege: s10 Contempt of Court Act 1981.

Suggested Solution

There are three main situations in which evidence can be withheld on grounds of privilege. Broadly, they are first, where by giving the evidence a witness exposes himself to the possibility of criminal proceedings (the privilege against self-incrimination), second, evidence of communications between party to proceedings and his lawyer or by a third party with either (legal professional privilege) and third, privilege arising on grounds of public interest (public interest immunity).

Confidentiality does not therefore of itself feature as a basis for exclusion. That said, it is true that confidentiality plays a substantial role in excluding evidence on grounds of public interest. This role will now examined.

Until comparatively recent times, establishing a claim to privilege on grounds of public interest was a relatively simple business. The minister or other political head of the organ of state claiming a privilege would submit a certificate and the courts regarded that certificate as final. This approach was approved by the House of Lords in *Duncan* v *Cammell Laird* [1942] AC 624. The approach changed with the subsequent decision of the House of Lords in *Conway* v *Rimmer* [1968] AC 910. That case established that the minister's view of the public interest was not conclusive and that the courts have a residual power to decide where that interest lies. It is in the evaluation that confidentiality plays a leading, though not necessarily explicit, part.

The approach adopted depends upon the type of document for which immunity is claimed. It has become the practice since *Duncan* v *Cammell Laird* [1942] AC 624 for a claim of public interest privilege to be made on a contents or class basis. In the former case, the claim is that the particular document in question should not be disclosed in the public interest. It is clear from *Conway* v *Rimmer* [1968] AC 910 that such a claim is very unlikely to be interfered with by the courts. Accordingly, the basis of the claim is unlikely to be investigated though it is readily apparent that the underlying reason for the claim for privilege and the reason for upholding it is the requirement of confidentiality for highly sensitive documents. For a class claim (where a claim is made on the basis that the document falls within a class of documents which should be withheld from production in the public interest) the role of confidentiality is even more evident. For class claims relative to 'high grade' documents such as Cabinet papers, privilege is very likely, subject to inspection of the relevant documents by the court, to be upheld and the usual basis is the sensitive nature of the material and the consequent need for confidentiality. This much is clear from *Conway* v *Rimmer* and subsequent authorities including *Burmah Oil* v *Bank of England* [1980] AC 1090 and *Air Canada* v *Secretary of State for Trade (No 2)* [1983] 2 AC 394. On the other hand, for lower grade documents or routine reports, a class claim based on confidentiality arising from the assertion that officials would feel inhibited from expressing their views if they thought that the information was to be disclosed (the 'candour' principle) is unlikely to be successful. The House of Lords in *Conway* v *Rimmer* made this clear and the courts have since rejected such claims consistently if based on this premise.

There are, however, circumstances where confidentiality in respect of routine information will found a successful claim for privilege in the public interest. These arise where disclosure might result in the drying up of information on which a public agency depends for undertaking work in the public interest. *Alfred Crompton Amusement Machines Ltd* v *Customs and Excise Commissioners (No 2)* [1974] AC 405 referred to in the question and *D* v *NSPCC* [1978] AC 171 are examples. In the latter case, an order for disclosure of the identity of the individual who supplied information to the NSPCC about alleged cruelty to a child was refused. The information was routine but if disclosed people would be dissuaded from volunteering information to the NSPCC. If that happened, the work of the NSPCC in protecting children, manifestly in the public interest, would be seriously impeded. Similar principles can be seen in exclusion of evidence of the identity of police informers which can also be claimed under public interest privilege. *Marks* v *Beyfus* (1890) 25 QBD 494 is authority for that proposition. The principle has been extended in *R* v *Rankine* [1986] QB 861 to premises from which police conduct surveillance, although *R* v *Johnson* [1989] 1 All ER 121 makes clear that the need for confidentiality must be made out on the evidence; such evidence should include the attitude of the occupier of the premises to be identified. Disclosure may also be ordered if it is necessary to establish an accused's innocence – *R* v *Agar* (1990) 90 Cr App R 318.

The final area of public interest which requires comment arises in the context of the role of confidentiality in journalistic information. This is now subject to statutory intervention in the form of s10 Contempt of Court Act 1981. Under that section, journalistic sources are provided with protection in the public interest unless it is established to the satisfaction of the court that disclosure is necessary in the interests of justice, national security or the prevention of disorder or crime. The requirement for confidentiality in the public interest is nowhere stated in the section, but it is clear from the common law which preceded it and from *Secretary of State for Defence* v *Guardian Newspapers* [1984] 3 All ER 601 that the protection of journalistic information by reason of confidentiality in the public interest forms its basis. Indeed, that is perhaps obvious because in the absence of such protection sources might well be reluctant to come forward to the media and the public would thereby be deprived of information which may be a matter of legitimate concern to them.

Chapter 14
Proof Without Evidence

14.1 Introduction

14.2 Key points

14.3 Key cases and statute

14.4 Questions and suggested solutions

14.1 Introduction

In some circumstances a court may be satisfied that facts are established without requiring them to be proved by relevant evidence. In some cases the facts may be established with virtually no evidence, eg the facts are formally admitted or judicially noticed; in others the facts are presumed in favour of the party alleging them and therefore may be established by less evidence than would otherwise be required. These three exceptional areas, therefore, are formal admissions, judicial notice and presumptions.

14.2 Key points

Formal admissions

Where a fact is formally admitted for the purpose of the proceedings, then no proof is necessary as that fact is no longer in issue between the parties.

In civil cases, formal admissions may be made at various pre-trial stages or at trial. Such formal admissions bind those making them only for the purpose of those proceedings, but in those proceedings are conclusive of the facts which are admitted.

In criminal cases, provision is made for formal admissions by s10 Criminal Justice Act 1967. If such admissions are made otherwise than in court they must comply with the requirements of s10(2) as to their form. Formal admissions in court may be made orally by counsel: *R v Lewis* [1989] Crim LR 61. Formal admissions may be withdrawn, but only with leave of the court: s10(4).

Whether in civil or criminal proceedings, formal admissions, which are conclusive, must be distinguished from informal admissions and confessions which are by no means conclusive but rather may be rejected as inadmissible after the party against whom they are tendered has adduced rebutting evidence – or in the case of confessions, the criminal court of its own motion may put the prosecution to proof of admissibility.

Judicial notice

In both civil and criminal cases the court will acknowledge the truth of some facts without any need for proof. This creates no problems in civil cases, but in criminal cases there is the problem, when the judge takes judicial notice of a fact, as to how the jury ought to be directed; it appears to be accepted that although in the jury's realm of fact rather than the judge's realm of law, the judge must nevertheless direct the jury to take the fact as proved: *R v Simpson* [1983] 1 WLR 1494; *Gibson v Wales* [1983] 1 WLR 393.

Judicial notice may be taken of notorious facts, or may be taken after reference.

Notoriety

Where the fact is a matter of common knowledge (universally, or in the case of magistrates it may be locally) which is so notorious as not to be open to any serious dispute, then judicial notice will be taken of it without reference to any source. Classic examples of a miriad of such facts include a fortnight being too short a period for human gestation, criminals leading unhappy lives, postcards being correspondence which may be read by anyone.

Notice after reference

The party seeking such judicial notice of a fact must provide any required source of reference. Most of these cases of judicial notice relate to political matters, such as the existence of a state of war; the meaning of the classification 'secret' on a government document; the extent of territorial sovereignty (and therefore jurisdiction of English courts). Others have involved professional practice, eg that of the Ordnance Survey (in interpreting map references), and readily demonstrable public facts, eg the meaning of words in common usage, or geographical facts, where reference may be made to dictionaries, maps etc.

Problems arise where judicial notice is taken after receiving evidence, and where personal knowledge of the judge is involved. In the classic case of *McQuaker v Goddard* [1940] 1 KB 687, the judge consulted books and heard evidence on the issue before taking judicial notice of the fact that a camel was a domestic animal. This is on the borderline of judicial notice/proof by evidence, but can be justified as being the former given that it is confined to constant facts which are therefore not determined by the special facts of any case. The problem of the extent to which a judge can utilise his personal knowledge has spawned a lot of case law, yet the basic distinction is between the judge properly applying his general knowledge of the subject matter to his understanding, and evaluation, of the evidence which has been adduced, and his improperly using his personal knowledge in place of evidence adduced. But in this latter situation a distinction must be drawn between judges and on the other hand magistrates and jurors whose local knowledge may be of something so notorious in the locality that judicial notice may be taken rather than evidence: *Ingram* v *Percival* [1969] 1 QB 548.

Presumptions

When a presumption operates, then the court either must, or may, come to the conclusion which the presumption points to, unless there is evidence (or sufficient evidence) to the contrary. All true presumptions are rebuttable by evidence to the contrary; there are two so-called 'irrebuttable presumptions', ie that a child under ten cannot commit an offence. This is not a presumption but a rule of substantive law. In addition there are presumptions which do not depend on proof of a basic fact, but are rather rules governing the incidence of the evidential and legal burdens of proof, and to some extent the standard in criminal cases; for example the presumption of sanity and of innocence – the former dictates that the defence has a legal burden of proving a defence of insanity or insane automatism and the latter dictates that the prosecution must prove beyond reasonable doubt every element of the offence charged and any other fact in issue such as the admissibility of a confession.

Further presumptions of fact need not detain the student of Evidence for long – they are merely commonly recurring examples of circumstantial evidence, ie illustrations of evidence relevant to the facts in issue. For example, if a party destroys or conceals evidence the court may infer that the evidence was unfavourable to his case; or the 'presumption of continuance', to the effect that any proven state of affairs may be assumed to have continued for some time, the duration depending on all the circumstances (examples being the question of the speed of a vehicle at a specific time and the continued existence of a person proved to be alive at some earlier time than that in question); and the inference which the court may draw as to whether the natural and probable consequences of an act of the accused were intended or foreseen by him.

All the above are often classed as not being 'true presumptions', in that rules of substantive law, rules governing the incidence of the burdens of proof, and pieces of circumstantial evidence, do not amount to presumptions in the true sense. 'True' presumptions are said to be rebuttable presumptions of law, ie on proof of a basic fact the presumption arises, and in the absence of sufficient evidence in rebuttal the prescribed conclusion must be drawn by the court. How much evidence is required in rebuttal determines whether the presumption is persuasive or evidential; conversely, whether the rebuttable presumption of law is persuasive or evidential dictates whether the party seeking to rebut must discharge a legal burden of proof or merely an evidential burden. If the appropriate burden is not discharged the court must draw the prescribed conclusion; if the burden is discharged the presumption is rebutted and the issue must be proved by admissible evidence without the aid, or hindrance, of the presumption.

The most frequently recurring, and therefore examinable, rebuttable presumptions of law are marriage, legitimacy, death, regularity, res ipsa loquitur.

Presumption of marriage

On proof of a marriage ceremony, the law presumes the formal validity of the marriage: *Piers* v *Piers* (1849) 2 HL Cas 331. The presumption is persuasive in civil cases, but only evidential in criminal cases when the prosecution bears the legal burden of proving validity. The law will also assume the essential validity of the marriage – ie that the parties had the capacity to marry (16 years old and not already validly married). This presumption of essential validity appears to be persuasive in civil cases, but the standard of proof in rebuttal, albeit the civil standard, is lower than that imposed in respect of rebuttal of the presumption of formal validity: *Re Peete; Peete* v *Crompton* [1952] 2 All ER 599. On proof of cohabitation, a presumption arises that the couple were living together as lawful spouses. In civil proceedings this presumption of marriage is persuasive: *Re Taylor* [1961] 1 WLR 9, but when relied on by the prosecution, proof of cohabitation does not even raise an evidentiary presumption unless coupled with production of a marriage certificate: *R* v *Birtles* (1911) 6 Cr App R 177.

Presumption of legitimacy

On proof of the basic fact that a child was born, or conceived, in wedlock, it is presumed that he is the legitimate issue of the spouses. In civil proceedings, the presumption is persuasive – to the civil standard of proof: s26 Family Law Reform Act 1969. In criminal proceedings, eg a charge of incest by the accused with a child born to or conceived by his wife during the subsistence of their marriage, the presumption can only be evidential. On general criminal law principles, the accused merely has to raise a reasonable doubt as to an element of the offence to ensure an acquittal, therefore evidence sufficient to raise such a doubt as to the legitimacy of the daughter must suffice, as opposed to proving illegitimacy in a civil dispute over paternity, custody, access, maintenance, etc.

Presumption of death

The rebuttable presumption of death arises on proof of basic facts which were stipulated in *Chard* v *Chard* [1956] P 259, ie there were persons likely to have heard of the person whose death is an issue, but they have not heard of him for at least seven years immediately preceding the proceedings and all due, appropriate, enquiries have been made, then the person will be presumed to have died at some time within the seven year period of silence and absence. The presumption is evidential only. There is conflict, however, as to whether, without evidence in rebuttal, death will be assumed to have occurred at some time during the seven years immediately preceding the hearing, or whether death can be assumed at the end of the seven year period of continuous silence and absence and at all times thereafter. Whichever view prevails, if a specific date of death must be established (for purposes of succession etc), then evidence must be adduced to prove the actual time of death.

Presumption of regularity

On proof of the basic fact that some person acted as the holder of a public office (eg judge, magistrate, police constable) it is presumed that he was duly appointed. It is presumed that devices which are usually efficient (eg speedometers of police vehicles, intoximeters, radar speed meters, radar guns) were working properly at the relevant time. On proof of necessary business transactions being carried out, it is presumed that they were carried out in the correct sequence. The presumption is evidential only, but in criminal proceedings the defence must adduce evidence to discharge the evidential burden borne by them on proof of the basic fact; it is not enough merely to challenge the regularity: see *Hill* v *Baxter* [1958] 1 QB 277 regarding discharge of the evidential burden by defence.

Res ipsa loquitur

On proof by the plaintiff in a negligence action that the accident which caused his injuries is one which in the normal course of events would not occur without negligence on the part of the person in control of the relevant operation, and that he, the plaintiff, cannot prove it was caused by the defendant's negligence, then the plaintiff may seek assistance from the principle res ipsa loquitur, ie 'the thing speaks for itself'. Given that, in the circumstances of the accident, the sole control by the defendant or his employees, and the ignorance of the plaintiff as to the defendant's conduct is proved, then it may be presumed that the accident was caused by the defendant's negligence (primary or vicarious). But whether the presumption is merely one of fact, or whether it is an evidential, or a persuasive, presumption of law is open to debate as the law is far from clear. If a presumption of fact, then in the absence of evidence from the defendant, the court may reach the conclusion prescribed by the presumption but does not have to. If the presumption is an evidential presumption of law, then it is rebutted if the defendant adduces evidence consistent equally with negligence and pure accident. If the presumption is persuasive, the defendant must disprove negligence. There are authorities in support of all three contentions, but this could be the result of the wide variance in the basic facts which give rise to the presumption in the reported cases.

Conflicting presumptions

Where there are two presumptions in conflict in the proceedings, then if they are of equal effect (eg both are persuasive presumptions) the court may decide that they cancel each other and the parties must discharge their burdens of proof by admissible evidence only: *Monckton* v *Tarr* (1930) 23 BWCC 504. Alternatively, the court may take account of public policy considerations in determining which presumption prevails: *Taylor* v *Taylor* [1965] 1 All ER 872. The classic case of *R* v *Willshire* (1881) 6 QBD 366 on conflicting presumptions can be interpreted as being purely a case of deciding which party had to discharge a legal, as opposed to evidential, burden of proof; but where presumptions arise they will have a bearing by their nature, on the incidence of the legal and/or evidential burden.

14.3 Key cases and statute

- *Chard* v *Chard* [1956] P 259

- *Hill* v *Baxter* [1958] 1 QB 277

- *Piers* v *Piers* (1849) 2 HL Cas 331

- *R* v *Simpson* [1983] 1 WLR 1494

- Criminal Justice Act 1967, s10

14.4 Questions and suggested solutions

QUESTION ONE

'Every writer of sufficient intelligence to appreciate the difficulties of the subject matter has approached the topic of presumptions with a sense of hopelessness and left it with a feeling of despair.' (Morgan)

Why are presumptions so difficult to analyse and classify?

University of London LLB Examination
(for External Students) Law of Evidence June 1985 Q3

General Comment

This question calls for a general discussion of presumptions, with a focus on the difficulties of analysis and classification. It will be important to avoid producing a catalogue of case law or a merely descriptive answer.

Skeleton Solution

Introduction: different effects of presumptions; scope of discussion – the general context: definition of terms; stages of a trial – traditional classification, introduction: irrebuttable presumptions of law – rebuttable presumptions of law: two types; new names; Lord Denning and Lord Bridge; two types – presumptions of fact: definition; Lord Denning and Lord Bridge; distinction between evidential and factual presumptions; permissive presumptions – criminal cases: burden placed on accused – conclusion: reasons for confusion.

Suggested Solution

Introduction

The area of presumptions has given rise to a great deal of division of terminology and of conceptual thinking. These differences among many eminent academic and practising lawyers has come about because of the three-part role of presumptions in English law. Presumptions sometimes alter the normal rules on burden of proof, for policy reasons; at other times they allow the proof of fact 'A' to be the result of proving fact 'B'; at other times they act simply to direct the mind of the trier of fact towards possible inferences which may be drawn from the evidence adduced. Indeed at time a presumption may do all three of these things. This complex role can only be understood if the rules on burden of proof are borne in mind, together with the procedure at each stage of a trial. These will be discussed below.

There are many different presumptions and many policy reasons behind those presumptions. As conceptions of public policy change, so the effect of presumptions will change; this makes the task of classification all the more difficult. It is proposed to deal with the traditional, or orthodox, classification and to show how each old category has been altered in terminology by recent commentators. The following discussion will be in relation to civil cases only, when covering basic principles; the rules applicable to criminal cases will be dealt with separately.

The general context

Although there is a considerable variation in terminology in the area of burdens of proof, this answer will use that favoured by Cross (*Cross on Evidence* (8th edition, 1995)). In other words the burden of proving an issue will be referred to as the legal burden of proof; the onus of raising an issue not already raised will be called the evidential burden; the risk of not calling evidence on an issue which one's opponent has already raised is the tactical burden; and the overall burden of persuading the court to find in one's favour will be called the ultimate burden.

It must be remembered that burdens and standards of proof are irrelevant unless the trier of fact or law actually has to make a decision. Throughout the calling of evidence it is naive to assume that the trier of fact takes each piece of evidence in turn and considers whether the case has been proved – that decision is only taken at the end of the case, when all the evidence has been called, so that everything can be seen in context. There are only three stages of a trial at which burdens are important. The first is at the end of the plaintiff's case, when the judge has to decide whether the evidential burden on the plaintiff has been discharged, in other words whether he has called evidence from which a reasonable jury could find for him (the rare case where the defendant has the right to begin works on the same principle). The second is when all evidence has been called and the judge has to consider whether sufficient evidence has been called on each issue for that issue to need to be decided. The third stage comes immediately after the second and is when the trier of fact (usually the judge in a civil case) has to decide whether the ultimate burden has been satisfied. At the first two stages questions of the discharge of evidential burdens arise, at the final stage it is the legal burden on each issue which is important.

The traditional classification – introduction

The traditional classification on presumptions is into three categories, ie irrebuttable presumptions of law, rebuttable presumptions of law and presumptions of fact. Irrebuttable presumptions of law are not true presumptions at all (this is one of the few statements on this topic with which all commentators agree!). Rather they are rules of law put into presumptive form. For example s50 Children and Young Persons Act 1933 (as amended by s16(1) Children and Young Persons Act 1963) states that 'it shall be conclusively presumed that no child under the age of ten years can be guilty of any offence'. This could be amended by the omission of the first six words so as to be the same rule, but not in presumptive form: 'no child under the age of ten years can be guilty of an offence'. Clearly nothing is added, or lost, by stating the rule in terms of a presumption, but it is not really a presumption at all. Therefore irrebuttable presumptions of law will not be discussed further.

Rebuttable presumptions of law

Rebuttable presumptions of law all follow the same logical form. On proof of fact 'A', fact 'B' is presumed to be true. The traditional classification of presumptions does not further divide these presumptions, but as has been pointed out many times there are two types of rebuttable presumption of law. The first type is the presumption which says that on proof of fact 'A' fact 'B' shall be taken to be true unless it is proved that fact 'B' is not true. The other type is the presumption which says that on proof of fact 'A' fact 'B' shall be taken to be true unless sufficient evidence is raised to throw doubt on whether fact 'B' really is true. The distinction can be illustrated by the following example.

A child is born to Mrs X while she is married to Mr X. Mr X leaves Mrs X and refuses to pay any maintenance for the child, because he claims he is not the father. Mrs X sues for maintenance.

There is a presumption that a child born in wedlock is the child of the mother's husband (*Banbury Peerage Case* (1811) 1 Sim & St 153). Theoretically this presumption could be rebutted by Mr X (the defendant) proving that he was not the father, or by him adducing evidence which showed a 50–50 chance of him not being the father. Since the burden of proving the right to maintenance will be on Mrs X (the plaintiff), so if Mr X could show an equal chance of him not being the father then he would have prevented Mrs X proving on balance of probabilities that she was entitled to maintenance money from him. So the presumption could require proof to the contrary or it could require the defendant merely to prevent the plaintiff proving her case, without proving his case himself. In fact the presumption of legitimacy places a legal burden on the party rebutting the presumption (see now s26 Family Law Reform Act 1969). But the theoretical position of rebuttable presumption is clear – they are of two types.

This failure of the traditional classification to distinguish between the two types of rebuttable presumption of law led to various attempts to adopt a two-part classification.

Lord Denning called the presumptions which put a legal burden on the rebutter 'compelling presumptions' ((1945) 61 MLR 379; see also Carter, *Cases and Statutes on Evidence* (2nd edition, 1990, pp78–79) though the more common terminology is 'persuasive presumptions' (*Cross on Evidence* (8th edition, 1995)); Heydon, *Evidence Cases and Statutes* (2nd edition, 1984, p43)). This new title is useful in that it distinguishes such presumptions from those which impose a lesser burden on the rebutter. But it has not gone without criticism. Lord Bridge ((1949) 12 MLR 272) has argued that the classification of such rules as presumptions is all wrong. He pointed out that these compelling or persuasive presumptions are rules of law which determine that a certain result must follow from the proof of certain facts. In the example given above, on proof by Mrs X of birth in wedlock the law stipulates that legitimacy must be found unless there is proof to the contrary. Lord Bridge's argument was that this is not a presumption at all, it is a rule of law dressed up as a presumption. It is certainly true that there is little difference between a common law rule that says the burden of proving illegitimacy is on the defendant once the plaintiff has proved birth in wedlock. Each of the rules is really in the same form – on the happening of a certain event, certain consequences follow; on the happening of the start of the case the ultimate burden is on the plaintiff, on the happening of proof of birth in wedlock the legal burden of proving illegitimacy is on the defendant. Each rule can be put into the same pattern. Therefore the question arises whether it is right to classify 'compelling' or 'persuasive' presumptions as presumptions. Lord Bridge argued that one should bear in mind the stages of the trial at which the issue of legitimacy will arise. The plaintiff must produce evidence on which a reasonable jury could find birth in wedlock; then the defendant has to prove illegitimacy. No question of presumption arises, he argued; there are two distinct issues – has the plaintiff prove birth in wedlock, has the defendant proved illegitimacy? It is submitted that Lord Bridge's approach does not properly explain the concept of the persuasive presumption. It is certainly true that the effect of the 'presumptions' is to state a rule of law, that the defendant bears the burden of proving illegitimacy; but that burden only arises once the basis for it has been established by the plaintiff. If the plaintiff calls no evidence relating to birth in wedlock, then her case would be rejected on the defendant making a submission of no case. It is artificial to separate the cases where a presumption places a legal burden of proof on the rebutter and those where only an evidential burden is placed on him, by arguing that the former category is not a presumption but is a rule of law. Both are presumptions and both presumptions arise because the law says they arise. In both cases the trier of fact must draw a certain conclusion unless some evidence is called to the contrary. The only difference between the two is the amount of evidence required to rebut the presumption.

The classification of the second type of rebuttable presumption of law is not subject to the same difficulties. This second category – the presumption that on proof of fact 'A', the trier of fact must conclude fact 'B' unless the other party can balance the probability of 'B' being true and being not true – has been defined by Cross as the 'evidential presumption' (*Cross on Evidence* (8th edition, 1995)) but Lord Bridge simply called these 'presumptions'; this being the result of his basic thesis that there is only one sort of presumption, all other things which are called presumptions being defined using other terminology (12 MLR 272, 279).

The effect of an evidential presumption, as mentioned above, is to place a burden on the rebutter to adduce sufficient evidence to prevent the proponent from proving his case. In other words a tactical burden is placed on the rebutter.

Evidential presumptions may be of two types. The first type reflects common sense by requiring fact 'B' to be presumed on the proof of fact 'A' even though as a matter of common sense the natural conclusion is that fact 'B' is true; the second type gives additional weight to fact 'A that common sense would always indicate. For example, the common law presumption of regularity states that if a person acts in an office for which certain formal qualifications are needed it is to be presumed that he has those qualifications (*Berryman* v *Wise* (1791) 4 Term Rep 366). As a matter of common sense proof that a man sat as a judge at the Old Bailey would be clear proof that he was qualified to do so; after all, if he were not qualified then he would have been found out. In such a case there is no need for there to be any legal presumption, the trier of fact would draw the required conclusion anyway. But, it could be that the use of a church for a wedding ceremony would not, necessarily, be construed by a reasonable man to be proof that it was properly licensed for weddings; nonetheless the presumption of regularity applies so that the trier of fact must find that it was licensed unless the opponent on the issue can show that there was an equal chance of the church not being licensed (*R* v *Cresswell* (1876) 1 QBD 446). Despite these two types of evidential presumptions, there seems to be no need to divide them into separate categories of presumptions because they both work in the same way. They both place a tactical burden on the opponent of the issue once the proponent has proved the basic facts.

There has, though, been some difference of terminology in that Lord Denning did not give evidential presumptions a separate name, but classed them together with presumptions of fact, as 'provisional' presumptions. This analysis will be discussed below, when dealing with presumptions of fact.

Presumptions of fact

The traditional presumption of fact has two aspects. The first is that there are some inferences which a trier of fact will draw because common sense tells him to. For example, if evidence is given that a man walking alongside a golf course was hit by a golf ball the trier of fact will conclude, in the absence of other evidence, that the ball came from the golf course. The second aspect of presumptions of fact is that there are certain issues of fact which arise regularly in trials and the courts have stated that the jury is entitled to draw certain conclusions in those cases. For example, there is a presumption of continuance of life, which states that a life is presumed to continue for a reasonable time. This is a commonsense inference from proof of the fact that someone is alive and well, but arises so frequently that the appellate courts have from time to time identified it as a presumption (*R v Lumley* (1869) LR 1 CCR 196). It is interesting to note that it has been said that presumptions of fact only arise in this second sense of the commonly recurring fact. The argument here seems to be that some presumptions of fact are recognised by the appellate courts so often that it would be an error of law by the trial judge if he failed to make a direction that the presumption can be made.

Furthermore, it must be noted that Lord Denning called presumptions of fact 'provisional' presumptions, on the basis that they put a tactical burden on the opponent of the issue, and this tactical burden can be satisfied by calling evidence which throws doubt on the truth of the presumed fact. In other words, the presumption will only be drawn when the proponent's evidence is called and may be displaced before the final decision has to be made; it is provisional not permanent. He seemed to group evidential presumptions (presumptions of law placing a tactical burden on the rebutter) and presumptions of fact together in that they both place a tactical burden only on the rebutter. But, as Lord Bridge pointed out, evidential presumptions must be drawn as a matter of law, whereas factual presumptions are permissive only, they may be drawn (12 MLR 272, 278–279). It is submitted, with respect, that Lord Denning failed to appreciate the true effect of the evidential and factual presumptions. Both presumptions only arise at the end of the case; they help the discharge of the legal burden on an issue, by allowing the trier of fact to draw an inference from the evidence presented. But what if no evidence is given by the defendant, must he necessarily fail? Is there a difference between the evidential and factual presumptions? It is submitted that there is a difference. In order to appreciate the difference it is necessary to go back to basics and consider the essence of a presumption.

All presumptions can be written in the same form: on proof of fact 'A' fact 'B' is proved. There are two elements – the proof of fact 'A'; and the proof of fact 'B'. In the case of a conclusive or irrebuttable presumption of law it is not possible to call evidence disproving fact 'B', once fact 'A' has been established. For example, it is not possible to prove that a 13-year-old boy committed rape (*R v Waite* [1892] 2 QB 600). But it is possible to call evidence that the boy in question was over 13 at the time of the alleged rape. In other words, although the presumption cannot be rebutted, it is possible to prevent the presumption arising in the first place.

Applying that principle to evidential and factual presumptions, the trier of fact could always conclude that the evidence called is not strong enough to prove that a certain man sat as a judge at the Old Bailey. If the trier of fact is not satisfied that he sat, then no presumption as to his qualifications must be drawn. Similarly, if the judge is asked to presume that a 35-year-old man was likely to live for a further ten years, the judge may find on the evidence presented that the man was not 35 at the time alleged. In both cases the failure to prove the basic fact means that the presumed fact is not proved. But the converse case shows the difference between evidential and factual presumption. Say the judge is satisfied that the man in the first case sat at the Old

Bailey, or that the man in the second case was aged 35 at the relevant time; in the first case if the party who wishes to dispute the man's qualifications calls no evidence then, as a matter of law, the trial judge would have to find that the man in question was qualified to sit. In other words once the basic fact is established the presumed fact must be found to be true. In the second case, though, even if the trial judge is satisfied that the man in question was 35 and in good health at the relevant time he would still be free to find that he would not be expected to live for a further ten years if, for example, there was a war on and the man was likely to be conscripted for dangerous duties. The second case illustrates that the trier of fact may draw a presumption once the basic facts are proved, but does not have to as a matter of law; whereas when dealing with evidential presumptions the presumed fact must be found to be true in the absence of rebutting evidence, once the basic fact is established. Therefore, it is submitted, Lord Denning was wrong to argue that there is no difference between evidential presumptions and presumptions of fact.

There is a further difficulty in the area of presumptions of fact, in that certain rules of law state that the trier of fact may draw a certain conclusion on the proof of certain basic facts. These instances are different from evidential presumptions in that the trier of fact is not bound to find the presumed fact once the basic fact is true and they are different from presumptions of fact in that the law stipulates that the conclusion may be drawn from the basic fact, rather than that being the result of applying commonsense. For example, if an employer has issued an employee with a timetable which directs him to drive from one place to another in an unreasonably short time, then by virtue of s78A Road Traffic Regulations Act 1967, the timetable 'may be produced as prima facie evidence' of incitement to commit a speeding offence. There is no requirement that the jury must find the employer guilty in the absence of proof or evidence to the contrary. The effect of this sort of statutory provision is clear if the stages of the trial mentioned above are remembered. The prosecution must make out a prima facie case, fit to be left to the jury. If they cannot do so then the accused may make a submission of no case, which would lead to his acquittal. Section 78A provides that the evidential burden on the prosecution will be satisfied by the timetable being adduced. In other words, the trier of law must draw the presumption that there is a case to answer, even though the trier of fact would be free to reject the timetable as being insufficient evidence to found a conviction.

Such a statutory presumption is not classified by most writers. Lord Denning did not mention them, nor Lord Bridge, nor Cross, nor Heydon, nor Nokes. Carter has labelled them 'permissive' presumptions because the trier of fact is permitted but not obliged, to conclude that there was incitement once the timetable has been adduced (*Cases and Statutes* (2nd edition, 1990, p77)).

Criminal cases

Although the occasional criminal example has been given above, the general rules stated are only applicable to civil cases. This point is not always appreciated. The reason for it is simple. In a civil case there is no conceptual difficulty in placing a legal burden of proof on the defendant once the plaintiff has adduced some evidence on an issue (nor on the plaintiff if the defendant raises the issue). But in a criminal case the accused only bears a legal burden in two instances – if he wishes to prove insanity (*M'Naghten's Case* (1843) 10 Cl & Fin 200) and where a statute requires him to prove his defence (*R v Carr-Briant* [1943] KB 607; *R v Edwards* [1975] QB 27). In all other cases the burden on him can be evidential only. Therefore if the prosecution wishes to rely on a presumption, the accused never has to disprove the presumed fact.

Conclusion

It can be seen from the above discussion that presumptions cover many areas of the law and have been subject to many differences in analysis. It is submitted that the difficulty of analysis and classification is caused by six main factors. Firstly, the failure to distinguish between criminal and civil cases has caused confusion to those who have attempted to set out rules of presumption applicable across the board. Secondly the use of the word presumption can cause a reaction, as with Lord Bridge, that a presumption is a conclusion drawn from the proof of basic facts and anything which does not fit into that model must be called something else – even if it has been called a presumption by other writers for many years. Thirdly, it is not always fully appreciated that some presumptions place a legal burden on the party rebutting and sometimes merely a tactical burden. In this area more than any other the terminology of writers tends to confuse. Williams talked of evidential presumptions because of his definition of the evidential burden; others define that burden as the tactical burden, but retain the term 'evidential presumption', the potential for confusion then is clear. Fourthly, the place of presumptions of fact is changing. The so-called doctrine of recent possession (someone found in possession of stolen goods shortly after they were stolen may be presumed to have come by them dishonestly) has been classified as a presumption of law (*R v Hepworth & Fearnley* [1955] 2 QB 600) but the Court of Appeal has recently made it clear that it is a presumption of fact only (*R v Ball* [1983] 2 All ER 1089). Similar confusion has been caused with the presumption that a man intends the natural and probable consequences of his acts; this started out as a presumption of fact (*R v Steane* [1947] KB 997), was turned into a presumption of law (*DPP v Smith* [1961] AC 290) and is now a presumption of fact again (s8 Criminal Justice Act 1967). This sort of change makes the use of older definitions of presumptions dangerous. Fifthly, presumptions of law are random rules affecting the way cases are proved and the way burdens of proof are distributed. The lack of any system of policy behind the presumptions misleads some commentators to attempt to over-simplify the categories. It is submitted that Lord Denning's classification of certain presumptions as 'provisional' falls within this point. Sixthly, the use by the judges of the term 'shifting of the burden of proof' is so widespread, and in many instances so misconceived, that one is tempted to look for a presumption to justify the supposed shift. For example, the 'doctrine' of res ipsa loquitur is treated as a presumption of fact in all parts of the world, where it is recognised that if the only logical inference to draw from the facts proved is that there was negligence then that conclusion must be drawn. But nowhere other than this country has consistently held that the doctrine creates a persuasive presumption placing a legal burden of proof on the rebutter. The confusion has been caused by inexact use of burden of proof terminology.

It is interesting to note that of all the major works on evidence only Carter has pointed out the true effect of what he calls 'permissive' presumptions – rules of law which allow the trier of law no right to reject a piece of evidence as insufficiently probative to be left to the trier of fact. But, even he does not make the point that such a presumption is useless by itself. To use the example given above, s78A Road Traffic Regulations Act 1967 allows the prosecution of an employer for incitement to exceed the speed limit, to use a timetable issued by the employer as evidence against him. This prevents the trial judge withdrawing the case from the jury for lack of evidence on the issue of incitement, but if the case is one where the judge would be minded to withdraw the case for lack of evidence and the jury convicts, then surely the convicted employer would have a ground for appeal in the same way that any appeal should be allowed where the evidence against the accused should, at common law, have been ruled to be insufficient. This new category of presumption, therefore, also has its problems. It only need be relied on if there is no other evidence against the employer, but in that case any conviction could well be perverse. By dressing-up s78A as a presumption there is every possibility that it will be given more significance than it deserves.

Finally, it cannot be stated that the existence of so many classifications and names of presumptions is of any real use unless and until the courts start to put one terminology or another into practice. Although Lord Denning introduced his own terminology and analysis in several cases (eg *Emmanuel* v *Emmanuel* [1946] P 115; *Huyton-with-Roby UDC* v *Hunter* [1955] 1 WLR 603) such usage has not been uniform. The source of confusion in the absence of judicial guidance is clear once the many sources of the word 'presumption' have been seen.

QUESTION TWO

a) What place has judicial notice in the context of our trial system?

b) How much use may a judge or magistrate make of his or her personal knowledge?

University of London LLB Examination
(for External Students) Law of Evidence June 1985 Q4

General Comment

A good answer to this question will describe relevant case law and will also provide some commentary or analysis. It is important to write a brief plan so that the answer has a unifying theme relevant to the question.

Skeleton Solution

The place of judicial notice; introduction – defining the problem – judicial notice of facts: notice without inquiry; notice after inquiry – judicial notice of law: scope of rule;

rationale – theory of judicial notice: two principles; policy; function of judge place of judicial notice – personal knowledge; introduction – definition of the problem – knowledge of the law: tacit notice – knowledge of fact: introduction – judge's personal knowledge of fact: limited scope of use; practical considerations – magistrates' personal knowledge: knowledge of local matters; expert knowledge; difference in treatment of judge and justices.

Suggested Solution

a) *Introduction*

The principle that questions of fact are for the jury and questions of law for the judge is so well established that no authority need be cited in its support. There is, though, a significant area where the judge decides questions of fact and directs the jury to reach a decision in accordance with his direction. This is the area of judicial notice. In this answer the place of judicial notice will be examined from three angles. Firstly will be considered the extent to which a judge in a criminal case may decide issues of fact. The second perspective will involve discussion of the way matters of law are proved. Thirdly will be examined whether there is any consistent theory as to the proper place for judicial notice.

Judicial notice of facts

There are some facts of such common knowledge that it is thought improper to leave the jury any scope for diversion from accepted wisdom. (This discussion will assume that there is a judge and jury, for the sake of convenience.) For example, the Court of Common Pleas once held that it was right for a judge to direct a jury that rain falls (*Fay v Prentice* (1845) 14 LJ CP 298). To allow the jury the possibility of disagreeing in such a case may be harmless in that it could be said with some confidence that no jury would disagree. Nonetheless, just to be sure, no evidence is allowed to go to the jury to give them cause for doubt.

Clearly this is a usurpation of the function of the jury by the trial judge. He directs them that an issue of fact must be decided in a certain way. As has already been mentioned, there is no harm in this in such an obvious case. But the right of the judge to direct the jury on questions of fact goes beyond cases where the fact is obvious to anyone. There are some facts of which judicial notice will be taken even though the trial judge may not have been able to state the fact without help from a work of reference. In such cases he is said to take notice after inquiry (*Cross on Evidence* (8th edition, 1995)). For example in *Duff Development Co v Government of Kelantan* [1924] AC 797 the House of Lords held that judicial notice should be taken of the fact that Kelantan was a sovereign state once the Secretary of State for the Colonies had certified that this was so. There is a clear policy element to such a decision, namely that the courts should not reach decisions which might upset the comity of nations. Notice after inquiry is not limited to such cases, though, it applies also to questions of fact which arise frequently and so should be decided in a consistent manner by the courts. To leave such questions to juries may lead to embarrassing conflicts of decisions. For example, in *Davey* v *Harrow Corporation* [1958] 1 QB 60 the Court of Appeal stated that judicial notice could be taken of the practice of the Ordnance Survey, primarily to prevent different juries reaching different decisions where similar points of the interpretation of maps arise.

Judicial notice of law

It is no usurpation of the function of the jury for a trial judge to direct them on the law, because that is his exclusive province. It is frequently said that everyone is presumed to know the law (the closes thing we have to be an authority on this is *Bilbie* v *Lumley* (1802) 2 East 469). To expect every trial judge to know the full contents of every statute and precedent is, obviously, quite unreasonable, though. Therefore the judge is allowed to 'refresh his memory' by references to statutes, precedents and works of authority. The formal rules of admissibility of evidence do not apply to legal argument, because the judge does not hear 'evidence'. Rather he refers to various authorities in order to remind himself of what he is seemed to know already.

Judicial notice is taken of English law, but not of other jurisdictions, except in certain special circumstances (for which see Nokes, 'The Limits of Judicial Notice' (1958) 74 LQR 59, 61–62). Judicial notice is also taken of the contents of statutes (s3 Interpretation Act 1978 and s4(2) European Communities Act 1972 for the taking of judicial notice of the contents of the Community Treaties) and of general customs (*Brandao* v *Barnett* (1846) 12 Cl & Fin 787). In some instances even local customs have been the proper subject of judicial notice; for example the local custom that markets in the City of London are market overt for the sale of goods, but not for their purchase by the shopkeeper (*Hargreave* v *Spink* [1892] 1 QB 25).

The rationale behind all these cases seems to be that the judge must decide questions of law in a way which allows for accuracy of decision and consistency from case to case (see Carter, *Cases and Statutes on Evidence* (2nd edition, 1990, pp123–125)). To impose rules of evidence on the adduction of law reports, for example, would exclude them as hearsay (subject to civil cases where the statutory exceptions, ss2 and 4 Civil Evidence Act 1968, apply). Such a result would be absurdly inconvenient, so by making questions of law the subject of judicial notice this inconvenience can be circumvented.

Theory of judicial notice

It will be seen from the above discussion that there are three common areas within which the rules of judicial notice apply. Firstly to questions of fact which are known to all; secondly to questions of fact which need to be decided uniformly from case to case, but which need inquiry to be established; and thirdly questions of law which are within the judge's exclusive domain. The question arises whether there is a consistent policy behind all three areas.

It is often asserted that the underlying principle of the rules of judicial notice is that 'notorious' matters should not be the subject of dispute, instead they should be recognised as notorious and applied the same in every case (see, for example, *Phipson on Evidence* (14th edition, 1990, paras 2–21)). This theory is supported to an extent by the history of judicial notice (Nokes, 74 LQR 59, 63–70), but there are, in fact, two distinct principles which are applied. The first is that for reasons of policy certain facts should not be challenged by evidence. An example is given above in *Duff Development Co* v *Government of Kelantan* [1924] AC 797 and this principle also explains such cases as *Fay* v *Prentice* (1845) 14 LJ CP 298. The other principle, which applies to the taking of judicial notice of questions of law, is that the function of the judge to decide questions of law should not be hampered by technical arguments over the admissibility of reference works.

The place of judicial notice in the trial system, therefore, is to provide a degree of consistency of decision to everyday questions of fact and to allow judges to reach decisions on questions of law in the most effective way. Judicial notice can thus be seen as a set of rules providing for the saving of time and the increase of efficiency in the courts.

b) *Introduction*

The above discussion of judicial notice divides the subject into two parts – notice of fact and notice of law. This distinction is maintained in the rules relating to the use which may be made of personal knowledge by a judge or magistrate.

Personal knowledge of law

If a judge has to decide a question of law he will not always need to be referred to statutes or authorities. Some areas of the law will be well known to him and his memory of these will not need to be refreshed. Clearly it would be unsatisfactory for a judge to have to be referred to statutes and authorities every time, therefore he is allowed to rely on his personal knowledge of the law. Cross has pointed out that some reliance on personal knowledge is inevitable in the decision by a judge or jury of any issue (*Cross on Evidence* (8th edition, 1995)). For example, if a judge has to decide whether a particular house is covered by the Rent and Housing Acts provisions which give tenants statutory rights against their landlord, he would not have to be referred to a dictionary in order to know what 'dwelling' means because he will already know what it means. In every case where a legal point arises it will be discussed in English, the judge relies on his personal knowledge of the English language in order to understand the argument. This is what Cross called a 'tacit' application of judicial notice.

Personal knowledge of fact

The decision of questions of fact by a judge raises different principles, though. In criminal cases it is, of course, the function of the jury to consider questions of fact, subject to directions of fact of which judicial notice has been taken. In civil cases the virtual extinction of the jury means that the judge has to decide both law and fact. The judge when deciding questions of fact is in essentially the same position as a jury or a bench of magistrates. It is not yet clear whether judges and magistrates are in the same position when it comes to the use of personal knowledge in the reaching of a decision of fact.

Judge's knowledge of fact

It is clear that a judge may rely on his personal knowledge of matters of general, or common, knowledge. The problem arises when he had to deal with an issue on which he has local knowledge. Is he allowed to rely on that local knowledge?

The start of the discussion must be the normal rule that questions of fact must be decided according to the evidence called, the trier of fact being entitled to draw any legitimate logical inference from that evidence. If, for example, the question arises whether the defendant trespassed on the plaintiff's land and the plaintiff calls evidence that the defendant was seen entered the land by climbing over a particular gate, and the defendant calls no evidence in rebuttal; then it would appear that the judge would have no option but to find for the plaintiff.

The position is made difficult if the judge knows that the gate is twenty feet high and covered from top to bottom in barbed wire. Is he allowed to rely on this knowledge and use it as the basis of rejecting the evidence called by the plaintiff? The old position was that the trier of fact, whether judge or jury, was not allowed to rely on personal local knowledge (*R* v *Sutton* (1816) 4 M & S 532). But this was altered gradually, so that in 1841 the trier of fact was allowed to make limited reference to his personal knowledge, and over 100 years later the general rule was stated that personal knowledge of notorious local matters could be relied on provided it was properly used and reasonably applied (*Reynolds* v *Llanelly Associated Tinplate Co* [1948] 1 All ER 140). The rule laid down is very wide and vague, indeed this was accepted by the judge who decided the *Reynolds* case. The position of the trained judge does not appear to have altered since 1948. Therefore it can be said, albeit tentatively, that a judge may rely on his personal knowledge of notorious local facts when it is proper and reasonable so to do. The test of when it is proper and reasonable is, necessarily, wide because much would depend on the availability of cogent evidence to prove the point and on whether time and expense would be saved by the judge relying on his knowledge rather than hearing such evidence. In the example give above, therefore, the trial judge would only be allowed to rely on his personal knowledge of the state of the gate if it was a matter which was notorious in the locality.

It may be useful to add that many County Court actions are heard by local judges who, it seems, must from time to time rely on their personal knowledge of the area. But the judges in such cases will not usually give detailed judgments, so the reliance on personal knowledge may be greater in practice than the Court of Appeal has ever had the opportunity to appreciate.

Certainly in principle, there is little to commend any distinction between a professional judge acting as a trier of fact and any other tribunal; nonetheless, such a distinction is drawn, as will now be shown.

Magistrates' knowledge of fact

It has been stated above that magistrates are treated differently to professional judges in the respect that they may rely on personal knowledge to a greater extent. Two Divisional Court decisions uphold a distinction between magistrates and judges.

In *Ingram* v *Percival* [1969] 1 QB 548 it was held that local magistrates were entitled to rely on their own knowledge of the tidal limits of local waters. In *Wetherall* v *Harrison* [1976] QB 773 the Divisional Court held that a magistrate was allowed to rely on his professional knowledge as a doctor when considering a medical defence put forward by the accused. The reasoning in both cases was similar and was that magistrates are local justices untrained in the law; as such their local expertise should be used to the advantage of the administration of justice, as should any other specialist knowledge which they have to offer. In *Wetherall* v *Harrison* [1976] QB 773 the position of the professional judge and the lay magistrate was said to be different because the professional judge is trained to put certain matters out of his mind, whereas the layman was not. Manchester (42 MLR 22, 28) has argued that there was no authority to support this distinction between the use by the different tribunals of personal knowledge. Perhaps it is not fair to counter this with the trite argument that there is never an authority for any proposition until the first authority is created. His point is that the Divisional Court when drawing this distinction assumed that it should be drawn, without sufficiently citing reasons why it should be drawn.

The position of magistrates, therefore, can be summarised in two propositions. Firstly, they may rely on their knowledge of local matters and are not limited, as are judges, to local matters which are 'notorious' (note: there is a signal failure in the authorities to define 'notorious', see 74 LQR 59, 59–70). Secondly they may rely on their professional knowledge in assessing the weight to give evidence called. The first principle has been criticised on the ground that no adequate reason has been given why the distinction should be drawn. Indeed it is hard to see why one trier of fact should be in any different position to any other. Perhaps the rule does not apply very often in practice, though. If evidence is called as to the circumstances of the case then there will be little scope for the justices to rely on their local knowledge. In *Ingram* v *Percival* they only relied on their own knowledge because no evidence had been called on the extent of the tidal waters. It may be that such a position will only rarely arise, usually evidence would be called. The trained judge, unlike the lay magistrates, would be able to direct the parties towards the lack of evidence if he feels that there is a relevant matter which requires to be proved. Perhaps this is the true reason behind the distinction – ability of the trier of fact to determine whether the case is better proved by relying on personal knowledge or by requiring evidence to be called.

The second principle may, in fact, reflect less of a difference in treatment between justices and judges than Manchester suggests. He argues that *Wetherall v Harrison* [1976] QB 773 allows justices to rely on professional knowledge to a greater extent than judges (42 MLR 22, 28). It is arguable that this is not so. A professional judge is allowed to rely on his professional instincts and experience when assessing the credibility of a witness. He would have seen and heard more witnesses in his career than any magistrate. Inevitably he would have developed a 'feel' for when a witness is honest or untruthful. There has never been any suggestion that he cannot rely on that experience. Is this any different to the position of the lay justice who is a doctor who does not believe a witness because professional experience tells him that the story told is untrue? It is submitted that there is no difference.

QUESTION THREE

What is the relationship between the burden of proof and presumptions? It is possible to classify presumptions by reference to their impact on the burden of proof? Give reasons.

University of London LLB Examination
(for External Students) Law of Evidence June 1986 Q2

General Comment

This question asks the student to describe and comment on the relationship between two areas of the syllabus and demonstrates how integrated those areas are.

Skeleton Solution

Burden of proof: two types; definition – standard rule on burden of proof in civil and criminal cases: exceptions – presumptions: definition; examples; effect on burden of proof – challenge of basic facts or challenge of conclusion – classifying presumptions according to their effect on burden of proof.

Suggested Solution

The burden of proof in any trial, civil or criminal, involves two elements, namely, the evidential burden and the legal burden. Indeed, these two burdens arise on each issue in the trial, as well as on the overall issue of which party is to win the case. The evidential burden lies on the party who has to adduce sufficient evidence to make an issue a live issue (*Cross on Evidence* (8th edition, 1995)). In other words it is the burden of raising sufficient evidence such that the issue involved could be decided in his favour. The legal burden is the burden of raising sufficient evidence to prove the issue, in other words sufficient evidence to satisfy the trier of fact that the issue in question should be decided in his favour (*Cross on Evidence* (8th edition, 1995)).

The normal rule in both civil and criminal trials is that the party who first raises an issue should prove it (*Abrath v North Eastern Railway Co* (1886) 11 App Cas 247); *Woolmington v DPP* [1935] AC 462). So, for example, if a prosecution is brought accusing a man of rape, it is for the prosecution to adduce sufficient evidence on all the elements of the offence which could satisfy a reasonable jury of the accused's guilt and it is also for the prosecution to prove guilt before it will win its case. Similarly the plaintiff in a negligence case must adduce sufficient evidence upon which a reasonable trier of fact could be satisfied that a duty of care was owed, that that duty was broken and that the damage incurred was non-remote, and must also satisfy the judge that all three elements were present.

Sometimes this normal rule is altered, however. On occasion it is for the defendant to raise an issue before the prosecution must disprove it – here the defendant bears an evidential burden and the prosecution the legal burden once that evidential burden has been satisfied. At other times the defendant bears a legal burden once the prosecution has raised an issue. At other times, still, the defendant bears both evidential and legal burdens on an issue; the most important examples of this later case are where the defendant argues insanity (*M'Naghten's Case* (1843) 10 Cl & Fin 200) and where he seeks to rely in his defence upon some exception, exemption, proviso, excuse or qualification to a statutory offence tried in the magistrates court (s101 Magistrates' Courts Act 1980 and see *R v Edwards* [1975] QB 27).

In civil cases it is more difficult to be precise about the incidents of the legal and evidential burdens, because, in almost all cases, the whole matter will be tried by judge alone and there is limited scope for a submission of no case to answer. The submission of no case is the stage of the criminal trial at which the prosecution has to satisfy the judge that it has adduced evidence upon which a reasonable jury could convict the accused (*R v Galbraith* [1981] 2 All ER 1060). In civil trials the defendant's election to make a submission of no case is tantamount to a decision not to call evidence (*Alexander v Rayson* [1936] 1 KB 169) and is, therefore, only rarely employed; in criminal trials, however, the submission is made in the absence of the trier of fact (the jury) and there is no bar on calling evidence afterwards in the event that the submission fails.

There is another burden which is of great practical importance, but does not form part of the strict theory of the law of evidence. Whenever one party has seen his opponent put forward evidence which could persuade a reasonable trier of fact that an issue should be decided in his (the opponent's) favour, the party has a choice, he could sit back and call no evidence, hoping that in fact the trier of fact will not be persuaded, or he could put forward evidence himself so as to counteract the effect of the evidence already adduced. When the evidence against him is strong he knows that he is almost certain to lose unless he calls evidence, and it is not uncommon for it to be said that in such circumstances he bears a tactical burden – he does not have to prove anything and the issue has already been raised, but if he does not call evidence to rebut the evidence already called then his tactics will have failed because he will lose his case (*Cross on Evidence* (8th edition, 1995)).

A presumption is a device by which one party may be aided in the task of satisfying a burden. The basic position is that the judge or jury approaches each issue with an open mind and in the absence of evidence which would satisfy a reasonable man that the issue concerned is made out, that mind will not be swayed to decide in favour of the party bearing the burden. But, presumptions come to the assistance of the party bearing the burden by allowing, or requiring, the judge or jury to decide that the burden is satisfied once certain prescribed evidence has been adduced, even though that evidence may not satisfy the judge or jury in the absence of the presumption. For example, once it has been proved that a person has not been heard of for seven years by those who would normally be expected to hear from him and reasonable enquiries have been made to ascertain his whereabouts, it will be presumed that he is dead (*Chard* v *Chard* [1956] P 259). Of course it is by no means the case that such a person will be dead, he may just have disappeared from circulation, and therefore it may be that left alone a judge or jury may not be satisfied of his death, but the law prescribes as being conclusions which are drawn after the proof of certain basic facts. If we use the example already adverted to and assume that one party wants to prove that Mr A is dead; he could prove this by direct evidence, say, that his corpse was identified, and this will be direct proof of death; alternatively when proving the issue of death it is possible to prove the absence for seven years etc and from proof of those basic facts the conclusion will be drawn that Mr A is dead.

Generally, the nature of a presumption is that it prescribes a conclusion which could or should be drawn once the basic facts are proved, but it can be rebutted, either by proving that the basic facts are not made out or by direct evidence to contradict the conclusion which would otherwise be drawn from those basic facts. The rebuttal of presumptions may arise in one of two ways. Firstly it may be that once a presumption has been drawn it must be disproved in order to be rebutted, on the other hand it may be enough to rebut a presumption that it is shown that there was an equal chance of the conclusion drawn being untrue as there is of it being true. These are normally explained by saying that in the first type a legal burden is placed on the rebutter, whereas in the second an evidential burden only is imposed, but this explanation does not tell the full story. The true position is that sometimes a presumption must be drawn once the primary facts are proved, for example the presumption of death mentioned above – in such cases the only way in which the conclusion reached can be challenged is by challenging the basic facts. For example, if it is desired to rebut the presumption of death it will be necessary to show that the person in question is still alive, but once that has been shown the presumption simply never arises. It is not the case that the plaintiff can satisfy the judge that the three elements of the presumption are made out and then it is for the defendant to challenge that result, because the presumption can only ever be drawn after all the evidence has been heard, for plaintiff and defence. On the other hand some presumptions can be rebutted by leaving the basic facts intact and challenging the conclusion. For example, there is a presumption that a child born in wedlock is legitimate provided the husband had access to the wife at the likely time of conception (*Banbury Peerage Case* (1811) 1 Sim & St 153). It is quite possible for the husband to challenge the wife's evidence about access, but it is equally possible for the husband to accept the basic facts and rebut the presumption by more direct evidence of illegitimacy, for example blood group evidence which shows that he is definitely not the father. In such a case the presumption arises once the wife has called evidence on the basic facts and that evidence is not challenged, but the husband can still rebut the presumption.

Therefore, the position is that some presumptions arise only after all the relevant evidence on the fact in issue has been adduced, whereas others arise once the basic facts are proved and it is then open to rebuttal on the ground that despite the basic facts being proved the conclusion should not follow. It is in the context of this latter type of presumption that the different burdens on the rebutter arise. If it is proposed to challenge the basic facts of a presumption then all that the rebutter has to do is show that the basic facts are not proved, in other words he must show it equally likely that the basic facts are not true as that they are true. If, though, it is proposed to challenge the conclusion without challenging the basic facts, then it must be asked what is the standard of challenge required; sometimes the rebutter will have to prove that the conclusion is not merited on the facts of the case, at other times he will successfully rebut the presumption by showing that the conclusion is equally likely to be untrue as it is to be true.

Presumptions rarely have the effect of deciding the overall outcome of a trial, it is more likely that they will assist in the decision on one or more issues. But, in some cases, the only issue at trial is the very one on which the presumption assists.

It can be seen from what has been said above that a presumption may have one of five effects. A presumption may allow one party to satisfy his evidential burden on a particular issue without affecting his legal burden; or it may allow him to satisfy his legal burden on that issue and place a legal burden of disproof on his opponent; or it may allow him to satisfy his legal burden on that issue and place a burden on his opponent to show that the conclusion drawn is equally likely to be false as true; or it may allow him to satisfy his evidential burden on an issue on which he bears no legal burden; or it may allow him to satisfy his legal burden on an issue on which his opponent bears an evidential burden. There is no presumption which determines the whole outcome of a case except in cases where one issue is paramount and a presumption assists in the determination of that issue.

Following what has been said above, it becomes possible to classify presumptions according to their effect on the burden of proof. If a presumption helps a party to meet his evidential burden then it is 'permissive', though of the leading writers only Carter specifically covers this type of presumption (*Cases and Statutes on Evidence* (2nd edition, 1990, pp77–78)). No distinction is drawn between permissive presumptions where the party using the presumption bears the legal burden on the issue and where his opponent bears that burden once the presumption is drawn. If it allows a legal burden to be satisfied in the absence of proof to the contrary then a presumption may be called 'persuasive' (*Cross on Evidence* (8th edition, 1995)) or, as Lord Denning prefers 'compelling' ((1945) 61 LQR 379). If it allows a legal burden to be satisfied but can be rebutted by evidence that the conclusion is equally likely to be false as true then it is an 'evidential' presumption (*Cross on Evidence* (8th edition, 1995); Carter, *Cases and Statutes on Evidence* (2nd edition, 1990, p78)). Lord Bridge wrote of such presumptions that they should be known simply as 'presumptions' because if a legal burden is imposed on the rebutter then we are not concerned with a presumption but with a rule of law which determines that a certain result must follow the proof of certain basic fact ((1949) 12 MLR 272). Lord Bridge's classification, it is submitted, is artificial because almost all presumptions involve rules of law which give special weight to the proof of basic facts. In some cases the conclusion which is drawn on proof of the basic facts is one which common sense would dictate in any event, but in many more cases the conclusion is only drawn because the law requires it; and, in such cases, whether a legal burden of disproof is placed on the rebutter or just a burden to balance the probabilities makes no difference in as much as a rule of law is involved which gives artificial weight to the basic facts.

QUESTION FOUR

Consider whether the presumptions of legitimacy, death and marriage serve any practical purpose in the law in relation to:

a) facilitating proof of the presumed fact;

b) their impact on the burden of proof.

University of London LLB Examination
(for External Students) Law of Evidence June 1987 Q4

General Comment

It is important to remember that the question asks for analysis, as well as description of the law. A good answer will accordingly consider the purpose of presumptions, as well as their effect.

Skeleton Solution

Definition of the three types of presumption.

a) Presumption of legitimacy – other methods of proving legitimacy – effect on burden of proof – civil and criminal cases.

b) Presumption of death – alternative methods of proving that the person is alive – effect on burden of proof – evidential only.

c) Presumption of marriage – practical effect of presumption – relatively easy alternative proof – effect on burden of proof.

Suggested Solution

The three presumptions mentioned in the question provide means of proving certain facts for the purpose of legal proceedings without having to call evidence which actually proves them to be true. In outline the three presumptions operate as follows. The presumption of legitimacy provides that once it is proved that a child was born to a woman who was married either at the time of conception or at the time of birth then it will be presumed that it is her husband's child (*Banbury Peerage Case* (1811) 1 Sim & St 153). The presumption of death provides that once it is proved that someone has been unheard of for seven years by those who are most likely to have heard of him, then he will be presumed to be dead (*Chard* v *Chard* [1956] P 259). The presumption of marriage is more complicated since it can operate in two ways. Firstly, it will be presumed that a couple are married if it is proved that they have gone through a ceremony of marriage and that they have cohabited as man and wife (*Piers* v *Piers* (1849) 2 HL Cas 331). Secondly, it will be presumed that a couple are married if they cohabit as man and wife and are reputed to be married (*Sastry Velaider Aronegary* v *Sambecutty Vailalie* (1881) 6 App Cas 364). Indeed the first of the two aspects of the presumption of marriage itself has two aspects in that it will be presumed that the ceremony itself was effective and that the parties had the capacity to marry.

The presumption of legitimacy

The presumption of legitimacy as outlined above operated to allow proof of paternity without the need to call medical evidence to establish that the husband could be the father. Indeed there is little evidence that can ever be used to prove that a particular man is the father of a child. Blood group evidence can prove that he is not and can prove that someone with the same blood type is the father, but it cannot go any further than that. Other more technical medical evidence could be called to establish paternity (for example so-called 'genetic fingerprint' evidence) whether the case is criminal or civil.

The effect of the presumption on the burden of proof differs according to whether the case is criminal or civil. In criminal cases where the prosecution wishes to rebut the presumption it will always bear a legal burden of proof and if the defence wishes to rebut it then an evidential burden only must be satisfied. There appears to be no authority directly to point but this results from the normal common law rules of burden and standard of proof, namely that the defence only bears a legal burden where the defence is insanity or where statute imposes such a burden.

In civil cases the presumption places a legal burden of proof on the party seeking to rebut it, whether that be plaintiff or defendant. The standard of proof in civil cases is the balance of probabilities. There is a question whether the presumption itself carries any weight, in other words whether the judge should consider the presumption itself to be evidence which points towards legitimacy, but it is thought that it does not and that its only effect is to place the burden of proof on the rebutter. If the presumption were intended to have weight as evidence then its effect would be not just to dictate who bears the burden of proof but also to increase the standard of proof required from the rebutter, yet the standard is the balance of probabilities only by virtue of s26 Family Law Reform Act 1969.

The presumption of death

Of the three presumptions discussed the presumption of death probably has the most widespread application in practice. It is also the most effective of the three in terms of assisting the court to reach a conclusion on a matter on which there is likely to be no evidence. A person (X) will be presumed to be dead if it can be proved: (a) that there are persons who could be expected to have heard of him; (b) that those persons have not heard of him for seven years; and (c) that reasonable steps have been taken to ascertain whether he is still alive. On proof of these three basic facts the judge must conclude that X is dead unless there is direct evidence that he is not dead. The presumption of death operates to allow for death to be presumed in many cases where it simply cannot be proved one way or the other whether X is in fact dead.

It is, of course, quite possible that X will still be alive but the possibility of this is reduced by the need to prove the first of the three basic facts outlined above. Unless it can be proved that someone is likely to have heard of him then the presumption cannot arise. If X goes abroad, declaring that he wants no further contact with his family or friends and is not heard of for seven years by them then the presumption would not arise, because as a matter of common sense as much as anything else, it is not a compelling conclusion that the reason for not hearing of him is that he is dead.

The need to prove seven years' absence does not give rise to a presumption that X died seven years from the time he was last heard of. The presumption, according to *Re Phene's Trusts* (1870) 5 Ch App 139 operates only to establish that X is dead at the time of the legal proceedings. There is some authority to the contrary, notably *Chipchase* v *Chipchase* [1939] P 391, but the proper view of such cases is that there was some evidence to show the time of death.

The presumption of death places an evidential burden only on the rebutting party, not a legal burden. To this extent it differs in its operation from the presumption of legitimacy. This difference also means that the effect of the presumption is the same no matter which party it operates against and no matter whether the proceedings are civil or criminal. The presumption will not, of course, be rebutted simply because some evidence is called which shows that one of the basic facts may not be made out. If that evidence is sufficiently cogent then the presumption will not arise at all because the basic fact would not be proved by the party trying to establish death, but once the judge is satisfied on all the evidence that the basic facts are proved then it is only direct evidence that X is alive which can rebut it.

In addition to the formal presumption of death which must arise on the proof of the three basic facts outlined above, the court is always entitled to presume that someone is dead as a matter of inference from other facts. For example, if someone falls from a ship into the middle of the Atlantic ocean and despite attempts to find him he is declared lost, the possibility of him still being alive a year later when nothing has been heard to suggest that he had been picked up by another vessel is remote. The court would be entitled to draw the inference that he is dead from the circumstances of his disappearance. This is not a question of a formal presumption of law being applied, but is a purely factual exercise.

The presumption of marriage

Whether two people are married can have consequences in both criminal and civil cases. Today the compulsory registration of marriages allows little scope for the presumption to arise, save in cases where there is a question over the legitimacy of the ceremony. Whether the presumption arises on proof of a ceremony and cohabitation or on proof of cohabitation and repute the effect is the same – marriage is presumed unless there is strong evidence that the parties are not legitimately married.

The proof of a ceremony of marriage gives rise to two presumptions which together form the presumption of marriage. The first is the presumption that the ceremony was conducted by an authorised person and in an authorised place. The second is that the parties had the capacity to marry, in other words that they were over 16 years of age, had any parental consent that may have been necessary and were not already married. The practical effect of the presumption is to allow the court to consider a couple to be properly married. The practical effect of the presumption is to allow the court to consider a couple to be properly married without having to investigate all sorts of matters upon which evidence may not be available. For example where a couple underwent a ceremony of marriage 40 years prior to the court proceedings it is highly unlikely that it could be discovered whether the person who married them was properly authorised, so the presumption operates to allow a common sense conclusion to be drawn by the court.

To presume marriage from cohabitation and repute, in other words to presume marriage from evidence that the couple lived together and were reputed to be married, raises rather different issues. In such cases there may be no evidence before the court that any ceremony was entered into, but the presumption still allows a common sense conclusion to be drawn from the proof of the basic facts. In practical terms cases are rare where cohabitation and repute need to be relied upon because of the registration of marriages, but such cases can still arise for example where the parties originally came from a country where there is no such registration.

It is arguable that the presumption of marriage adds little to the right of a court to draw an inference from facts which are proved to it. Perhaps the only effect of it is to prevent the court from refusing to draw the inference of marriage where evidence of the basic facts is proved on balance of probabilities but not to any higher standard.

The presumption of marriage which arises from proof of a ceremony and cohabitation operates somewhat differently to the other presumptions discussed above. This is because the presumption itself is not really concerned with marriage but with the validity of appointment and certification of places and people. The presumption is that:

(a) the place in which some ceremony was carried out was licensed; (b) the person conducting it was authorised to do so; (c) the parties concerned were over 16; (d) neither party was already married; and (e) the parties had obtained any parental or other consent which was required. It is these formal matters which are presumed and once they are presumed it then follows that the ceremony was valid. There is no presumption applied directly to the marriage itself.

The effect of this presumption on the burden of proof is also somewhat difficult to state. It is often said that the party who wishes to show that the parties are not married bears a legal burden of proof. But this burden is usually a burden of proving that the basic facts are not established rather than a burden that the presumed fact is not established from the basic facts. The challenge may be made, for example, on the ground that the official who married the parties was not properly authorised or that one of the parties was already married. But that challenge goes to proof of the basic facts not of the presumed fact. In other words it prevents the basic facts being established. To put it another way, where a party to an action wishes to argue that the basic facts are not established then it is for him to prove it. The standard required is the balance of probabilities (*Blyth* v *Blyth* [1966] AC 643), but of course, the more unusual the argument being put forward the less probable it is that that argument is correct. For example if it is alleged that a ceremony carried out in a church was not valid because the church was not a proper place for the celebration of marriage then the burden will be very heavy because of the inherent unlikelihood of the allegation.

Once the basic facts of this presumption are established then the only way of rebutting the presumption of marriage is by proving that the marriage has been dissolved.

The presumption which arises out of proof of cohabitation and repute probably places a legal burden of disproof on the rebutter in civil cases. The scope for rebuttal of this presumption is greater because the basic facts can be established without having to prove any ceremony at all. Therefore the rebutter may successfully challenge the presumption by proving that the ceremony which was undergone was not valid. The effect of the cohabitation and repute presumption in many cases is to add to the other presumption of marriage. There are cases, like *R* v *Shepherd* [1904] 1 Ch 456, where a ceremony has been proved and cohabitation and repute have also been proved, and the judge has held that the challenge to the validity of the ceremony had failed because the evidence of cohabitation and repute is strong.

In criminal cases, as shown above in the case of the presumption of legitimacy, nothing more than an evidential burden can be placed on the accused and nothing less than a legal burden on the prosecution, although the prosecution's task may be made easier in bigamy cases because evidence of cohabitation and repute could be an admission by the defendant(s) that they are married.

QUESTION FIVE

'It is not only the adduction of prima facie evidence by the proponent which results in an evidential burden being cast on the opponent. The same effect may result from the operation of a presumption.' (Phipson and Elliot)

Discuss. To what extent do you agree that the operation of presumptions is based more on considerations of public policy than of logic?

University of London LLB Examination
(for External Students) Law of Evidence June 1991 Q4

General Comment

This rather long question requires a treatment in outline of the role of evidential burden under the general law and (as the main part of the answer) the effects of common law presumptions on the burden. The latter is best dealt with by reference to the principal rebuttable presumptions of law.

Skeleton Solution

Role of the evidential burden under the general law with particular reference to common law defences: distinction of tactical or provisional burden – effect of presumptions: res ipsa loquitur; death; legitimacy; marriage – the relationship in criminal trials with the *Woolmington* principle; the diffuseness of the language used to describe the evidential effects of presumptions and the variations of approach in the case law.

Suggested Solution

A party wishing to establish his case to the requisite standard of proof in civil or criminal proceedings has two hurdles to surmount. He must first ensure that the tribunal of fact considers his story. He must then ensure that the jury act on it in his favour. The second is the discharge of the burden of proof on the party. The first is the discharge of the evidential burden – sufficient evidence to make the party's case a live issue. Sufficient in other words, for the tribunal of fact to consider his story at all.

Clearly, if a party has to discharge the burden of proof, he must get his contentions considered by the tribunal of fact in the first place. The party having the legal burden also generally has the evidential burden. To this extent, therefore, the evidential burden is of little consequence. There are, however, cases where the evidential burden can be critical. Common law defences are a case in point. The prosecution have the legal burden to establish an accused's guilt, but before a jury is entitled to consider an accused's defence of provocation (*Mancini* v *DPP* [1942] AC 1), duress (*R* v *Gill* [1963] 1 WLR 841), self-defence (*R* v *Lobell* [1957] 1 QB 547) and, probably, accident (*Bratty* v *Attorney-General for Northern Ireland* [1963] AC 386) and alibi (*R* v *Johnson* [1961] 1 WLR 1478). The evidential burden must be discharged by the accused before the jury will be entitled to consider the defence. Indeed, it would appear that any defence which is more than the denial of an essential element of the prosecution's case is subject to such a burden.

But the fact that one party puts up a case which, in the absence of contradictory evidence, he may win does not result in an evidential burden being placed on that party, unless the term is being used as a description of the need by that opponent to produce factual controverting evidence, or to neutralise the evidence by cross-examination, or lose the case. It is submitted that this is not the meaning properly ascribed to the term evidential burden in its technical sense. The requirement for an opponent to meet unfavourable evidence is sometimes called a 'tactical' or 'provisional' burden and this is a source of confusion. It is not an evidential burden.

The field of presumptions does however provide examples for which the quotation in the question is apt. These presumptions have the effect of establishing certain facts ('the presumed facts') once other facts ('the basic facts') are proved. For the purposes of discussion, the presumptions of res ipsa loquitur, death, legitimacy and marriage will be examined.

Res ipsa loquitur applies only to civil proceedings. If a state of affairs is under control of a party and an accident occurs which would not in the ordinary course of events happen in the absence of negligence, then negligence will be presumed. The evidential effect is not entirely settled, and there are cases indicating that it is really no more than a label for circumstantial evidence – or a presumption of fact (*Langham* v *Governors of Wellingborough School* [1932] LJ KB 513). *The Kite* [1933] P 154 indicates that it is a rebuttable presumption of law casting an evidential burden on the opposing party. On the other hand, the presumption casts the legal burden on the party against whom it operates, according to *Barkway* v *South Wales Transport Executive* [1949] 1 KB 54. The most recent pronouncement from the Privy Council in *Ng Chun Pui* v *Lee Chuen Tat* (1988) The Times 25 May follows the proposition that the maxim casts an evidential burden on the opposing party.

Under the presumption of death, the fact of death is presumed on proof of an absence of seven years or more, nothing having been heard of the absentee by persons who might have heard of him, due enquiries having been made. It is apparent from the decision of the House of Lords in *Prudential Assurance Co* v *Edmonds* (1877) 2 AC 487 that this presumption operates to cast an evidential burden on the party against whom it operates.

The presumption of legitimacy is less straightforward in that it is overlaid by statute, and also reveals the need to consider the position in civil and criminal cases separately.

At common law, the presumed fact – legitimacy – was established by proof of the basic facts of birth or conception in lawful wedlock. The effect of the presumption according to *Morris* v *Davies* (1837) 5 Cl & Fin 163 was to place the legal burden (and not just an evidential burden) on the opposing party. Clearly, the former requirement is the important one, since to discharge the legal burden, the party must discharge the evidential burden on that issue.

But in criminal trials, the placing of the legal burden on an accused would appear to conflict with the *Woolmington* v *DPP* [1935] AC 462 principle. The exceptions under that rule (insanity raised by defence and statutory exceptions) clearly exclude presumptions. Thus, it might be that the presumption of legitimacy if deployed by the prosecution has the maximum effect of placing an evidential burden on the accused.

Finally, with the presumption of marriage, there are three different situations to consider, formal validity, essential validity and presumption of marriage by cohabitation and repute. A marriage proved to have complied with the necessary formalities of local law is presumed to be formally valid. Likewise, the parties are presumed to have had the capacity to enter into the marriage. *Piers* v *Piers* (1849) 2 HL Cas 331 applied *Morris* v *Davies* from which it is apparent that the evidential effect was to put the legal burden on the party against whom the presumption operated in civil trials. Essential validity is more ambiguous. *Tweny* v *Tweny* [1946] 1 All ER 564 indicates that the effect is to place evidential burden on the party against whom the presumption operates, though it hardly seems very sensible to invest in two related aspects of the same presumption with different evidential effects.

On the third aspect of the presumption, a cohabiting couple reputed in the community to have been married are taken at common law to have been through a valid marriage ceremony at some time in the past. *Sastry Velaider Aronegary* v *Sambecutty Vailalie* (1881) 6 App Cas 364 is authority for the view that this places the legal burden on the opposing party, although, as with the other aspects of the presumption, the language is less than clear. This aspect, together with formal validity, must be subject to the proviso that in criminal trials, the maximum effect of the presumption when relied on by the prosecution is to place an evidential burden on the accused, for the *Woolmington* v *DPP* [1935] AC 462 principle is otherwise infringed.

There is little doubt that public policy has played a significant part in development of presumptions. The sanctity of marriage and the stigma of illegitimacy were influential in establishing their evidential effects. It is also true that notwithstanding efforts to provide a coherent strategy for analysis of those evidential effects, satisfactory classification of them is still elusive. This is apparent from the above discussion, demonstrating, for example, seemingly different evidential effects for different aspects of the same presumption, and divergence in judicial views of the effects of the same presumption.

One explanation for this elusiveness is that they were developed to satisfy policy concerns rather than legal principle. If that is the case, establishing a coherent legal framework for the operation of presumptions may not be capable of achievement.

Law Update 2003 edition – due March 2003

An annual review of the most recent developments in specific legal subject areas, useful for law students at degree and professional levels, others with law elements in their courses and also practitioners seeking a quick update.

Published around March every year, the Law Update summarises the major legal developments during the course of the previous year. In conjunction with Old Bailey Press textbooks it gives the student a significant advantage when revising for examinations.

Contents

Administrative Law • Civil and Criminal Procedure • Commercial Law • Company Law • Conflict of Laws • Constitutional Law • Contract Law • Conveyancing • Criminal Law • Criminology • English and European Legal Systems • Equity and Trusts • European Union Law • Evidence • Family Law • Jurisprudence • Land Law • Law of International Trade • Public International Law • Revenue Law • Succession • Tort

For further information on contents or to place an order, please contact:

Mail Order
Old Bailey Press
at Holborn College
Woolwich Road
Charlton
London
SE7 8LN

Telephone No: 020 7381 7407
Fax No: 020 7386 0952
Website: www.oldbaileypress.co.uk

ISBN 1 85836 477 9
Soft cover 246 x 175 mm
450 pages approx
£10.95
Due March 2003

Unannotated Cracknell's Statutes for use in Examinations

New Editions of Cracknell's Statutes

£11.95 due 2002

Cracknell's Statutes provide a comprehensive series of essential statutory provisions for each subject. Amendments are consolidated, avoiding the need to cross-refer to amending legislation. Unannotated, they are suitable for use in examinations, and provide the precise wording of vital Acts of Parliament for the diligent student.

Commercial Law
ISBN: 1 85836 472 8

European Community Legislation
ISBN: 1 85836 470 1

Conflict of Laws
ISBN: 1 85836 473 6

Family Law
ISBN: 1 85836 471 X

Criminal Law
ISBN: 1 85836 474 4

Public International Law
ISBN: 1 85836 476 0

Employment Law
ISBN: 1 85836 475 2

For further information on contents or to place an order, please contact:

Mail Order
Old Bailey Press
at Holborn College
Woolwich Road
Charlton
London
SE7 8LN

Telephone No: 020 7381 7407
Fax No: 020 7386 0952
Website: www.oldbaileypress.co.uk

Suggested Solutions to Past Examination Questions 2000–2001

The Suggested Solutions series provides examples of full answers to the questions regularly set by examiners. Each suggested solution has been broken down into three stages: general comment, skeleton solution and suggested solution. The examination questions included within the text are taken from past examination papers set by the London University. The full opinion answers will undoubtedly assist you with your research and further your understanding and appreciation of the subject in question.

Only £6.95 Due December 2002

Constitutional Law
ISBN: 1 85836 478 7

Jurisprudence and Legal Theory
ISBN: 1 85836 484 1

Criminal Law
ISBN: 1 85836 479 5

Land Law
ISBN: 1 85836 481 7

English Legal System
ISBN: 1 85836 482 5

Law of Tort
ISBN: 1 85836 483 3

Elements of the Law of Contract
ISBN: 1 85836 480 9

For further information on contents or to place an order, please contact:

Mail Order
Old Bailey Press
at Holborn College
Woolwich Road
Charlton
London
SE7 8LN

Telephone No: 020 7381 7407
Fax No: 020 7386 0952
Website: www.oldbaileypress.co.uk

Old Bailey Press

The Old Bailey Press integrated student law library is tailor-made to help you at every stage of your studies from the preliminaries of each subject through to the final examination. The series of Textbooks, Revision WorkBooks, 150 Leading Cases and Cracknell's Statutes are interrelated to provide you with a comprehensive set of study materials.

You can buy Old Bailey Press books from your University Bookshop, your local Bookshop, direct using this form, or you can order a free catalogue of our titles from the address shown overleaf.

The following subjects each have a Textbook, 150 Leading Cases/Casebook, Revision WorkBook and Cracknell's Statutes unless otherwise stated.

Administrative Law
Commercial Law
Company Law
Conflict of Laws
Constitutional Law
Conveyancing (Textbook and 150 Leading Cases)
Criminal Law
Criminology (Textbook and Sourcebook)
Employment Law (Textbook and Cracknell's Statutes)
English and European Legal Systems
Equity and Trusts
Evidence
Family Law
Jurisprudence: The Philosophy of Law (Textbook, Sourcebook and
    Revision WorkBook)
Land: The Law of Real Property
Law of International Trade
Law of the European Union
Legal Skills and System
    (Textbook)
Obligations: Contract Law
Obligations: The Law of Tort
Public International Law
Revenue Law (Textbook,
    Revision WorkBook and
    Cracknell's Statutes)
Succession

Mail order prices:	
Textbook	£14.95
150 Leading Cases	£11.95
Revision WorkBook	£9.95
Cracknell's Statutes	£11.95
Suggested Solutions 1998–1999	£6.95
Suggested Solutions 1999–2000	£6.95
Suggested Solutions 2000–2001	£6.95
Law Update 2002	£9.95
Law Update 2003	£10.95

Please note details and prices are subject to alteration.

To complete your order, please fill in the form below:

Module	Books required	Quantity	Price	Cost
		Postage		
		TOTAL		

For Europe, add 15% postage and packing (£20 maximum).
For the rest of the world, add 40% for airmail.

ORDERING

By telephone to Mail Order at 020 7381 7407, with your credit card to hand.

By fax to 020 7386 0952 (giving your credit card details).

Website: www.oldbaileypress.co.uk

By post to: Mail Order, Old Bailey Press at Holborn College, Woolwich Road, Charlton, London, SE7 8LN.

When ordering by post, please enclose full payment by cheque or banker's draft, or complete the credit card details below. You may also order a free catalogue of our complete range of titles from this address.

We aim to despatch your books within 3 working days of receiving your order.

Name

Address

Postcode   Telephone

Total value of order, including postage: £

I enclose a cheque/banker's draft for the above sum, or

charge my   ☐ Access/Mastercard   ☐ Visa   ☐ American Express
Card number

☐☐☐☐ ☐☐☐☐ ☐☐☐☐ ☐☐☐☐

Expiry date   ☐☐☐☐

Signature: ....Date: ....